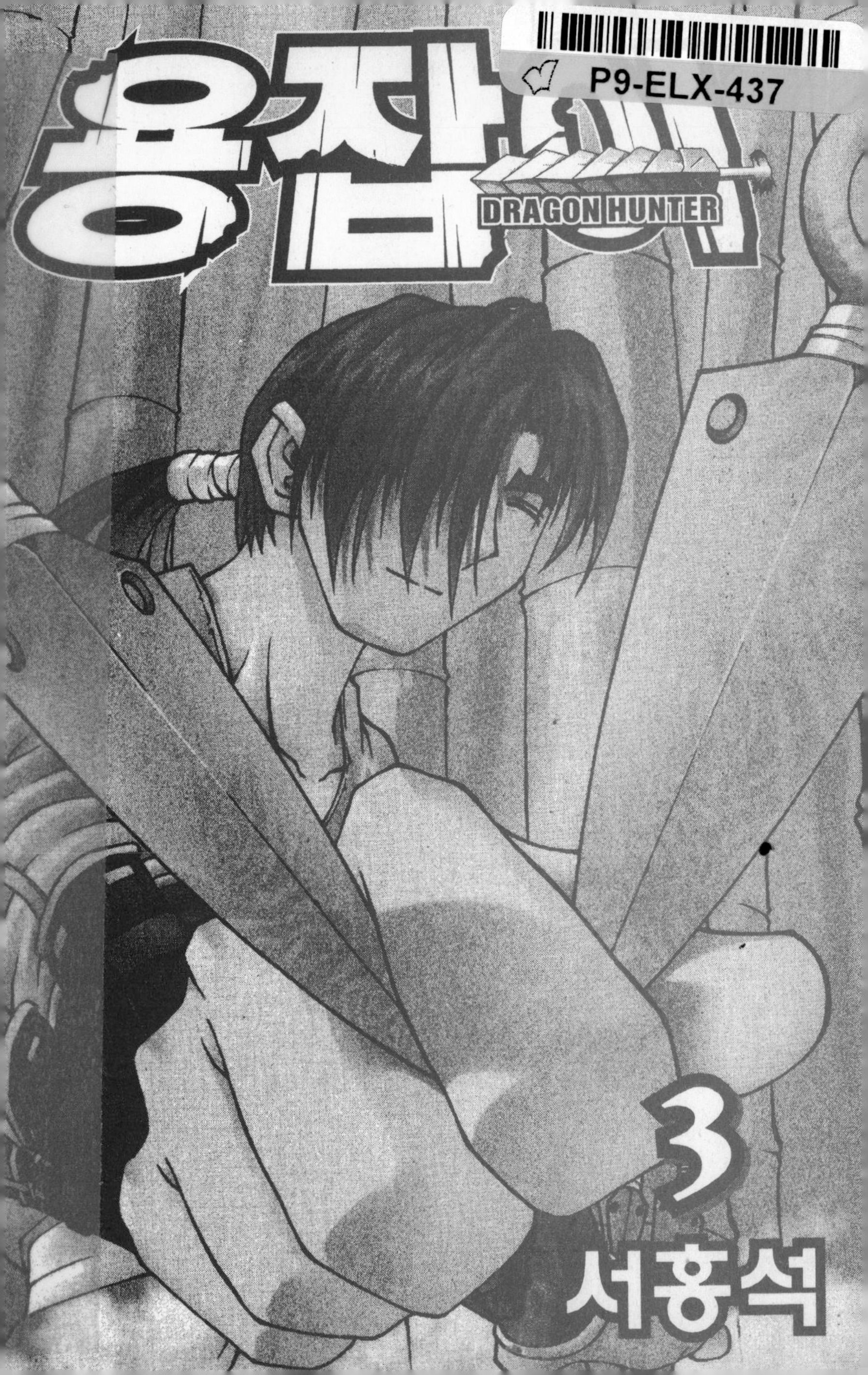
용잡
DRAGON HUNTER
3
서홍석

ALSO AVAILABLE FROM TOKYOPOP®

MANGA

.HACK//LEGEND OF THE TWILIGHT*
@LARGE (December 2003)
ANGELIC LAYER*
BABY BIRTH*
BATTLE ROYALE*
BRAIN POWERED*
BRIGADOON*
CARDCAPTOR SAKURA
CARDCAPTOR SAKURA: MASTER OF THE CLOW*
CHOBITS*
CHRONICLES OF THE CURSED SWORD
CLAMP SCHOOL DETECTIVES*
CLOVER
CONFIDENTIAL CONFESSIONS*
CORRECTOR YUI
COWBOY BEBOP*
COWBOY BEBOP: SHOOTING STAR*
CYBORG 009*
DEMON DIARY
DIGIMON*
DRAGON HUNTER
DRAGON KNIGHTS*
DUKLYON: CLAMP SCHOOL DEFENDERS*
ERICA SAKURAZAWA*
FAKE*
FLCL*
FORBIDDEN DANCE*
GATE KEEPERS*
G GUNDAM*
GRAVITATION*
GTO*
GUNDAM WING
GUNDAM WING: BATTLEFIELD OF PACIFISTS
GUNDAM WING: ENDLESS WALTZ*
GUNDAM WING: THE LAST OUTPOST*
HAPPY MANIA*
HARLEM BEAT
I.N.V.U.
INITIAL D*
ISLAND
JING: KING OF BANDITS*
JULINE
KARE KANO*
KINDAICHI CASE FILES, THE*
KING OF HELL
KODOCHA: SANA'S STAGE*
LOVE HINA*
LUPIN III*
MAGIC KNIGHT RAYEARTH*
MAGIC KNIGHT RAYEARTH II* (COMING SOON)
MAN OF MANY FACES*
MARMALADE BOY*
MARS*
MIRACLE GIRLS
MIYUKI-CHAN IN WONDERLAND*
MONSTERS, INC.
PARADISE KISS*
PARASYTE
PEACH GIRL
PEACH GIRL: CHANGE OF HEART*
PET SHOP OF HORRORS*
PLANET LADDER*
PLANETES*
PRIEST
RAGNAROK
RAVE MASTER*
REALITY CHECK
REBIRTH
REBOUND*
RISING STARS OF MANGA
SABER MARIONETTE J*
SAILOR MOON
SAINT TAIL
SAMURAI DEEPER KYO*
SAMURAI GIRL: REAL BOUT HIGH SCHOOL*
SCRYED*
SHAOLIN SISTERS*
SHIRAHIME-SYO: SNOW GODDESS TALES* (Dec. 2003)
SHUTTERBOX
SORCERER HUNTERS
THE SKULL MAN*
THE VISION OF ESCAFLOWNE*
TOKYO MEW MEW*
UNDER THE GLASS MOON
VAMPIRE GAME*
WILD ACT*
WISH*
WORLD OF HARTZ (November 2003)
X-DAY*
ZODIAC P.I. *

For more information visit www.TOKYOPOP.com

*INDICATES 100% AUTHENTIC MANGA (RIGHT-TO-LEFT FORMAT)

CINE-MANGA™

CARDCAPTORS
JACKIE CHAN ADVENTURES (November 2003)
JIMMY NEUTRON
KIM POSSIBLE
LIZZIE MCGUIRE
POWER RANGERS: NINJA STORM
SPONGEBOB SQUAREPANTS
SPY KIDS 2

NOVELS

KARMA CLUB (April 2004)
SAILOR MOON

TOKYOPOP KIDS

STRAY SHEEP

ART BOOKS

CARDCAPTOR SAKURA*
MAGIC KNIGHT RAYEARTH*

ANIME GUIDES

COWBOY BEBOP ANIME GUIDES
GUNDAM TECHNICAL MANUALS
SAILOR MOON SCOUT GUIDES

080103

Dragon Hunter

Volume 3

by

Hong Seock Seo

with

Studio Redstone

TOKYOPOP®

Los Angeles • Tokyo • London

Translator - Hye-Young Im
English Adaptation - J. Torres
Copy Editor - Bryce P. Coleman
Associate Editor - Jonathan Vankin
Retouch and Lettering - Jesse Ferneley
Logo Design - Patrick Hook

Editor - Rob Tokar
Managing Editor - Jill Freshney
Production Coordinator - Antonio DePietro
Production Manager - Jennifer Miller
Art Director - Matt Alford
Editorial Director - Jeremy Ross
VP of Production - Ron Klamert
President & C.O.O. - John Parker
Publisher & C.E.O. - Stuart Levy

Email: editor@TOKYOPOP.com
Come visit us online at www.TOKYOPOP.com

A  Manga

TOKYOPOP Inc.
5900 Wilshire Blvd. Suite 2000
Los Angeles, CA 90036

ISBN: 1-59182-163-0

First TOKYOPOP® printing: October 2003

10 9 8 7 6 5 4 3 2 1
Printed in the USA

THE STORY THUS FAR

...

SEUR-CHONG IS AN ELITE (AND CASH-OBSESSED) DRAGON HUNTER WHO, DUE TO AN INVOLUNTARY INFUSION OF DRAGON'S BLOOD, POSSESSES INCREDIBLE STRENGTH AND DURABILITY...ALONG WITH A SUBSTANTIALLY SHORTENED LIFESPAN. SEUR-CHONG'S PARTNER, MYUNG-HO, IS A SHAMAN WHO CAN USE MAGIC TO CONTROL DRAGONS--AND THUS MAKE THEM EASIER TO KILL.

ALWAYS SEEKING WAYS TO EARN MORE MONEY, THE DUO ACCEPTED AN ASSIGNMENT FROM THE RULERS OF THE KAYA PROVINCE TO DESTROY A WATER DRAGON. THIS ALREADY DIFFICULT TASK WAS MADE EVEN HARDER BY INTERFERENCE FROM THE CHUNJOO, A MYSTERIOUS BUT POWERFUL DRAGON-HUNTING GANG THAT DOESN'T TOLERATE COMPETITION. IN THE ENSUING MELEE, MYUNG-HO WAS MORTALLY WOUNDED.

IN RETALIATION, A VENGEFUL SEUR-CHONG VISITED THE LOCAL CHUNJOO HEADQUARTERS AND SINGLE-HANDEDLY WIPED OUT EVERYONE THERE. SEEING ONLY ONE WAY TO SAVE MYUNG-HO'S LIFE, SEUR-CHONG GAVE HIS DYING FRIEND A DRINK OF DRAGON'S BLOOD. THE YOUNG SHAMAN'S STRENGTH WAS RESTORED, BUT NOW MYUNG-HO MUST ENDURE THE DREADED DRAGON'S CURSE: POWER THAT WILL EVENTUALLY COST HIM HIS LIFE

MEANWHILE, THE SHAMAN PRIESTESS SO-CHUN HIRED A DRAGON HUNTER NAMED TAE-RANG TO BAG ANOTHER OF THE POWERFUL BEASTS. HOWEVER, IT WAS QUICKLY REVEALED THAT TAE-RANG IS REALLY KOK-JUNG--ONCE SEUR-CHONG'S BEST FRIEND, NOW HIS SWORN ENEMY. KOK-JUNG ENGAGED SEUR-CHONG IN MORTAL COMBAT BUT, WHEN AN ESPECIALLY FEARSOME DRAGON ATTACKED, THEY JOINED FORCES TO BATTLE IT. IN THE END, THE DRAGON FELL...RIGHT ON TOP OF KOK-JUNG!

TO SEUR-CHONG'S SURPRISE, KOK-JUNG SURVIVED BY DRINKING DRAGON'S BLOOD, DELIBERATELY TAKING ON THE DRAGON'S CURSE...AND THE INCREDIBLE POWERS THAT COME WITH IT. NOW, KOK-JUNG HAS BECOME ONE OF THE DEADLIEST FOES SEUR-CHONG HAS EVER FACED.

MEANWHILE, A RECOVERING MYUNG-HO COLLAPSED IN PAIN AS THE EFFECTS OF HIS OWN DRAGON'S CURSE BECAME EVIDENT...IN THE FORM OF A MONSTROUS THIRD EYE IN THE MIDDLE OF THE SHAMAN'S FOREHEAD!

DRAGON HUNTER

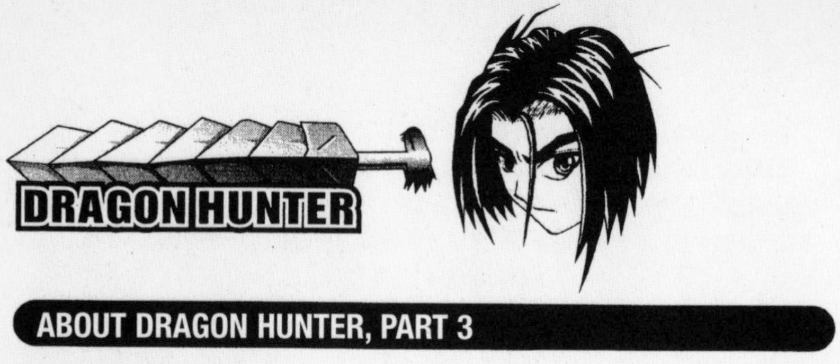

ABOUT DRAGON HUNTER, PART 3

This is the third volume.

Yet it's still not easy for me to draw people fighting dragons.

I'm starting to enjoy it. It's just that dragons, compared to Seur-Chong and the other characters who fight them, are too huge and the people turned out a lot smaller than I originally thought. So, I'm having a hard time coordinating the dragons and people on the page. But it's kind of fun to try and make sense of it all when I draw.

This comic book is Korean, so I try to include traditional Korean houses and clothes. However, the history is muddled, so I can't say all the details are 100 percent authentic Korean. My plan was to stick to Korean traditions but, since Korea is not the only country in this comic book, I thought it might be fun to draw dragons the way they look in Western mythology. Hmm… I wonder how Seur-Chong would do if he battled a Western dragon? I'm smiling just thinking about it — but I'm only thinking, that's all.

Lastly, I haven't explained enough about Seur-Chong's past, nor the different species of dragons. I have my reasons but I'll keep them to myself. Delving more deeply into Seur-Chong's past makes me nervous. There's so much there. The scale of this comic book is going to get bigger, too, because there are more dragons to come.

Anyway, for now, enjoy the story of the conflict between Seur-Chong and Kok-Jung in this volume!

Hong Seock Seo

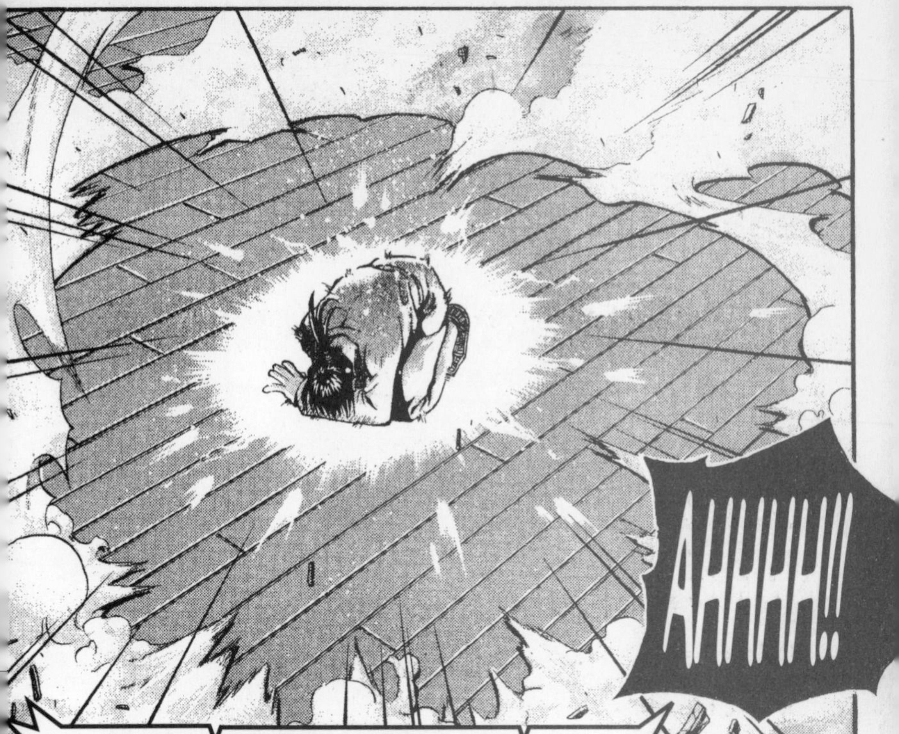
AHHHH!!

CHAPTER 10–CONTINUED

A COLLEAGUE AND A FRIEND

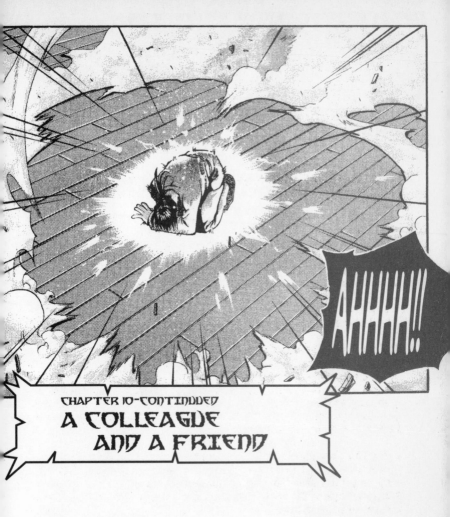

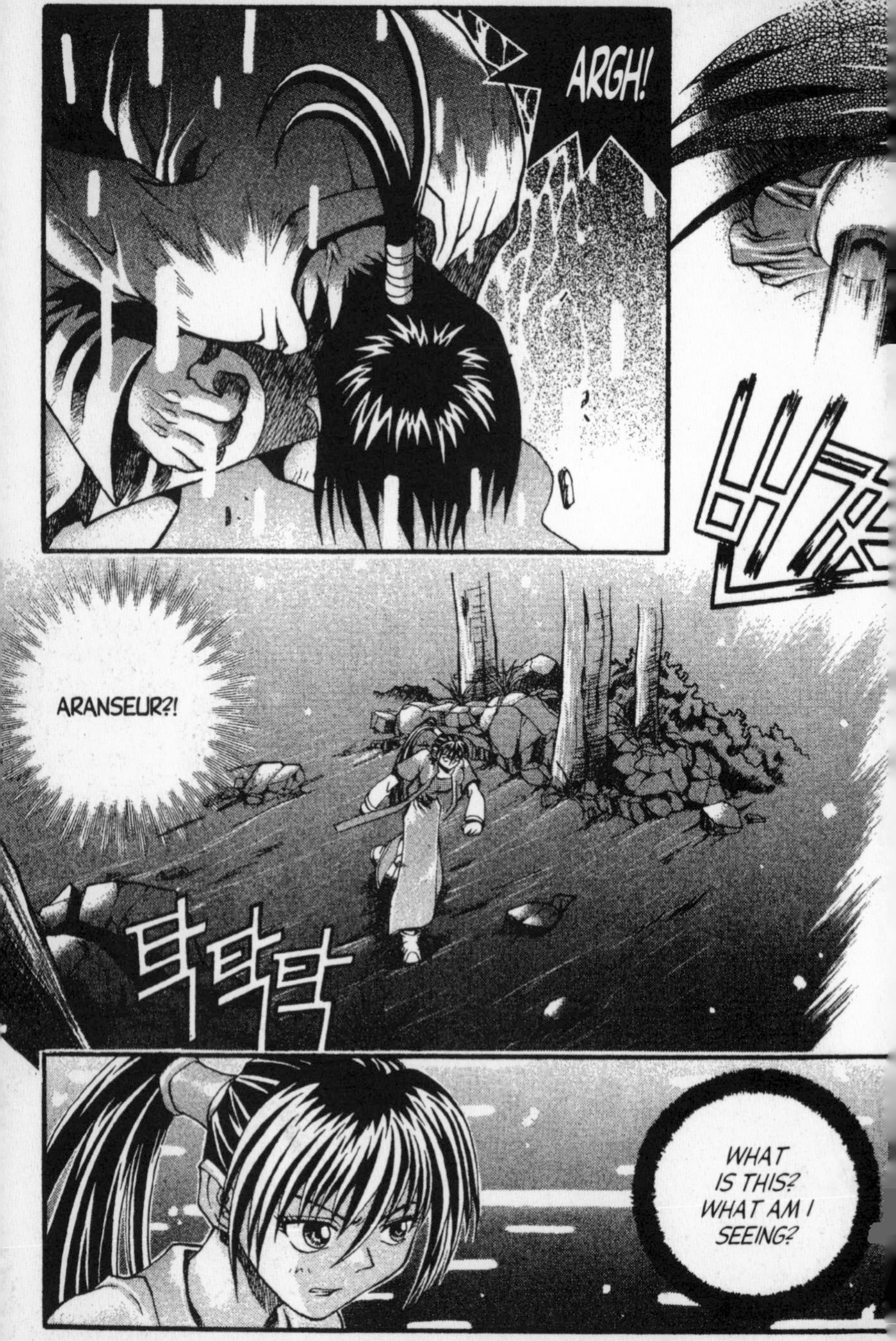
ARGH!
ARANSEUR?!
탁탁탁
WHAT IS THIS? WHAT AM I SEEING?

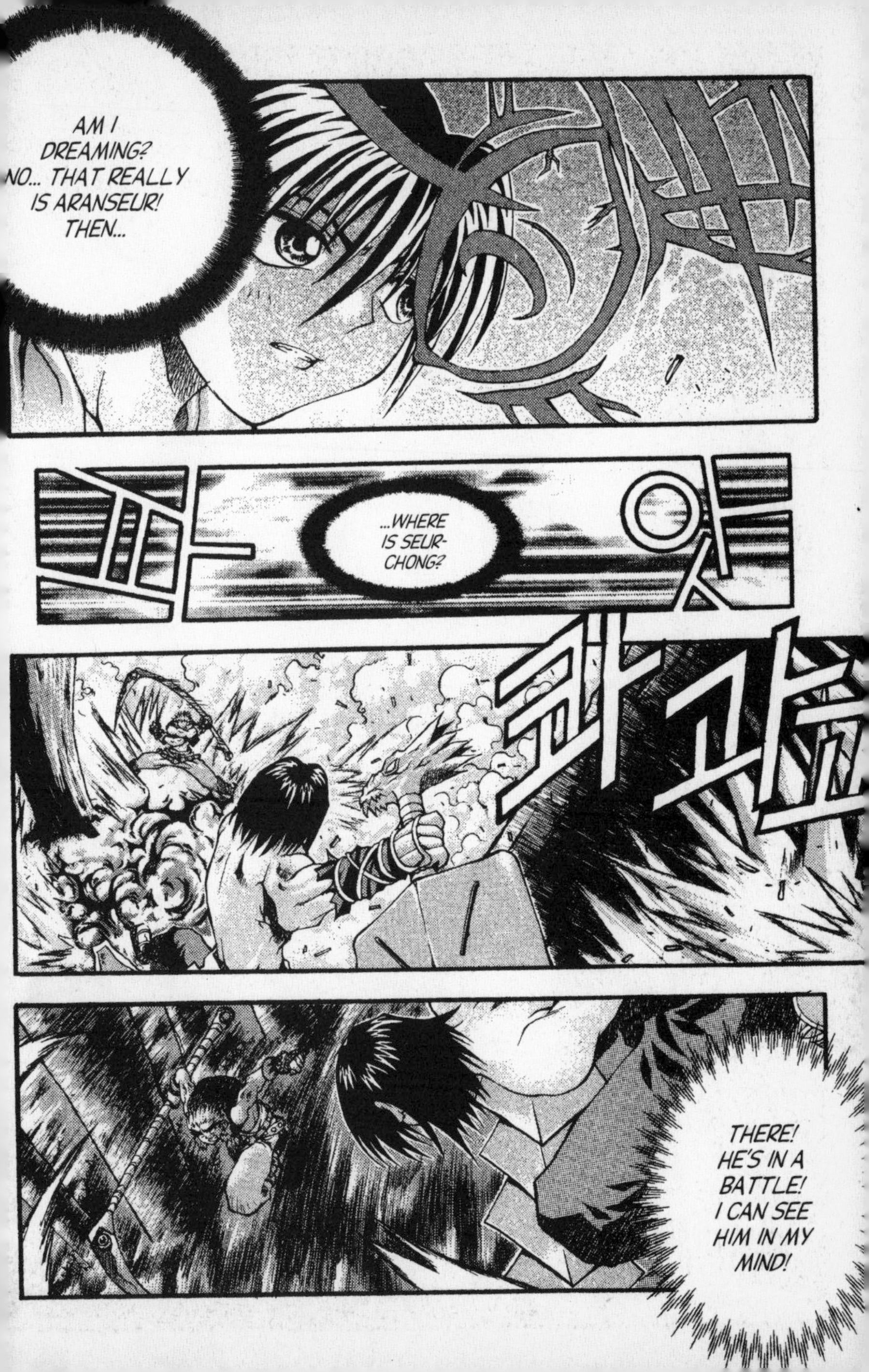
AM I DREAMING? NO... THAT REALLY IS ARANSEUR! THEN...
...WHERE IS SEUR-CHONG?
THERE! HE'S IN A BATTLE! I CAN SEE HIM IN MY MIND!

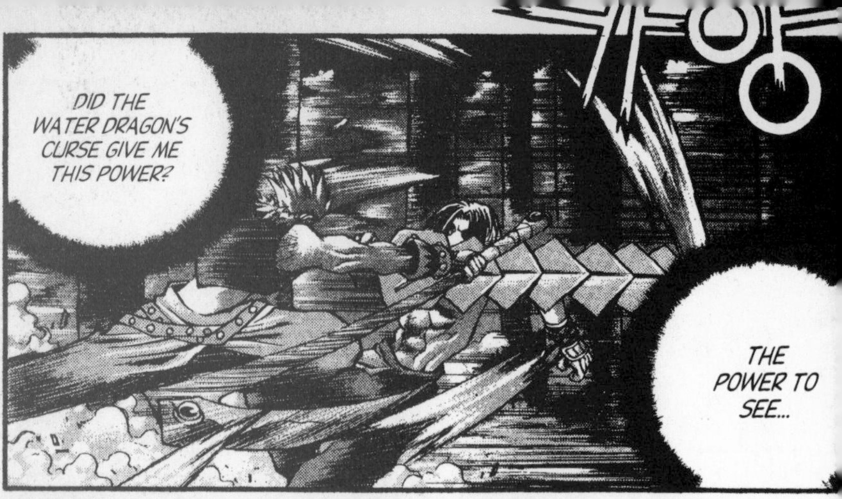
DID THE WATER DRAGON'S CURSE GIVE ME THIS POWER?
THE POWER TO SEE...
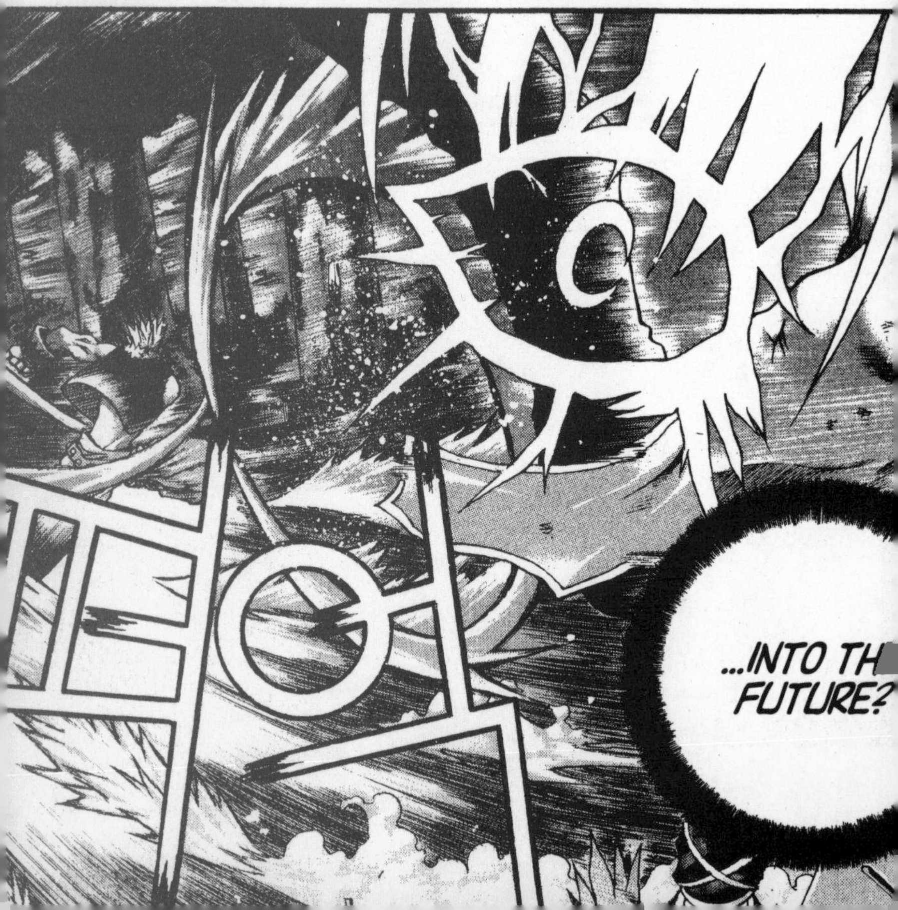
...INTO TH
FUTURE?

HUH? WHAT? THE VISION IS GONE. DOES THE POWER FAIL WHEN I'M OVERTIRED?
PANT
PANT
MASTER MYUNG-HO...?
PANT

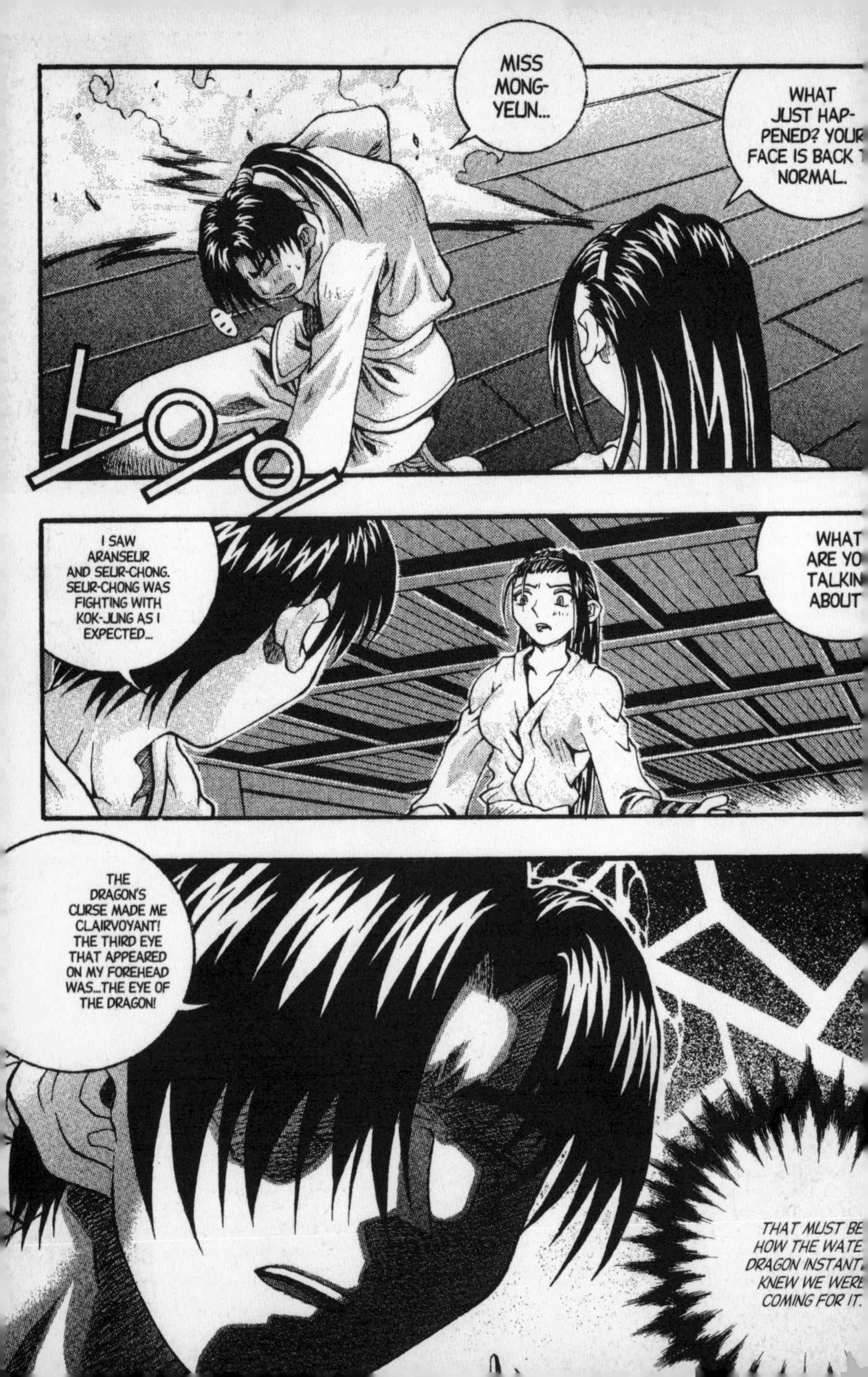
MISS MONG-YEUN...
WHAT JUST HAP-PENED? YOUR FACE IS BACK T NORMAL.
I SAW ARANSEUR AND SEUR-CHONG. SEUR-CHONG WAS FIGHTING WITH KOK-JUNG AS I EXPECTED...
WHAT ARE YO TALKIN ABOUT
THE DRAGON'S CURSE MADE ME CLAIRVOYANT! THE THIRD EYE THAT APPEARED ON MY FOREHEAD WAS...THE EYE OF THE DRAGON!
THAT MUST BE HOW THE WATE DRAGON INSTANT KNEW WE WERE COMING FOR IT.

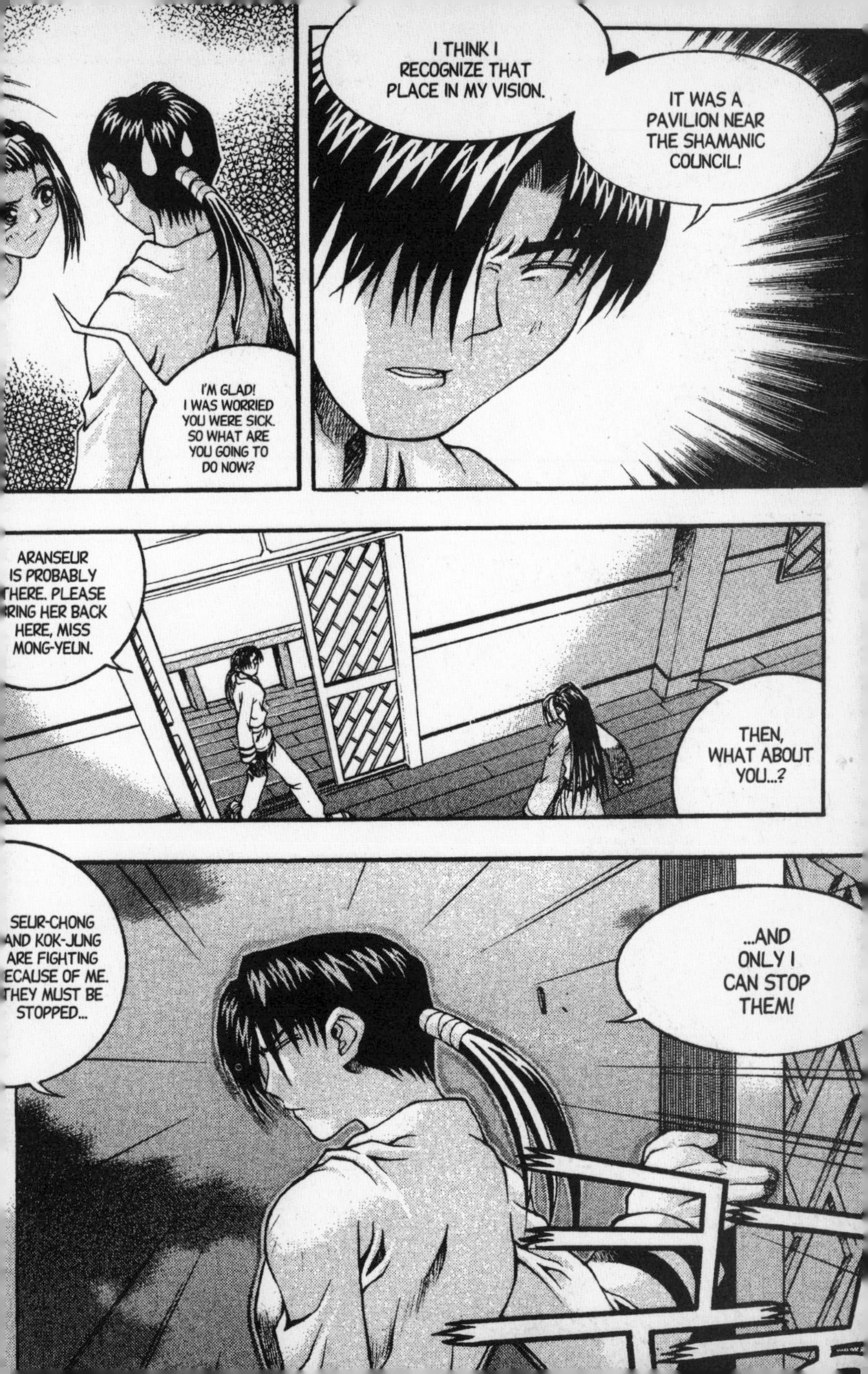
I'M GLAD! I WAS WORRIED YOU WERE SICK. SO WHAT ARE YOU GOING TO DO NOW?
I THINK I RECOGNIZE THAT PLACE IN MY VISION.
IT WAS A PAVILION NEAR THE SHAMANIC COUNCIL!
ARANSEUR IS PROBABLY THERE. PLEASE RING HER BACK HERE, MISS MONG-YEUN.
THEN, WHAT ABOUT YOU...?
SEUR-CHONG AND KOK-JUNG ARE FIGHTING ECAUSE OF ME. THEY MUST BE STOPPED...
...AND ONLY I CAN STOP THEM!

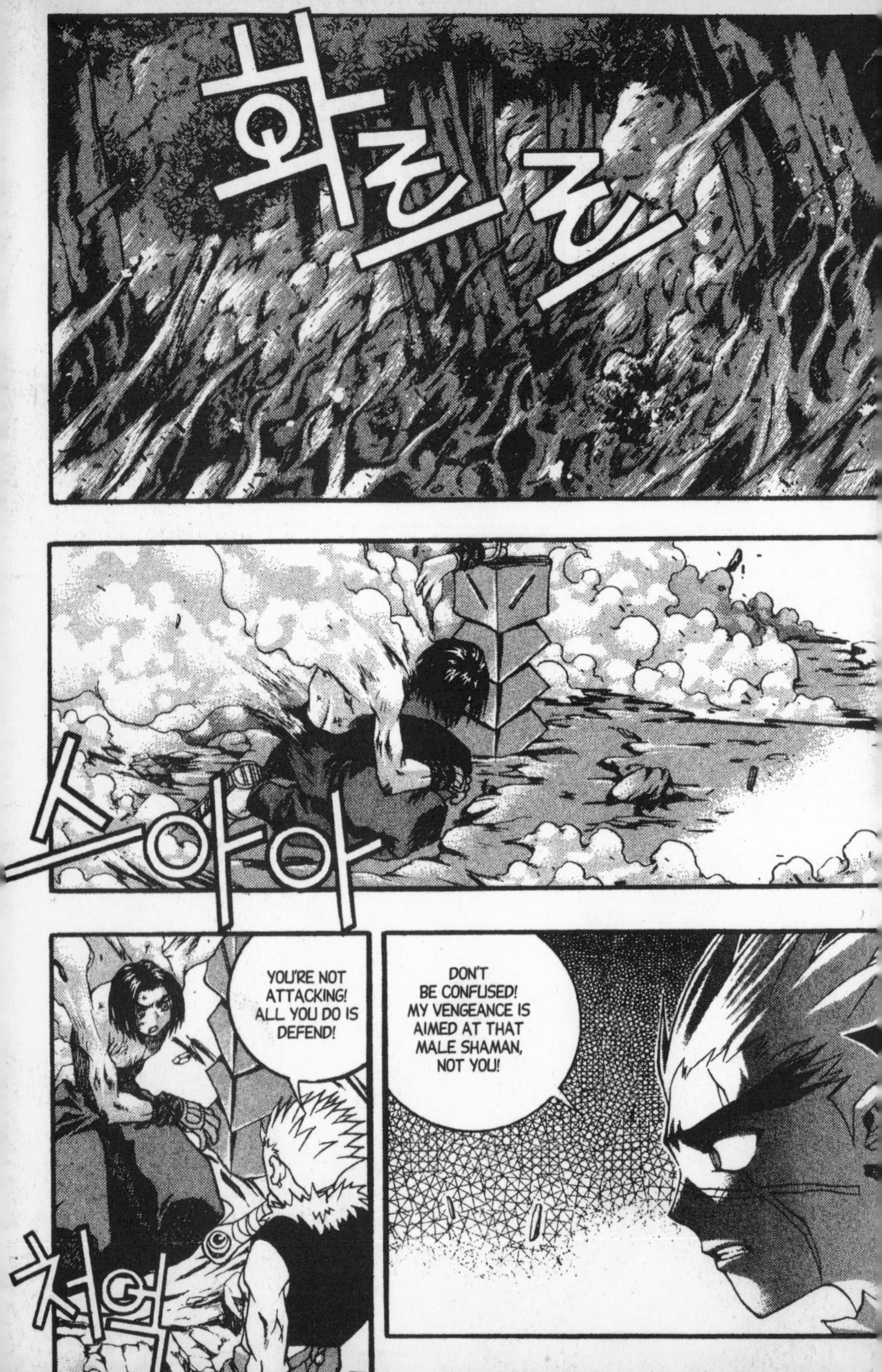
YOU'RE NOT ATTACKING! ALL YOU DO IS DEFEND!
DON'T BE CONFUSED! MY VENGEANCE IS AIMED AT THAT MALE SHAMAN, NOT YOU!

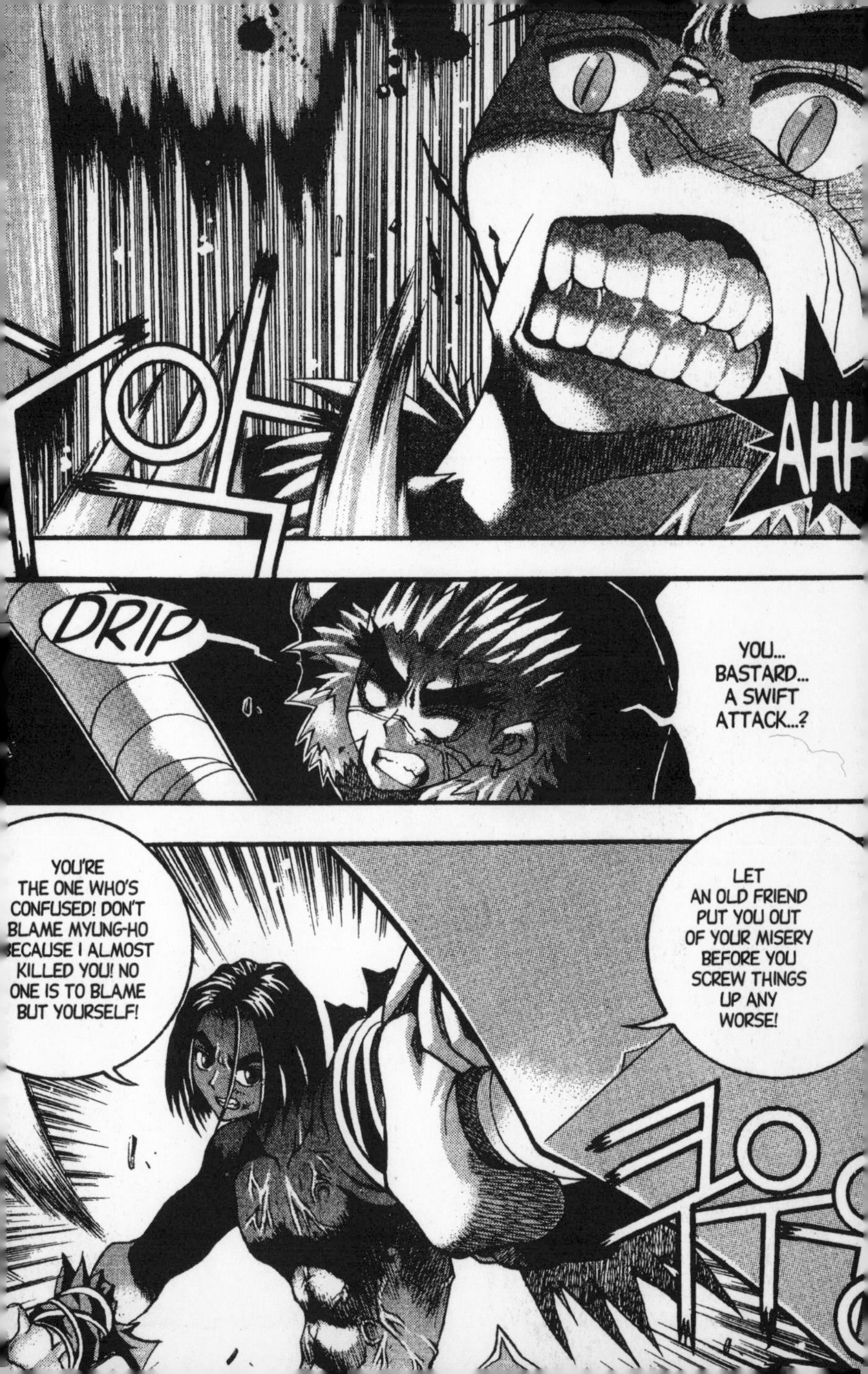
AHH
DRIP
YOU... BASTARD... A SWIFT ATTACK...?
YOU'RE THE ONE WHO'S CONFUSED! DON'T BLAME MYUNG-HO BECAUSE I ALMOST KILLED YOU! NO ONE IS TO BLAME BUT YOURSELF!
LET AN OLD FRIEND PUT YOU OUT OF YOUR MISERY BEFORE YOU SCREW THINGS UP ANY WORSE!

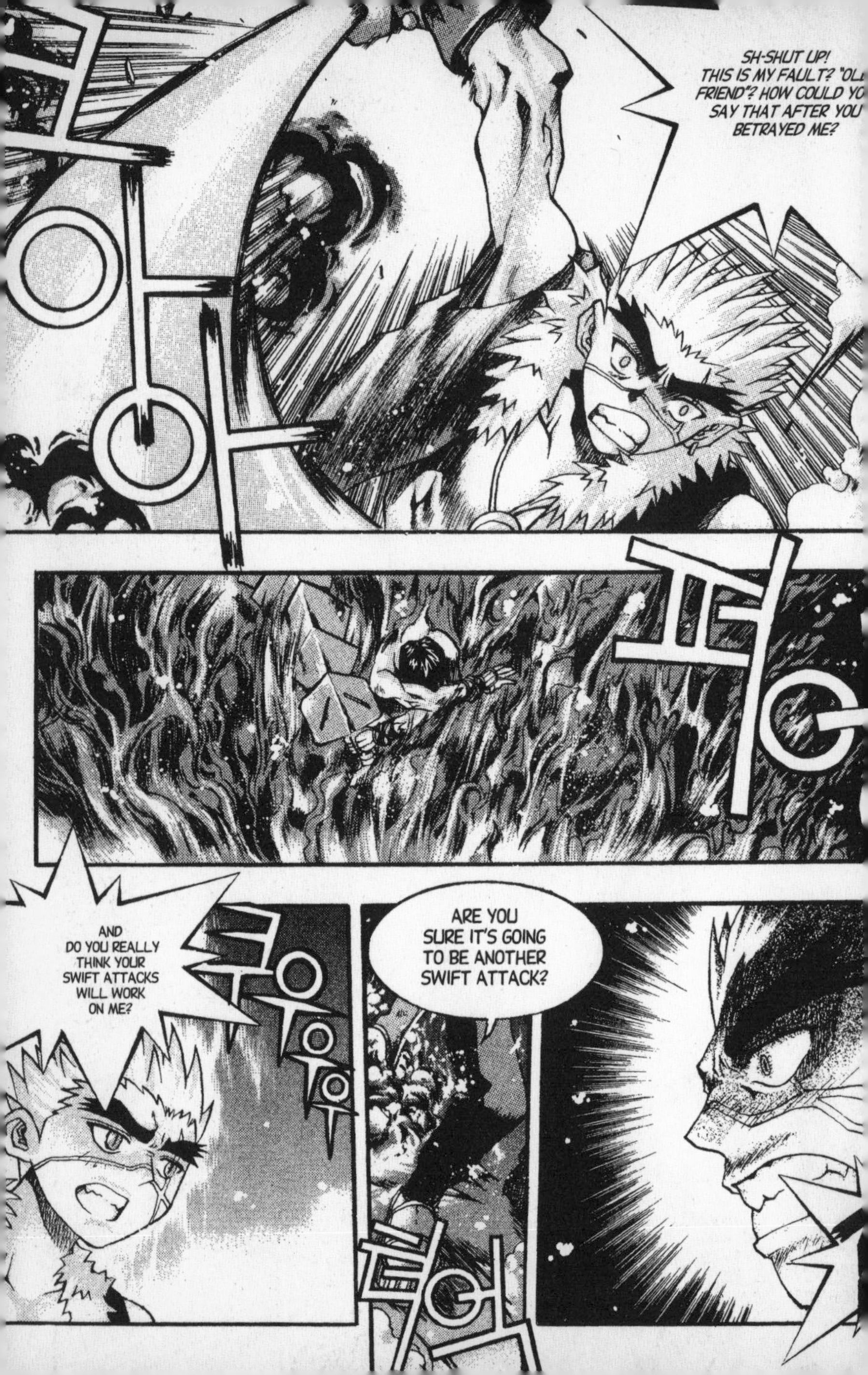
SH-SHUT UP! THIS IS MY FAULT? "OL FRIEND"? HOW COULD YO SAY THAT AFTER YOU BETRAYED ME?
AND DO YOU REALLY THINK YOUR SWIFT ATTACKS WILL WORK ON ME?
ARE YOU SURE IT'S GOING TO BE ANOTHER SWIFT ATTACK?

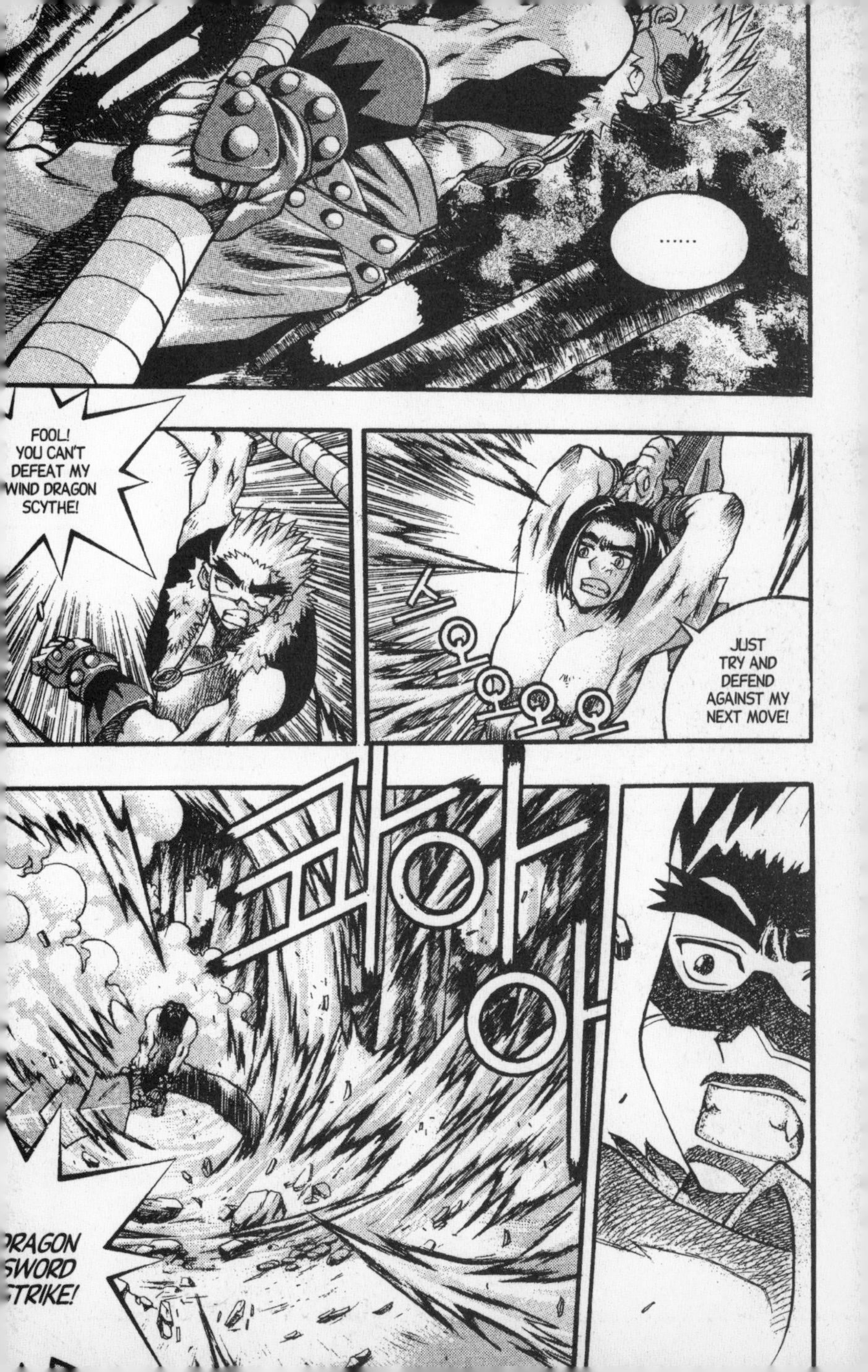
......
FOOL! YOU CAN'T DEFEAT MY WIND DRAGON SCYTHE!
JUST TRY AND DEFEND AGAINST MY NEXT MOVE!
DRAGON SWORD STRIKE!

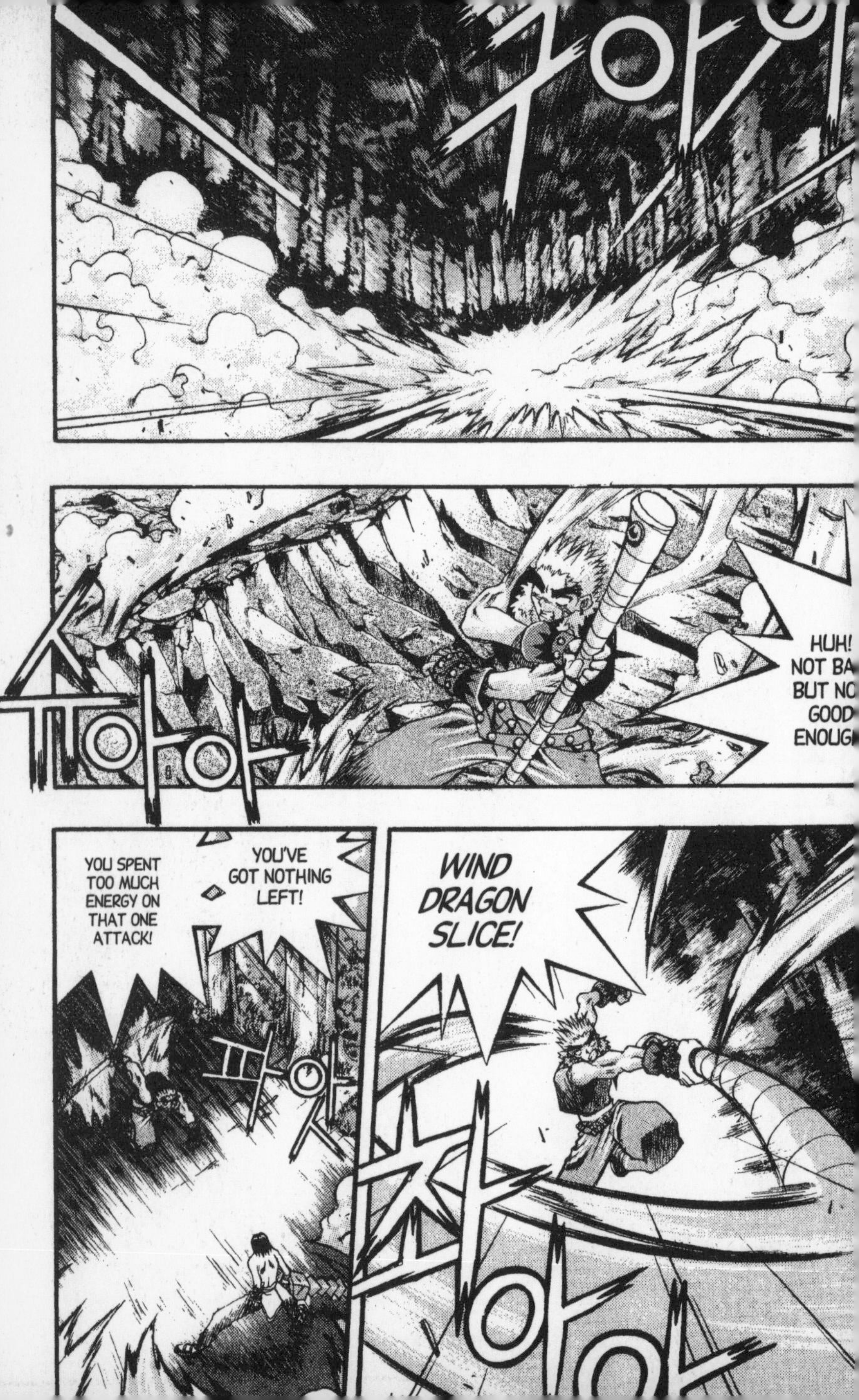
HUH! NOT BA
BUT NO
GOOD
ENOUG
YOU SPENT TOO MUCH ENERGY ON THAT ONE ATTACK!
YOU'VE GOT NOTHING LEFT!
WIND DRAGON SLICE!

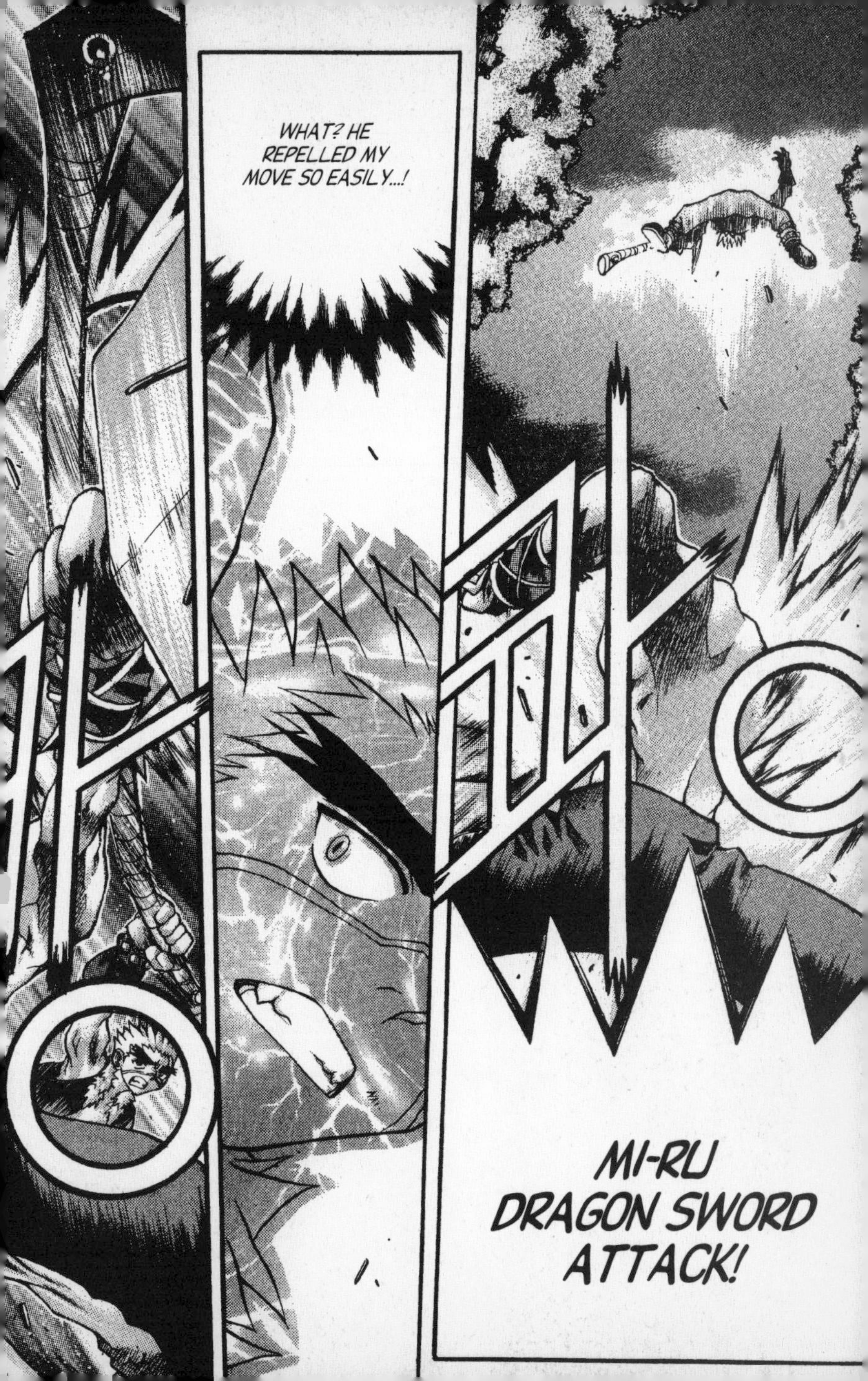
WHAT? HE REPELLED MY MOVE SO EASILY...!
MI-RU DRAGON SWORD ATTACK!

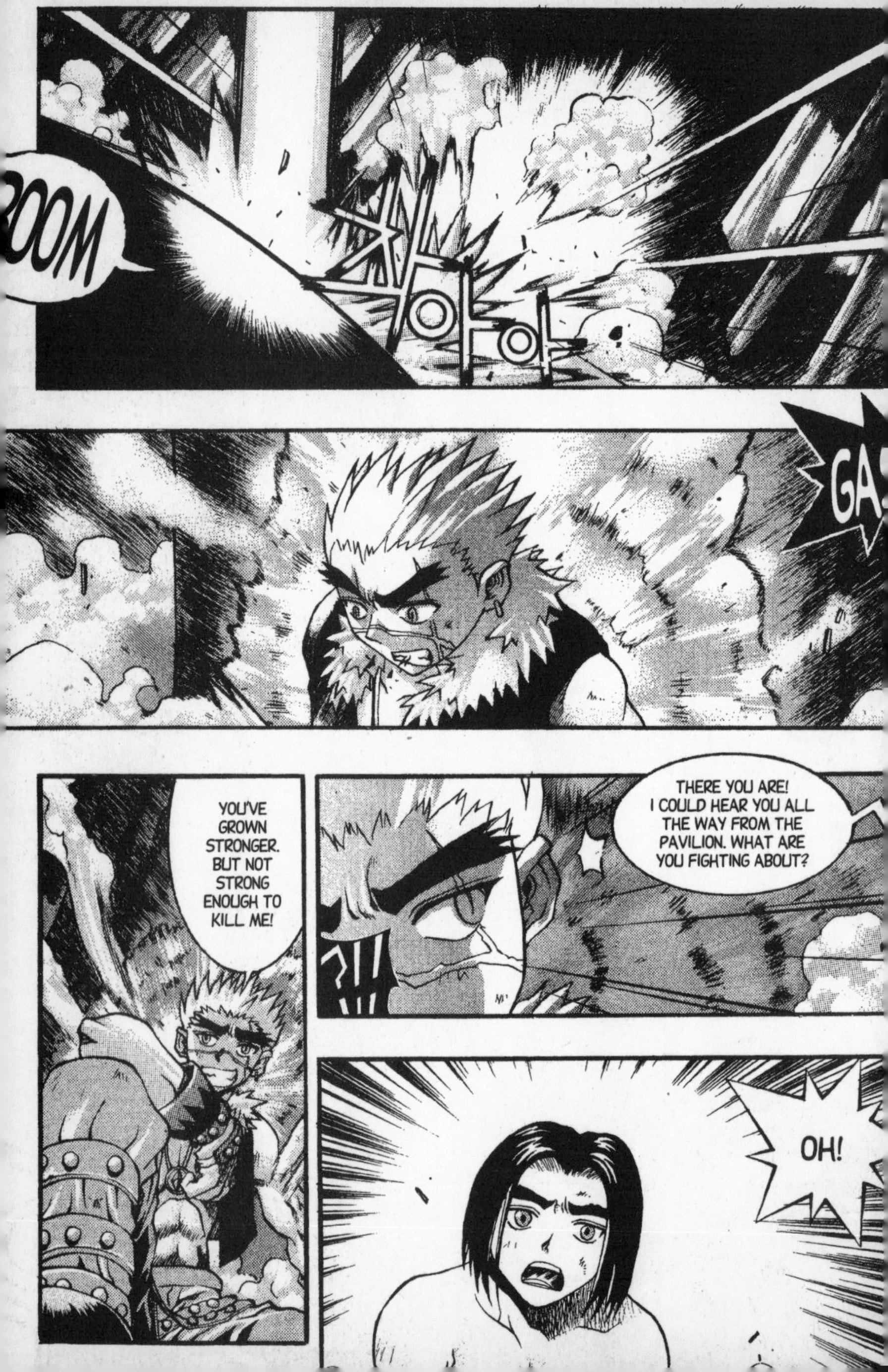

OOM
GA
YOU'VE GROWN STRONGER. BUT NOT STRONG ENOUGH TO KILL ME!
?!!
THERE YOU ARE! I COULD HEAR YOU ALL THE WAY FROM THE PAVILION. WHAT ARE YOU FIGHTING ABOUT?
OH!

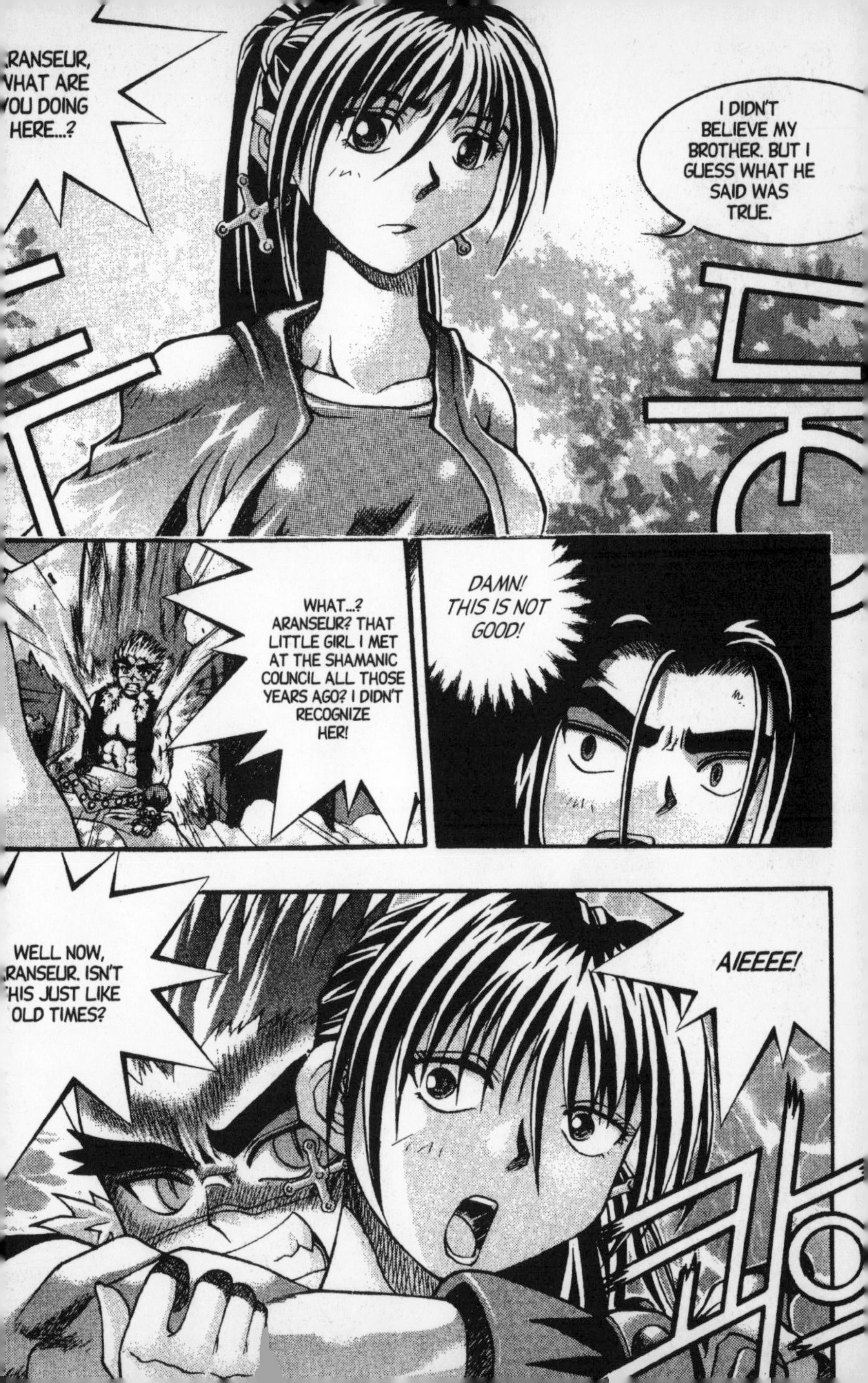
ARANSEUR, WHAT ARE YOU DOING HERE...?
I DIDN'T BELIEVE MY BROTHER. BUT I GUESS WHAT HE SAID WAS TRUE.
WHAT...? ARANSEUR? THAT LITTLE GIRL I MET AT THE SHAMANIC COUNCIL ALL THOSE YEARS AGO? I DIDN'T RECOGNIZE HER!
DAMN! THIS IS NOT GOOD!
WELL NOW, ARANSEUR. ISN'T THIS JUST LIKE OLD TIMES?
AIEEEE!

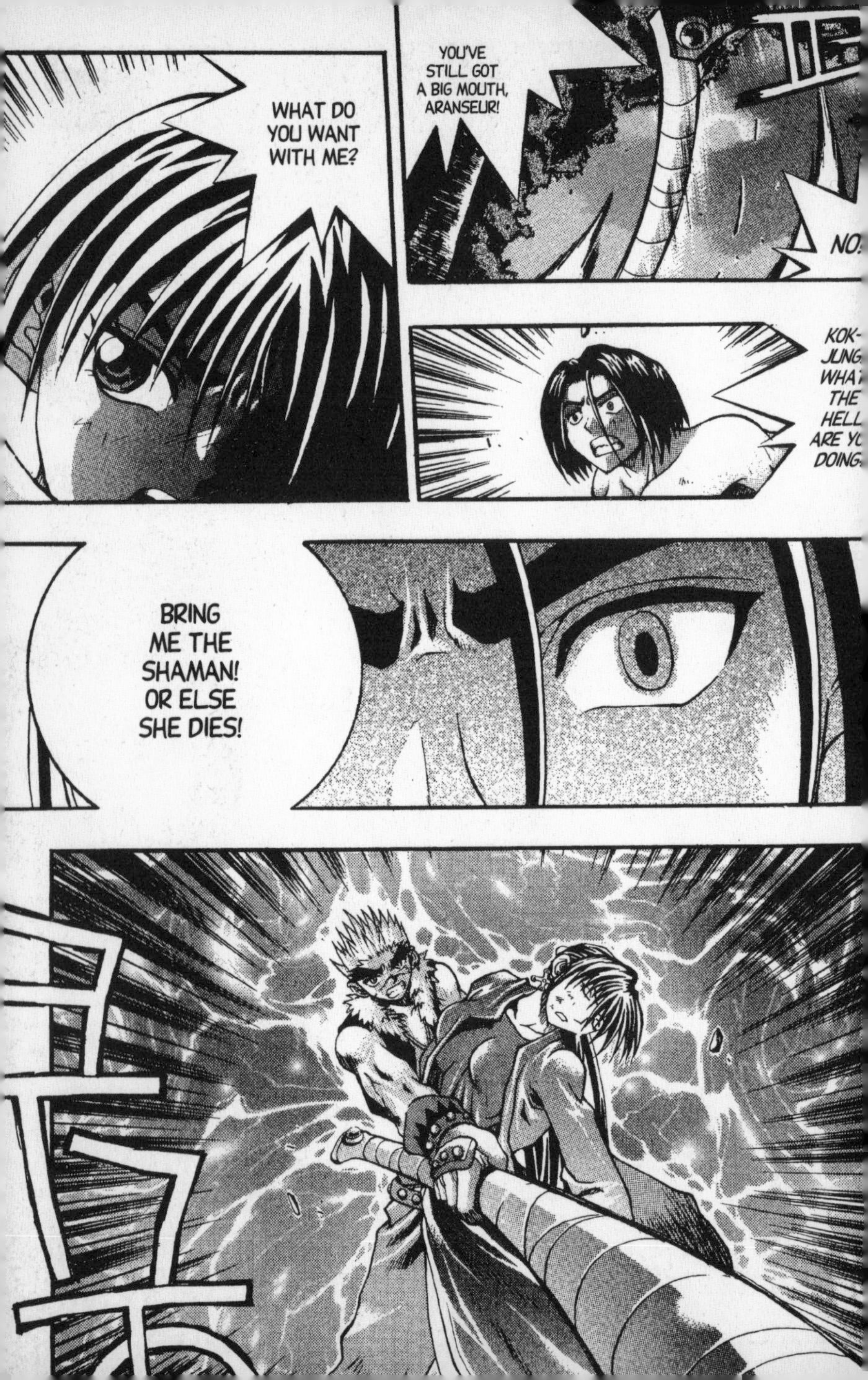
WHAT DO YOU WANT WITH ME?
YOU'VE STILL GOT A BIG MOUTH, ARANSEUR!
NO
KOK-JUNG WHA THE HELL ARE YO DOING
BRING ME THE SHAMAN! OR ELSE SHE DIES!

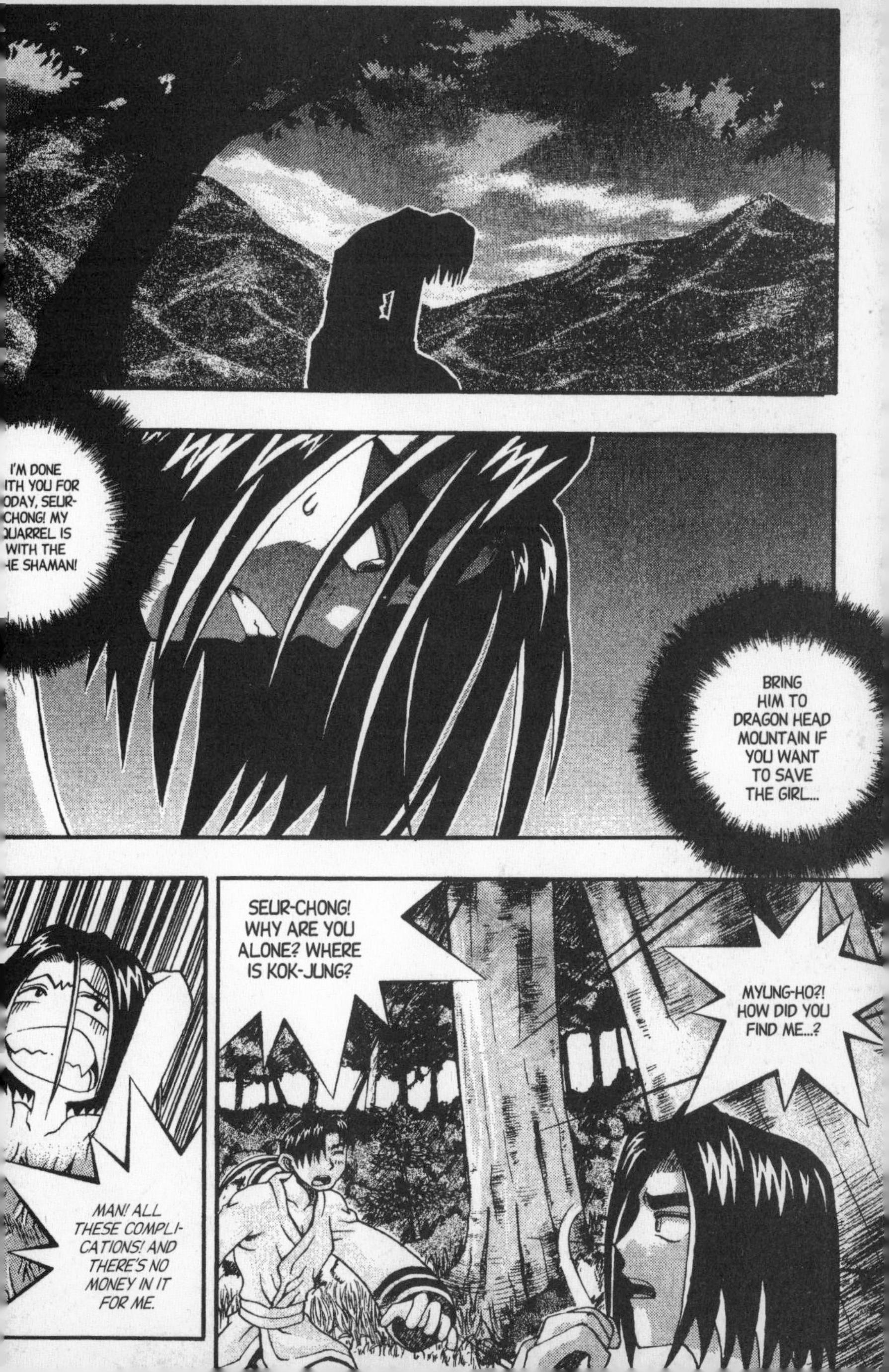
I'M DONE ITH YOU FOR ODAY, SEUR-CHONG! MY QUARREL IS WITH THE HE SHAMAN!
BRING HIM TO DRAGON HEAD MOUNTAIN IF YOU WANT TO SAVE THE GIRL...
MAN! ALL THESE COMPLI-CATIONS! AND THERE'S NO MONEY IN IT FOR ME.
SEUR-CHONG! WHY ARE YOU ALONE? WHERE IS KOK-JUNG?
MYUNG-HO?! HOW DID YOU FIND ME...?

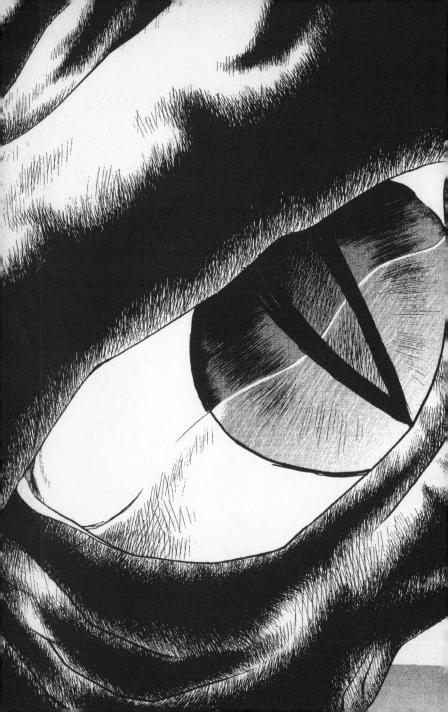

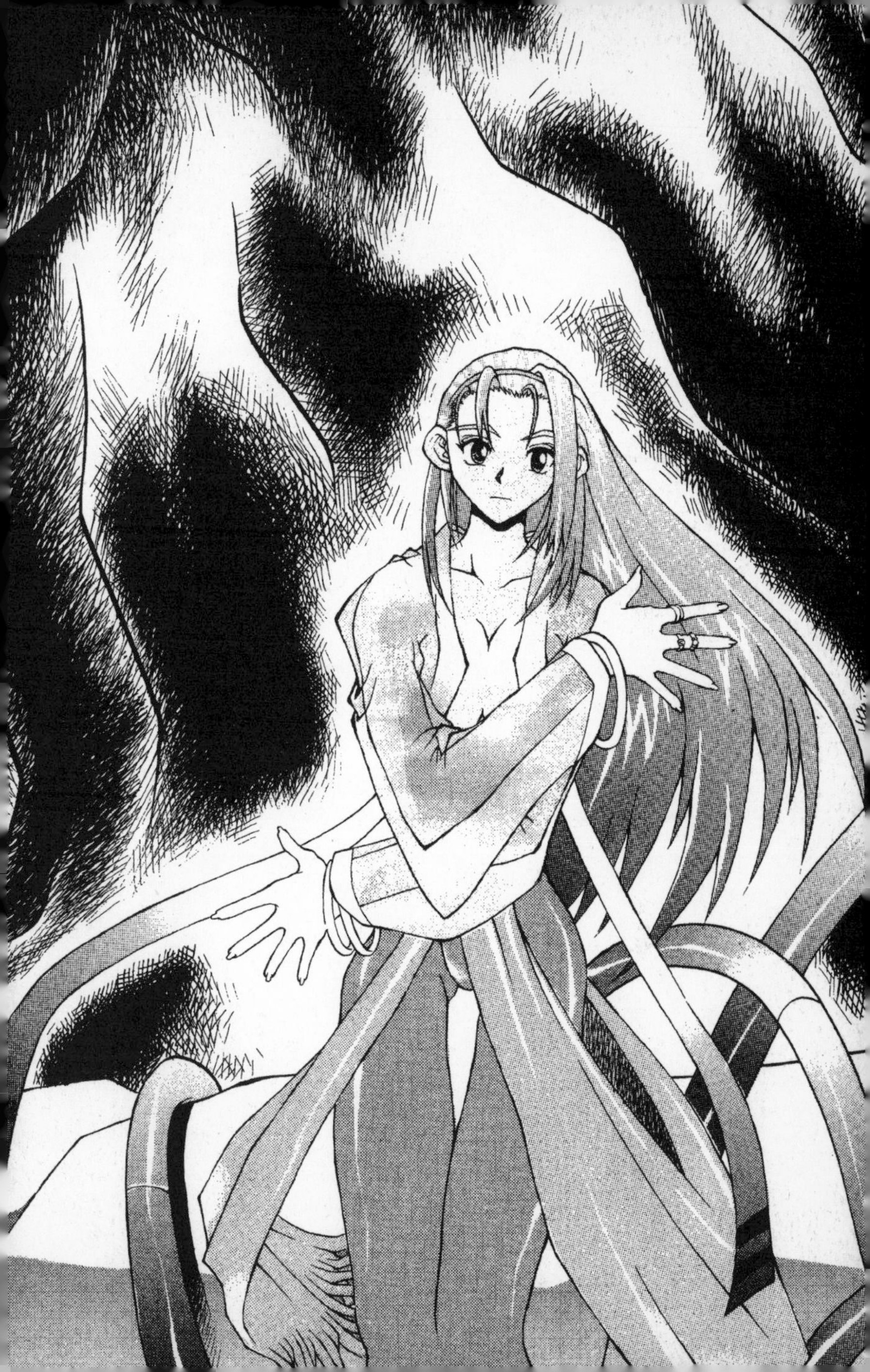

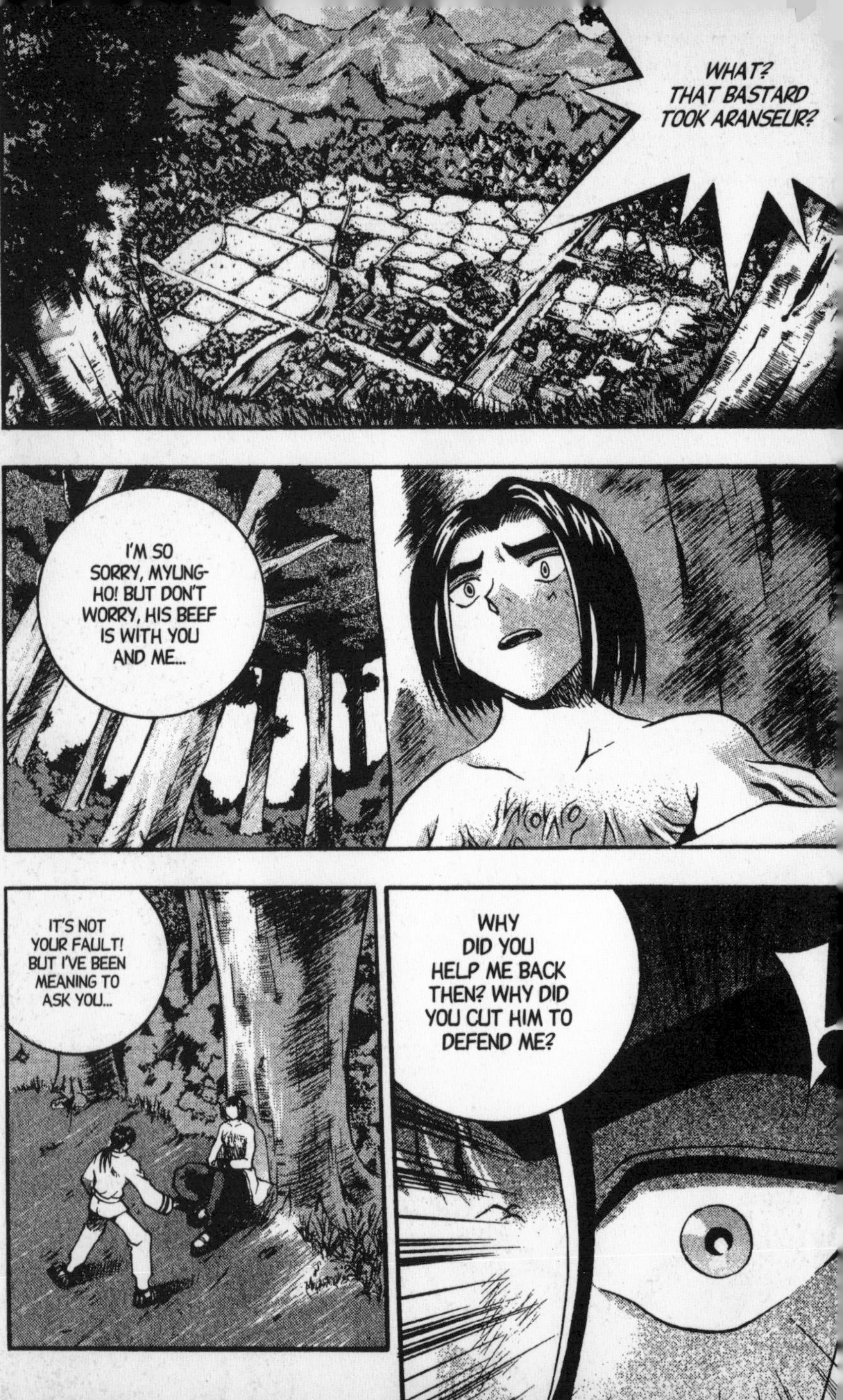
WHAT? THAT BASTARD TOOK ARANSEUR?
I'M SO SORRY, MYUNG-HO! BUT DON'T WORRY, HIS BEEF IS WITH YOU AND ME...
IT'S NOT YOUR FAULT! BUT I'VE BEEN MEANING TO ASK YOU...
WHY DID YOU HELP ME BACK THEN? WHY DID YOU CUT HIM TO DEFEND ME?

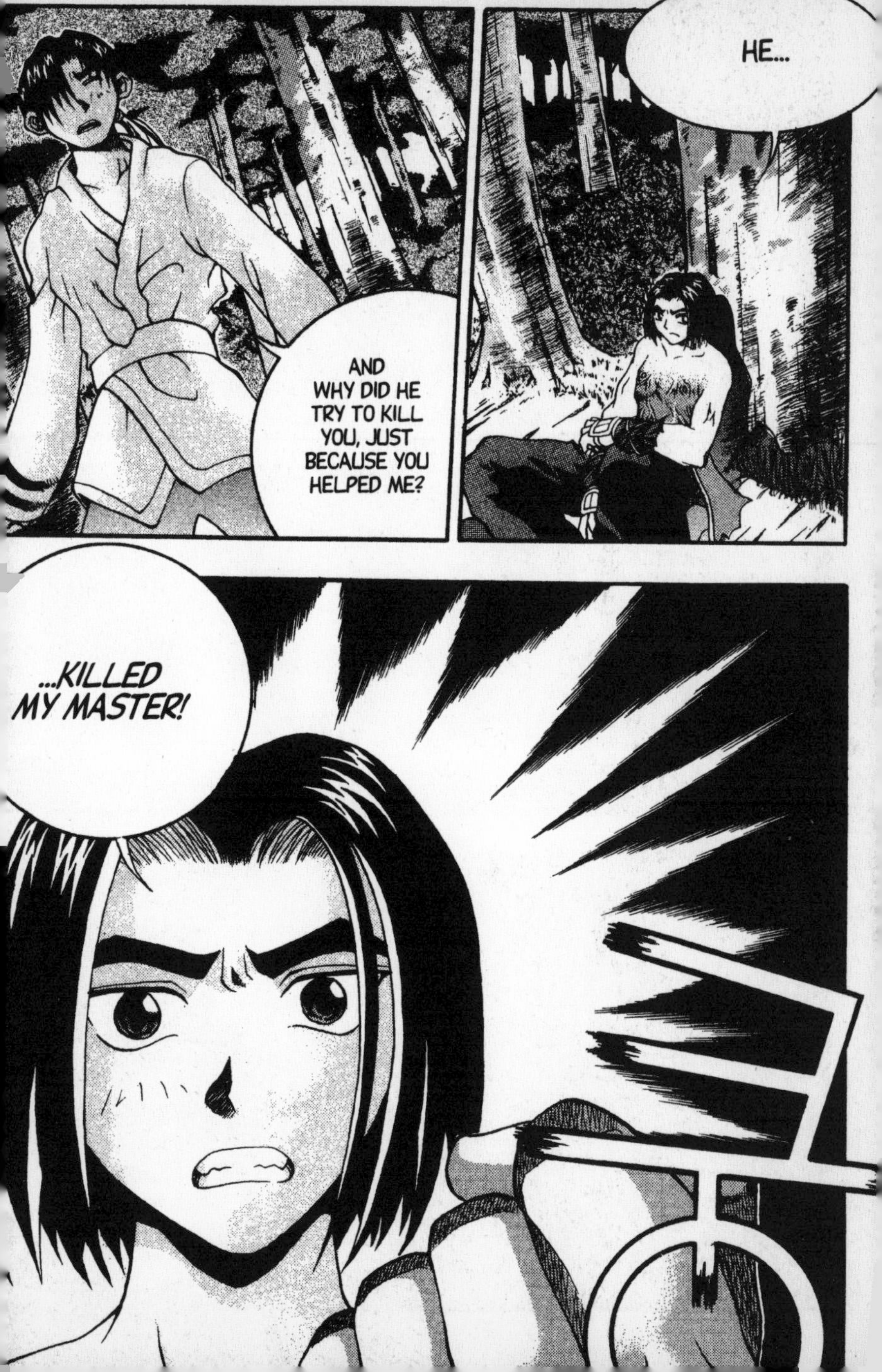
AND WHY DID HE TRY TO KILL YOU, JUST BECAUSE YOU HELPED ME?
HE...
...KILLED MY MASTER!

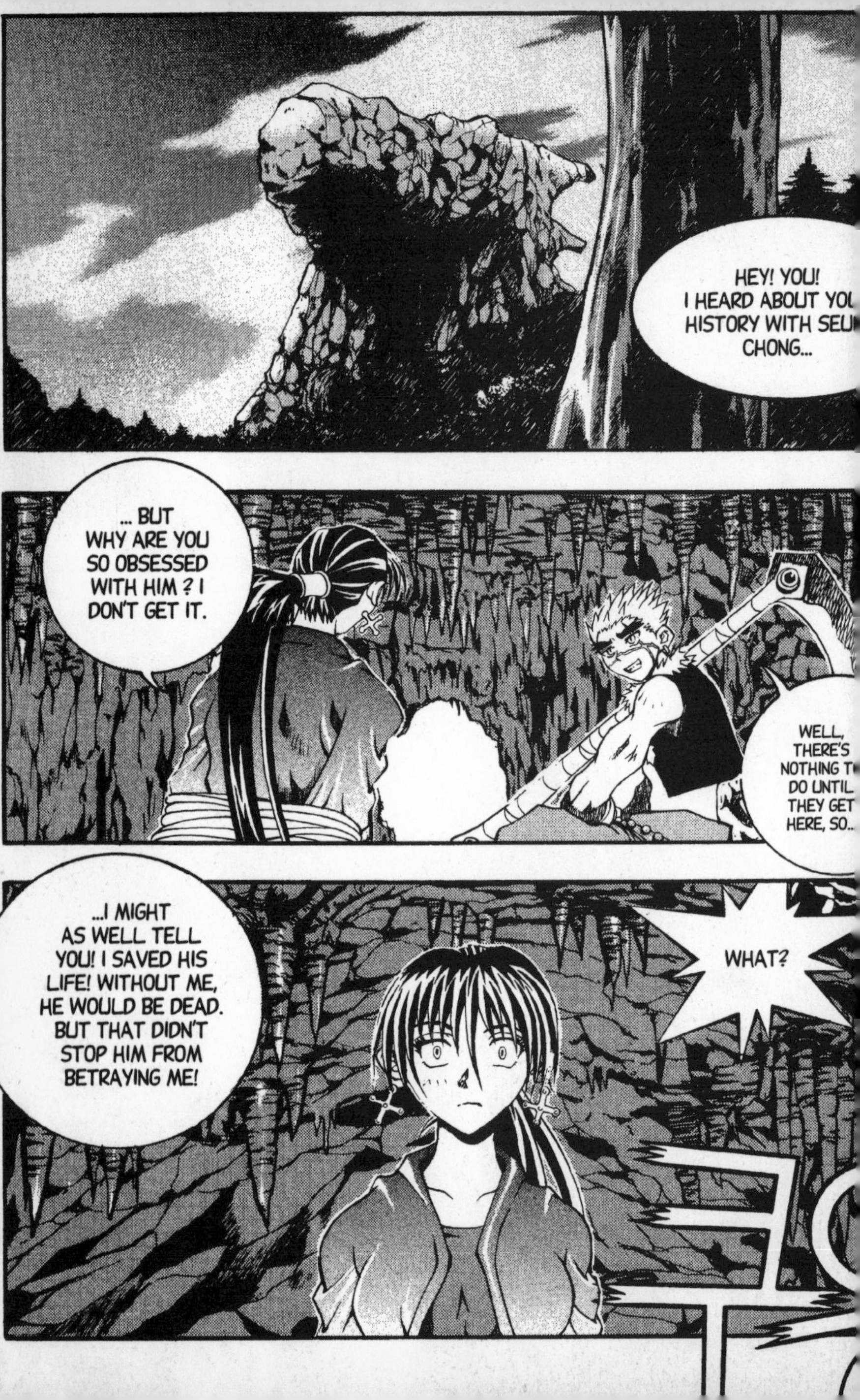
HEY! YOU! I HEARD ABOUT YOU HISTORY WITH SEU CHONG...
... BUT WHY ARE YOU SO OBSESSED WITH HIM ? I DON'T GET IT.
WELL, THERE'S NOTHING T DO UNTIL THEY GET HERE, SO...
...I MIGHT AS WELL TELL YOU! I SAVED HIS LIFE! WITHOUT ME, HE WOULD BE DEAD. BUT THAT DIDN'T STOP HIM FROM BETRAYING ME!
WHAT?

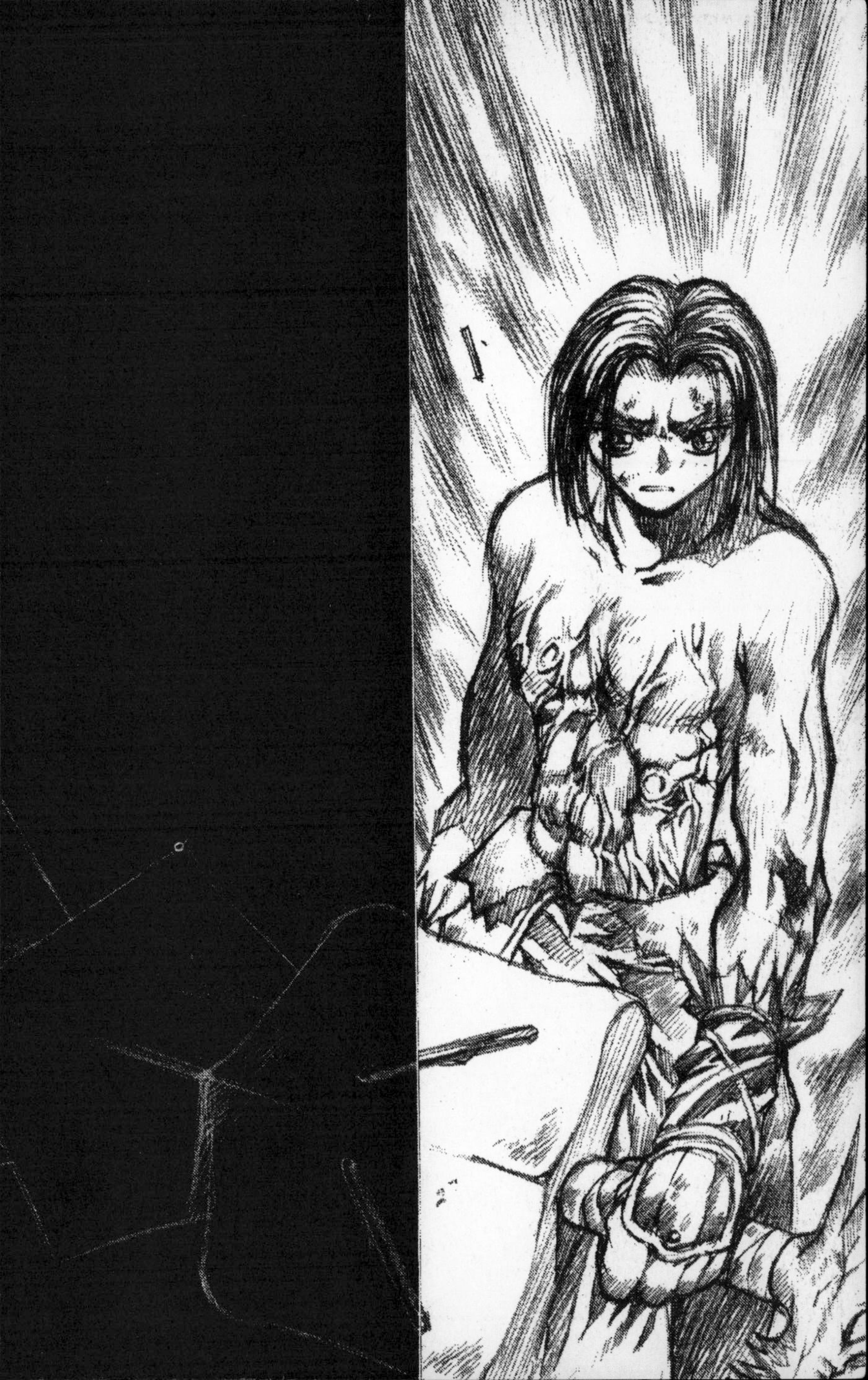

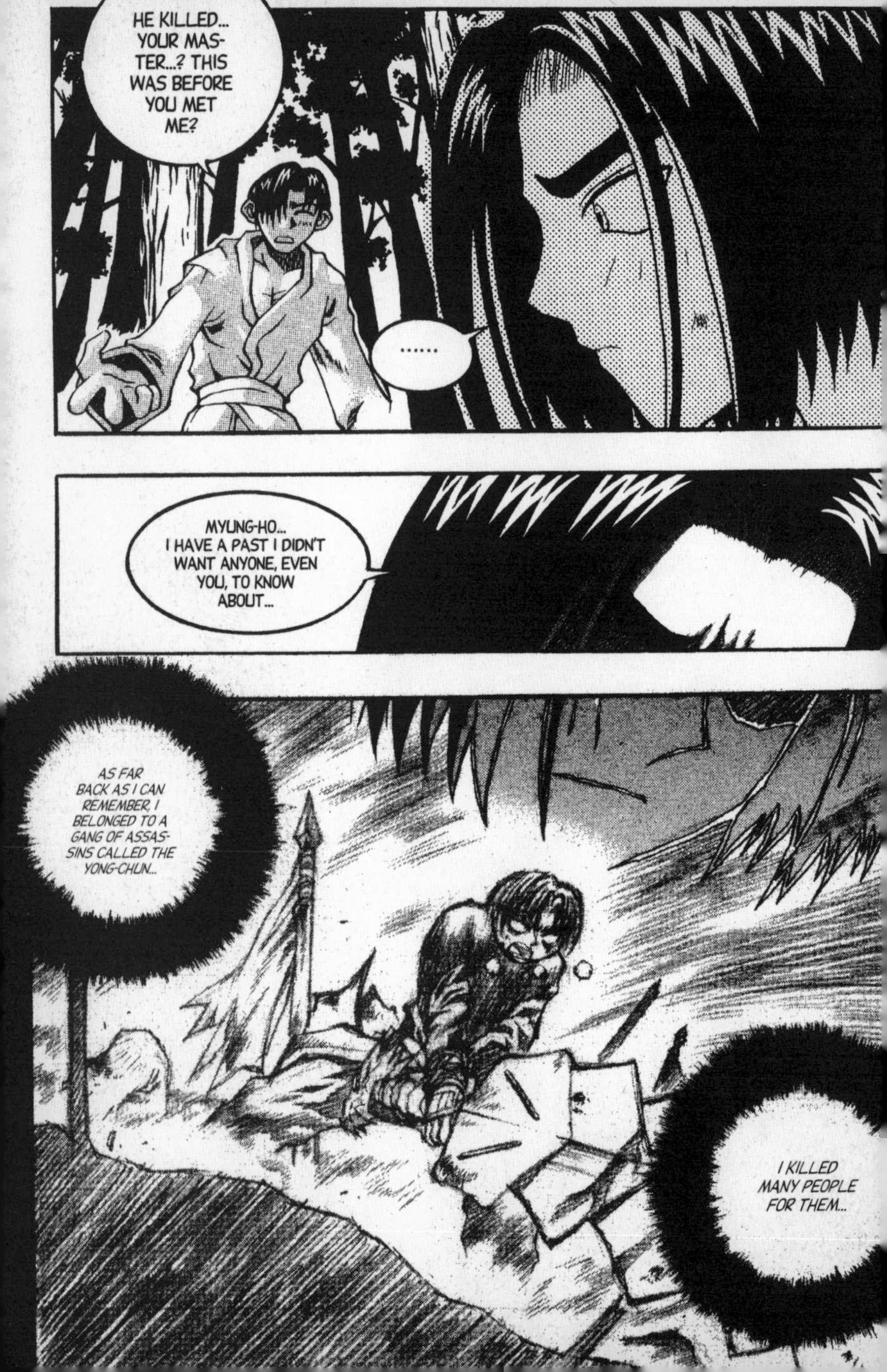
HE KILLED... YOUR MASTER...? THIS WAS BEFORE YOU MET ME?
......
MYUNG-HO... I HAVE A PAST I DIDN'T WANT ANYONE, EVEN YOU, TO KNOW ABOUT...
AS FAR BACK AS I CAN REMEMBER, I BELONGED TO A GANG OF ASSASSINS CALLED THE YONG-CHUN...
I KILLED MANY PEOPLE FOR THEM...

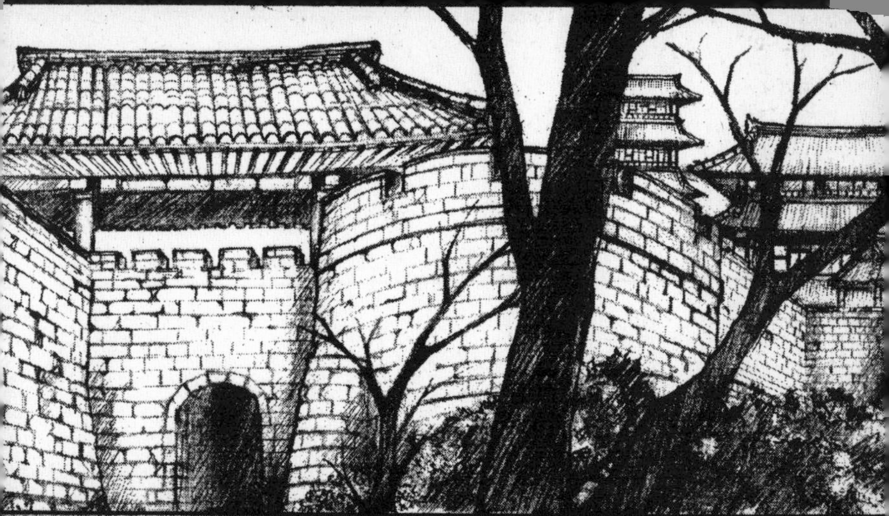

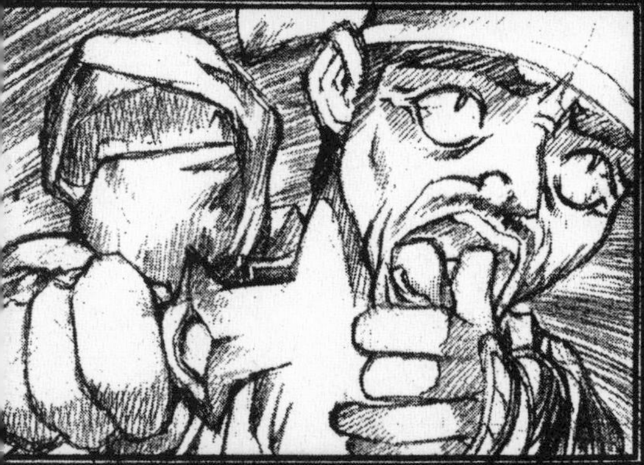

OUR MISSIONS INVOLVED GATHERING INTELLIGENCE, PROTECTING CERTAIN POLITI-CIANS AND KILLING OTHERS.

I WORKED FOR THAT GANG AS LONG AS I COULD REMEMBER.

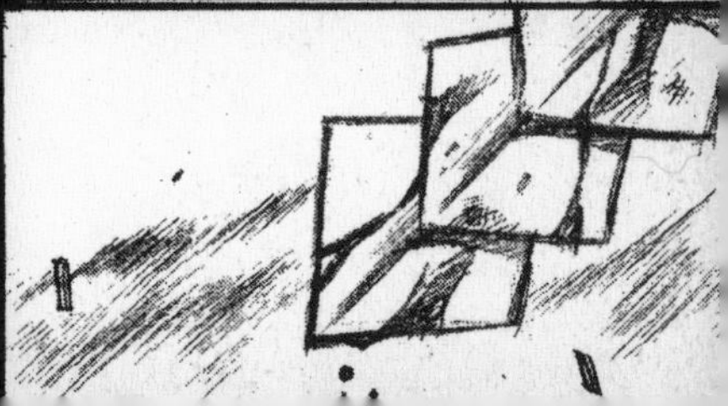

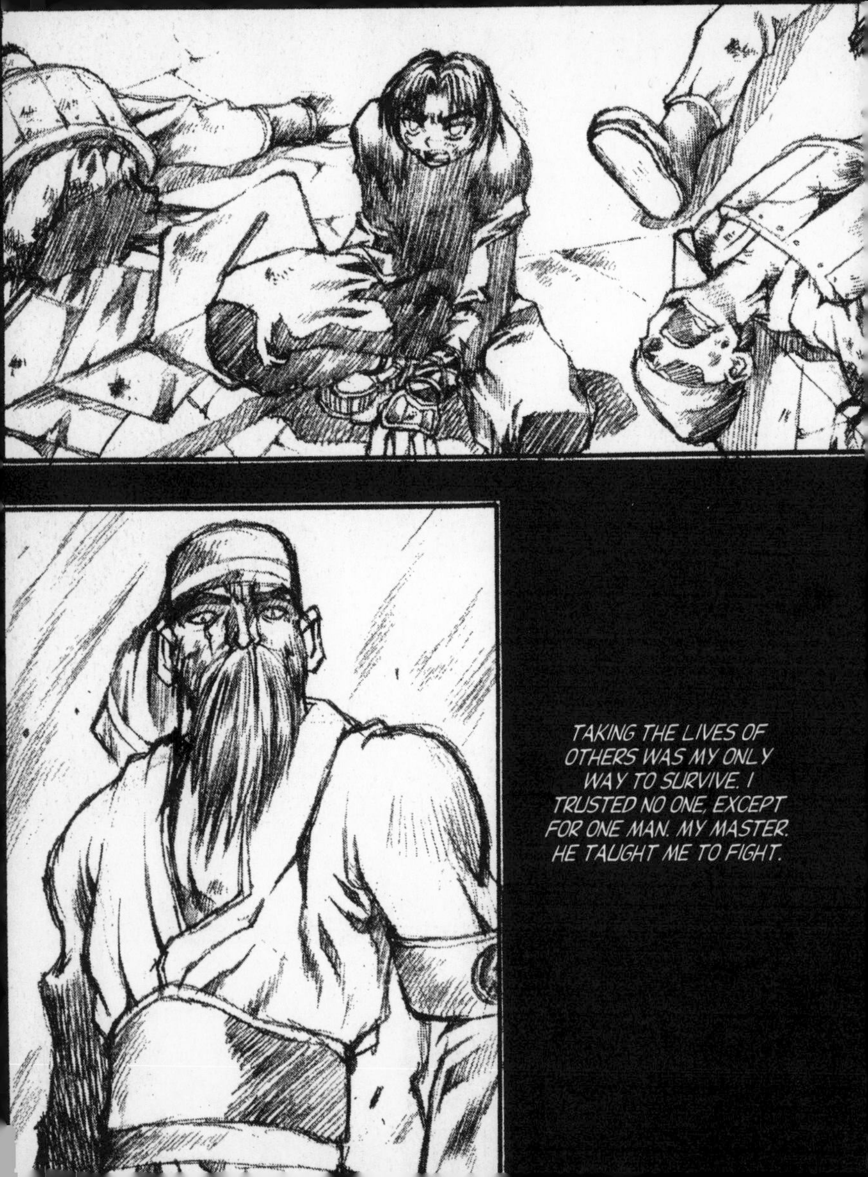
TAKING THE LIVES OF OTHERS WAS MY ONLY WAY TO SURVIVE. I TRUSTED NO ONE, EXCEPT FOR ONE MAN. MY MASTER. HE TAUGHT ME TO FIGHT.

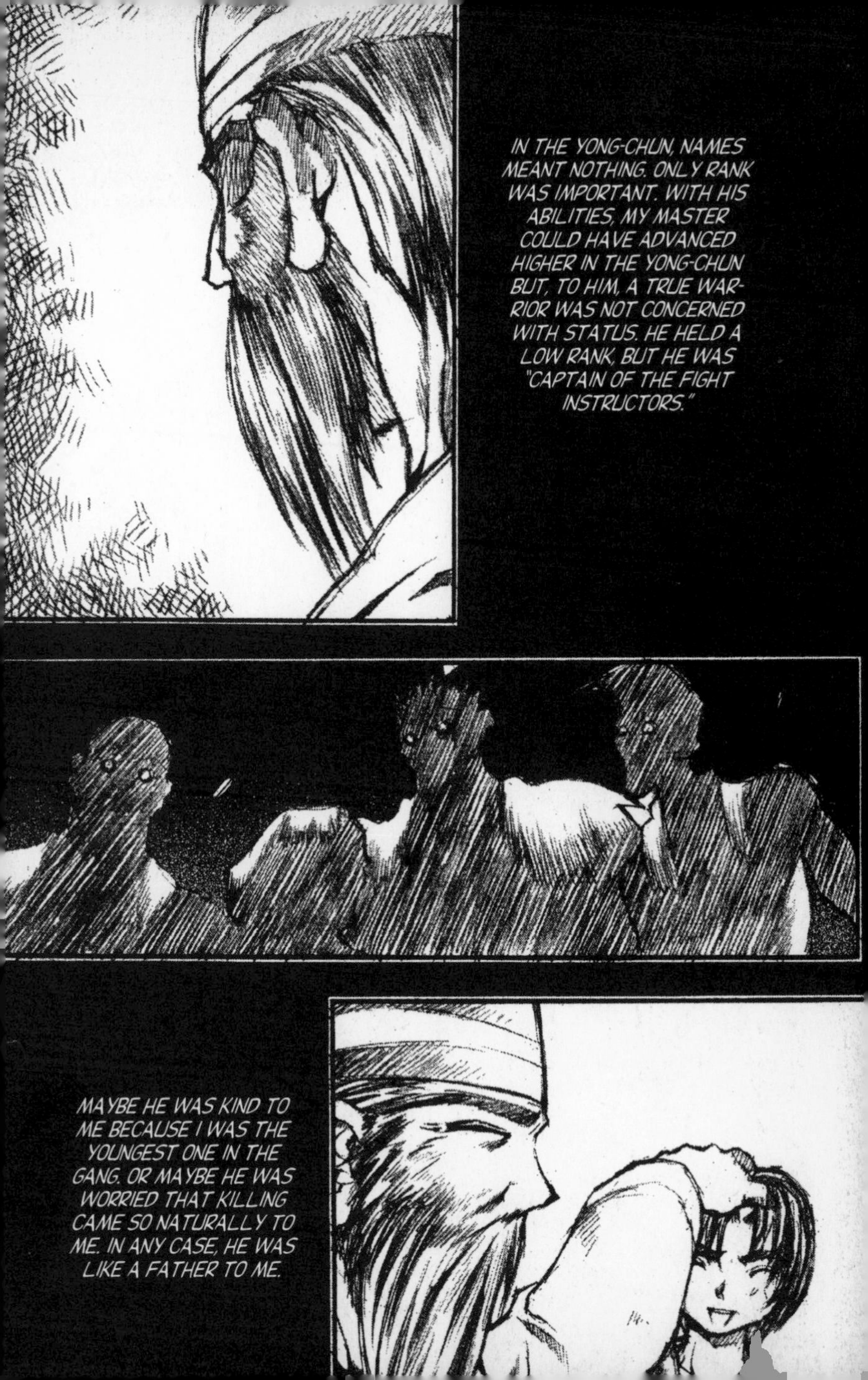
IN THE YONG-CHUN, NAMES MEANT NOTHING. ONLY RANK WAS IMPORTANT. WITH HIS ABILITIES, MY MASTER COULD HAVE ADVANCED HIGHER IN THE YONG-CHUN BUT, TO HIM, A TRUE WARRIOR WAS NOT CONCERNED WITH STATUS. HE HELD A LOW RANK, BUT HE WAS "CAPTAIN OF THE FIGHT INSTRUCTORS."
MAYBE HE WAS KIND TO ME BECAUSE I WAS THE YOUNGEST ONE IN THE GANG. OR MAYBE HE WAS WORRIED THAT KILLING CAME SO NATURALLY TO ME. IN ANY CASE, HE WAS LIKE A FATHER TO ME.

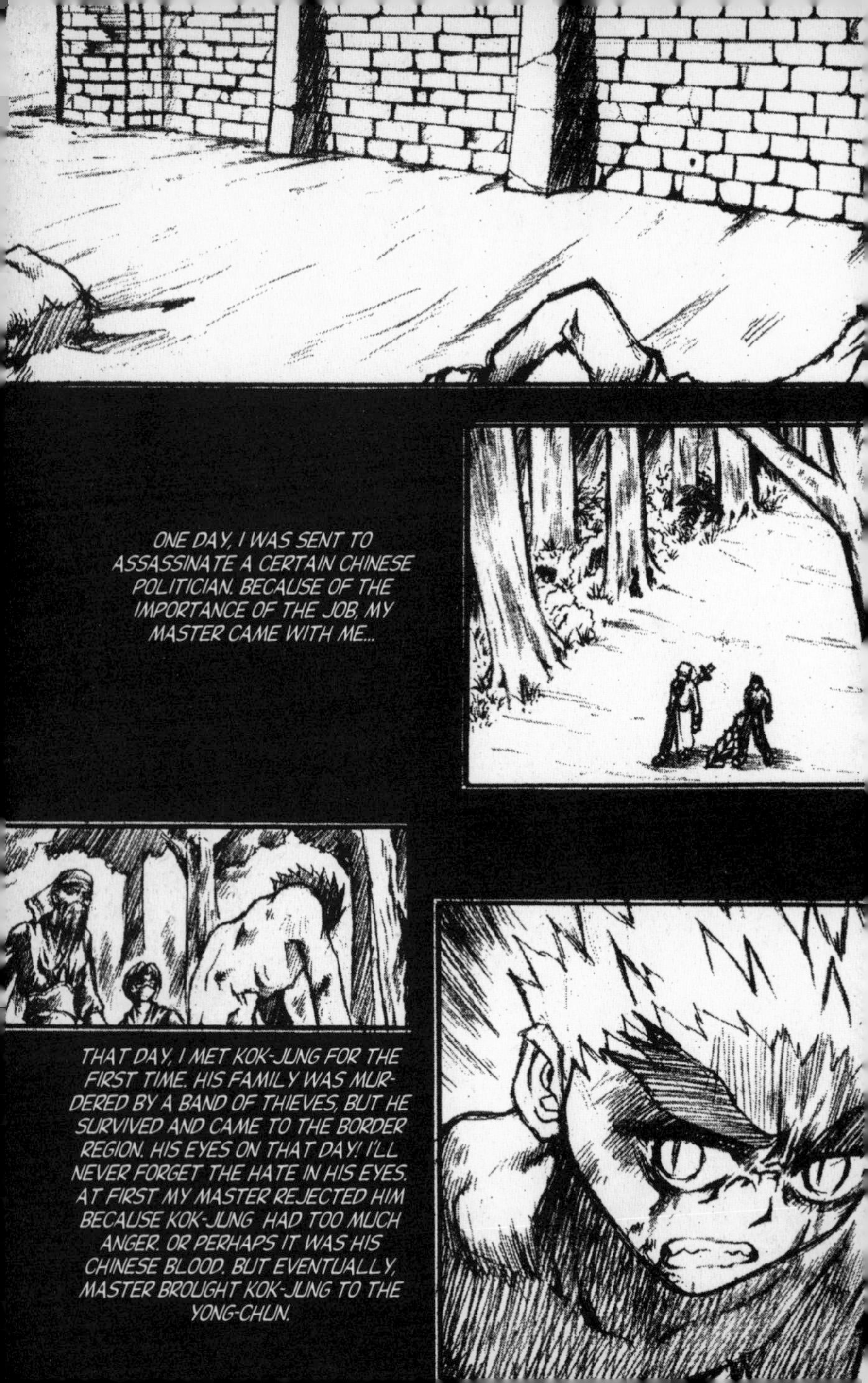
ONE DAY, I WAS SENT TO ASSASSINATE A CERTAIN CHINESE POLITICIAN. BECAUSE OF THE IMPORTANCE OF THE JOB, MY MASTER CAME WITH ME...
THAT DAY, I MET KOK-JUNG FOR THE FIRST TIME. HIS FAMILY WAS MURDERED BY A BAND OF THIEVES, BUT HE SURVIVED AND CAME TO THE BORDER REGION. HIS EYES ON THAT DAY! I'LL NEVER FORGET THE HATE IN HIS EYES. AT FIRST MY MASTER REJECTED HIM BECAUSE KOK-JUNG HAD TOO MUCH ANGER. OR PERHAPS IT WAS HIS CHINESE BLOOD. BUT EVENTUALLY, MASTER BROUGHT KOK-JUNG TO THE YONG-CHUN.

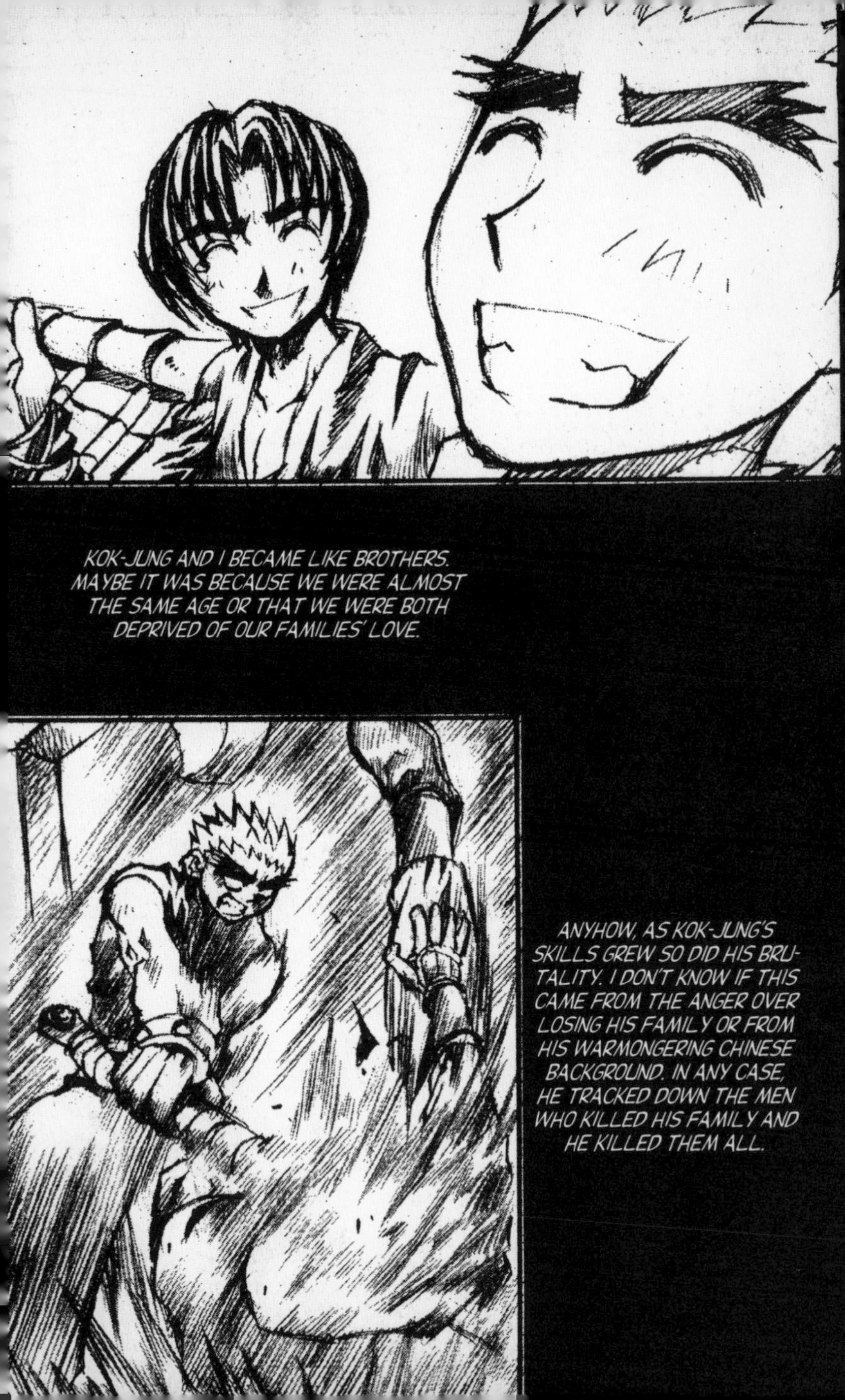
KOK-JUNG AND I BECAME LIKE BROTHERS. MAYBE IT WAS BECAUSE WE WERE ALMOST THE SAME AGE OR THAT WE WERE BOTH DEPRIVED OF OUR FAMILIES' LOVE.
ANYHOW, AS KOK-JUNG'S SKILLS GREW SO DID HIS BRUTALITY. I DON'T KNOW IF THIS CAME FROM THE ANGER OVER LOSING HIS FAMILY OR FROM HIS WARMONGERING CHINESE BACKGROUND. IN ANY CASE, HE TRACKED DOWN THE MEN WHO KILLED HIS FAMILY AND HE KILLED THEM ALL.

MASTER DIDN'T LIKE KOK-JUNG
BECAUSE OF HIS BRUTAL NATURE,
AND KOK-JUNG KNEW IT.

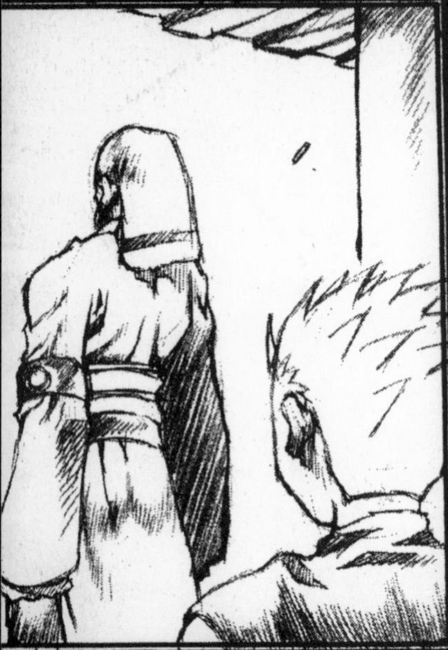

MEANWHILE THE COUNTRY
CONTINUED TO DIVIDE.

WE KILLED MORE AND MORE PEOPLE
BECAUSE OF THE GOVERNMENTAL
POWER STRUGGLES.

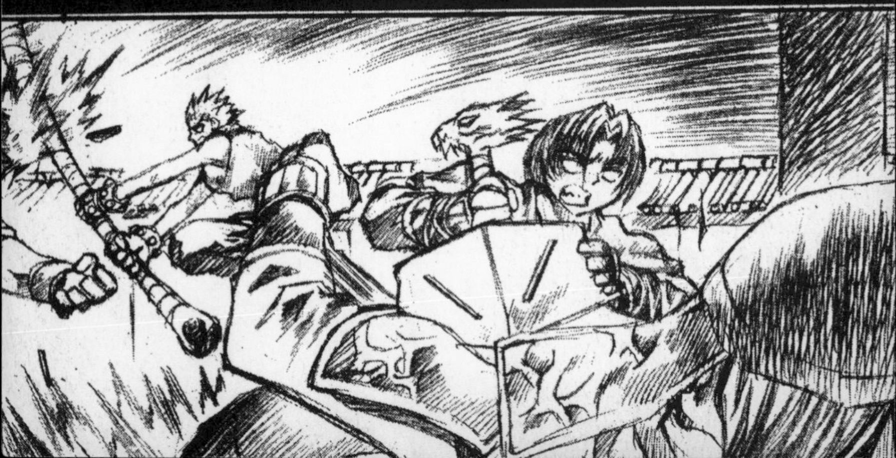

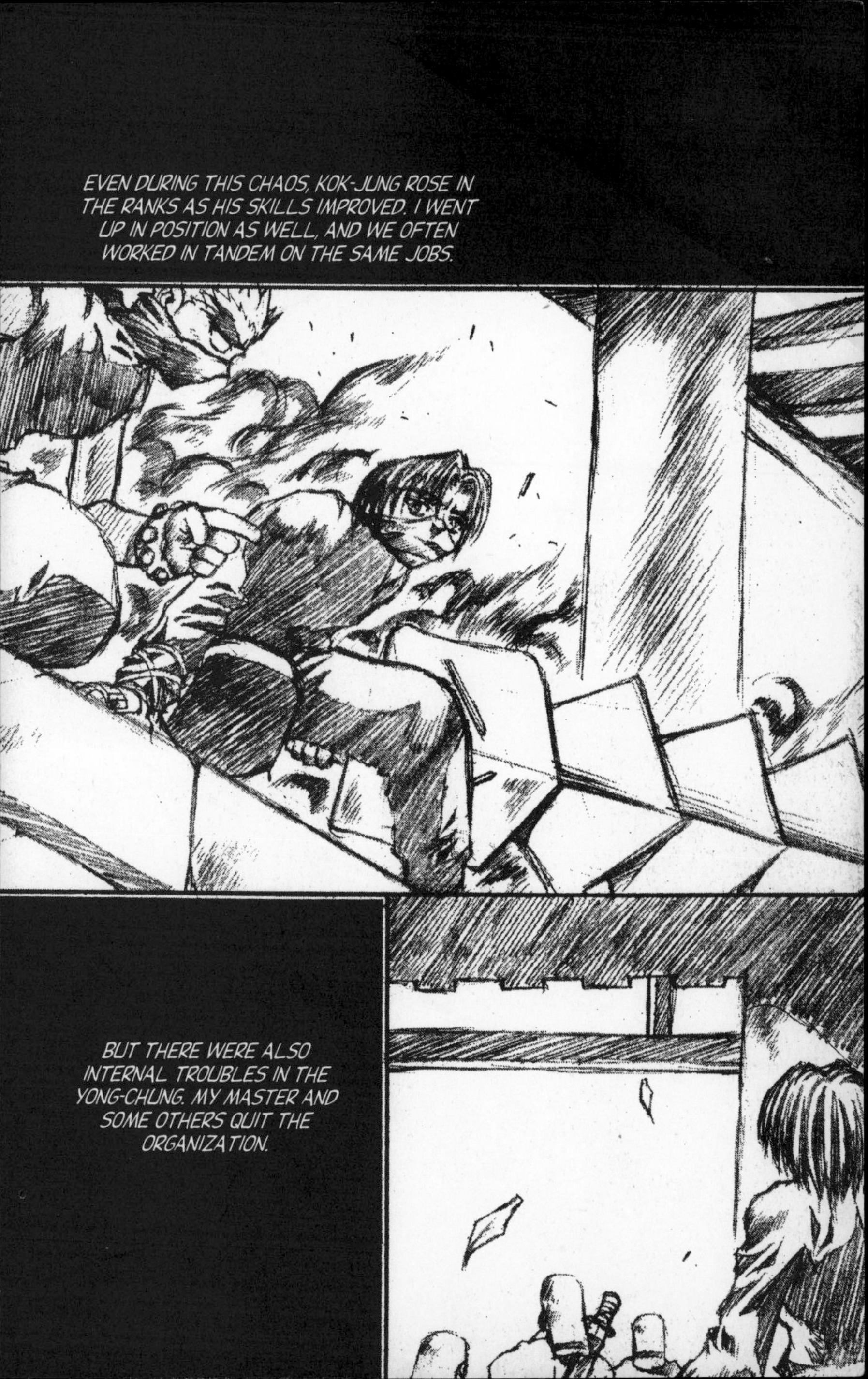
EVEN DURING THIS CHAOS, KOK-JUNG ROSE IN THE RANKS AS HIS SKILLS IMPROVED. I WENT UP IN POSITION AS WELL, AND WE OFTEN WORKED IN TANDEM ON THE SAME JOBS.
BUT THERE WERE ALSO INTERNAL TROUBLES IN THE YONG-CHUNG. MY MASTER AND SOME OTHERS QUIT THE ORGANIZATION.

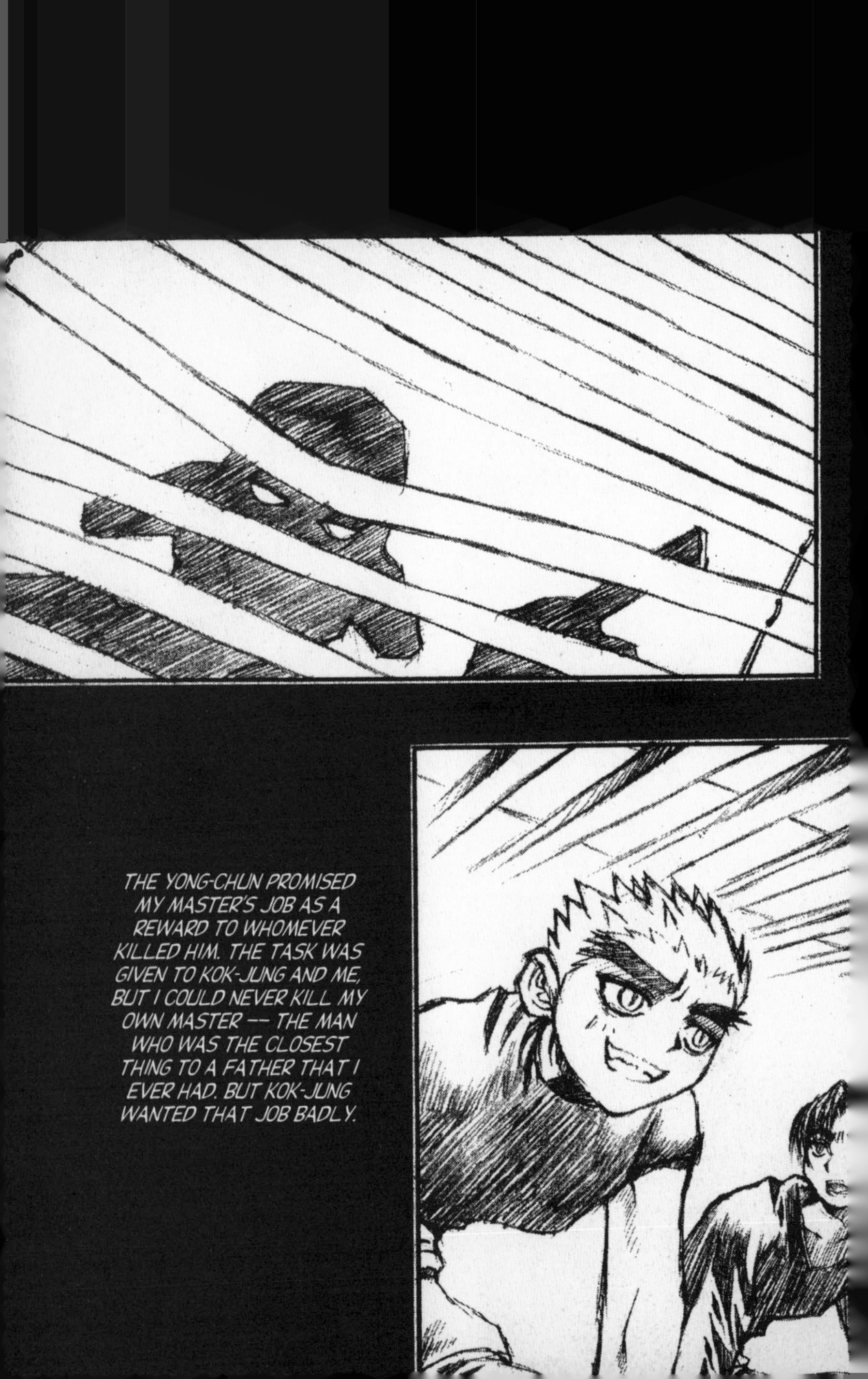
THE YONG-CHUN PROMISED MY MASTER'S JOB AS A REWARD TO WHOMEVER KILLED HIM. THE TASK WAS GIVEN TO KOK-JUNG AND ME, BUT I COULD NEVER KILL MY OWN MASTER -- THE MAN WHO WAS THE CLOSEST THING TO A FATHER THAT I EVER HAD. BUT KOK-JUNG WANTED THAT JOB BADLY.

EVENTUALLY, KOK-JUNG FOUND MY MASTER AND THE OTHER DESERTERS...

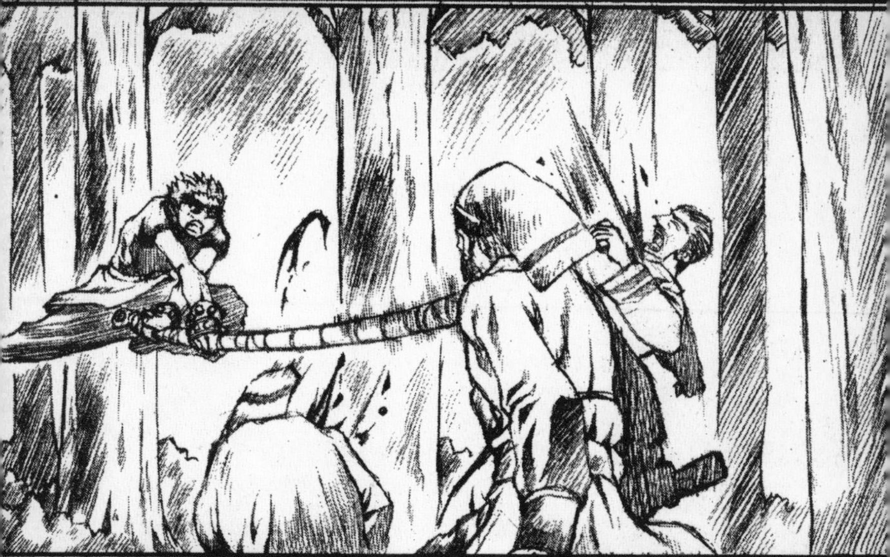

AND HE KILLED MY MASTER...

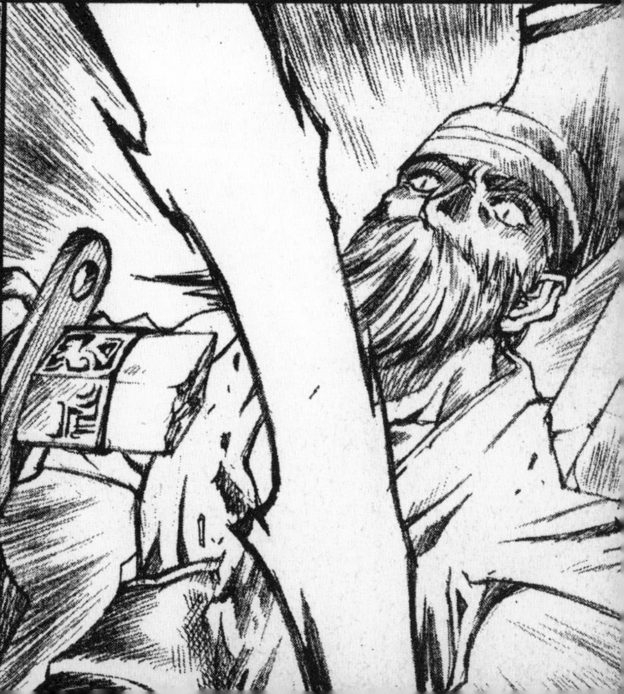

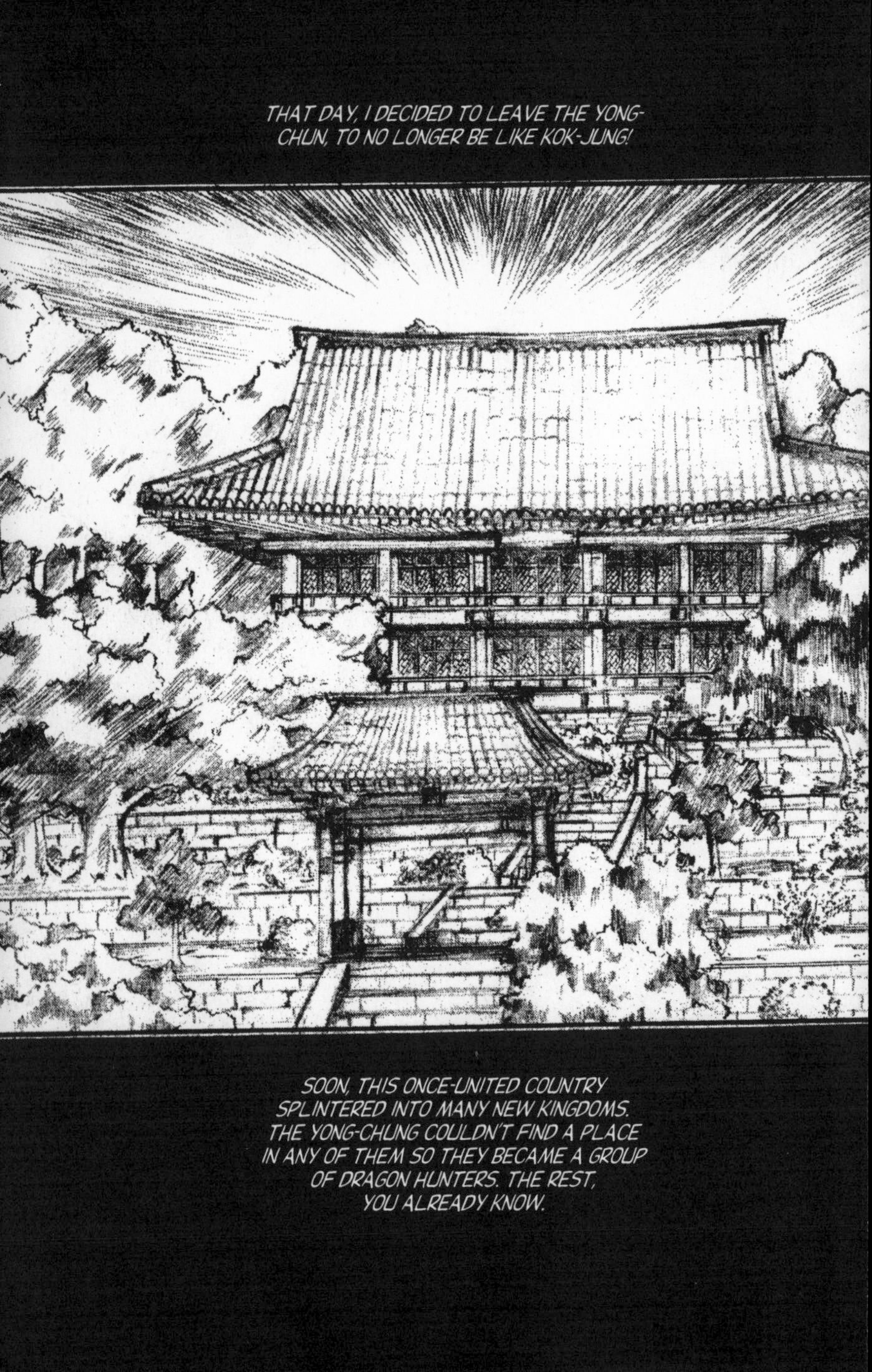
THAT DAY, I DECIDED TO LEAVE THE YONG-CHUN, TO NO LONGER BE LIKE KOK-JUNG!
SOON, THIS ONCE-UNITED COUNTRY SPLINTERED INTO MANY NEW KINGDOMS. THE YONG-CHUNG COULDN'T FIND A PLACE IN ANY OF THEM SO THEY BECAME A GROUP OF DRAGON HUNTERS. THE REST, YOU ALREADY KNOW.

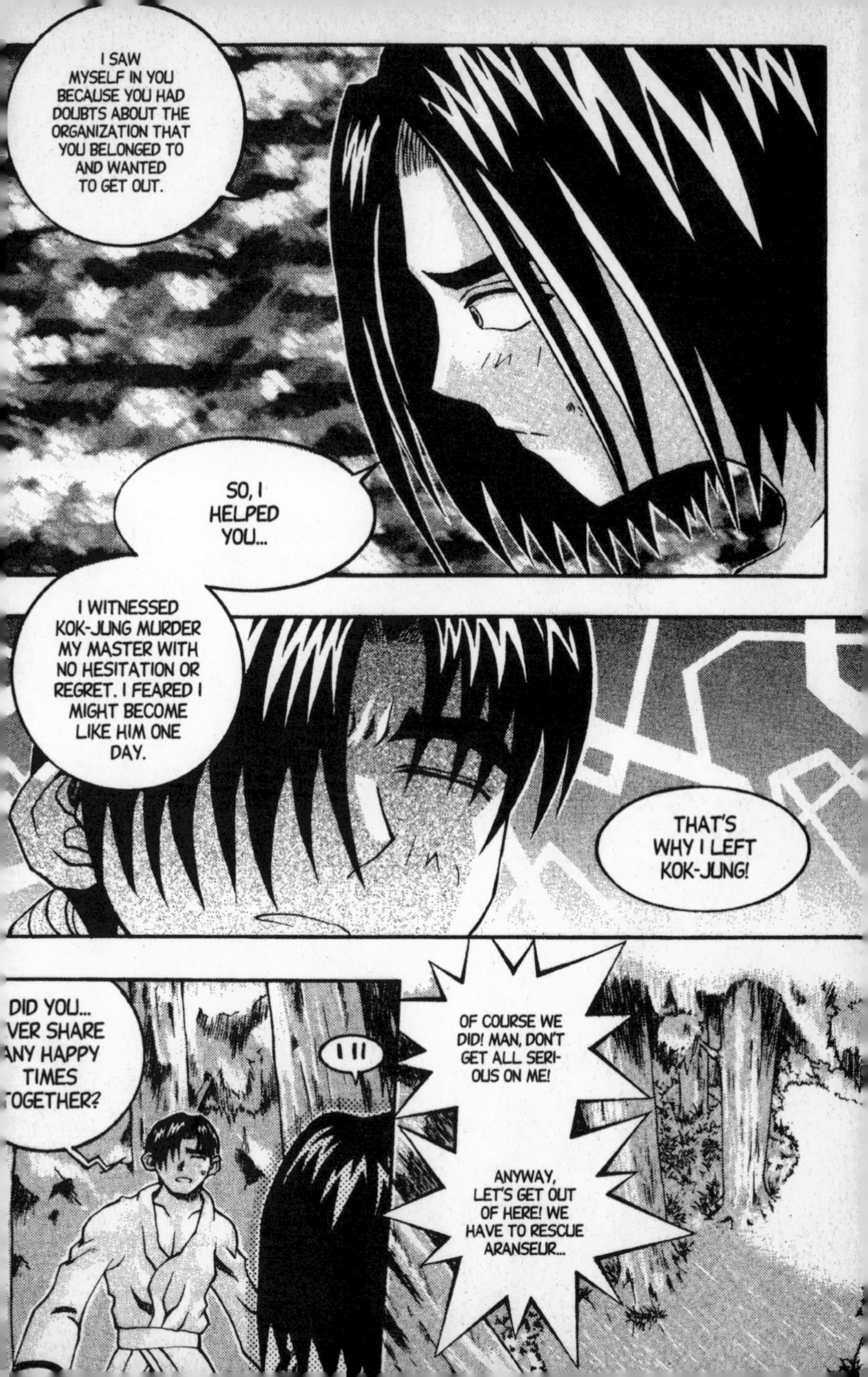
I SAW MYSELF IN YOU BECAUSE YOU HAD DOUBTS ABOUT THE ORGANIZATION THAT YOU BELONGED TO AND WANTED TO GET OUT.
SO, I HELPED YOU...
I WITNESSED KOK-JUNG MURDER MY MASTER WITH NO HESITATION OR REGRET. I FEARED I MIGHT BECOME LIKE HIM ONE DAY.
THAT'S WHY I LEFT KOK-JUNG!
DID YOU... VER SHARE NY HAPPY TIMES OGETHER?
!!!
OF COURSE WE DID! MAN, DON'T GET ALL SERI-OUS ON ME!
ANYWAY, LET'S GET OUT OF HERE! WE HAVE TO RESCUE ARANSEUR...

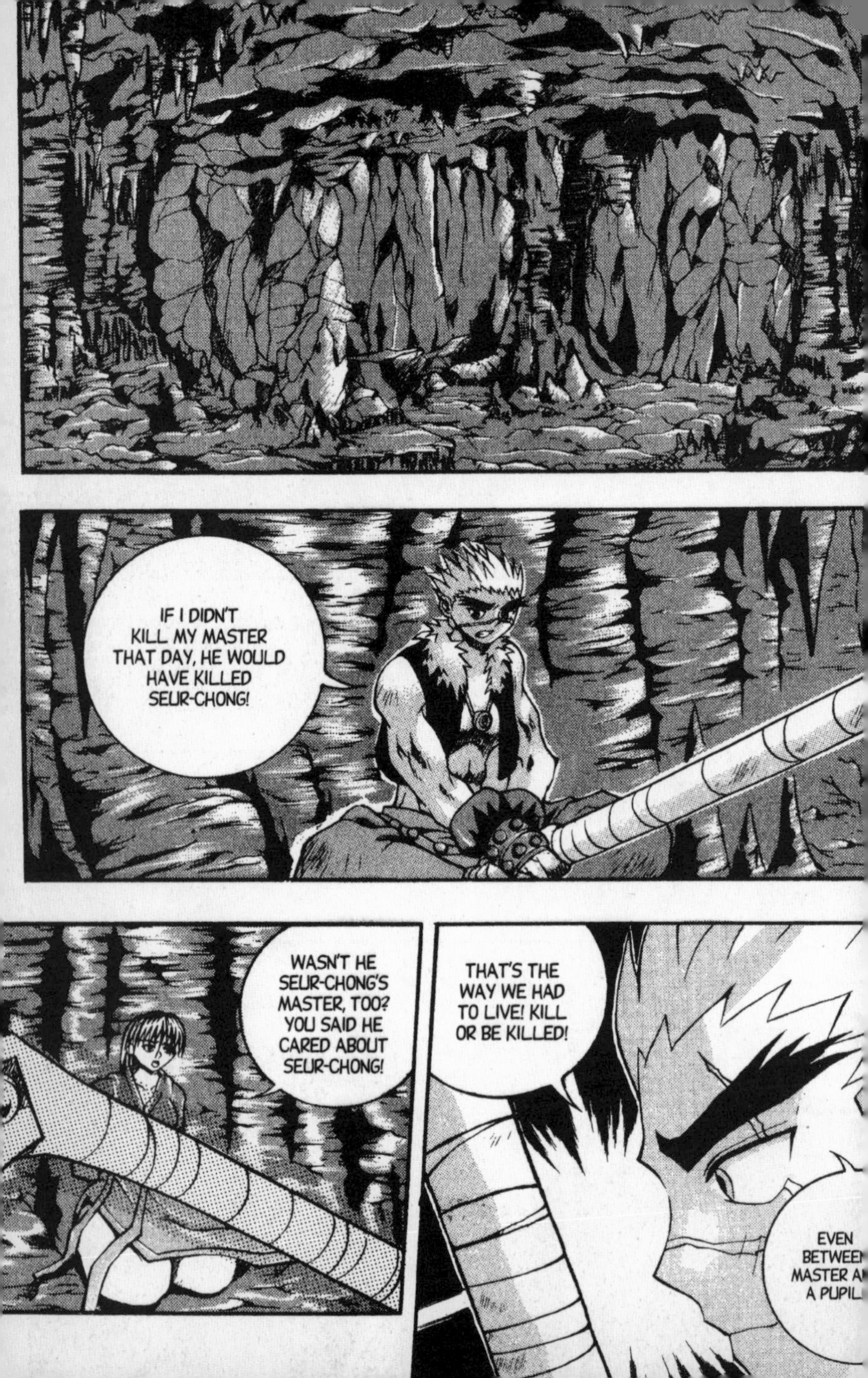
IF I DIDN'T KILL MY MASTER THAT DAY, HE WOULD HAVE KILLED SEUR-CHONG!
WASN'T HE SEUR-CHONG'S MASTER, TOO? YOU SAID HE CARED ABOUT SEUR-CHONG!
THAT'S THE WAY WE HAD TO LIVE! KILL OR BE KILLED!
EVEN BETWEEN MASTER A A PUPIL.

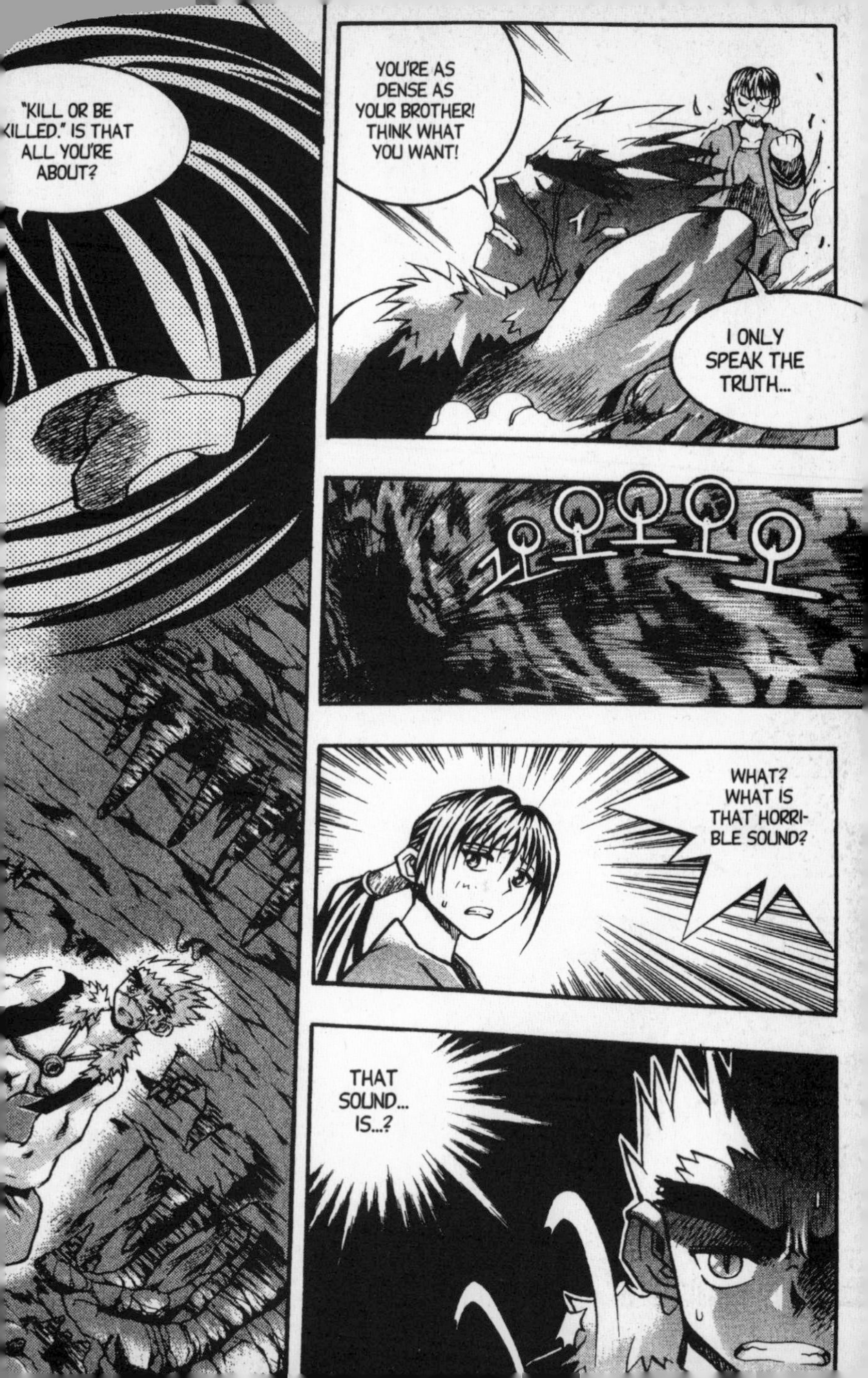
"KILL OR BE KILLED." IS THAT ALL YOU'RE ABOUT?
YOU'RE AS DENSE AS YOUR BROTHER! THINK WHAT YOU WANT!
I ONLY SPEAK THE TRUTH...
WHAT? WHAT IS THAT HORRIBLE SOUND?
THAT SOUND... IS...?

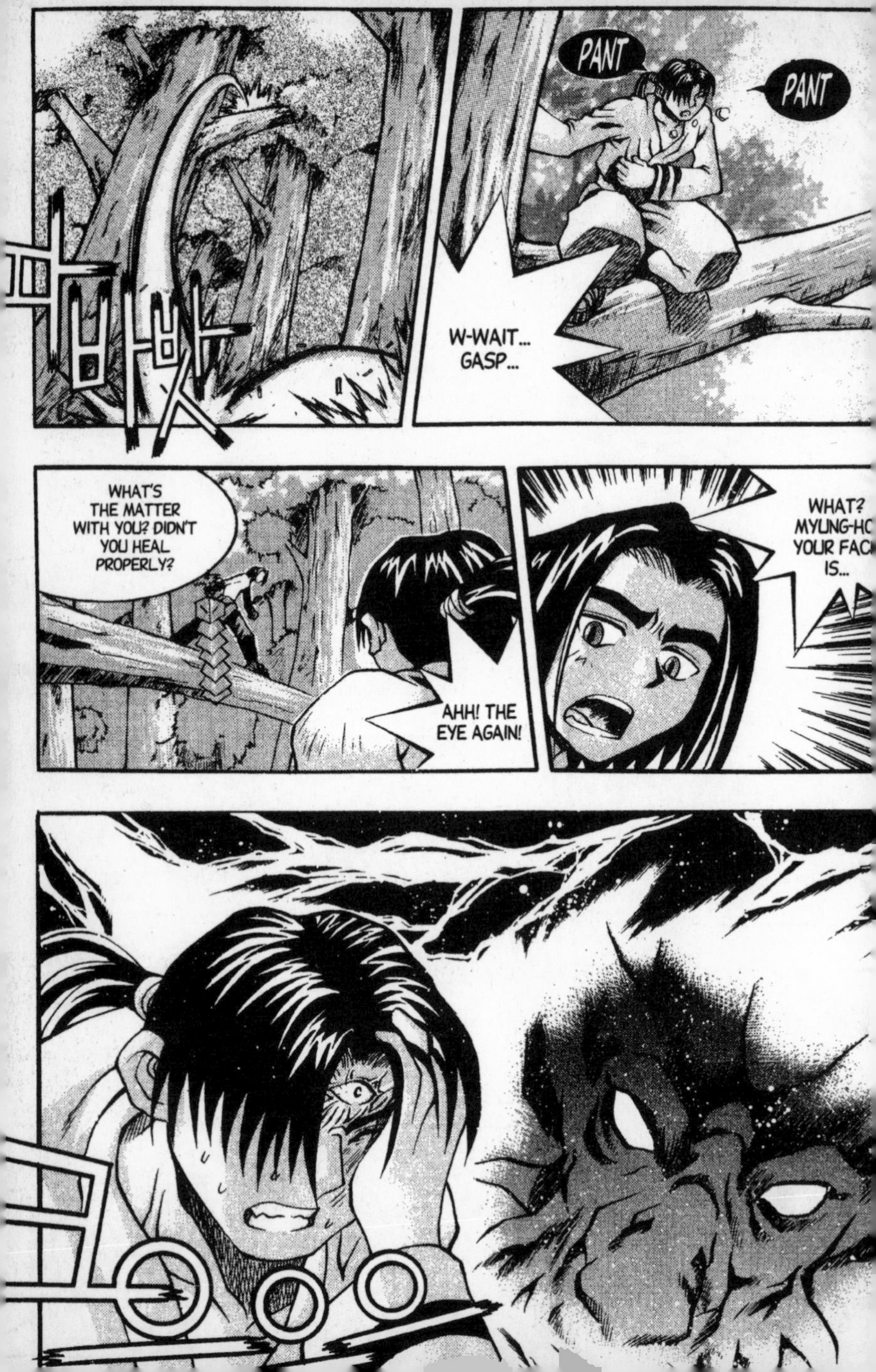
PANT
PANT
W-WAIT... GASP...
WHAT'S THE MATTER WITH YOU? DIDN'T YOU HEAL PROPERLY?
AHH! THE EYE AGAIN!
WHAT? MYUNG-HO YOUR FAC IS...

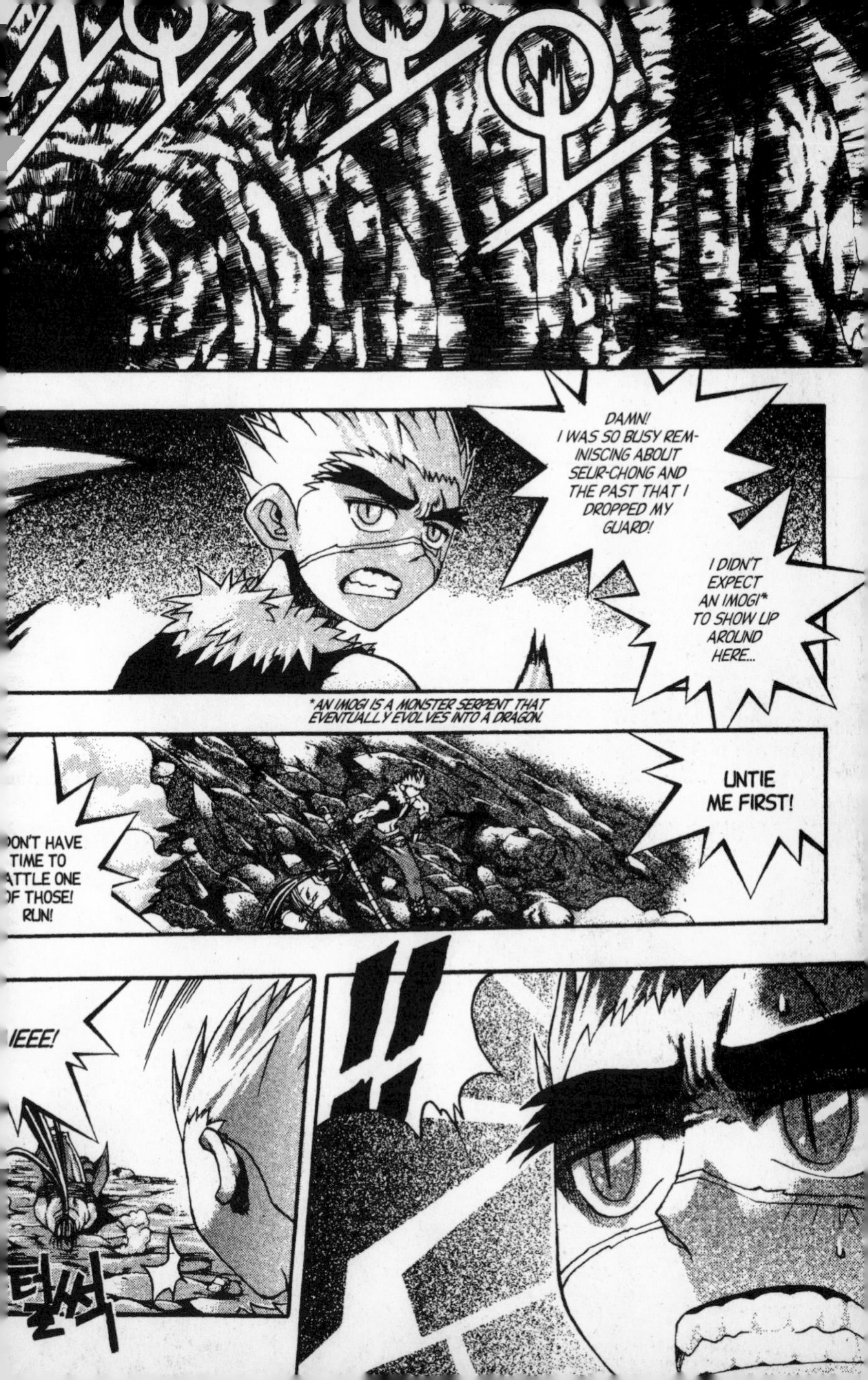
DAMN! I WAS SO BUSY REMINISCING ABOUT SEUR-CHONG AND THE PAST THAT I DROPPED MY GUARD!
I DIDN'T EXPECT AN IMOGI* TO SHOW UP AROUND HERE...
*AN IMOGI IS A MONSTER SERPENT THAT EVENTUALLY EVOLVES INTO A DRAGON.
ON'T HAVE TIME TO ATTLE ONE OF THOSE! RUN!
UNTIE ME FIRST!
IEEE!
!!

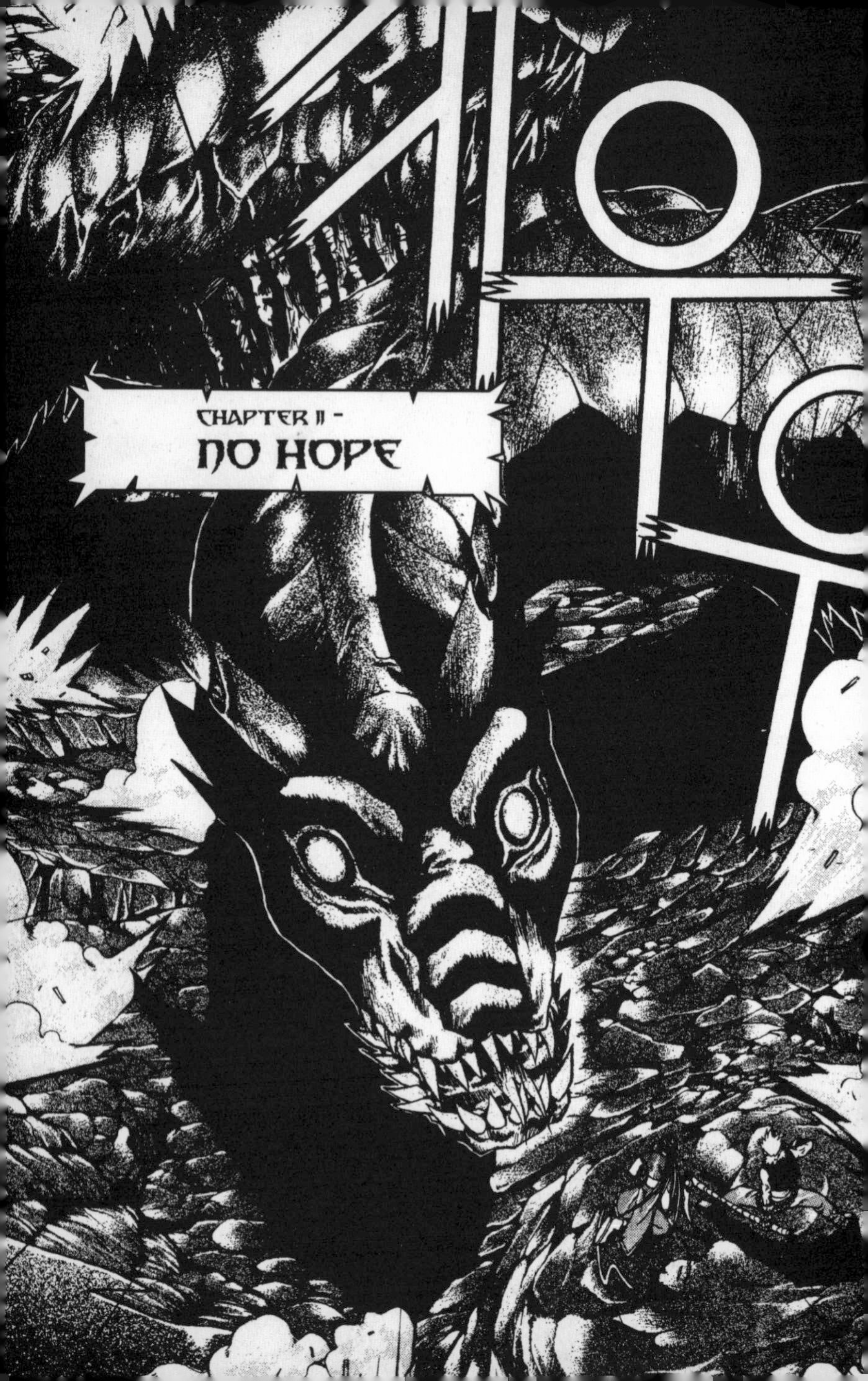
CHAPTER 11 -
NO HOPE

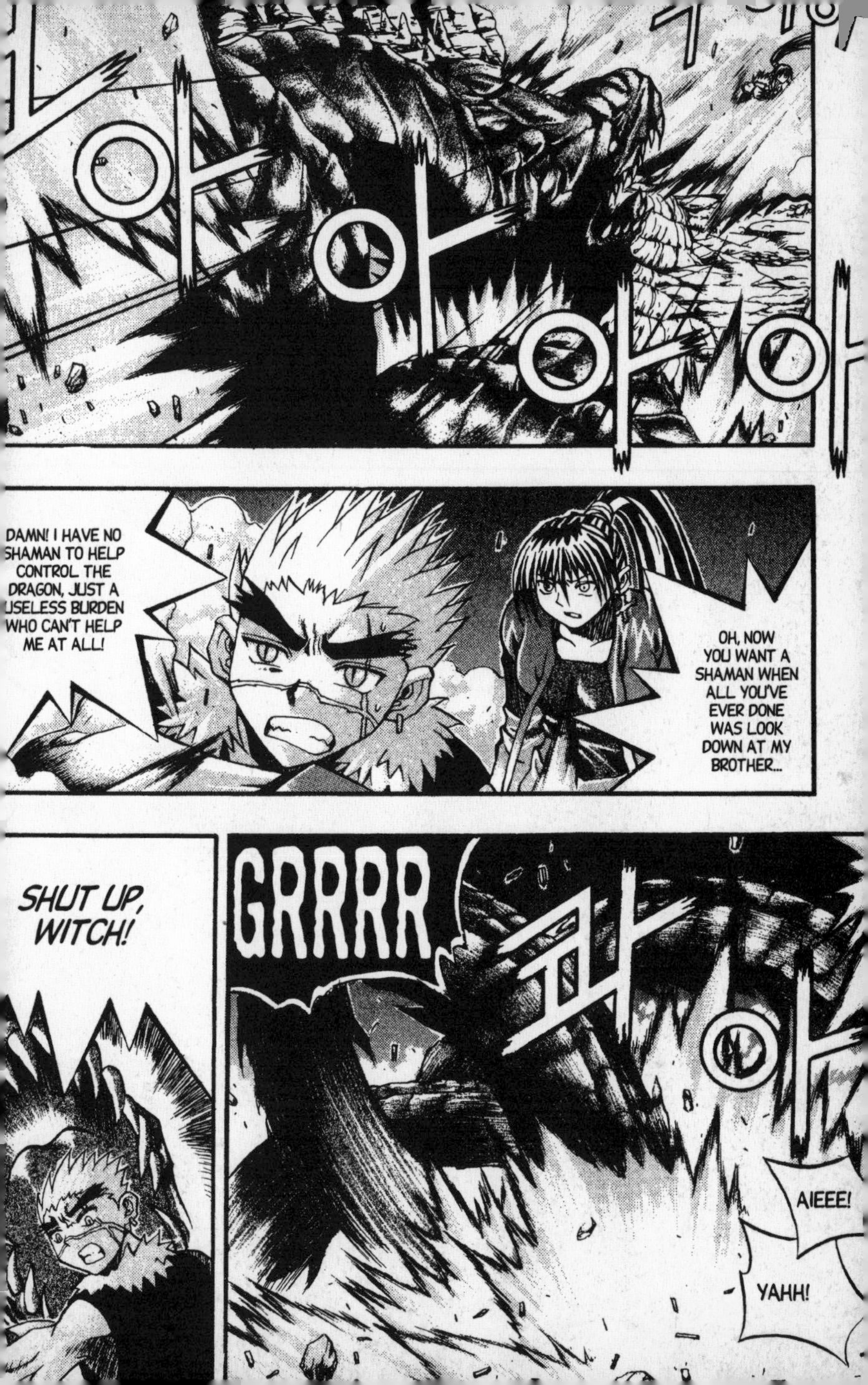
DAMN! I HAVE NO SHAMAN TO HELP CONTROL THE DRAGON, JUST A USELESS BURDEN WHO CAN'T HELP ME AT ALL!
OH, NOW YOU WANT A SHAMAN WHEN ALL YOU'VE EVER DONE WAS LOOK DOWN AT MY BROTHER...
SHUT UP, WITCH!
GRRRR
AIEEE!
YAHH!

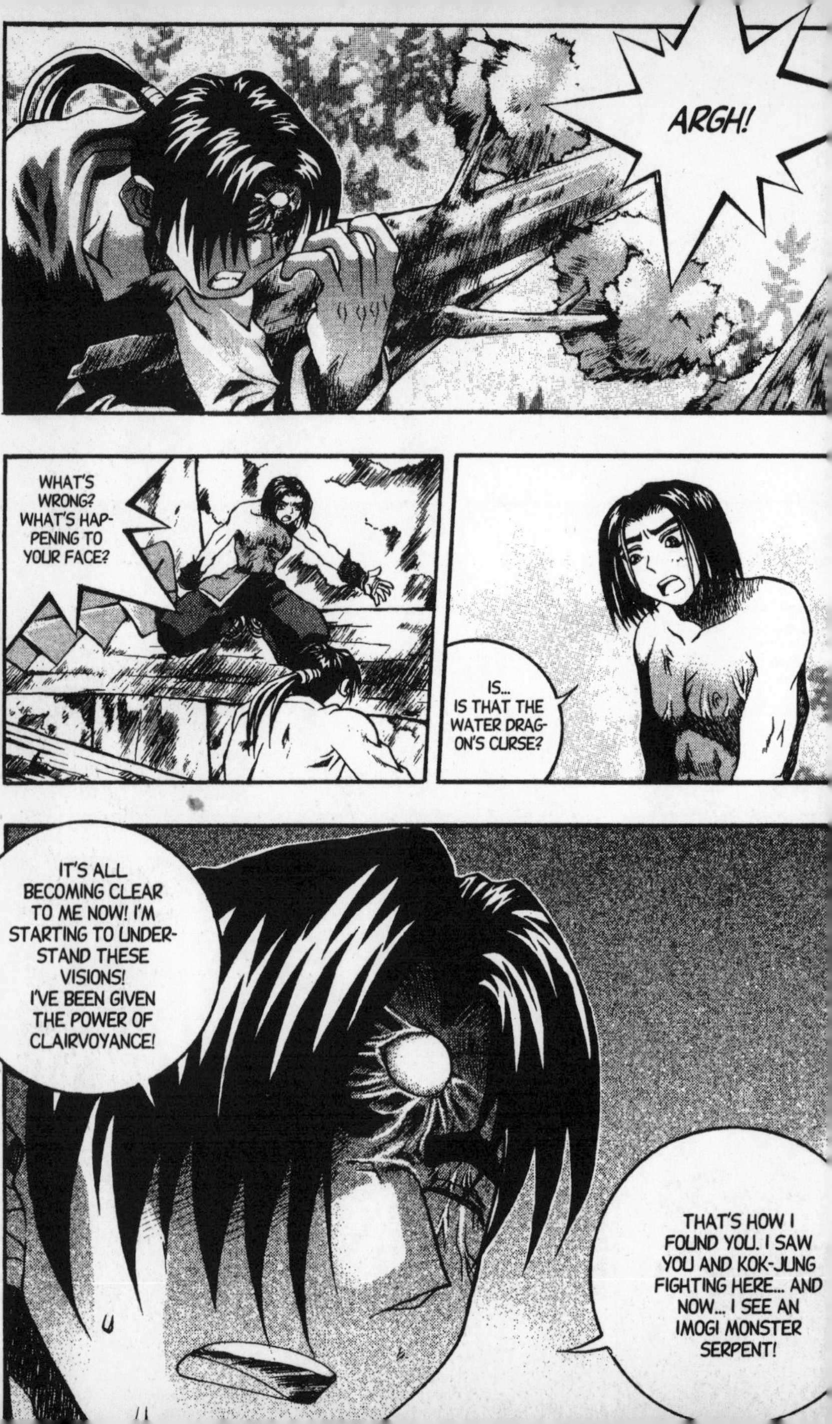
ARGH!
WHAT'S WRONG? WHAT'S HAP-PENING TO YOUR FACE?
IS... IS THAT THE WATER DRAG-ON'S CURSE?
IT'S ALL BECOMING CLEAR TO ME NOW! I'M STARTING TO UNDER-STAND THESE VISIONS! I'VE BEEN GIVEN THE POWER OF CLAIRVOYANCE!
THAT'S HOW I FOUND YOU. I SAW YOU AND KOK-JUNG FIGHTING HERE... AND NOW... I SEE AN IMOGI MONSTER SERPENT!

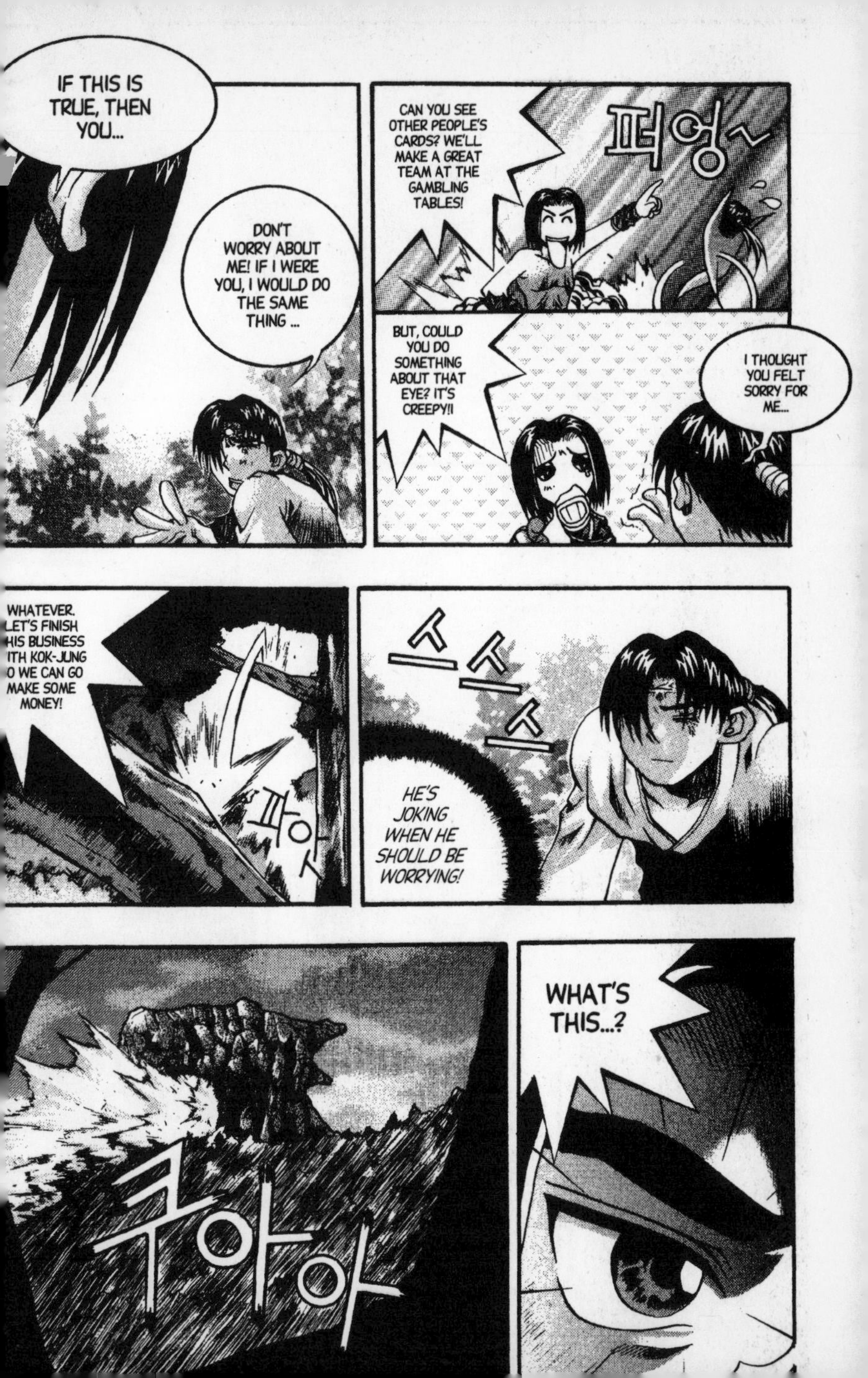
IF THIS IS TRUE, THEN YOU...
DON'T WORRY ABOUT ME! IF I WERE YOU, I WOULD DO THE SAME THING ...
CAN YOU SEE OTHER PEOPLE'S CARDS? WE'LL MAKE A GREAT TEAM AT THE GAMBLING TABLES!
BUT, COULD YOU DO SOMETHING ABOUT THAT EYE? IT'S CREEPY!!
I THOUGHT YOU FELT SORRY FOR ME...
WHATEVER. LET'S FINISH HIS BUSINESS ITH KOK-JUNG O WE CAN GO MAKE SOME MONEY!
HE'S JOKING WHEN HE SHOULD BE WORRYING!
WHAT'S THIS...?

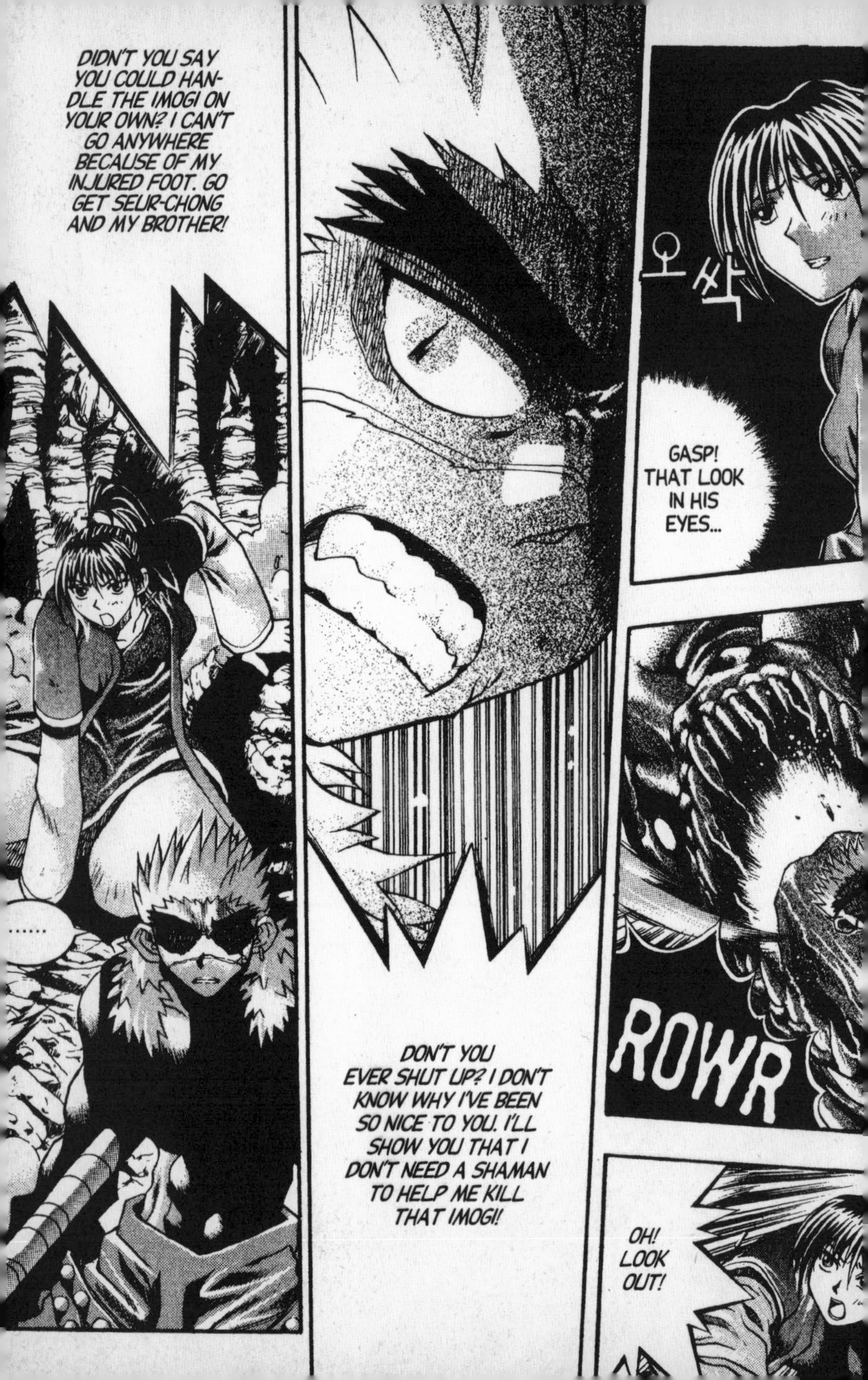
DIDN'T YOU SAY YOU COULD HAN-DLE THE IMOGI ON YOUR OWN? I CAN'T GO ANYWHERE BECAUSE OF MY INJURED FOOT. GO GET SEUR-CHONG AND MY BROTHER!
......
DON'T YOU EVER SHUT UP? I DON'T KNOW WHY I'VE BEEN SO NICE TO YOU. I'LL SHOW YOU THAT I DON'T NEED A SHAMAN TO HELP ME KILL THAT IMOGI!
오싹
GASP! THAT LOOK IN HIS EYES...
ROWR
OH! LOOK OUT!

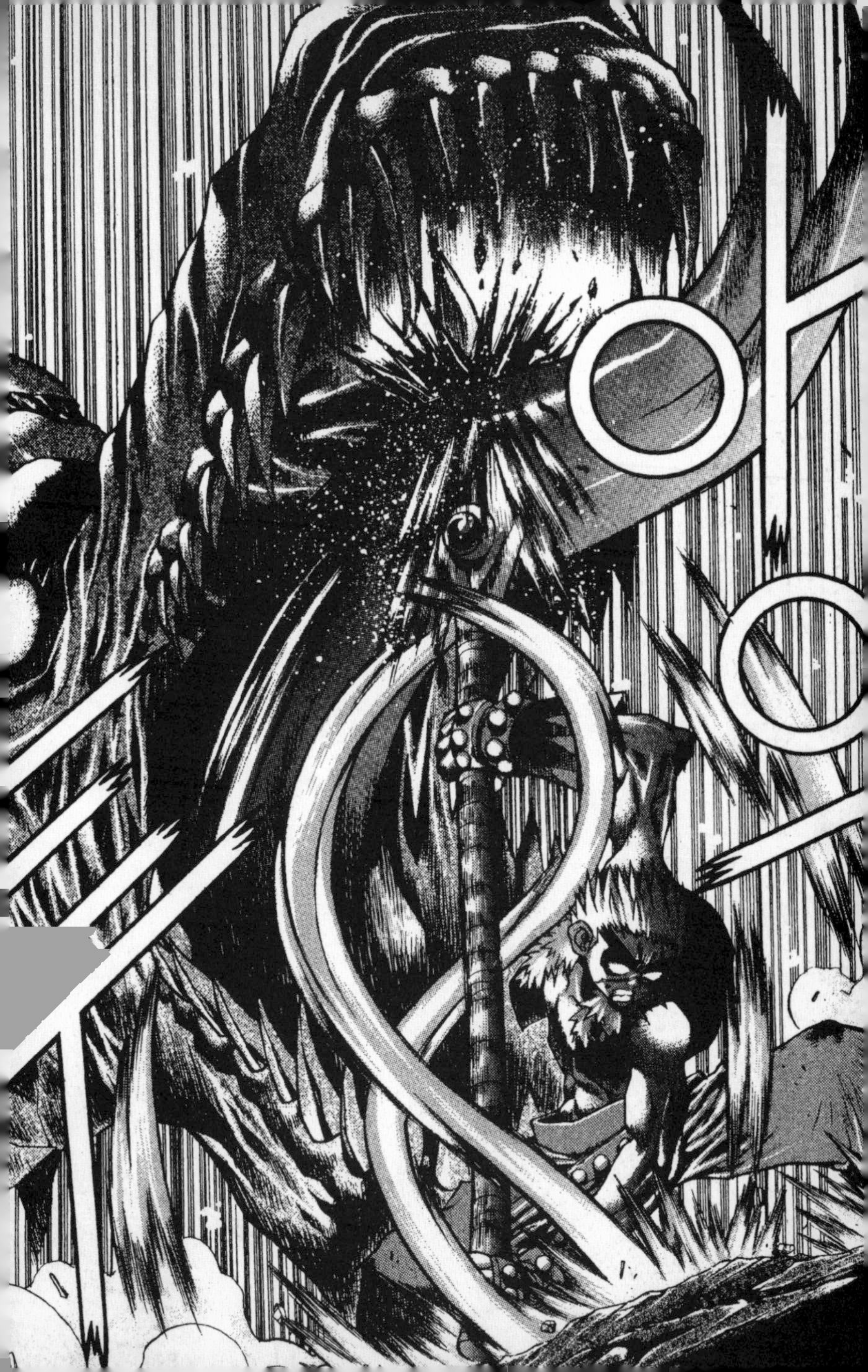

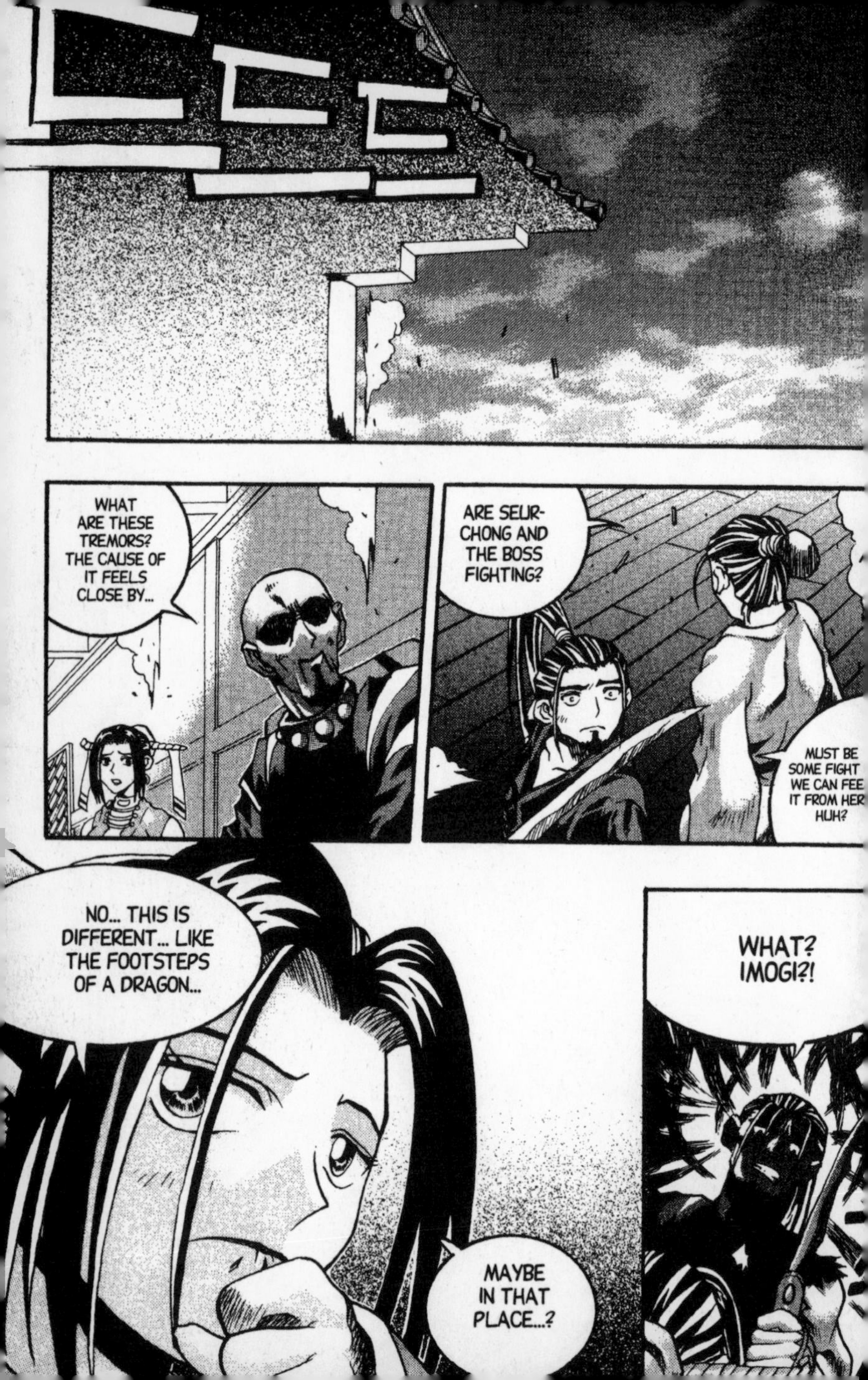
WHAT ARE THESE TREMORS? THE CAUSE OF IT FEELS CLOSE BY...
ARE SEUR-CHONG AND THE BOSS FIGHTING?
MUST BE SOME FIGHT WE CAN FEE IT FROM HER HUH?
NO... THIS IS DIFFERENT... LIKE THE FOOTSTEPS OF A DRAGON...
MAYBE IN THAT PLACE...?
WHAT? IMOGI?!

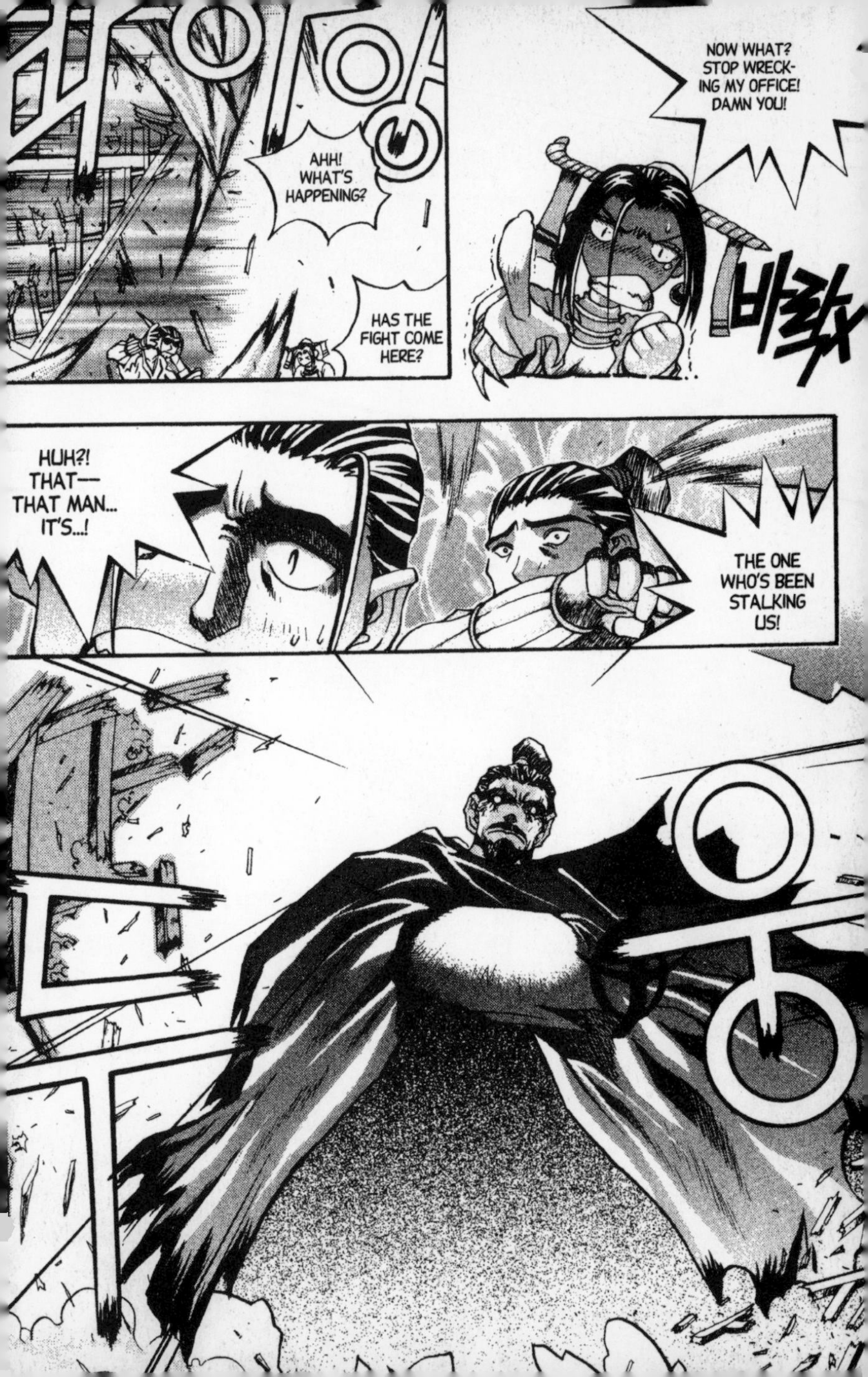
AHH! WHAT'S HAPPENING?
HAS THE FIGHT COME HERE?
NOW WHAT? STOP WRECKING MY OFFICE! DAMN YOU!
HUH?! THAT— THAT MAN... IT'S...!
THE ONE WHO'S BEEN STALKING US!

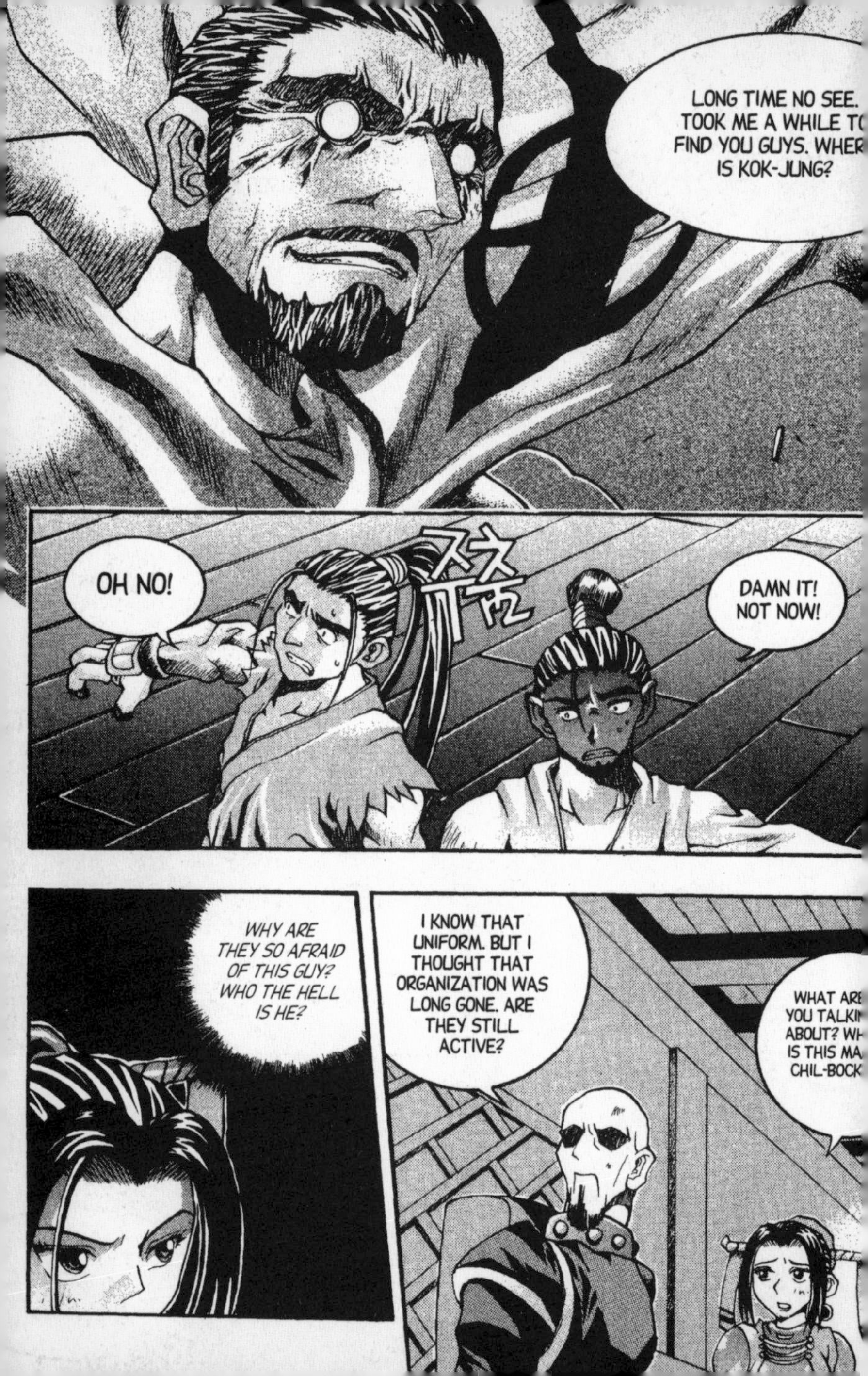

LONG TIME NO SEE. TOOK ME A WHILE T FIND YOU GUYS. WHER IS KOK-JUNG?
OH NO!
DAMN IT! NOT NOW!
WHY ARE THEY SO AFRAID OF THIS GUY? WHO THE HELL IS HE?
I KNOW THAT UNIFORM. BUT I THOUGHT THAT ORGANIZATION WAS LONG GONE. ARE THEY STILL ACTIVE?
WHAT AR YOU TALKI ABOUT? WH IS THIS MA CHIL-BOCK

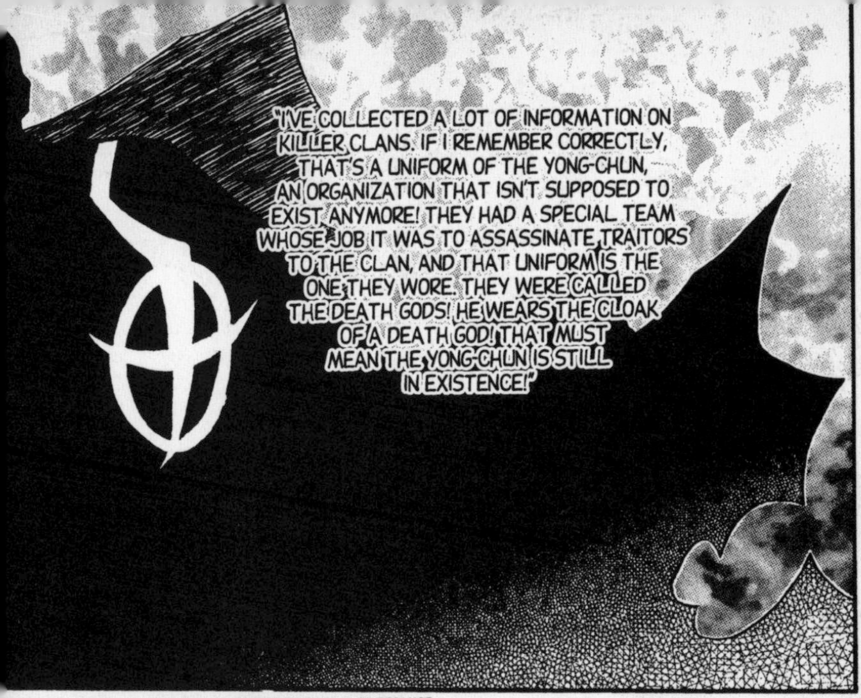
"I'VE COLLECTED A LOT OF INFORMATION ON KILLER CLANS. IF I REMEMBER CORRECTLY, THAT'S A UNIFORM OF THE YONG-CHUN, AN ORGANIZATION THAT ISN'T SUPPOSED TO EXIST ANYMORE! THEY HAD A SPECIAL TEAM WHOSE JOB IT WAS TO ASSASSINATE TRAITORS TO THE CLAN, AND THAT UNIFORM IS THE ONE THEY WORE. THEY WERE CALLED THE DEATH GODS! HE WEARS THE CLOAK OF A DEATH GOD! THAT MUST MEAN THE YONG-CHUN IS STILL IN EXISTENCE!"

* "TAE-RANG" IS AN ALIAS KOK-JUNG PREFERS TO BE CALLED BECAUSE EVERYONE MAKES FUN OF HIS REAL NAME WHICH MEANS "WORRY."

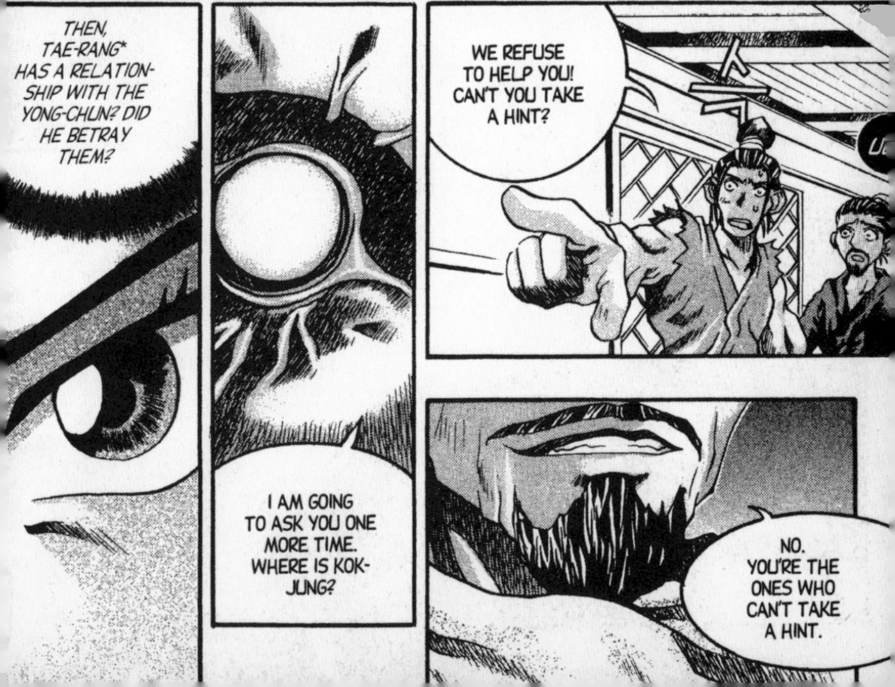
THEN, TAE-RANG* HAS A RELATIONSHIP WITH THE YONG-CHUN? DID HE BETRAY THEM?
I AM GOING TO ASK YOU ONE MORE TIME. WHERE IS KOK-JUNG?
WE REFUSE TO HELP YOU! CAN'T YOU TAKE A HINT?
NO. YOU'RE THE ONES WHO CAN'T TAKE A HINT.

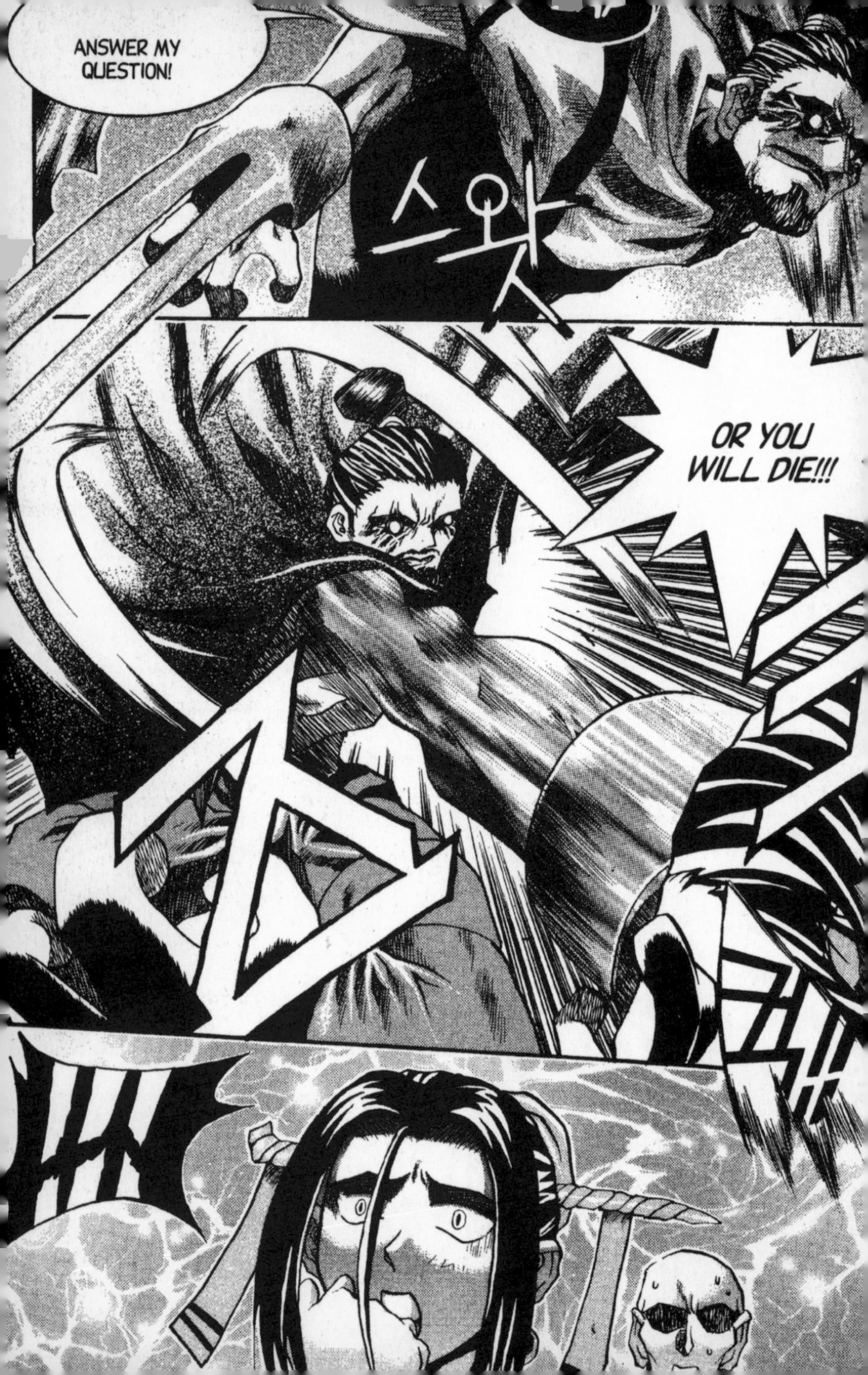
ANSWER MY QUESTION!
스왓
OR YOU WILL DIE!!!

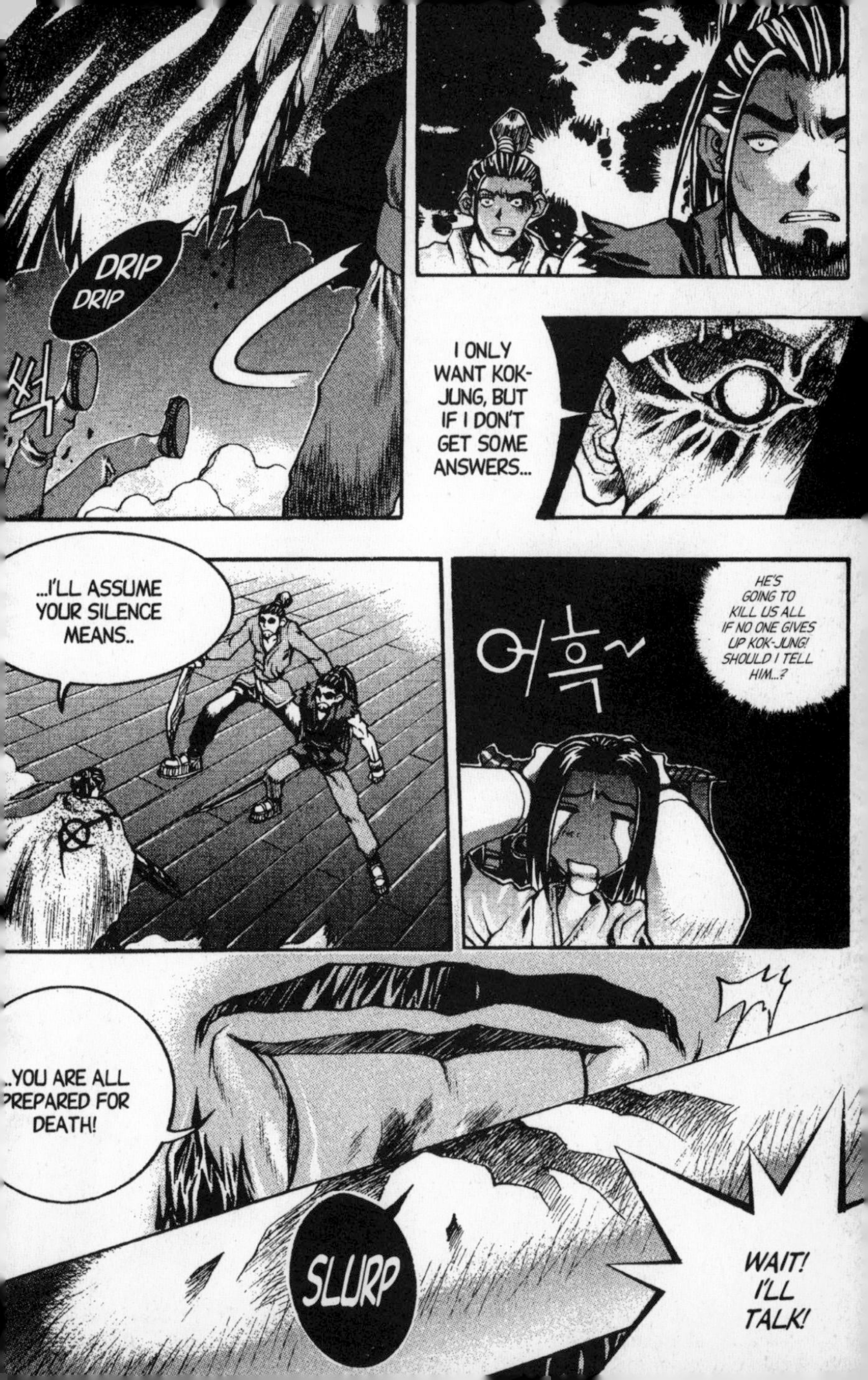
DRIP
DRIP
싹
I ONLY WANT KOK-JUNG, BUT IF I DON'T GET SOME ANSWERS...
...I'LL ASSUME YOUR SILENCE MEANS..
어흑~
HE'S GOING TO KILL US ALL IF NO ONE GIVES UP KOK-JUNG! SHOULD I TELL HIM...?
..YOU ARE ALL PREPARED FOR DEATH!
SLURP
WAIT! I'LL TALK!

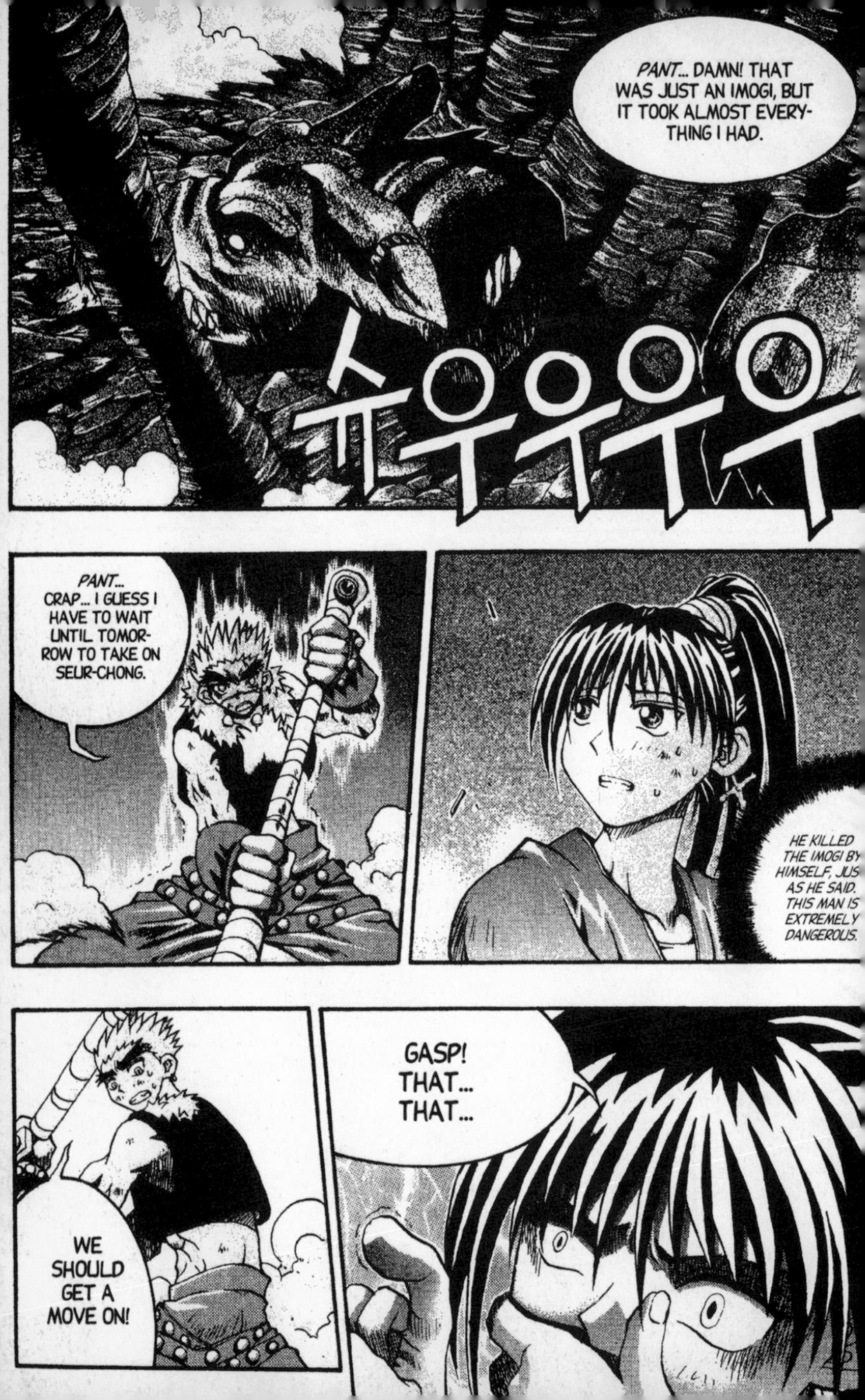
PANT... DAMN! THAT WAS JUST AN IMOGI, BUT IT TOOK ALMOST EVERY-THING I HAD.
PANT... CRAP... I GUESS I HAVE TO WAIT UNTIL TOMOR-ROW TO TAKE ON SEUR-CHONG.
HE KILLED THE IMOGI BY HIMSELF, JUS AS HE SAID. THIS MAN IS EXTREMELY DANGEROUS.
WE SHOULD GET A MOVE ON!
GASP! THAT... THAT...

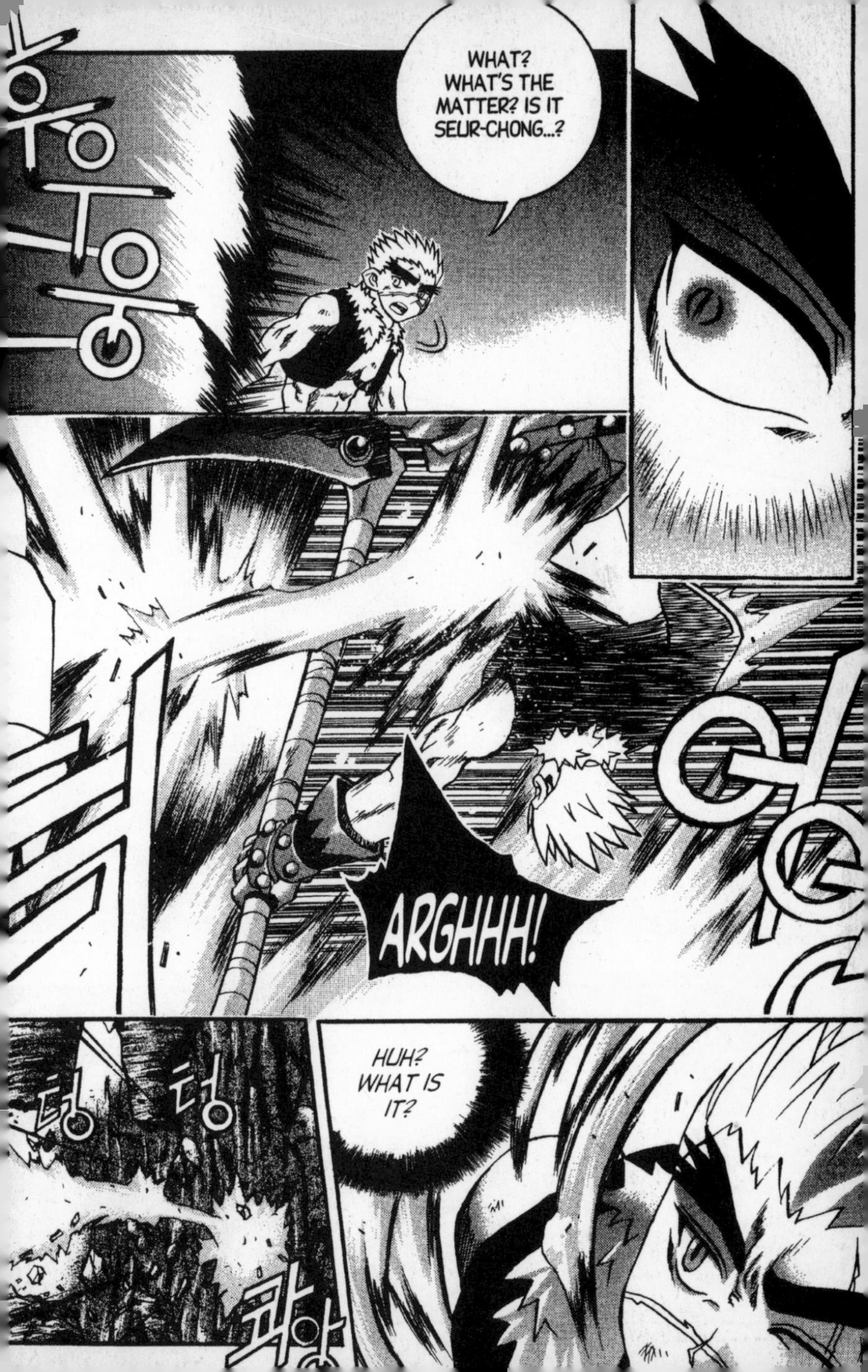
WHAT? WHAT'S THE MATTER? IS IT SEUR-CHONG...?
ARGHHH!
HUH? WHAT IS IT?

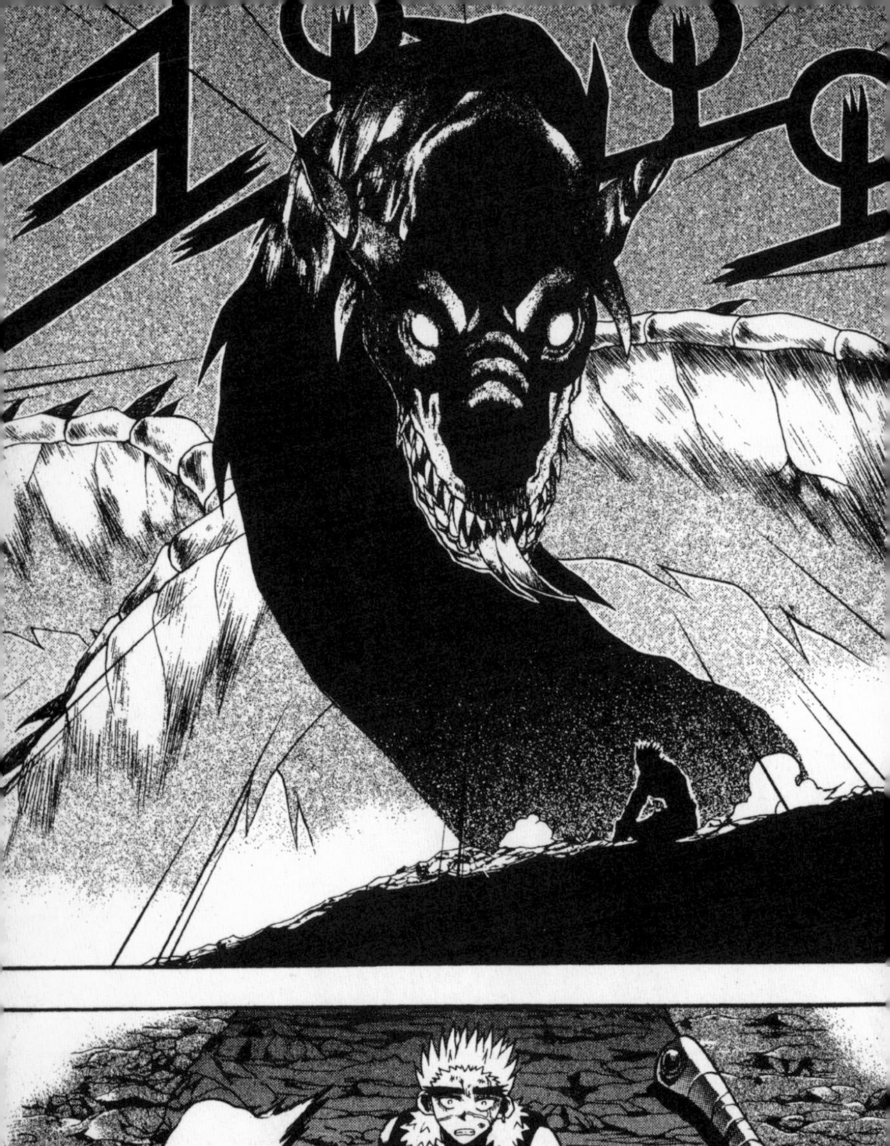
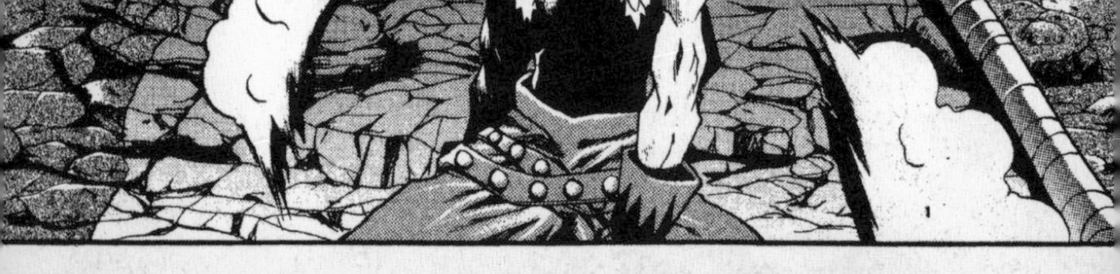

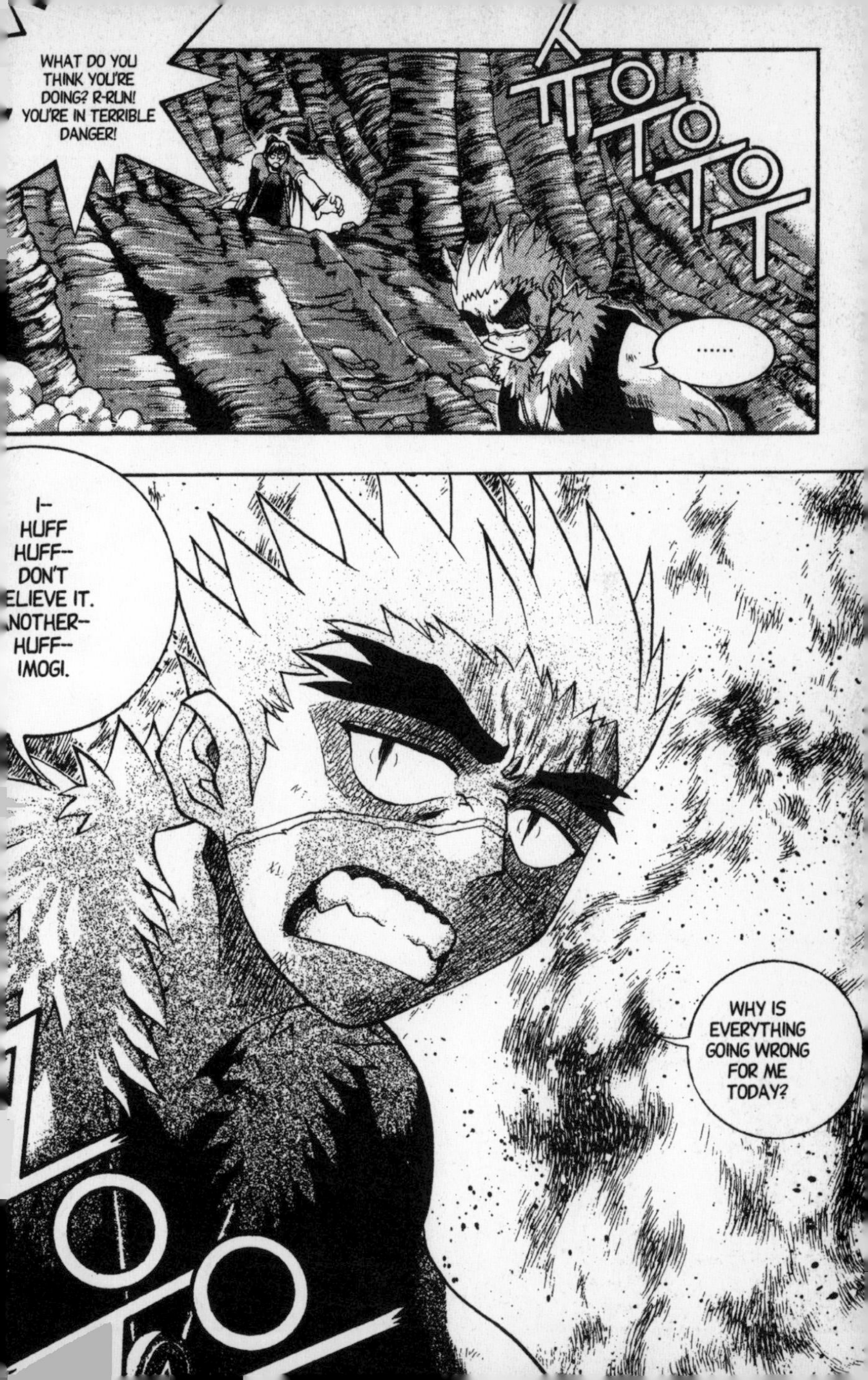
WHAT DO YOU THINK YOU'RE DOING? R-RUN! YOU'RE IN TERRIBLE DANGER!
......
I-- HUFF HUFF-- DON'T ELIEVE IT. NOTHER-- HUFF-- IMOGI.
WHY IS EVERYTHING GOING WRONG FOR ME TODAY?

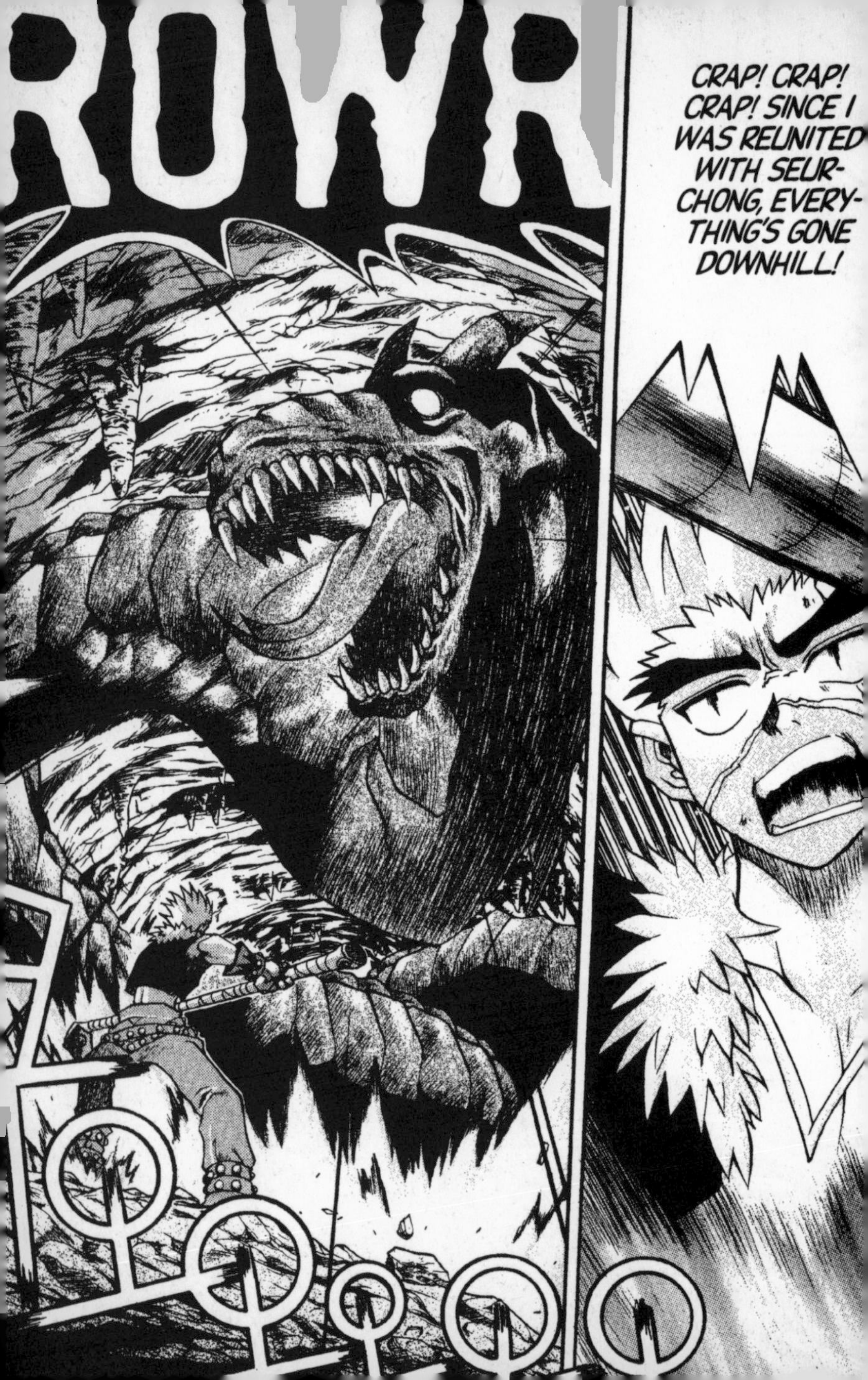
ROWR
CRAP! CRAP! CRAP! SINCE I WAS REUNITED WITH SEUR-CHONG, EVERY-THING'S GONE DOWNHILL!

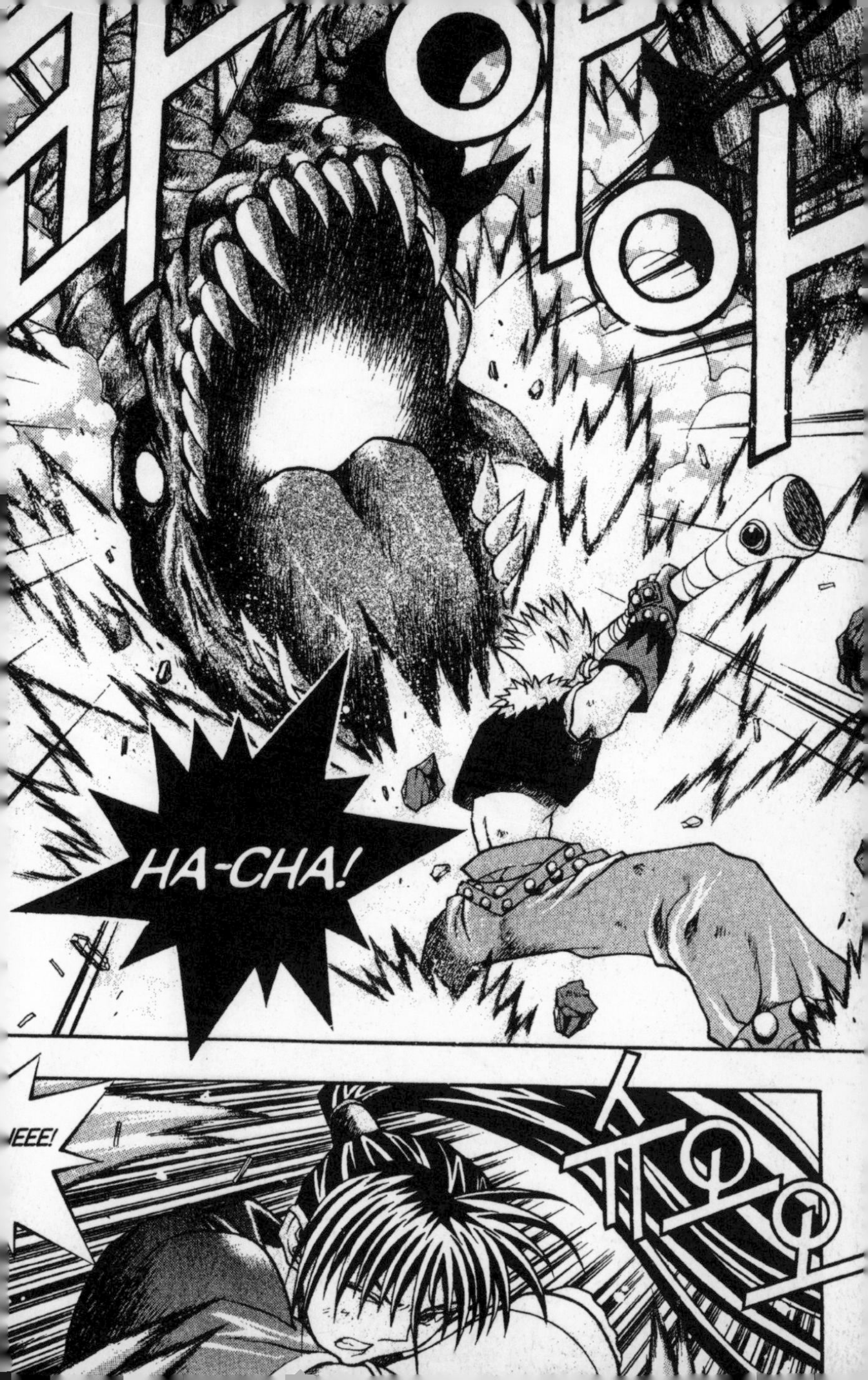
HA-CHA!
IEEE!

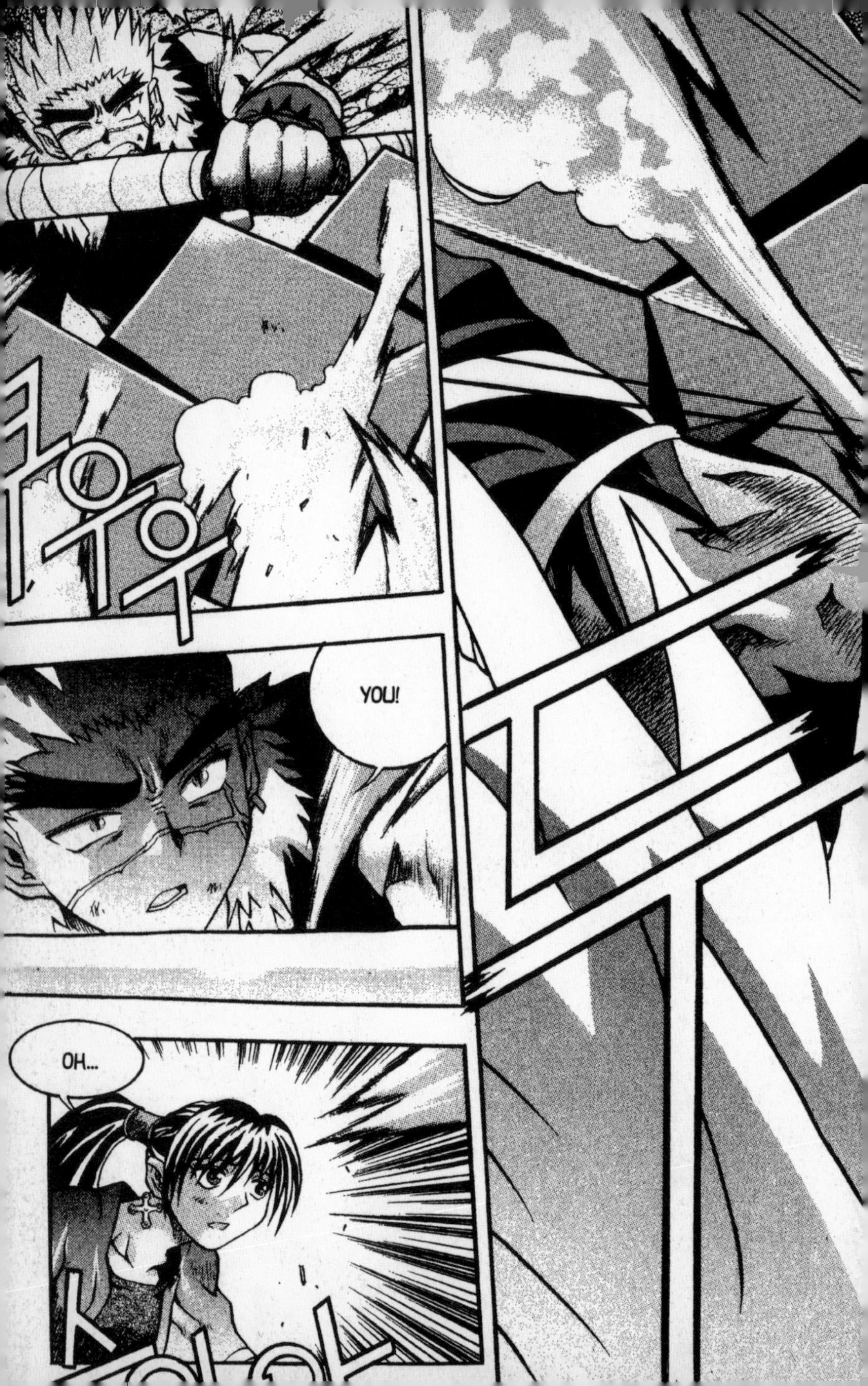
YOU!
OH...

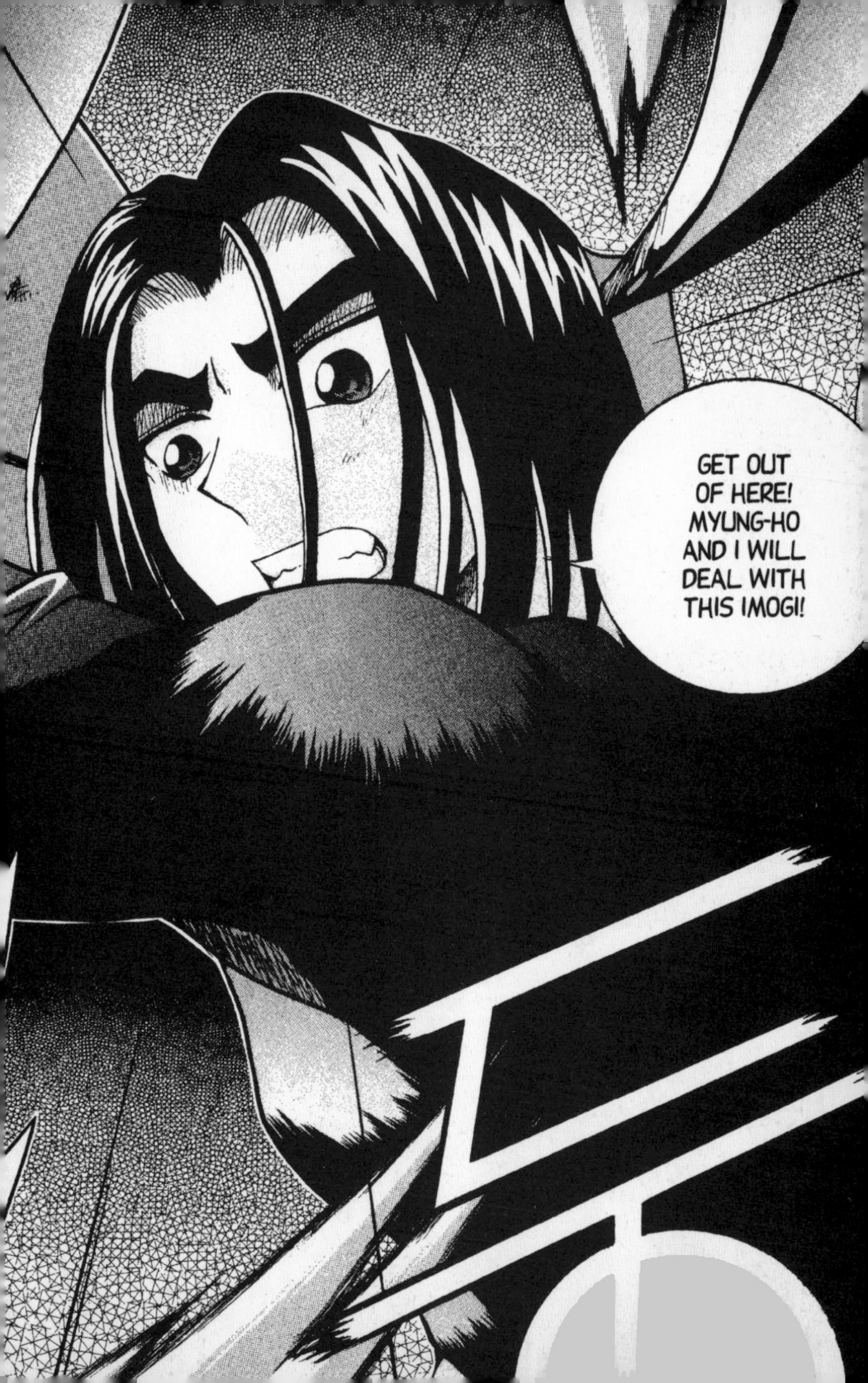
GET OUT OF HERE! MYUNG-HO AND I WILL DEAL WITH THIS IMOGI!

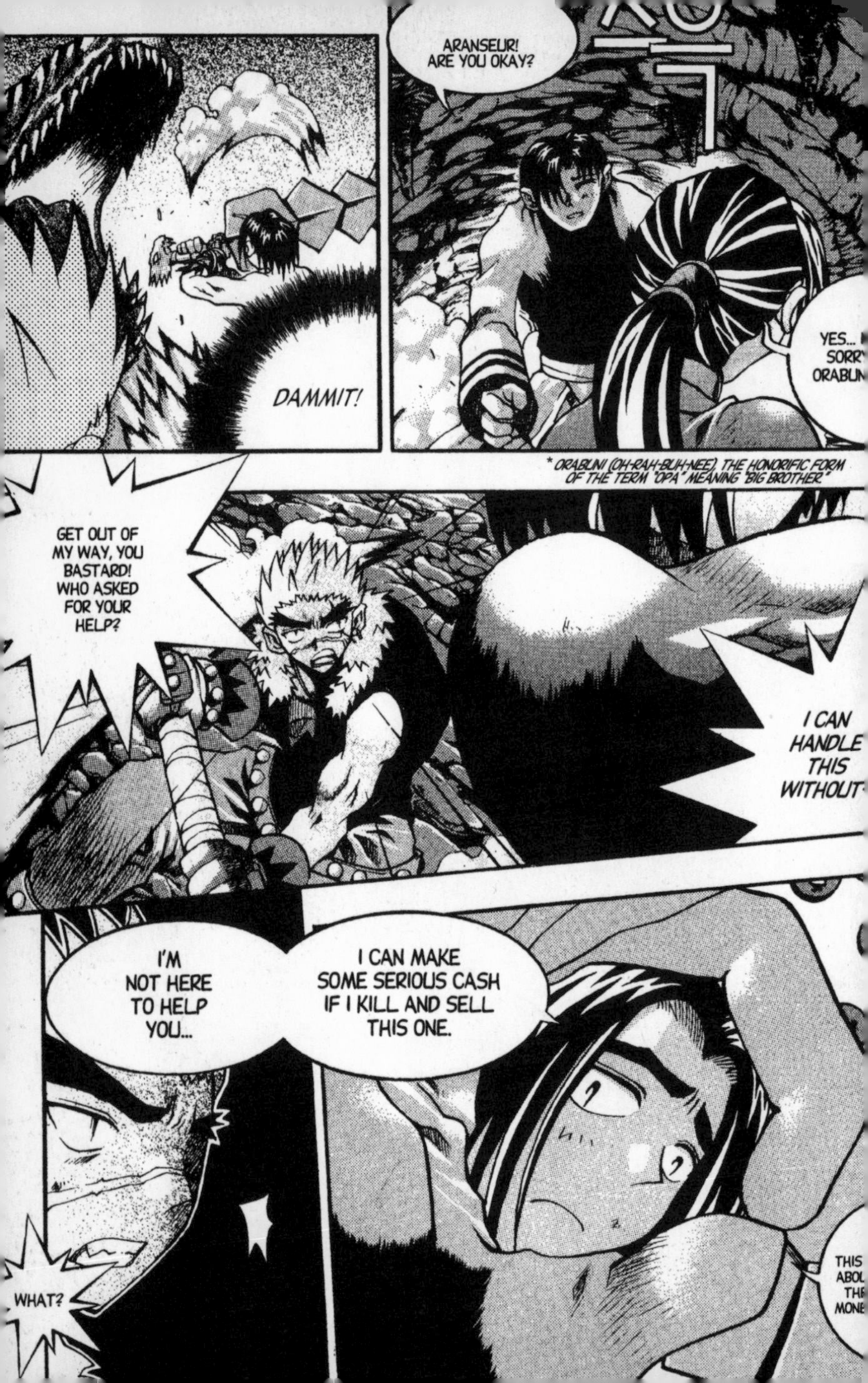
DAMMIT!
ARANSEUR! ARE YOU OKAY?
YES... SORRY ORABUNI
* ORABUNI (OH-RAH-BUH-NEE), THE HONORIFIC FORM OF THE TERM "OPA" MEANING "BIG BROTHER."
GET OUT OF MY WAY, YOU BASTARD! WHO ASKED FOR YOUR HELP?
I CAN HANDLE THIS WITHOUT-
I'M NOT HERE TO HELP YOU...
I CAN MAKE SOME SERIOUS CASH IF I KILL AND SELL THIS ONE.
WHAT?

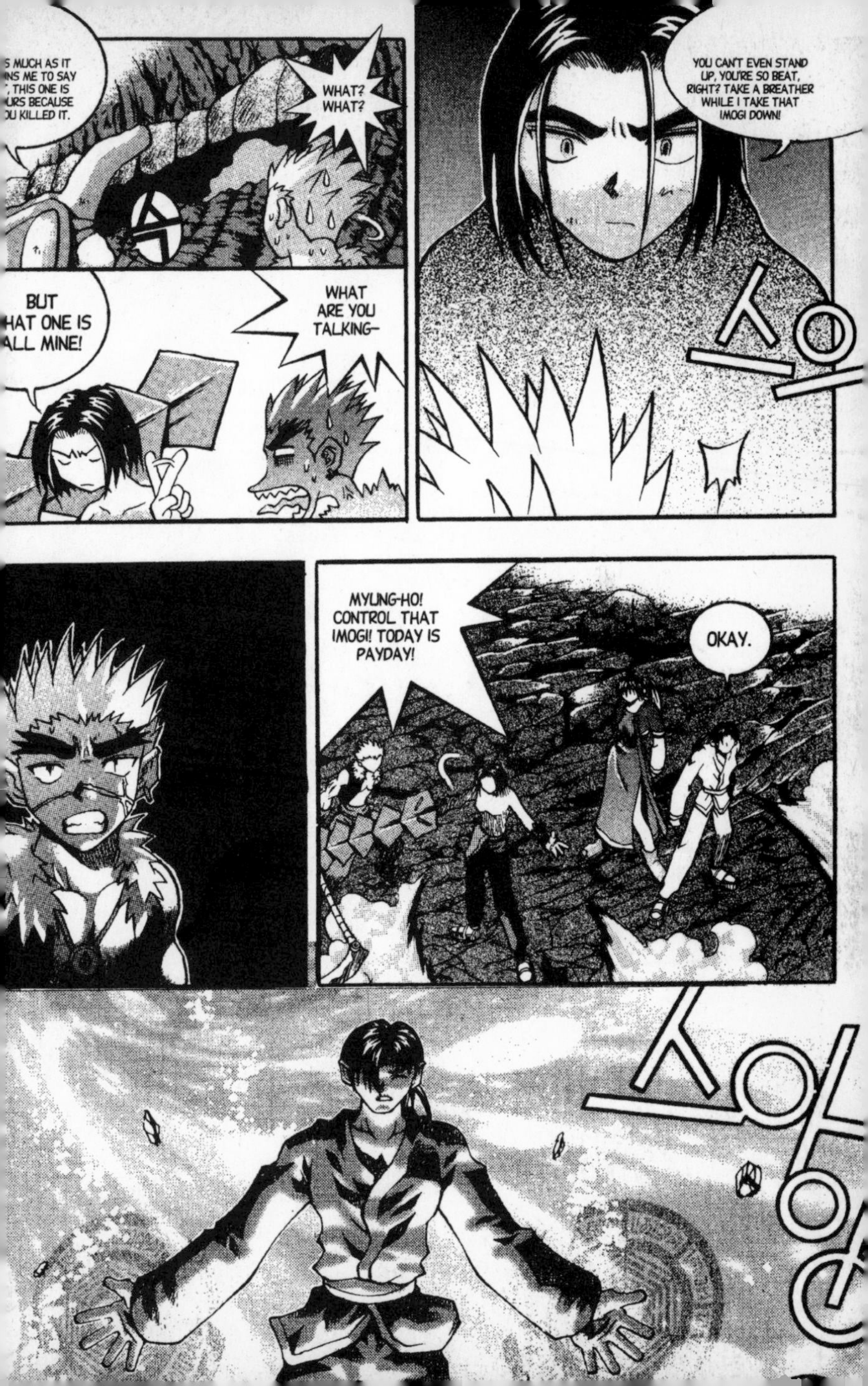
S MUCH AS IT INS ME TO SAY , THIS ONE IS URS BECAUSE OU KILLED IT.
WHAT? WHAT?
BUT HAT ONE IS ALL MINE!
WHAT ARE YOU TALKING–
YOU CAN'T EVEN STAND UP, YOU'RE SO BEAT, RIGHT? TAKE A BREATHER WHILE I TAKE THAT IMOGI DOWN!
MYUNG-HO! CONTROL THAT IMOGI! TODAY IS PAYDAY!
OKAY.

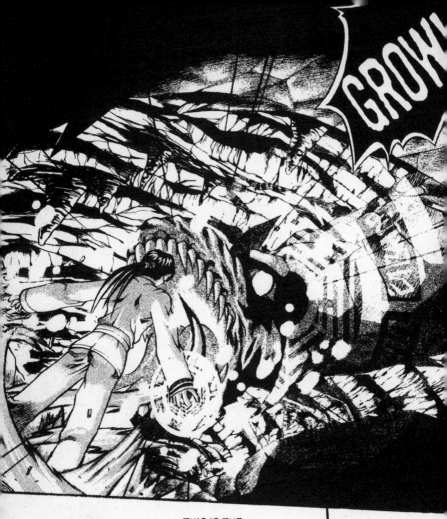

GROW!

THIS IS THE FIRST TIME I'VE EVER SEEN MY BROTHER CAST A CONTROL SPELL ON AN IMOGI!!

HE IS AMAZING!

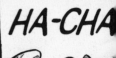

HA-CHA

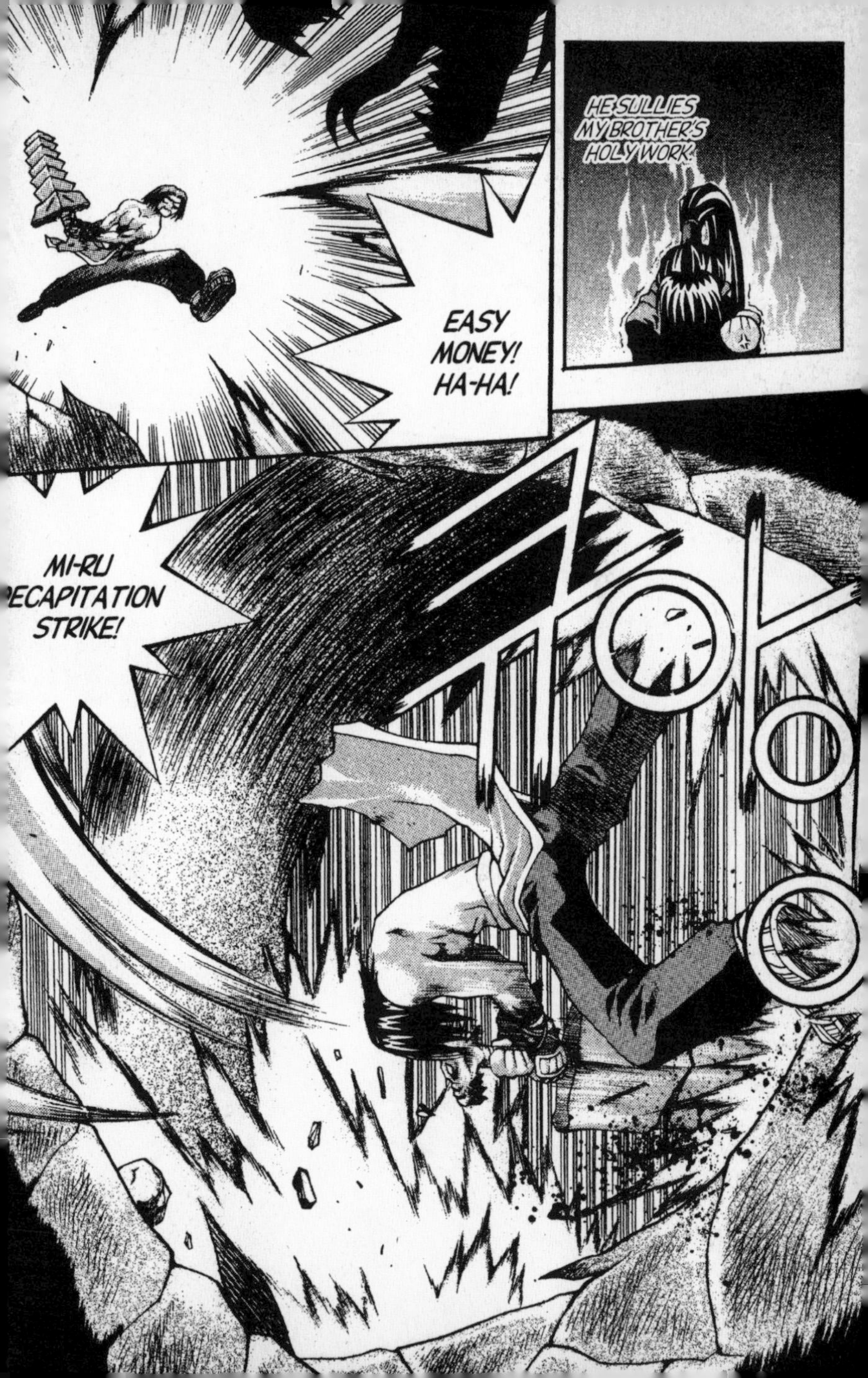
EASY MONEY! HA-HA!
HE SULLIES MY BROTHER'S HOLY WORK
MI-RU ECAPITATION STRIKE!

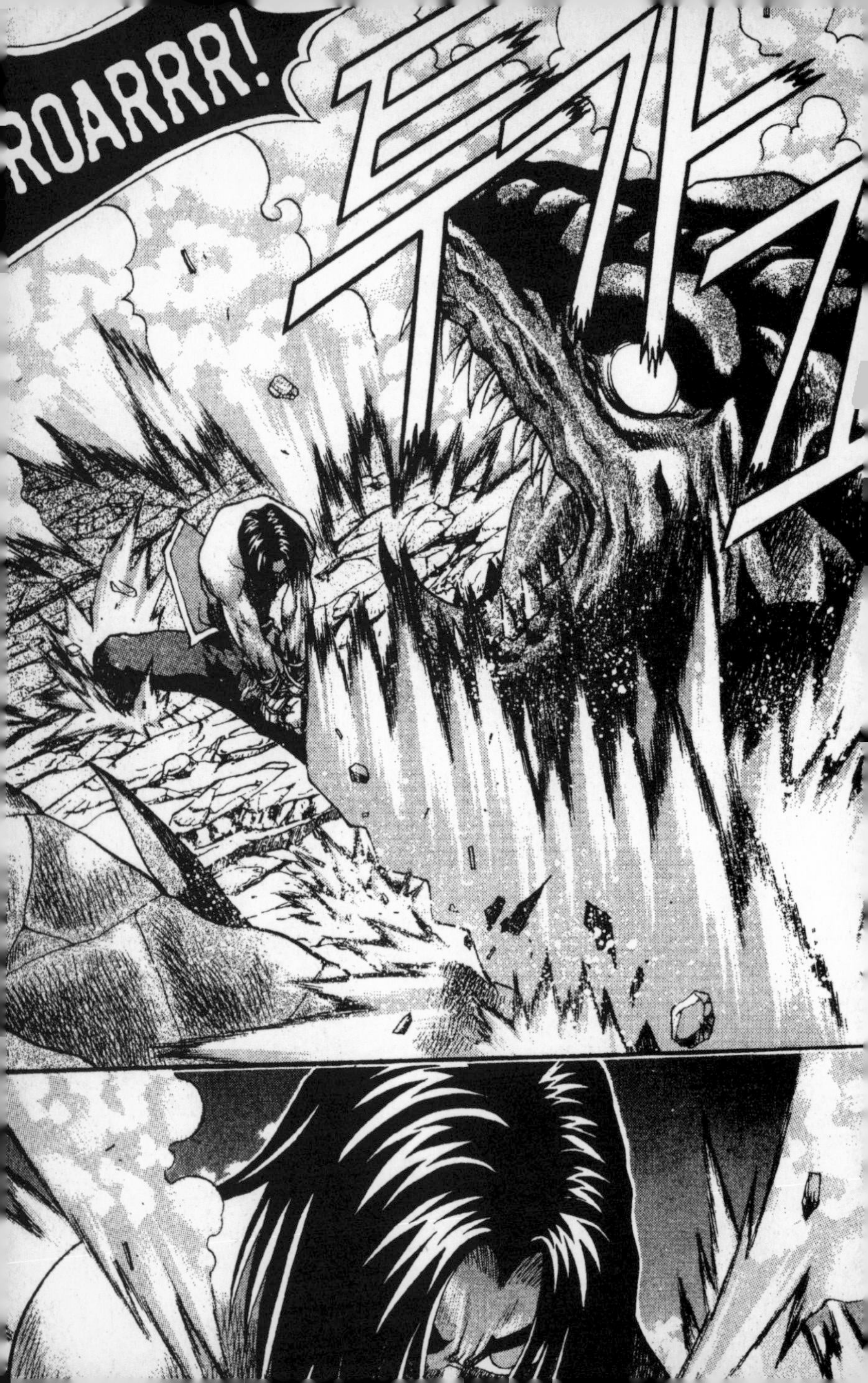
ROARRR!

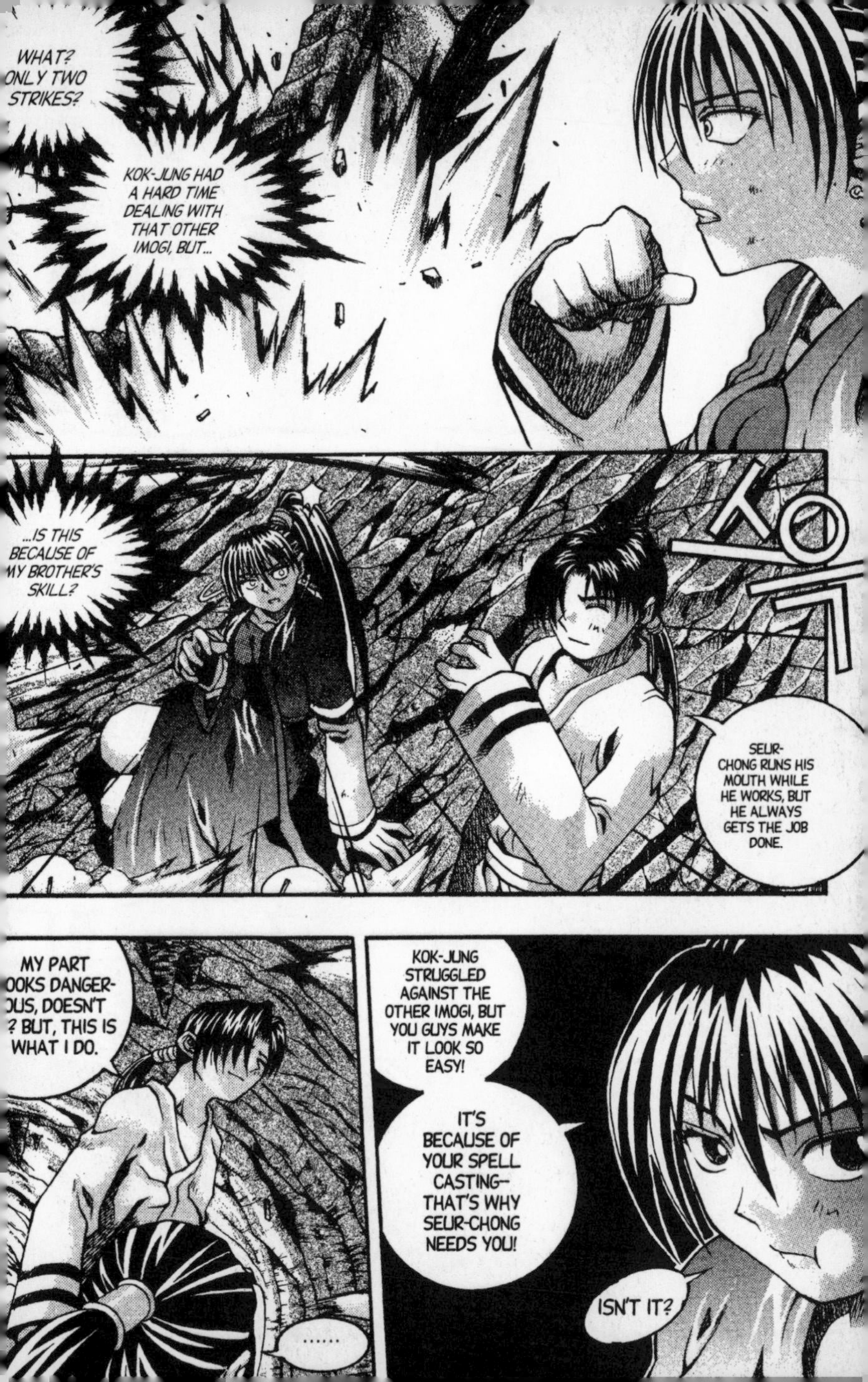
WHAT? ONLY TWO STRIKES?
KOK-JUNG HAD A HARD TIME DEALING WITH THAT OTHER IMOGI, BUT...
...IS THIS BECAUSE OF MY BROTHER'S SKILL?
SEUR-CHONG RUNS HIS MOUTH WHILE HE WORKS, BUT HE ALWAYS GETS THE JOB DONE.
MY PART OOKS DANGER-OUS, DOESN'T ? BUT, THIS IS WHAT I DO.
......
KOK-JUNG STRUGGLED AGAINST THE OTHER IMOGI, BUT YOU GUYS MAKE IT LOOK SO EASY!
IT'S BECAUSE OF YOUR SPELL CASTING--THAT'S WHY SEUR-CHONG NEEDS YOU!
ISN'T IT?

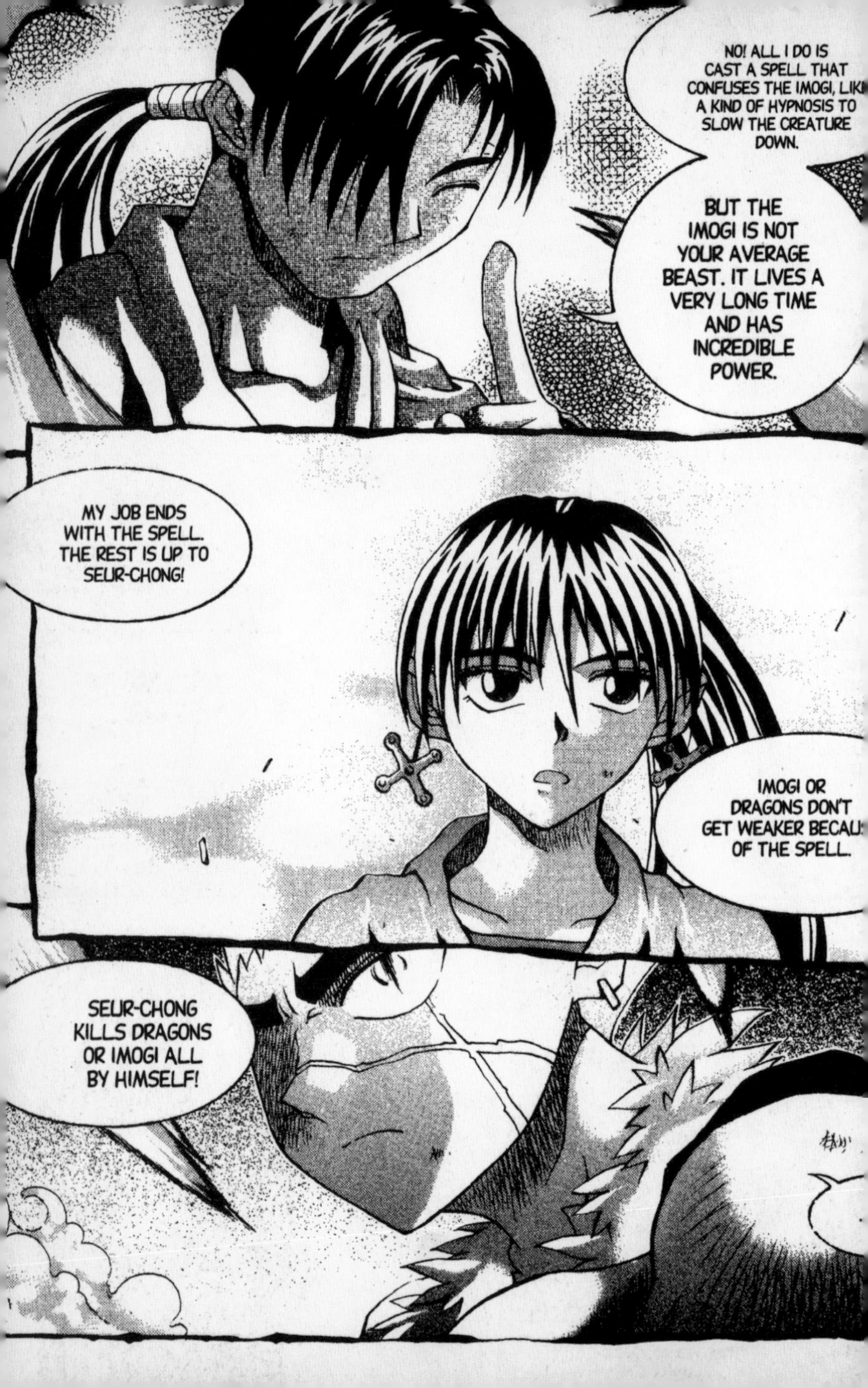
NO! ALL I DO IS CAST A SPELL THAT CONFUSES THE IMOGI, LIK A KIND OF HYPNOSIS TO SLOW THE CREATURE DOWN.
BUT THE IMOGI IS NOT YOUR AVERAGE BEAST. IT LIVES A VERY LONG TIME AND HAS INCREDIBLE POWER.
MY JOB ENDS WITH THE SPELL. THE REST IS UP TO SEUR-CHONG!
IMOGI OR DRAGONS DON'T GET WEAKER BECAU OF THE SPELL.
SEUR-CHONG KILLS DRAGONS OR IMOGI ALL BY HIMSELF!

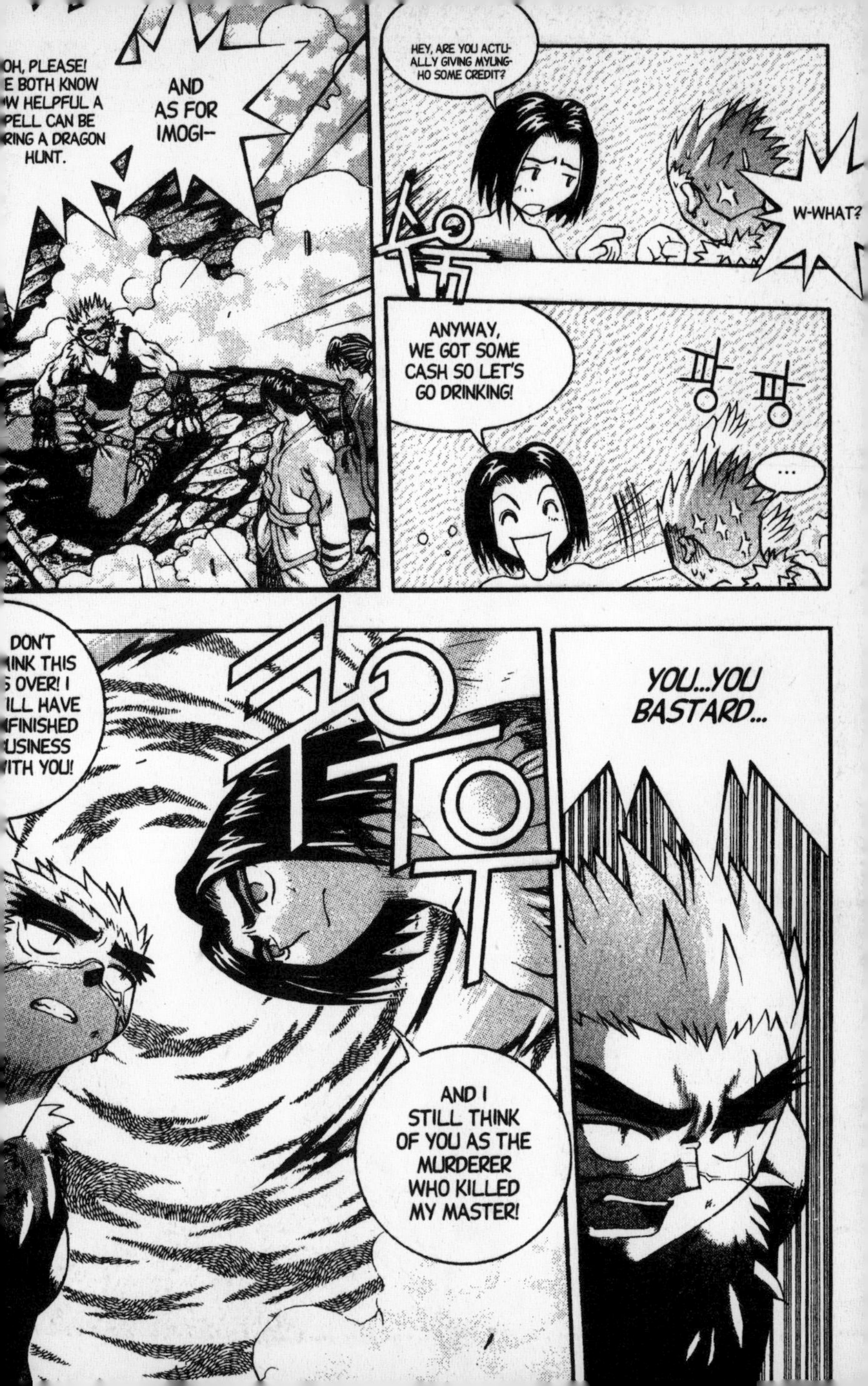
OH, PLEASE!
E BOTH KNOW
W HELPFUL A
PELL CAN BE
RING A DRAGON
HUNT.
AND AS FOR IMOGI--
HEY, ARE YOU ACTUALLY GIVING MYUNG-HO SOME CREDIT?
W-WHAT?
ANYWAY, WE GOT SOME CASH SO LET'S GO DRINKING!
...
DON'T
INK THIS
S OVER! I
ILL HAVE
FINISHED
USINESS
ITH YOU!
AND I STILL THINK OF YOU AS THE MURDERER WHO KILLED MY MASTER!
YOU...YOU BASTARD...

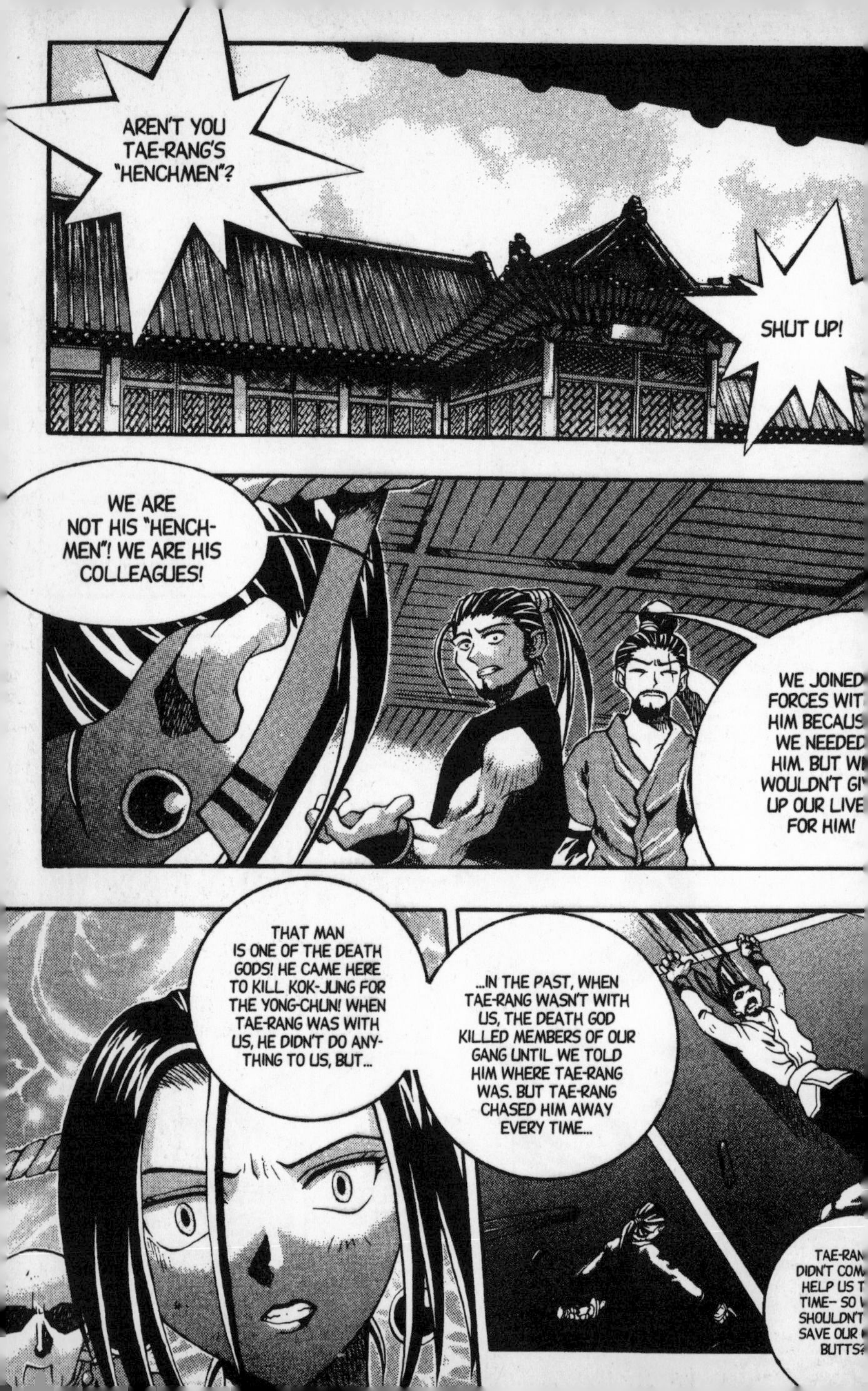
AREN'T YOU TAE-RANG'S "HENCHMEN"?
SHUT UP!
WE ARE NOT HIS "HENCH-MEN"! WE ARE HIS COLLEAGUES!
WE JOINED FORCES WIT HIM BECAUS WE NEEDED HIM. BUT W WOULDN'T GI UP OUR LIVE FOR HIM!
THAT MAN IS ONE OF THE DEATH GODS! HE CAME HERE TO KILL KOK-JUNG FOR THE YONG-CHUN! WHEN TAE-RANG WAS WITH US, HE DIDN'T DO ANY-THING TO US, BUT...
...IN THE PAST, WHEN TAE-RANG WASN'T WITH US, THE DEATH GOD KILLED MEMBERS OF OUR GANG UNTIL WE TOLD HIM WHERE TAE-RANG WAS. BUT TAE-RANG CHASED HIM AWAY EVERY TIME...
TAE-RAN DIDN'T COM HELP US T TIME-- SO SHOULDN'T SAVE OUR BUTTS?

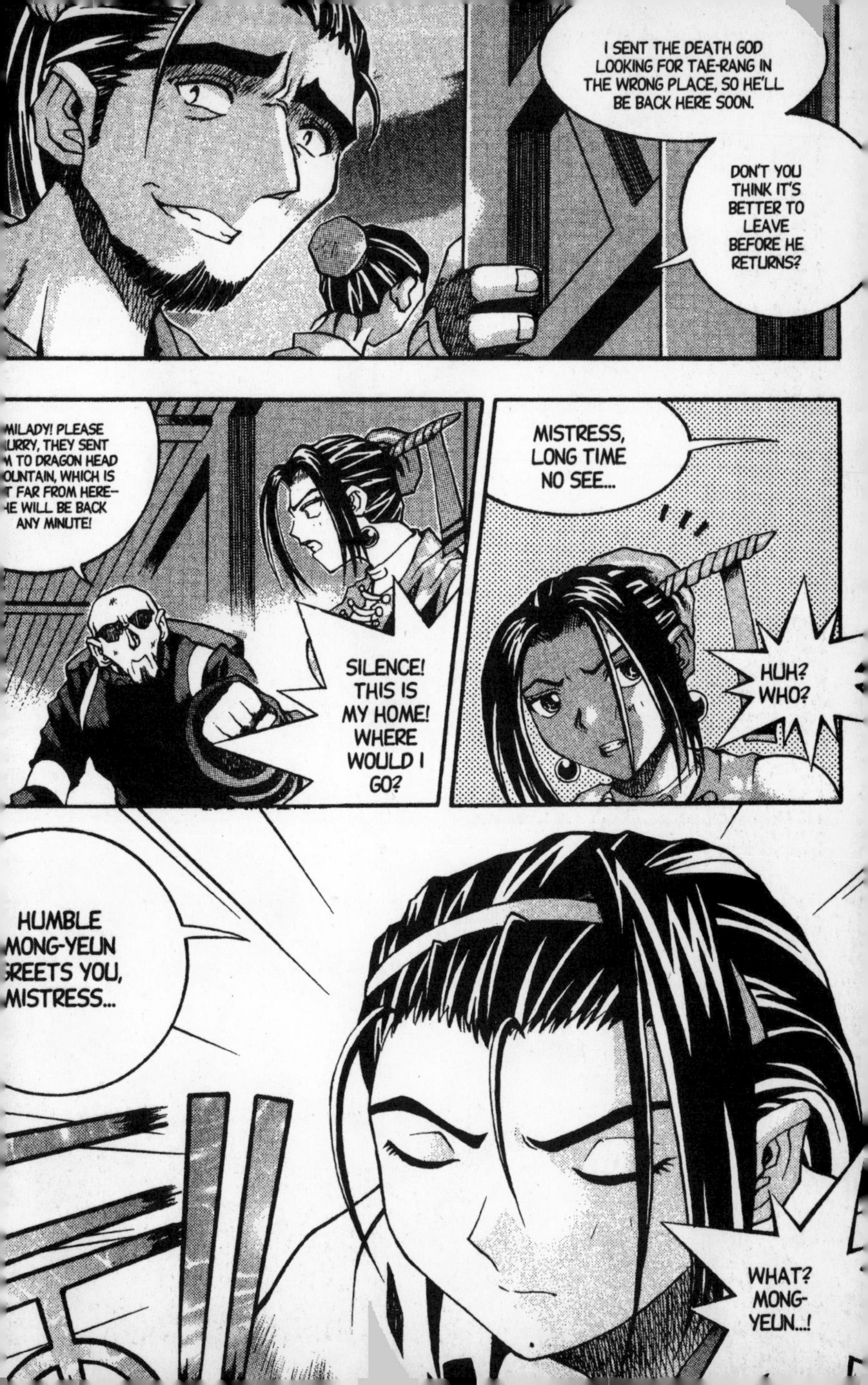

I SENT THE DEATH GOD LOOKING FOR TAE-RANG IN THE WRONG PLACE, SO HE'LL BE BACK HERE SOON.
DON'T YOU THINK IT'S BETTER TO LEAVE BEFORE HE RETURNS?
MILADY! PLEASE URRY, THEY SENT M TO DRAGON HEAD OUNTAIN, WHICH IS T FAR FROM HERE– IE WILL BE BACK ANY MINUTE!
SILENCE! THIS IS MY HOME! WHERE WOULD I GO?
MISTRESS, LONG TIME NO SEE...
HUH? WHO?
HUMBLE MONG-YEUN GREETS YOU, MISTRESS...
WHAT? MONG-YEUN...!

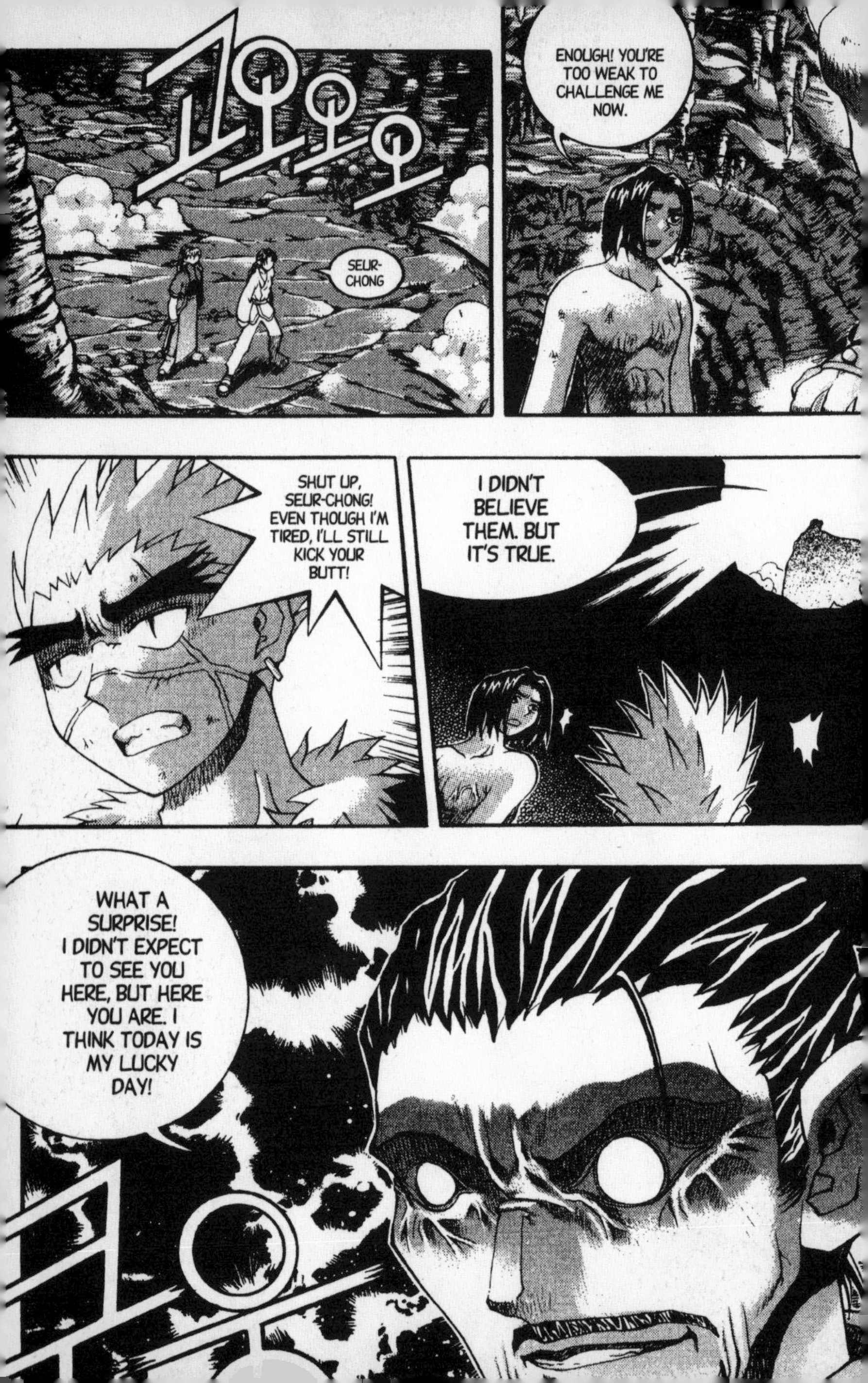
SEUR-CHONG
ENOUGH! YOU'RE TOO WEAK TO CHALLENGE ME NOW.
SHUT UP, SEUR-CHONG! EVEN THOUGH I'M TIRED, I'LL STILL KICK YOUR BUTT!
I DIDN'T BELIEVE THEM. BUT IT'S TRUE.
WHAT A SURPRISE! I DIDN'T EXPECT TO SEE YOU HERE, BUT HERE YOU ARE. I THINK TODAY IS MY LUCKY DAY!

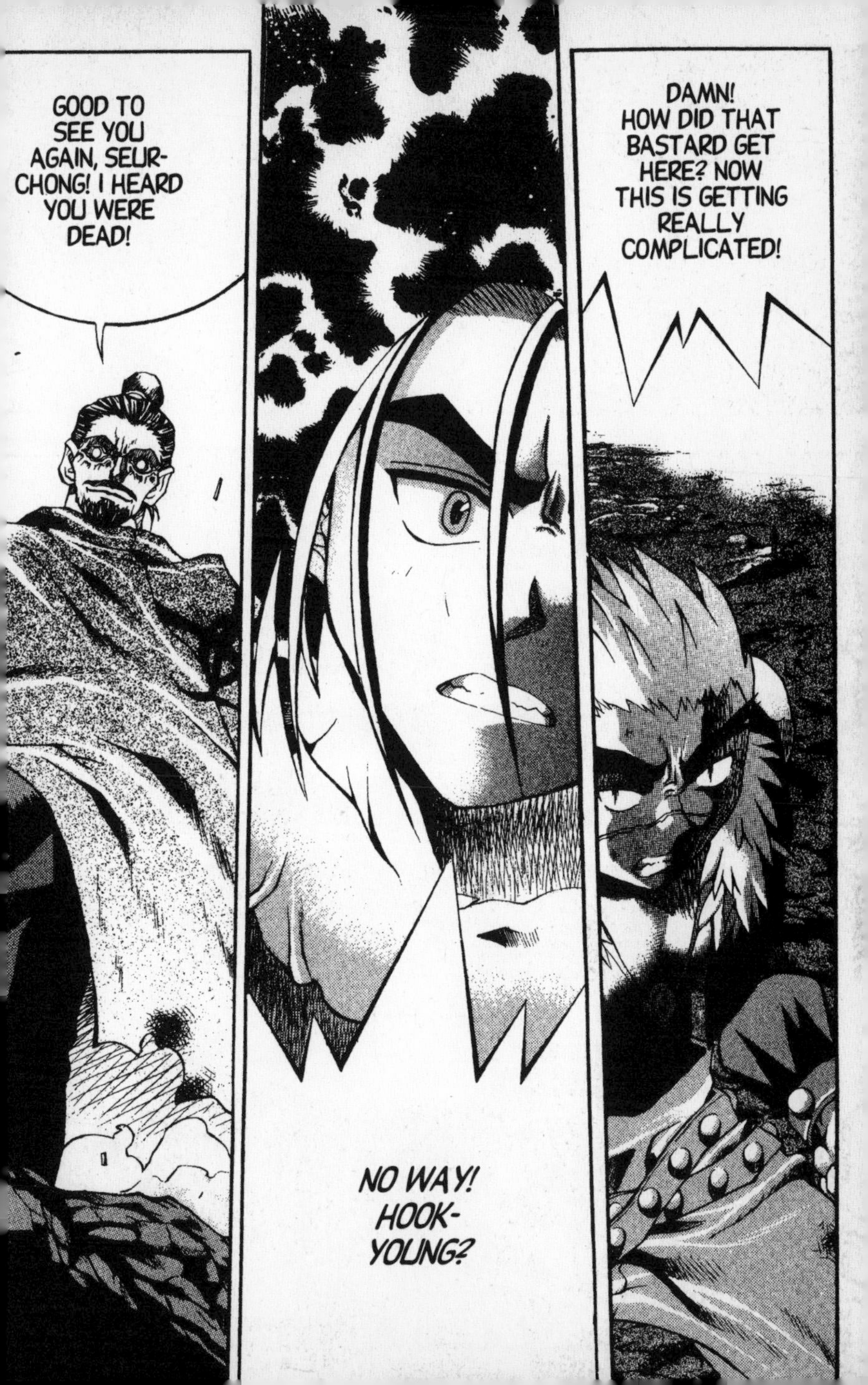
GOOD TO SEE YOU AGAIN, SEUR-CHONG! I HEARD YOU WERE DEAD!
NO WAY! HOOK-YOUNG?
DAMN! HOW DID THAT BASTARD GET HERE? NOW THIS IS GETTING REALLY COMPLICATED!

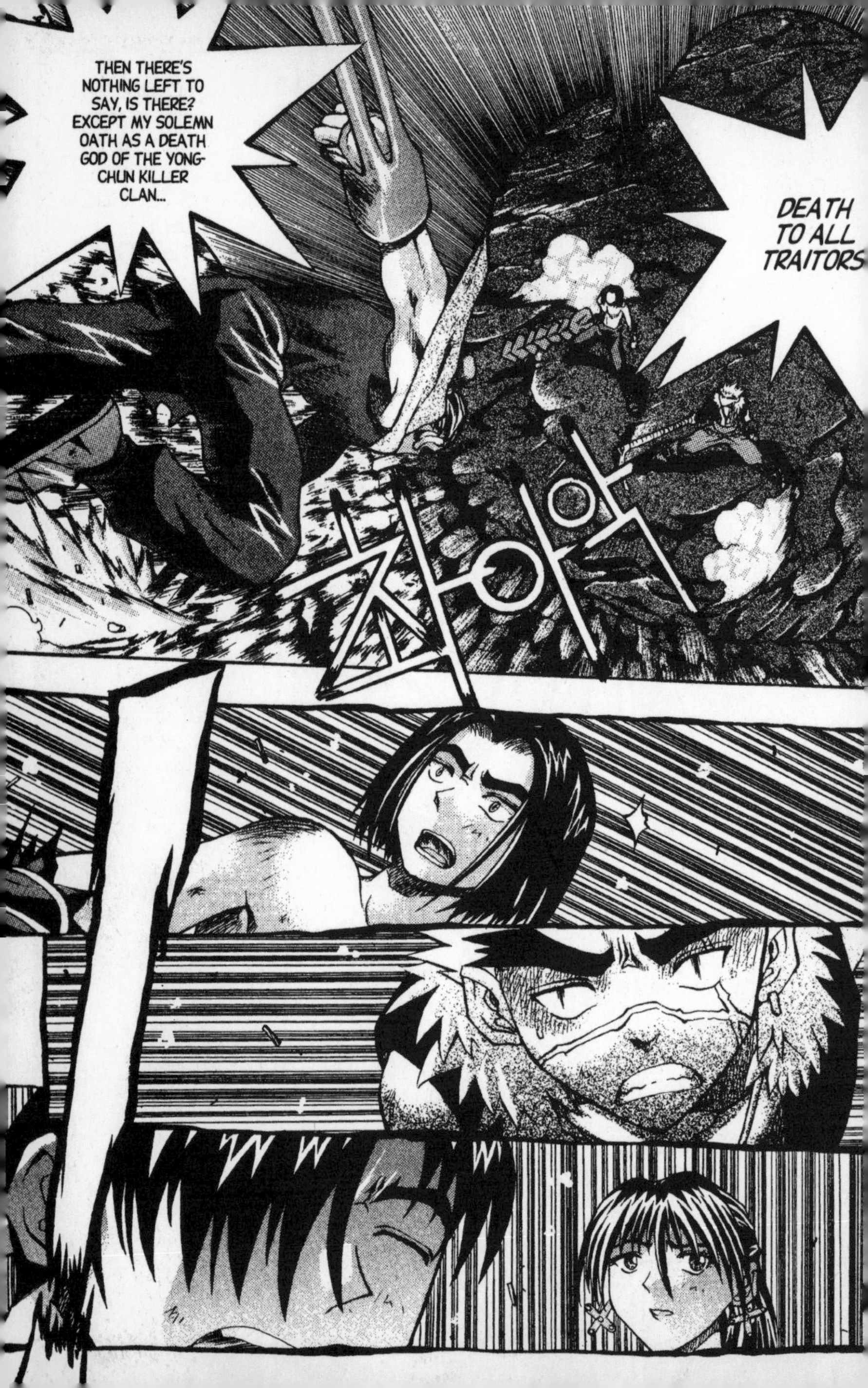
THEN THERE'S NOTHING LEFT TO SAY, IS THERE? EXCEPT MY SOLEMN OATH AS A DEATH GOD OF THE YONG-CHUN KILLER CLAN...
DEATH TO ALL TRAITORS

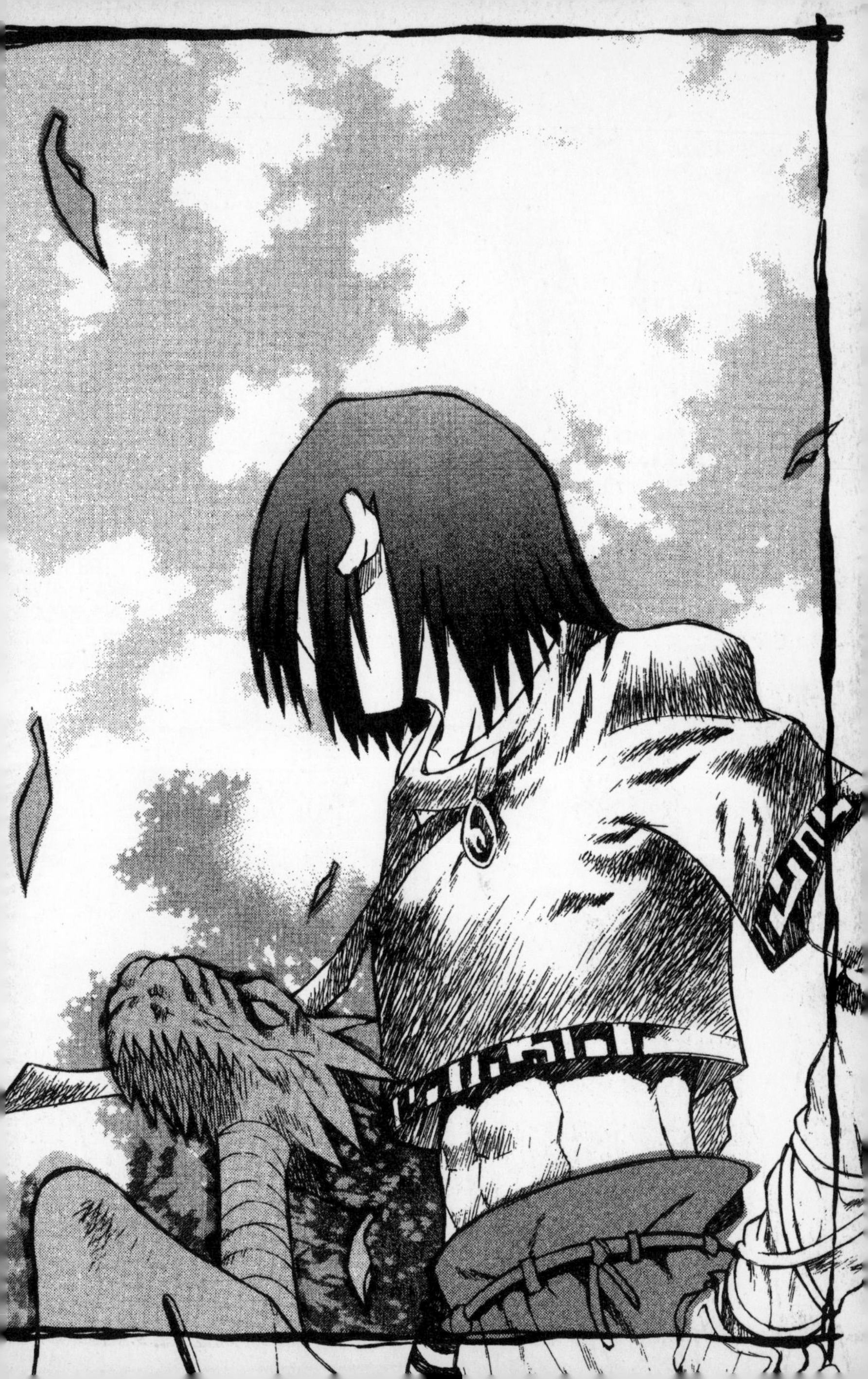

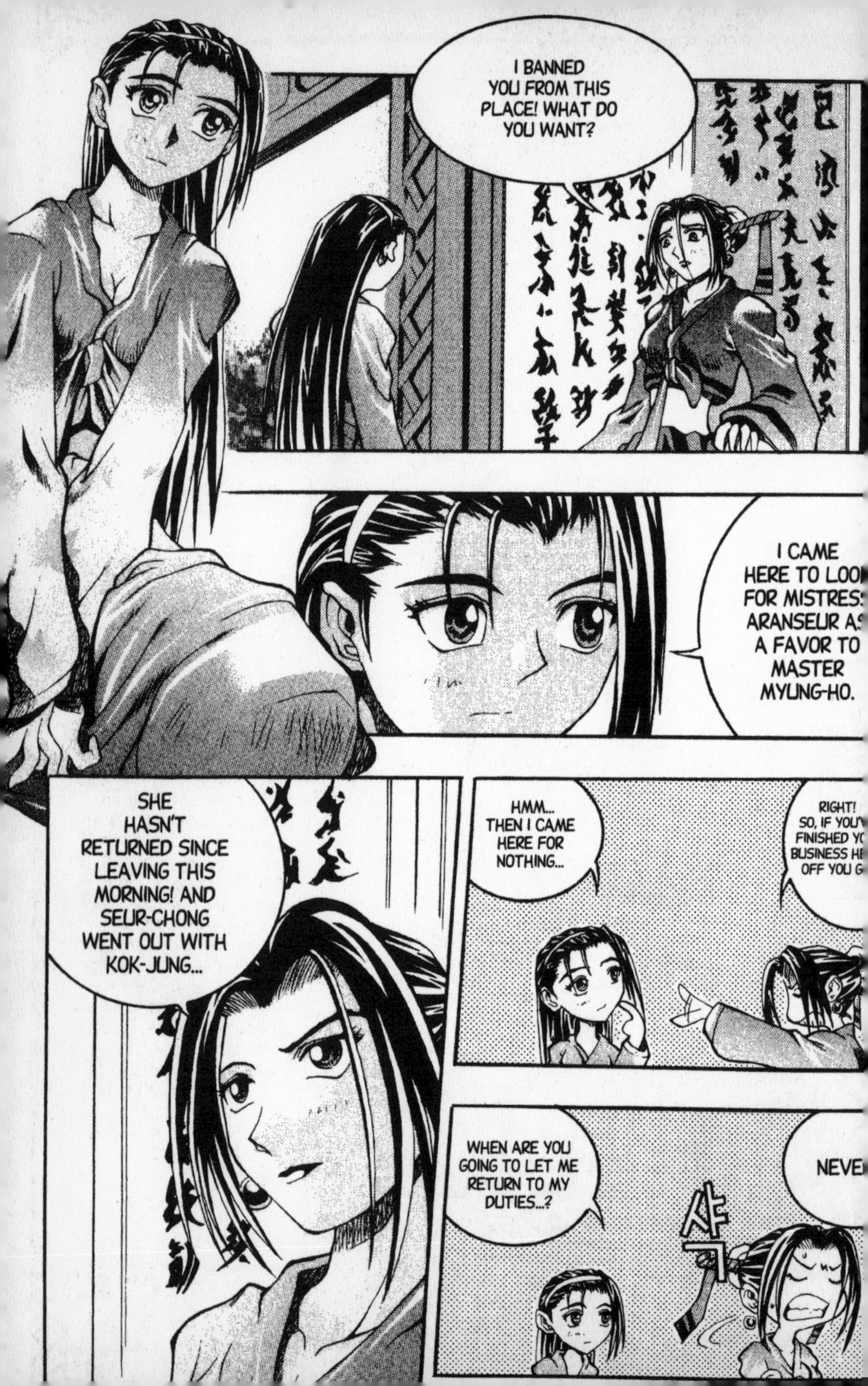
I BANNED YOU FROM THIS PLACE! WHAT DO YOU WANT?
I CAME HERE TO LOOK FOR MISTRESS ARANSEUR AS A FAVOR TO MASTER MYUNG-HO.
SHE HASN'T RETURNED SINCE LEAVING THIS MORNING! AND SEUR-CHONG WENT OUT WITH KOK-JUNG...
HMM... THEN I CAME HERE FOR NOTHING...
RIGHT! SO, IF YOU'VE FINISHED YOUR BUSINESS HERE, OFF YOU GO
WHEN ARE YOU GOING TO LET ME RETURN TO MY DUTIES...?
NEVER

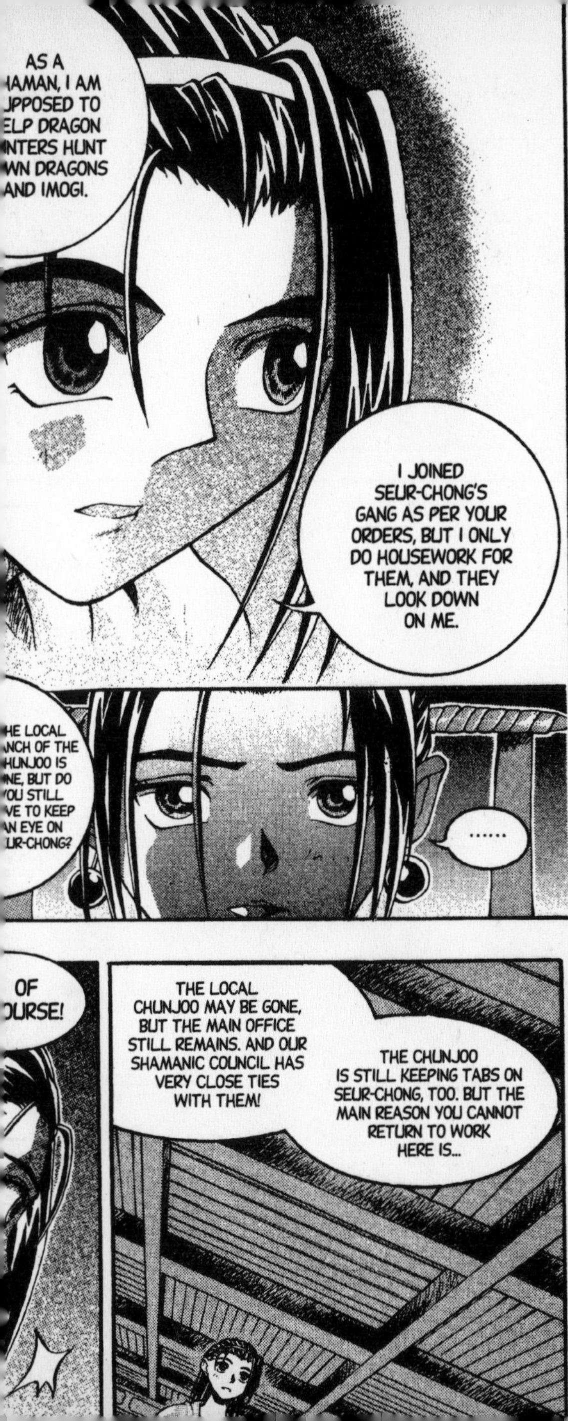
AS A
HAMAN, I AM
JPPOSED TO
ELP DRAGON
NTERS HUNT
WN DRAGONS
AND IMOGI.
I JOINED SEUR-CHONG'S GANG AS PER YOUR ORDERS, BUT I ONLY DO HOUSEWORK FOR THEM, AND THEY LOOK DOWN ON ME.
HE LOCAL
NCH OF THE
HUNJOO IS
NE, BUT DO
OU STILL
VE TO KEEP
N EYE ON
UR-CHONG?
......
OF
OURSE!
THE LOCAL CHUNJOO MAY BE GONE, BUT THE MAIN OFFICE STILL REMAINS. AND OUR SHAMANIC COUNCIL HAS VERY CLOSE TIES WITH THEM!
THE CHUNJOO IS STILL KEEPING TABS ON SEUR-CHONG, TOO. BUT THE MAIN REASON YOU CANNOT RETURN TO WORK HERE IS...

Dragon Hunter's Encyclopedia

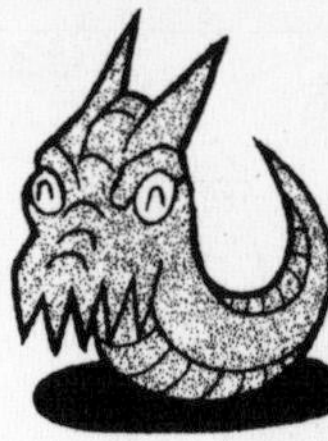

About Imogi, Part 1

Most people think that the Imogi is an old snake that has yet to become a dragon, but the Imogi appears often, in various forms, in many different myths. Even in traditional folk songs and plays, the Imogi is called by different names such as Isimi, Kwang-Chul, Young-Noh, etc. The Imogi hides from people in order to complete its metamorphosis into a dragon, so it is also known as a "Hidden Dragon." The Imogi looks very similar to a dragon, and its length is usually 3 meters or more. Imogi transform into dragons when they turn 1000 years old. It is said that Imogi who harm people are bitter about their long wait to transform into a dragon. There are two classes of Imogi, those with antlers (called the Chuk-Jok) and those without antlers. More on the Chuk-Jok in "About Imogi, Part 2."

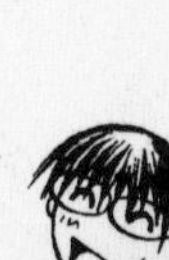

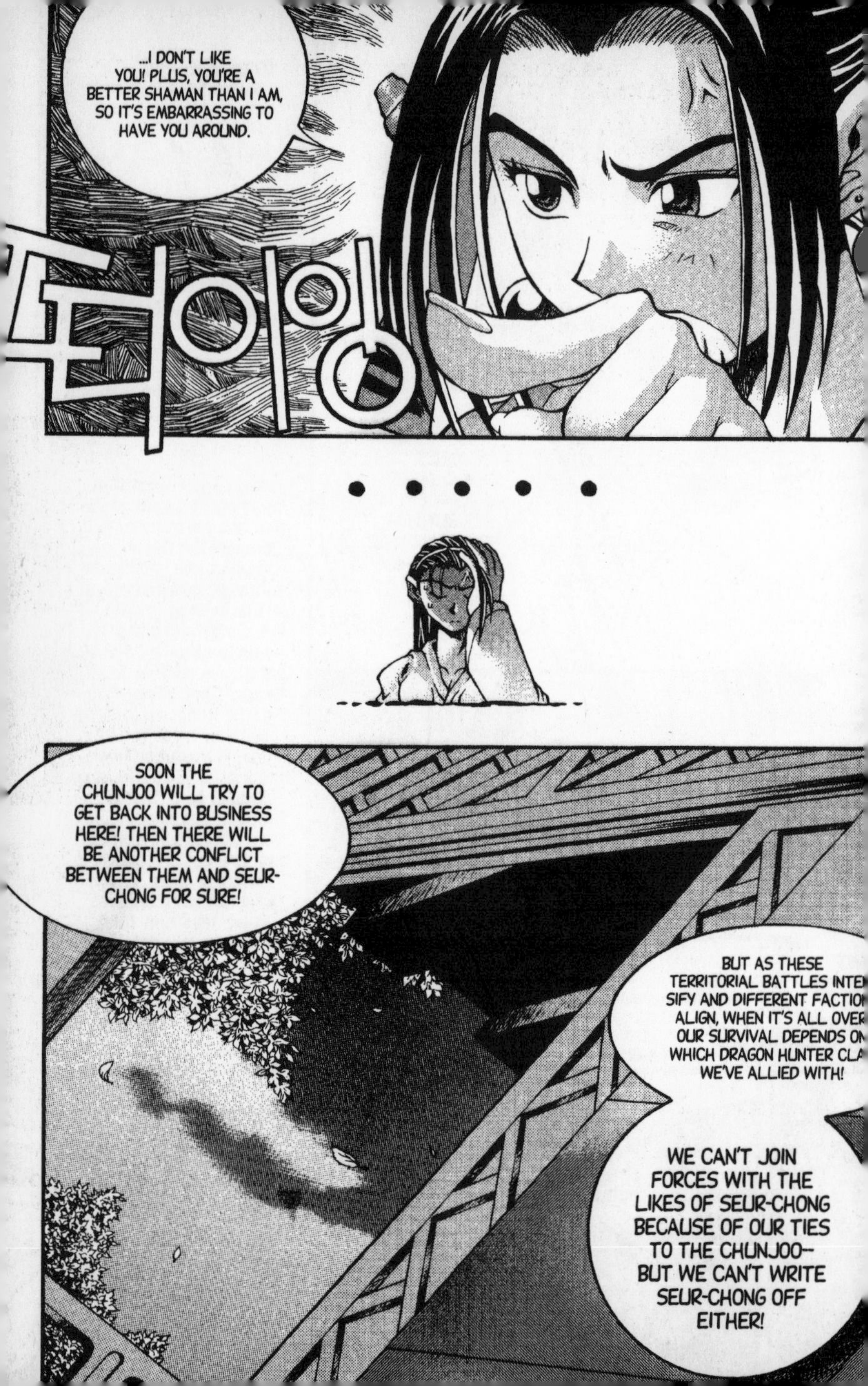
...I DON'T LIKE YOU! PLUS, YOU'RE A BETTER SHAMAN THAN I AM, SO IT'S EMBARRASSING TO HAVE YOU AROUND.
• • • • •
SOON THE CHUNJOO WILL TRY TO GET BACK INTO BUSINESS HERE! THEN THERE WILL BE ANOTHER CONFLICT BETWEEN THEM AND SEUR-CHONG FOR SURE!
BUT AS THESE TERRITORIAL BATTLES INTE SIFY AND DIFFERENT FACTIO ALIGN, WHEN IT'S ALL OVE OUR SURVIVAL DEPENDS O WHICH DRAGON HUNTER CL WE'VE ALLIED WITH!
WE CAN'T JOIN FORCES WITH THE LIKES OF SEUR-CHONG BECAUSE OF OUR TIES TO THE CHUNJOO-- BUT WE CAN'T WRITE SEUR-CHONG OFF EITHER!

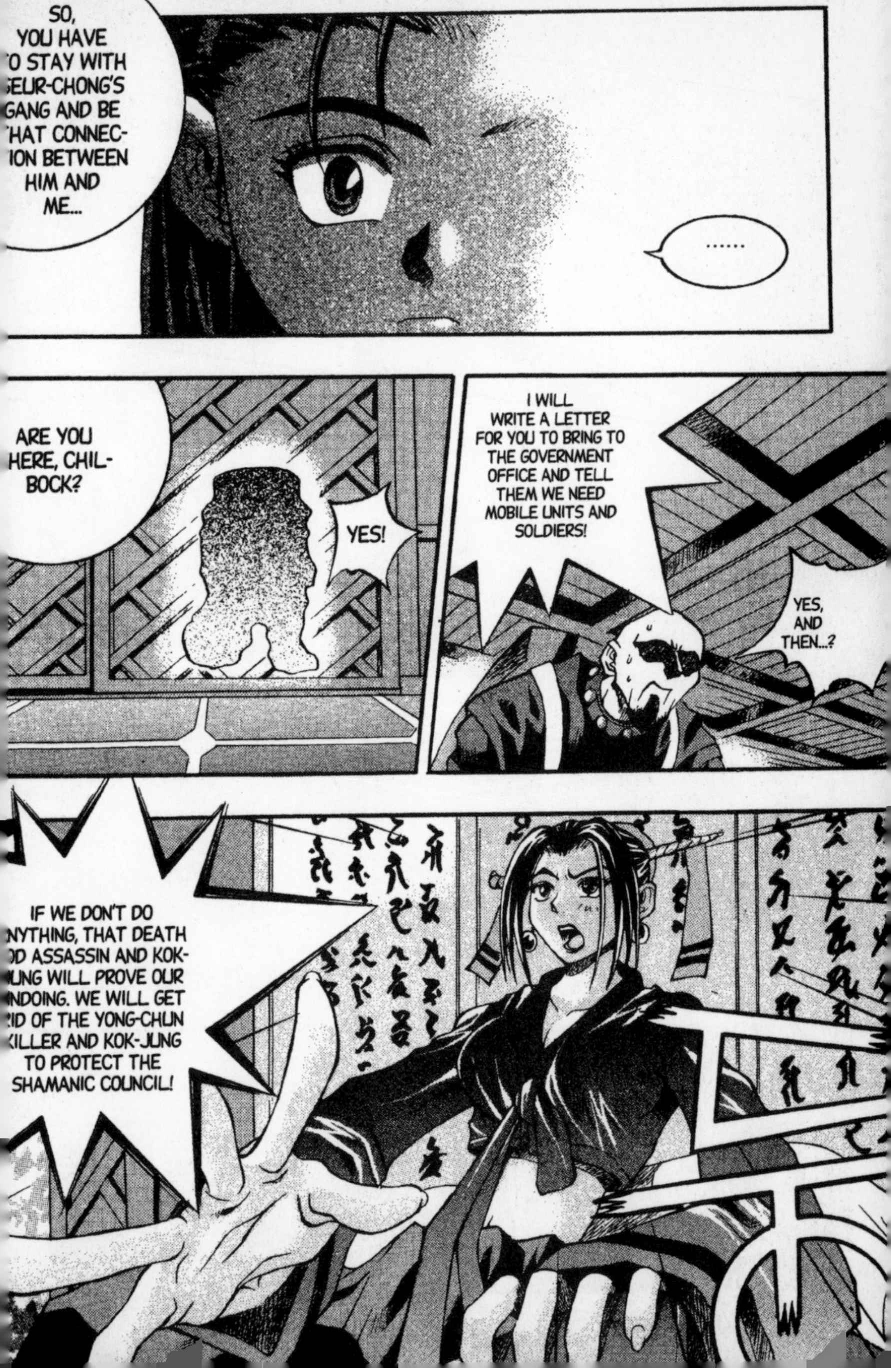
SO, YOU HAVE O STAY WITH EUR-CHONG'S GANG AND BE HAT CONNEC- ION BETWEEN HIM AND ME...
......
ARE YOU HERE, CHIL- BOCK?
YES!
I WILL WRITE A LETTER FOR YOU TO BRING TO THE GOVERNMENT OFFICE AND TELL THEM WE NEED MOBILE UNITS AND SOLDIERS!
YES, AND THEN...?
IF WE DON'T DO NYTHING, THAT DEATH OD ASSASSIN AND KOK- UNG WILL PROVE OUR NDOING. WE WILL GET RID OF THE YONG-CHUN KILLER AND KOK-JUNG TO PROTECT THE SHAMANIC COUNCIL!

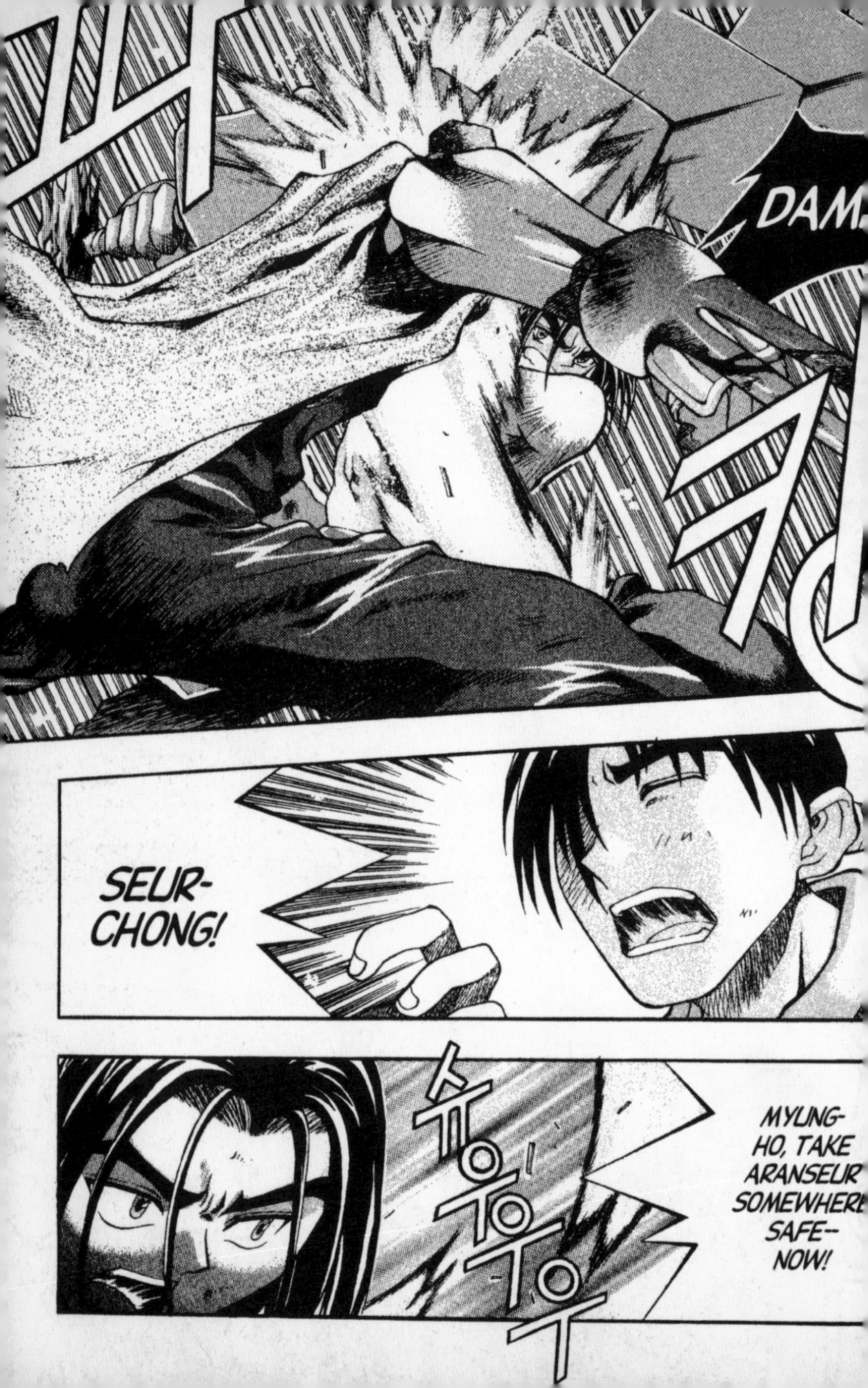
DAM-
SEUR-
CHONG!
MYUNG-
HO, TAKE
ARANSEUR
SOMEWHERE
SAFE--
NOW!

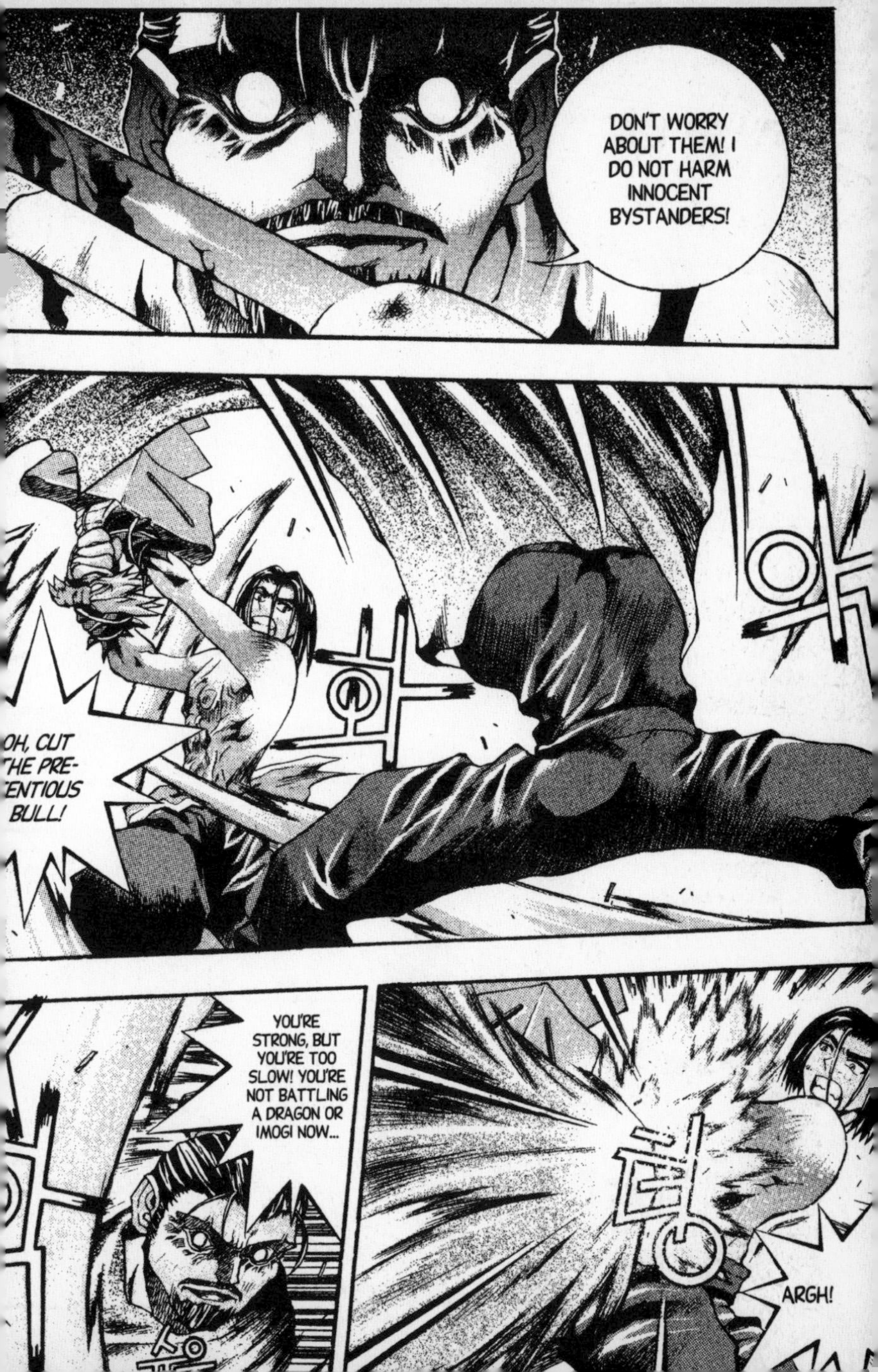
DON'T WORRY ABOUT THEM! I DO NOT HARM INNOCENT BYSTANDERS!
OH, CUT THE PRE-TENTIOUS BULL!
YOU'RE STRONG, BUT YOU'RE TOO SLOW! YOU'RE NOT BATTLING A DRAGON OR IMOGI NOW...
ARGH!

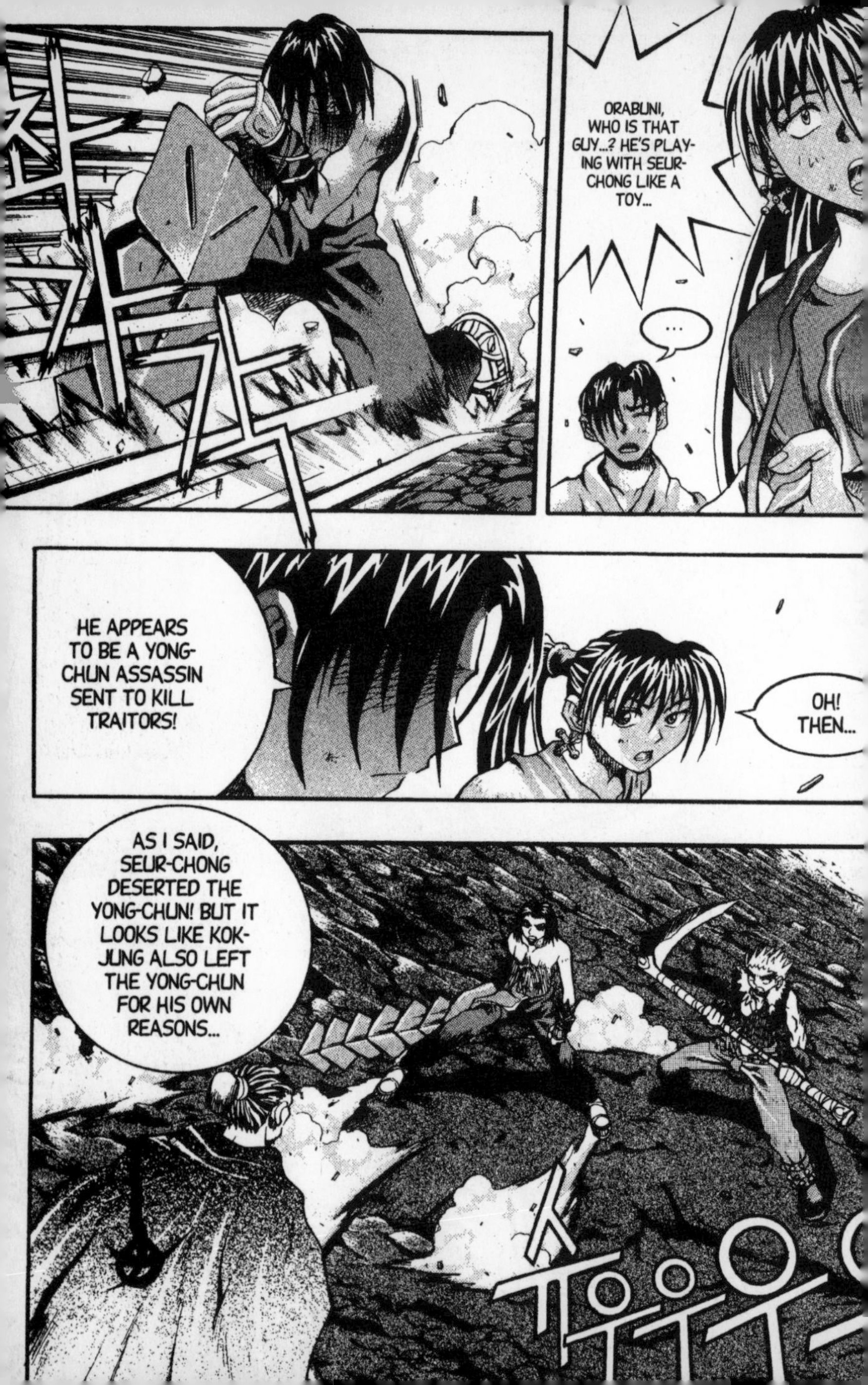
ORABUNI, WHO IS THAT GUY...? HE'S PLAYING WITH SEUR-CHONG LIKE A TOY...
...
HE APPEARS TO BE A YONG-CHUN ASSASSIN SENT TO KILL TRAITORS!
OH! THEN...
AS I SAID, SEUR-CHONG DESERTED THE YONG-CHUN! BUT IT LOOKS LIKE KOK-JUNG ALSO LEFT THE YONG-CHUN FOR HIS OWN REASONS...

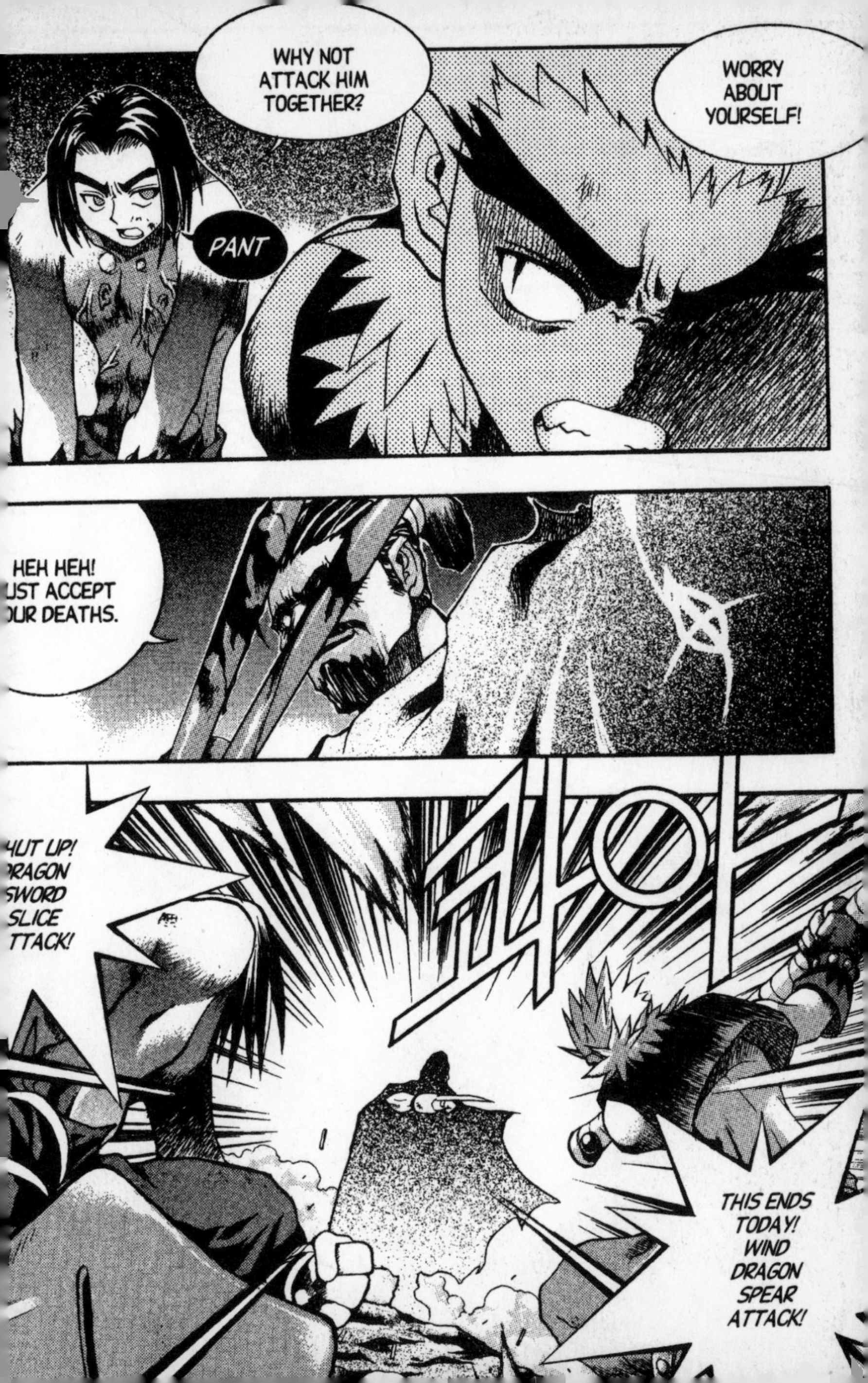

WHY NOT ATTACK HIM TOGETHER?
PANT
WORRY ABOUT YOURSELF!
HEH HEH! UST ACCEPT OUR DEATHS.
HUT UP! RAGON SWORD SLICE TTACK!
THIS ENDS TODAY! WIND DRAGON SPEAR ATTACK!

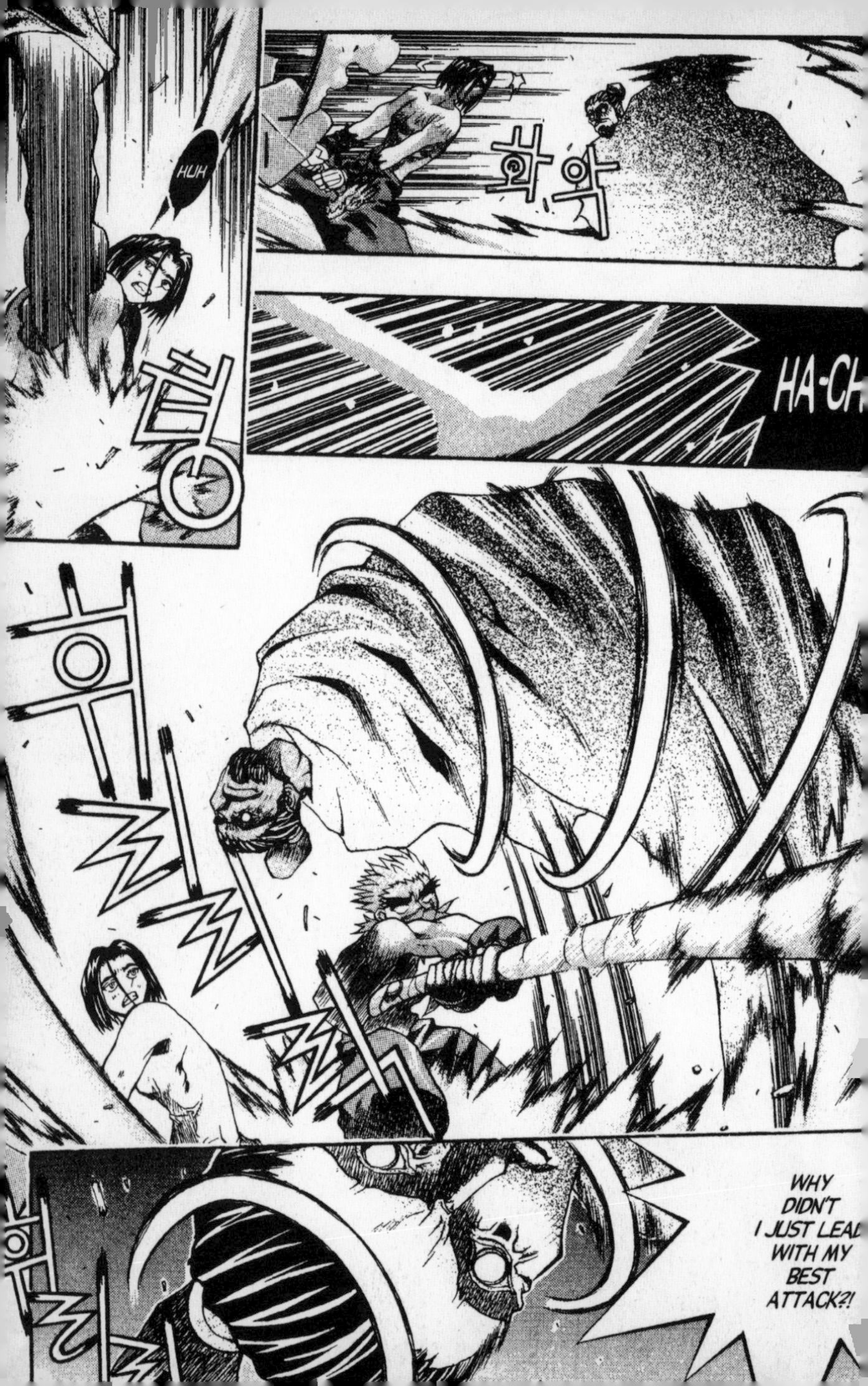
HUH
화악
HA-CH
WHY DIDN'T I JUST LEAD WITH MY BEST ATTACK?!

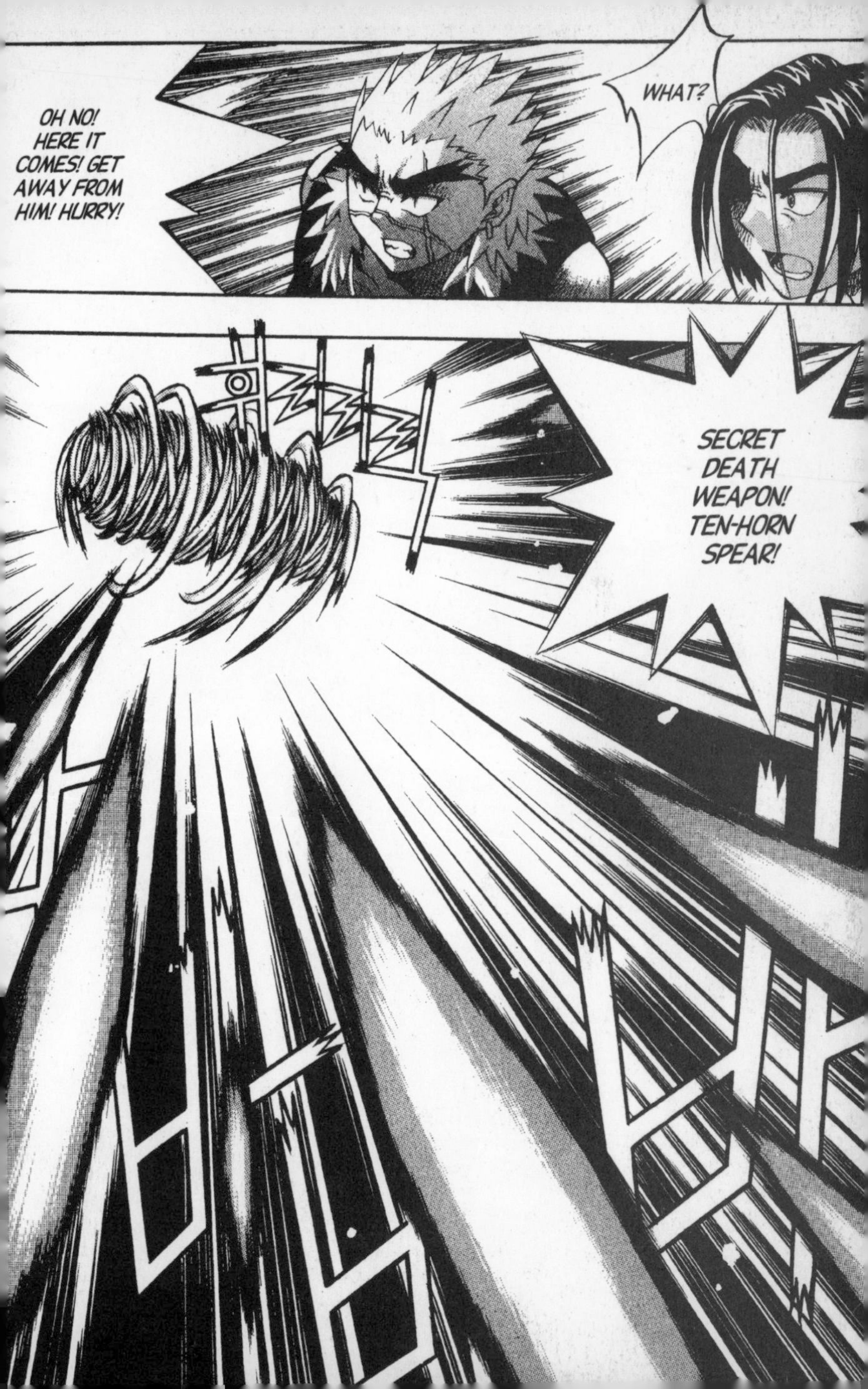
OH NO! HERE IT COMES! GET AWAY FROM HIM! HURRY!
WHAT?
SECRET DEATH WEAPON! TEN-HORN SPEAR!

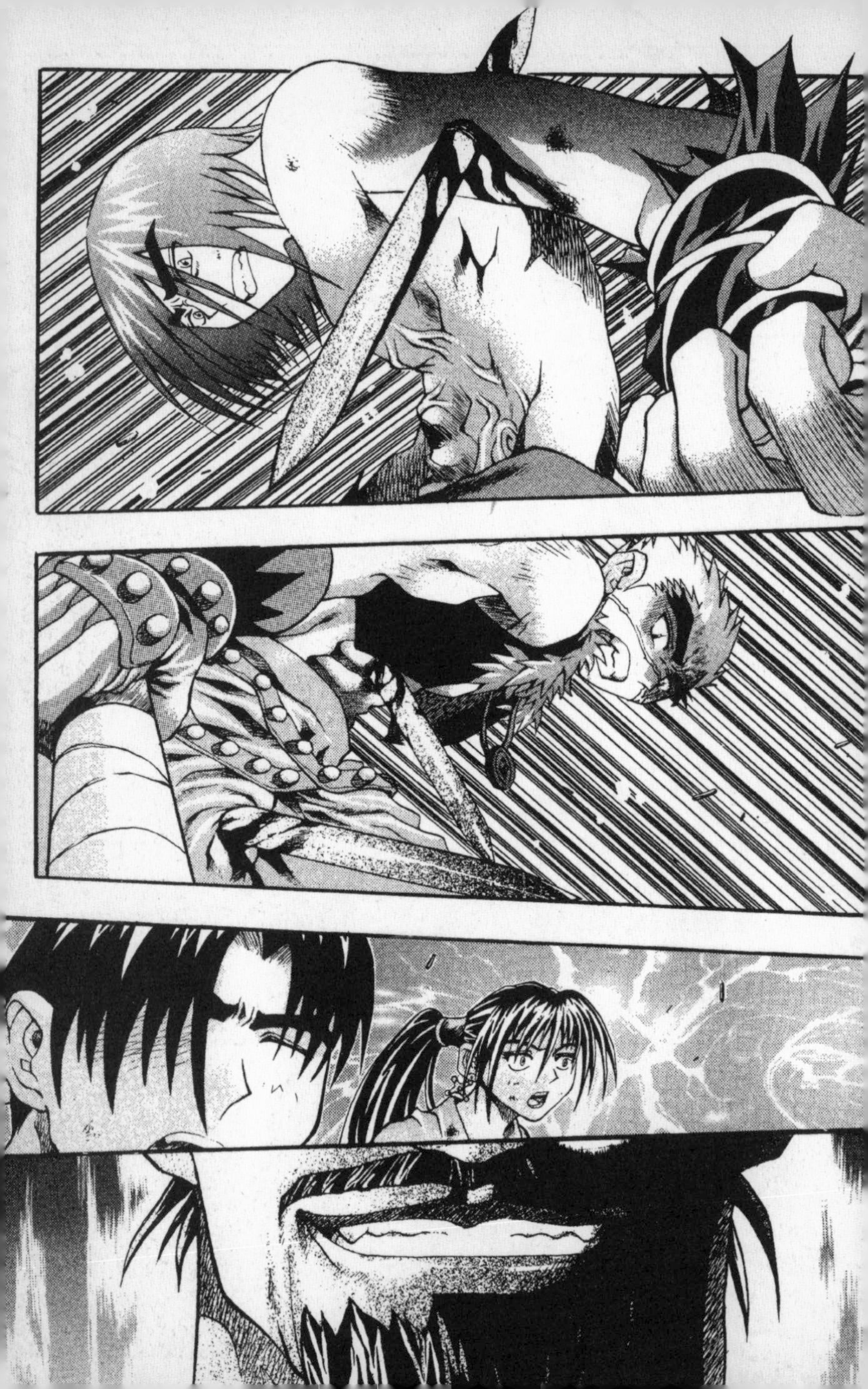

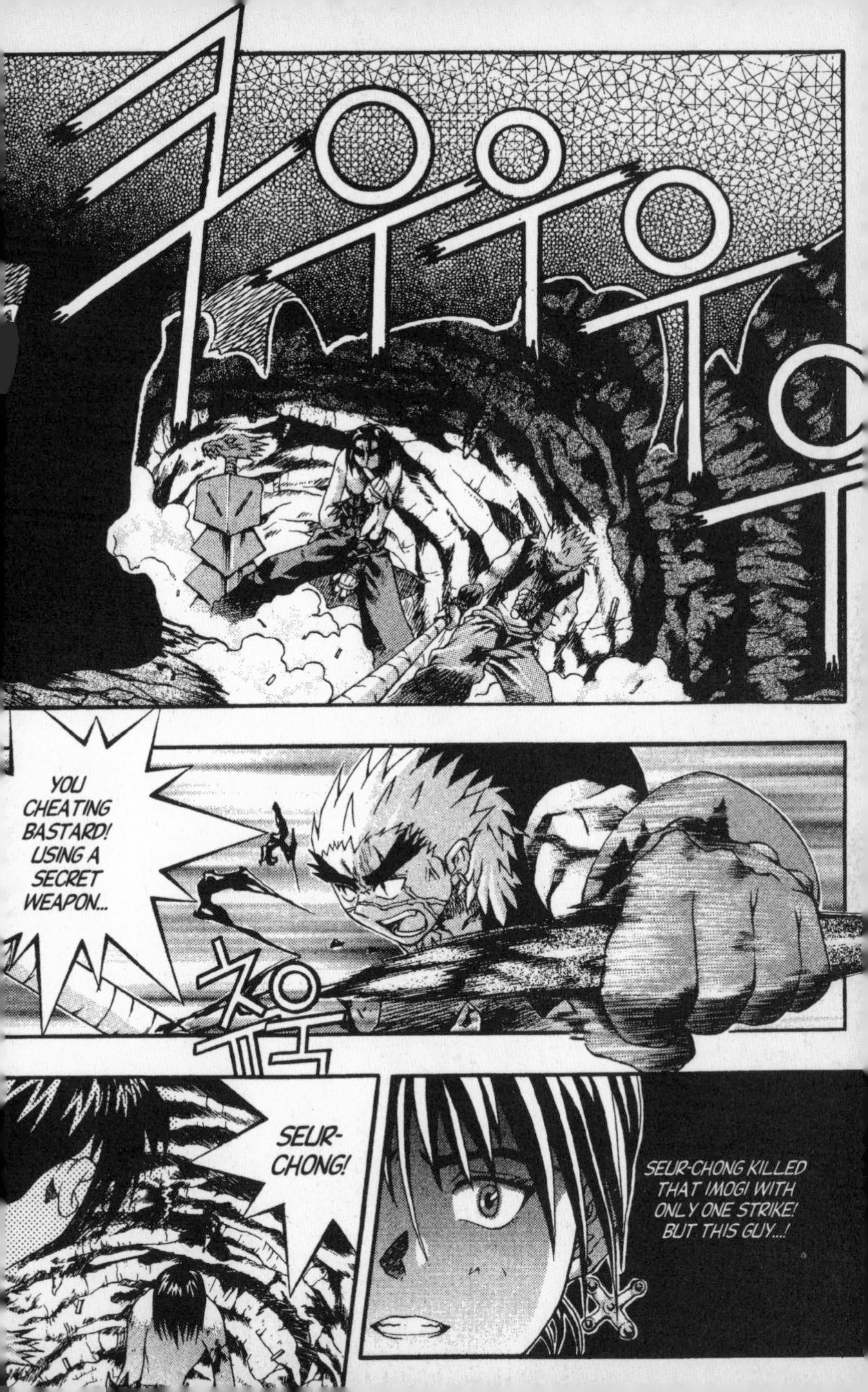
YOU CHEATING BASTARD! USING A SECRET WEAPON...
SEUR-CHONG!
SEUR-CHONG KILLED THAT IMOGI WITH ONLY ONE STRIKE! BUT THIS GUY...!

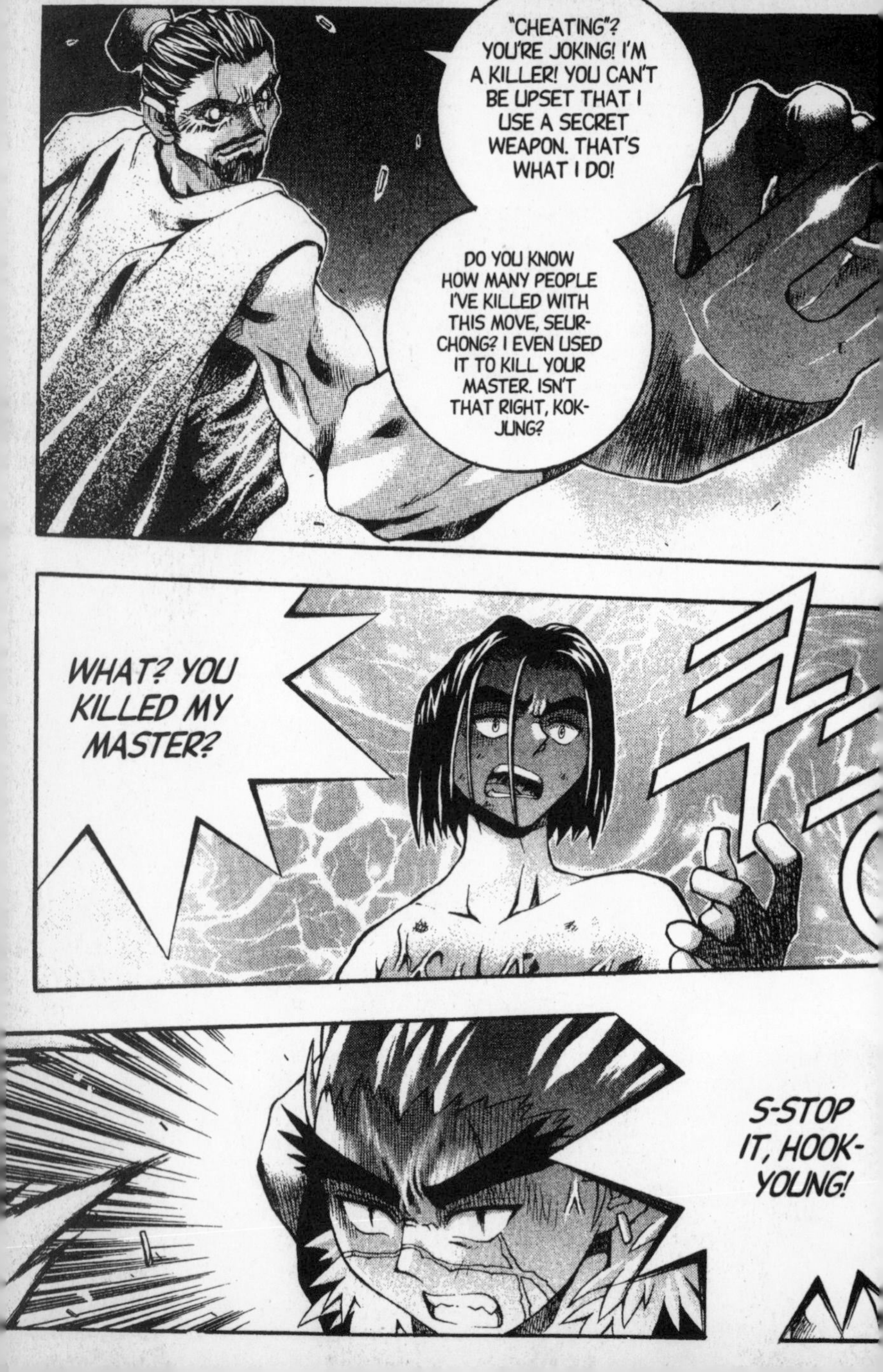
"CHEATING"? YOU'RE JOKING! I'M A KILLER! YOU CAN'T BE UPSET THAT I USE A SECRET WEAPON. THAT'S WHAT I DO!
DO YOU KNOW HOW MANY PEOPLE I'VE KILLED WITH THIS MOVE, SEUR-CHONG? I EVEN USED IT TO KILL YOUR MASTER. ISN'T THAT RIGHT, KOK-JUNG?
WHAT? YOU KILLED MY MASTER?
S-STOP IT, HOOK-YOUNG!

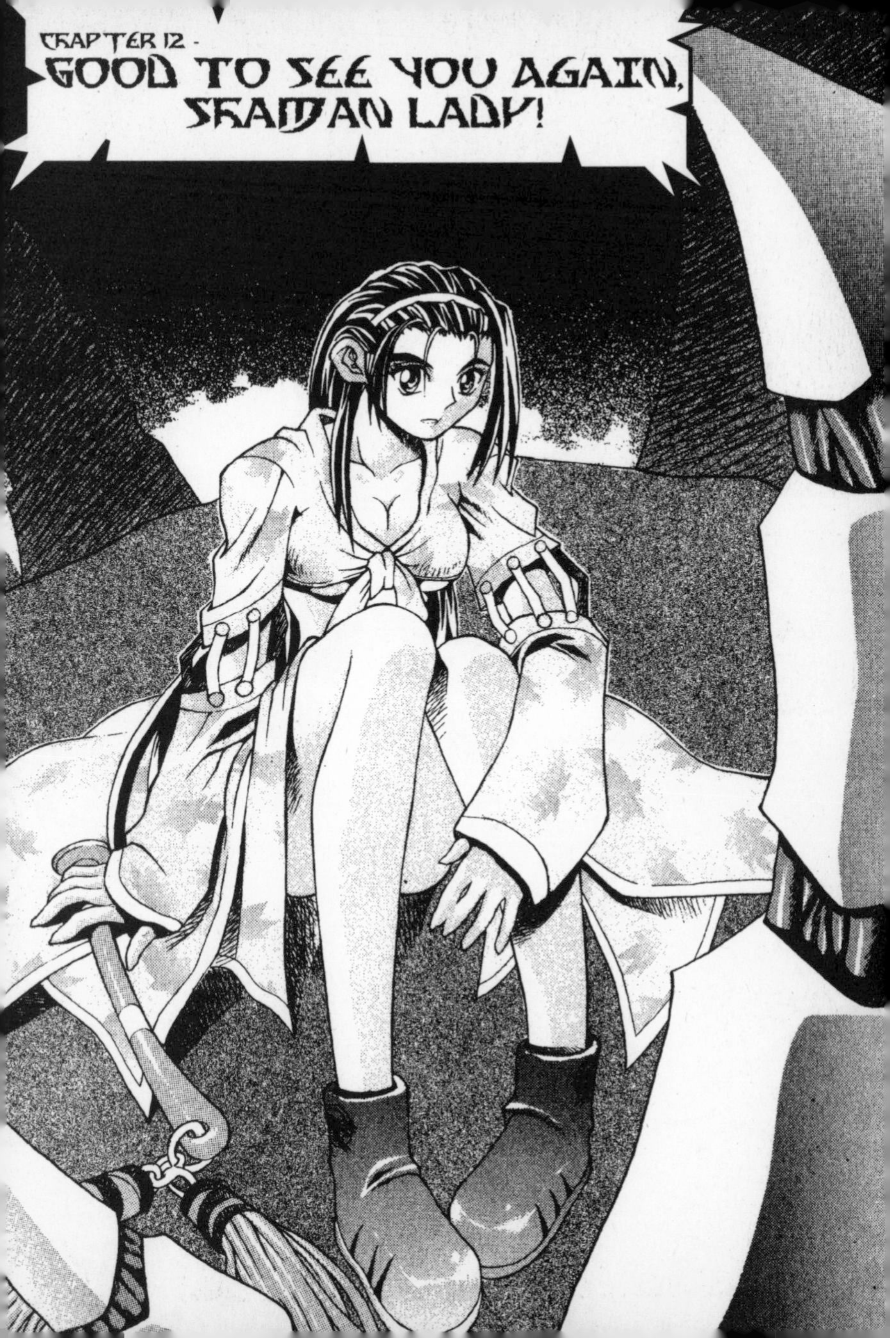
CHAPTER 12 -
GOOD TO SEE YOU AGAIN, SHAMAN LADY!

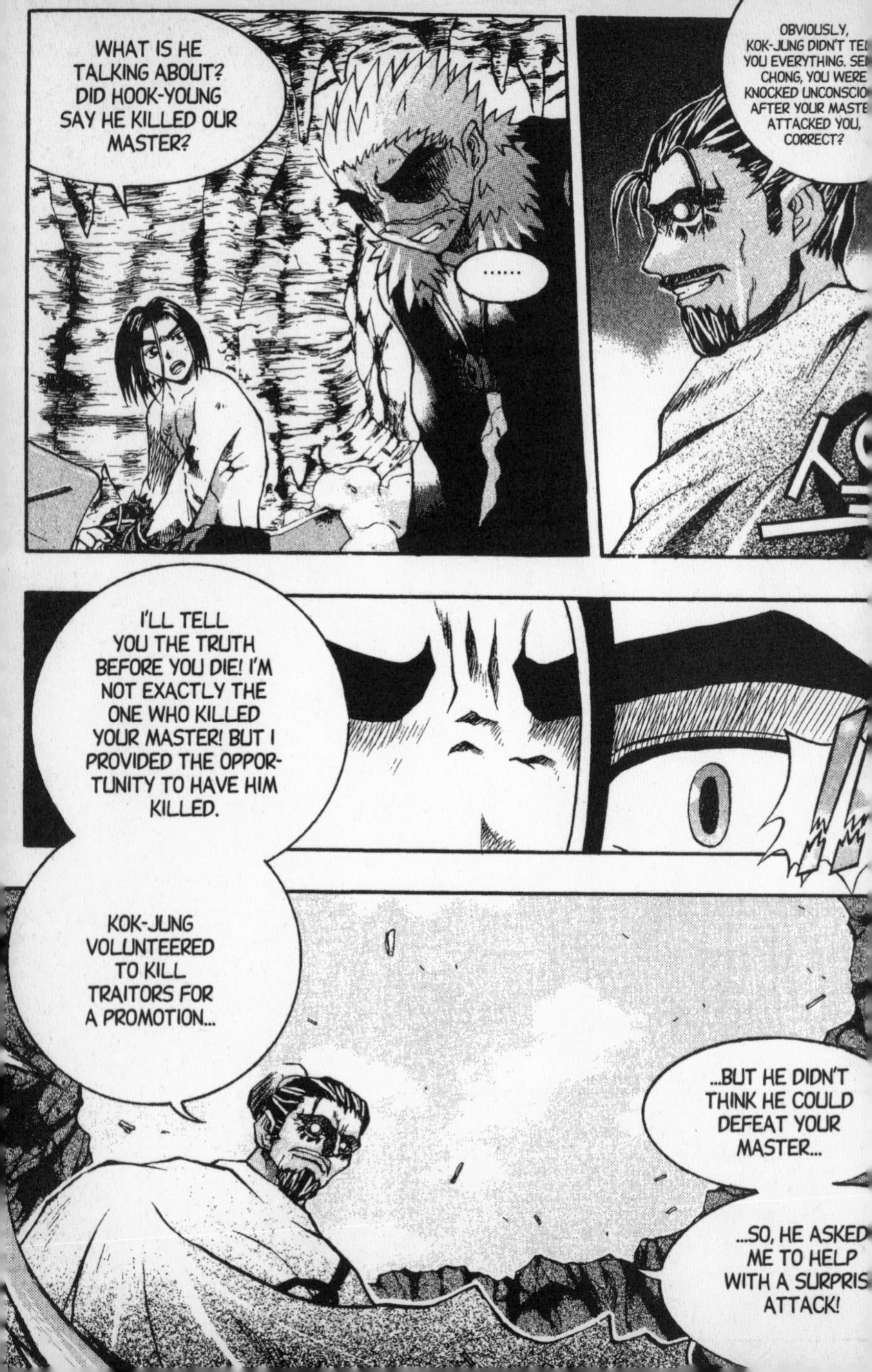
WHAT IS HE TALKING ABOUT? DID HOOK-YOUNG SAY HE KILLED OUR MASTER?
....
OBVIOUSLY, KOK-JUNG DIDN'T TE YOU EVERYTHING. SE CHONG, YOU WERE KNOCKED UNCONSCIO AFTER YOUR MASTE ATTACKED YOU, CORRECT?
I'LL TELL YOU THE TRUTH BEFORE YOU DIE! I'M NOT EXACTLY THE ONE WHO KILLED YOUR MASTER! BUT I PROVIDED THE OPPOR-TUNITY TO HAVE HIM KILLED.
KOK-JUNG VOLUNTEERED TO KILL TRAITORS FOR A PROMOTION...
...BUT HE DIDN'T THINK HE COULD DEFEAT YOUR MASTER...
...SO, HE ASKED ME TO HELP WITH A SURPRIS ATTACK!

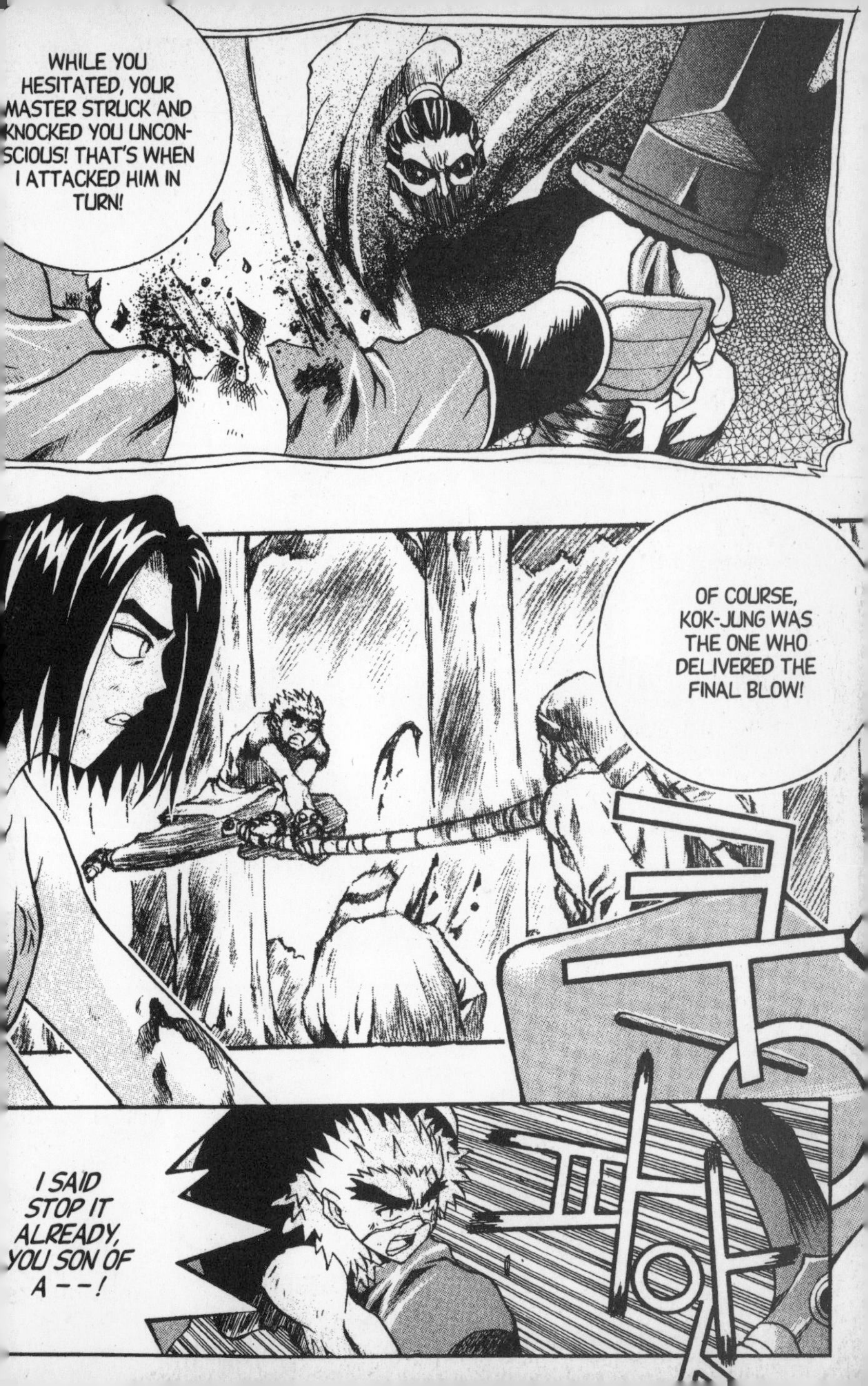
WHILE YOU HESITATED, YOUR MASTER STRUCK AND KNOCKED YOU UNCON-SCIOUS! THAT'S WHEN I ATTACKED HIM IN TURN!
OF COURSE, KOK-JUNG WAS THE ONE WHO DELIVERED THE FINAL BLOW!
I SAID STOP IT ALREADY, YOU SON OF A --!

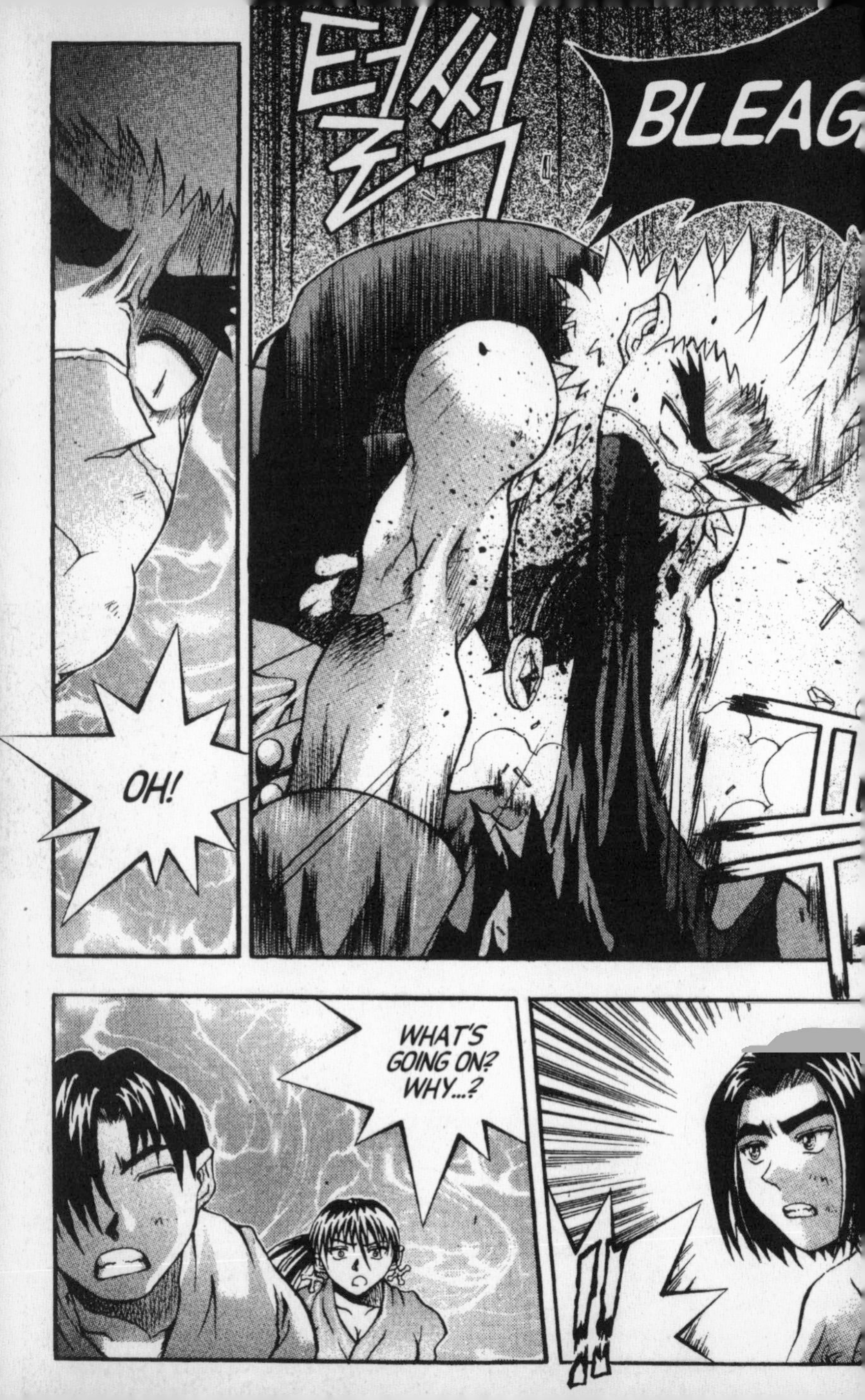
OH!
털썩
BLEAG
WHAT'S GOING ON? WHY...?

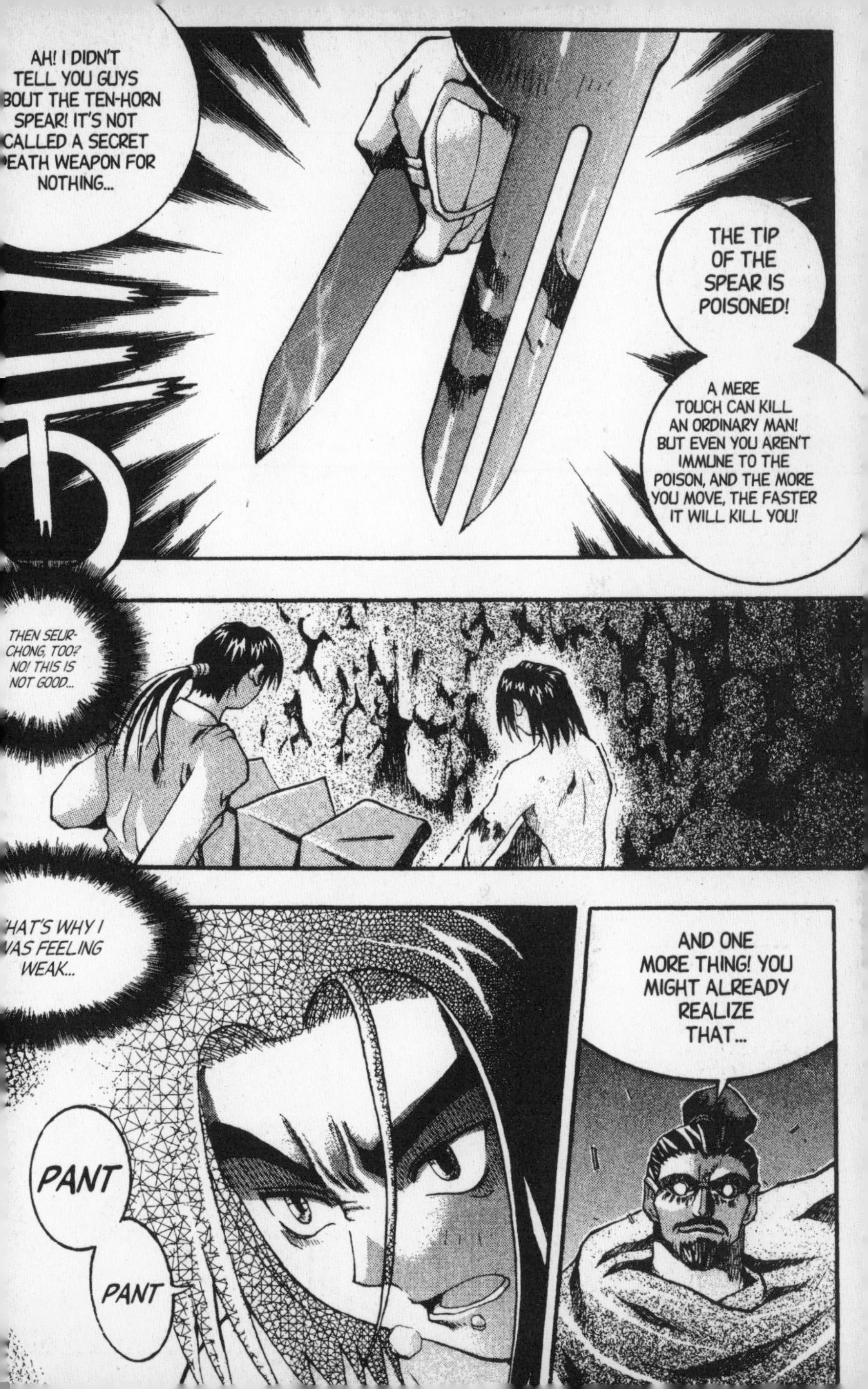
AH! I DIDN'T TELL YOU GUYS BOUT THE TEN-HORN SPEAR! IT'S NOT CALLED A SECRET EATH WEAPON FOR NOTHING...
THE TIP OF THE SPEAR IS POISONED!
A MERE TOUCH CAN KILL AN ORDINARY MAN! BUT EVEN YOU AREN'T IMMUNE TO THE POISON, AND THE MORE YOU MOVE, THE FASTER IT WILL KILL YOU!
THEN SEUR-CHONG, TOO? NO! THIS IS NOT GOOD...
HAT'S WHY I VAS FEELING WEAK...
PANT
PANT
AND ONE MORE THING! YOU MIGHT ALREADY REALIZE THAT...

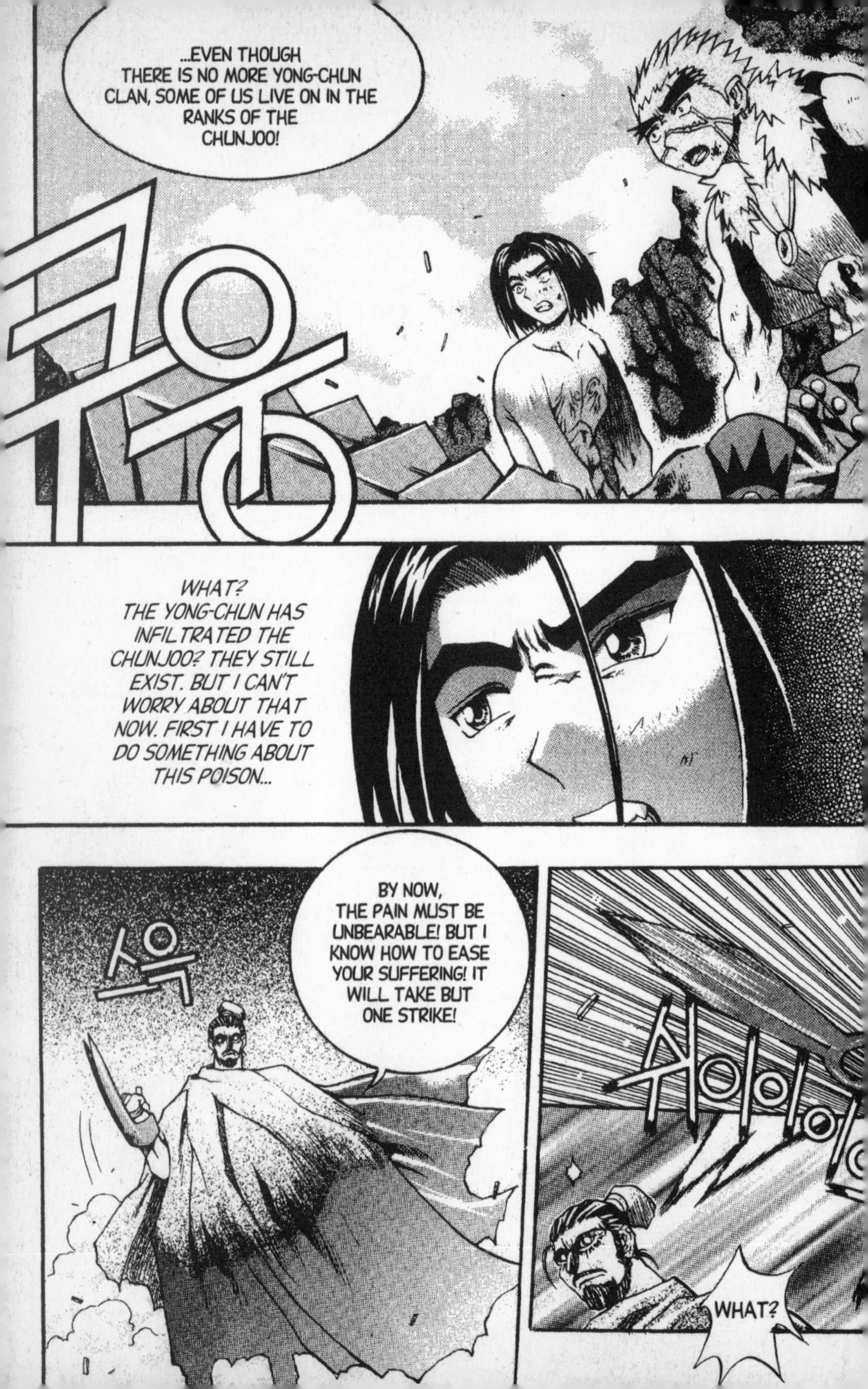
...EVEN THOUGH THERE IS NO MORE YONG-CHUN CLAN, SOME OF US LIVE ON IN THE RANKS OF THE CHUNJOO!
WHAT? THE YONG-CHUN HAS INFILTRATED THE CHUNJOO? THEY STILL EXIST. BUT I CAN'T WORRY ABOUT THAT NOW. FIRST I HAVE TO DO SOMETHING ABOUT THIS POISON...
BY NOW, THE PAIN MUST BE UNBEARABLE! BUT I KNOW HOW TO EASE YOUR SUFFERING! IT WILL TAKE BUT ONE STRIKE!
WHAT?

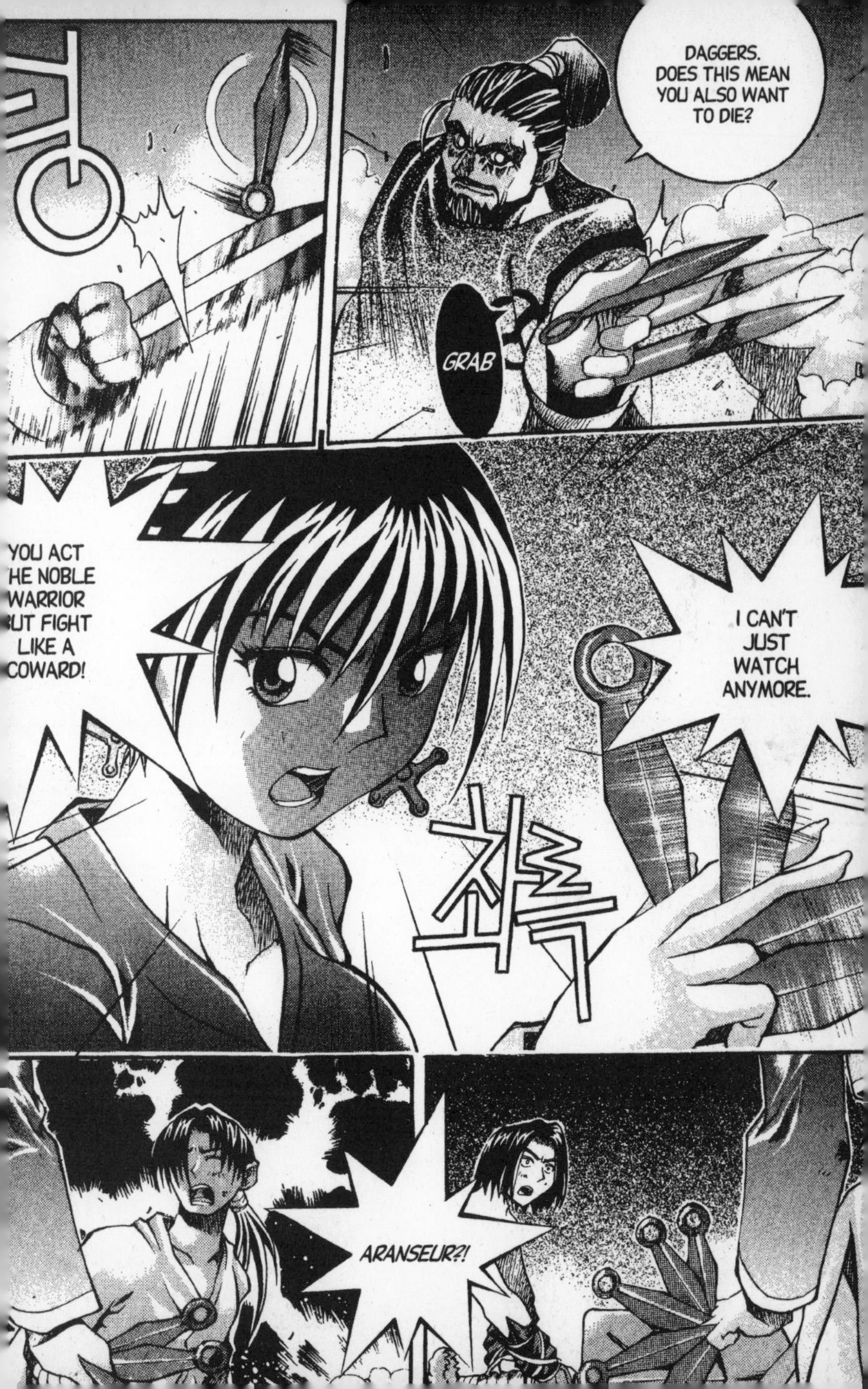
DAGGERS. DOES THIS MEAN YOU ALSO WANT TO DIE?
GRAB
YOU ACT HE NOBLE WARRIOR UT FIGHT LIKE A COWARD!
I CAN'T JUST WATCH ANYMORE.
ARANSEUR?!

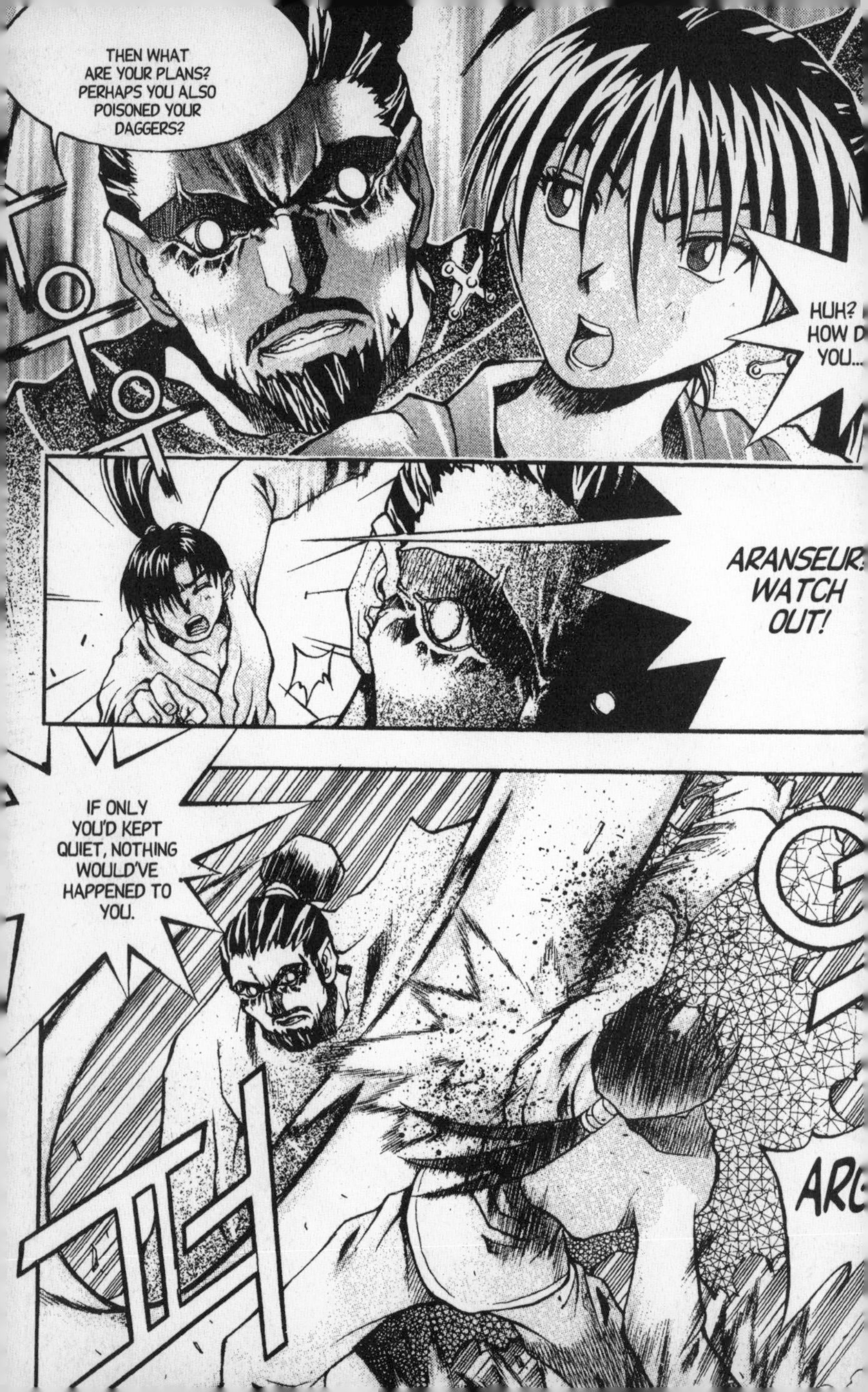
THEN WHAT ARE YOUR PLANS? PERHAPS YOU ALSO POISONED YOUR DAGGERS?
HUH? HOW D YOU...
ARANSEUR! WATCH OUT!
IF ONLY YOU'D KEPT QUIET, NOTHING WOULD'VE HAPPENED TO YOU.
ARG

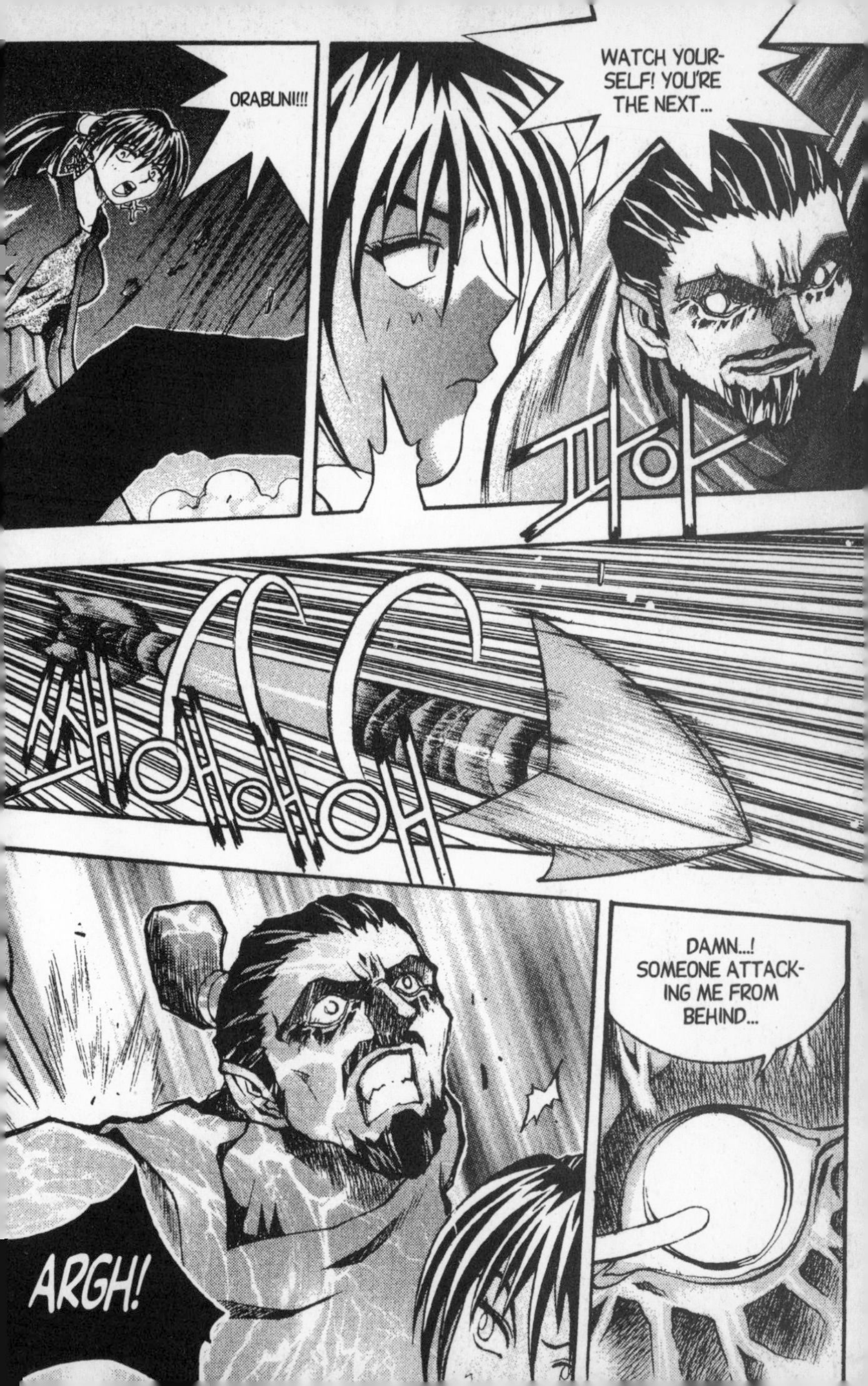
ORABUNI!!!
WATCH YOURSELF! YOU'RE THE NEXT...
ARGH!
DAMN...! SOMEONE ATTACKING ME FROM BEHIND...

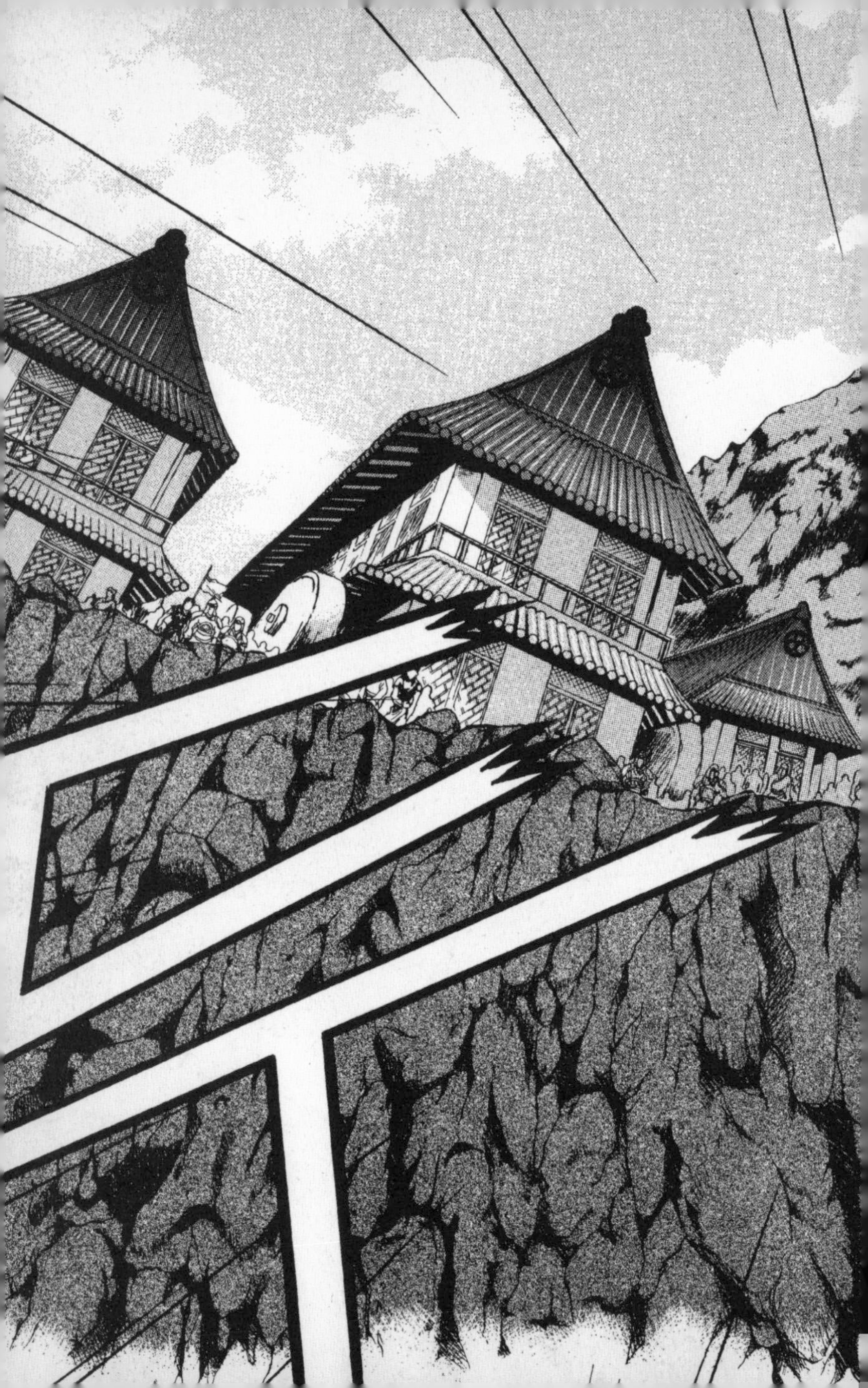

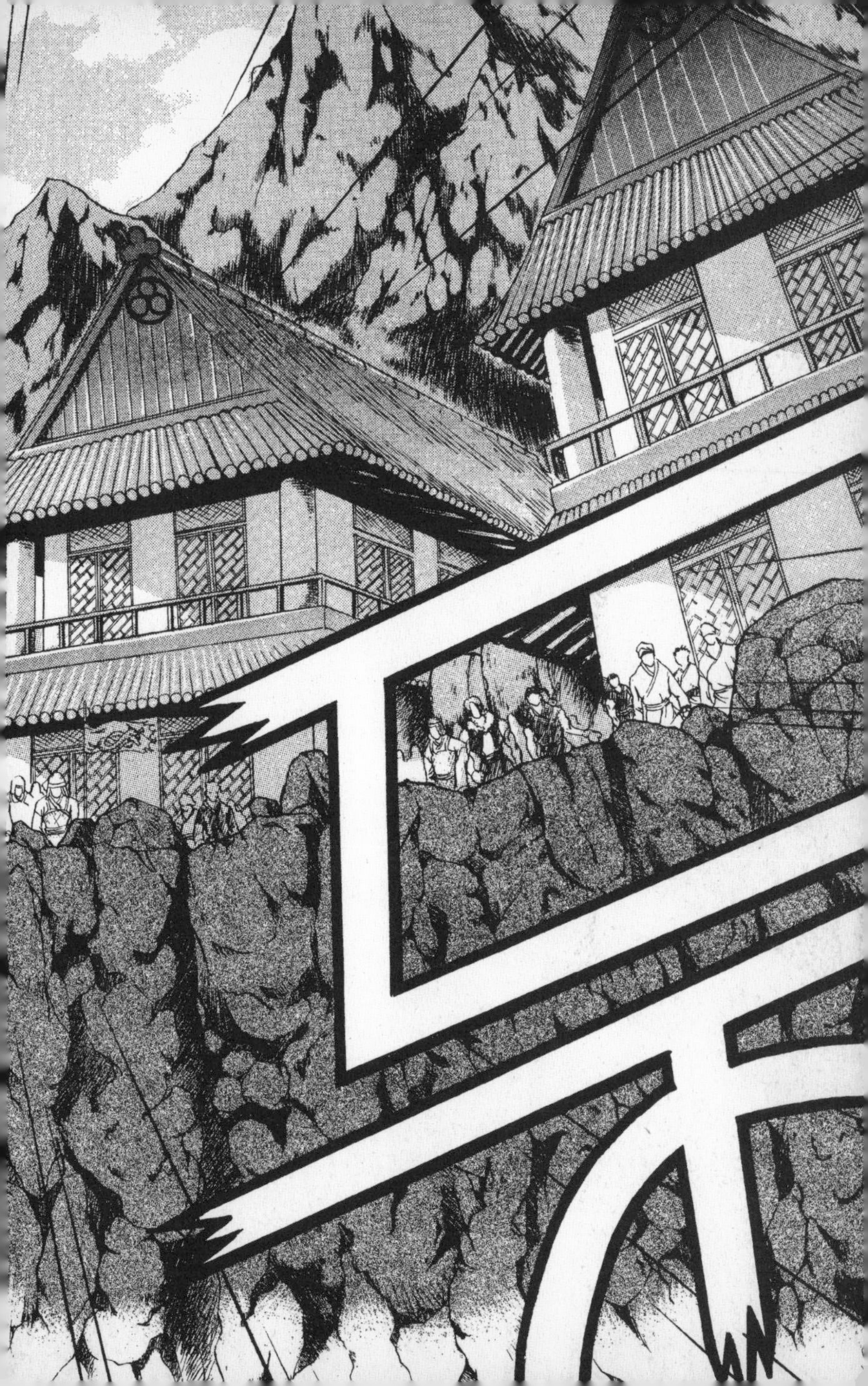

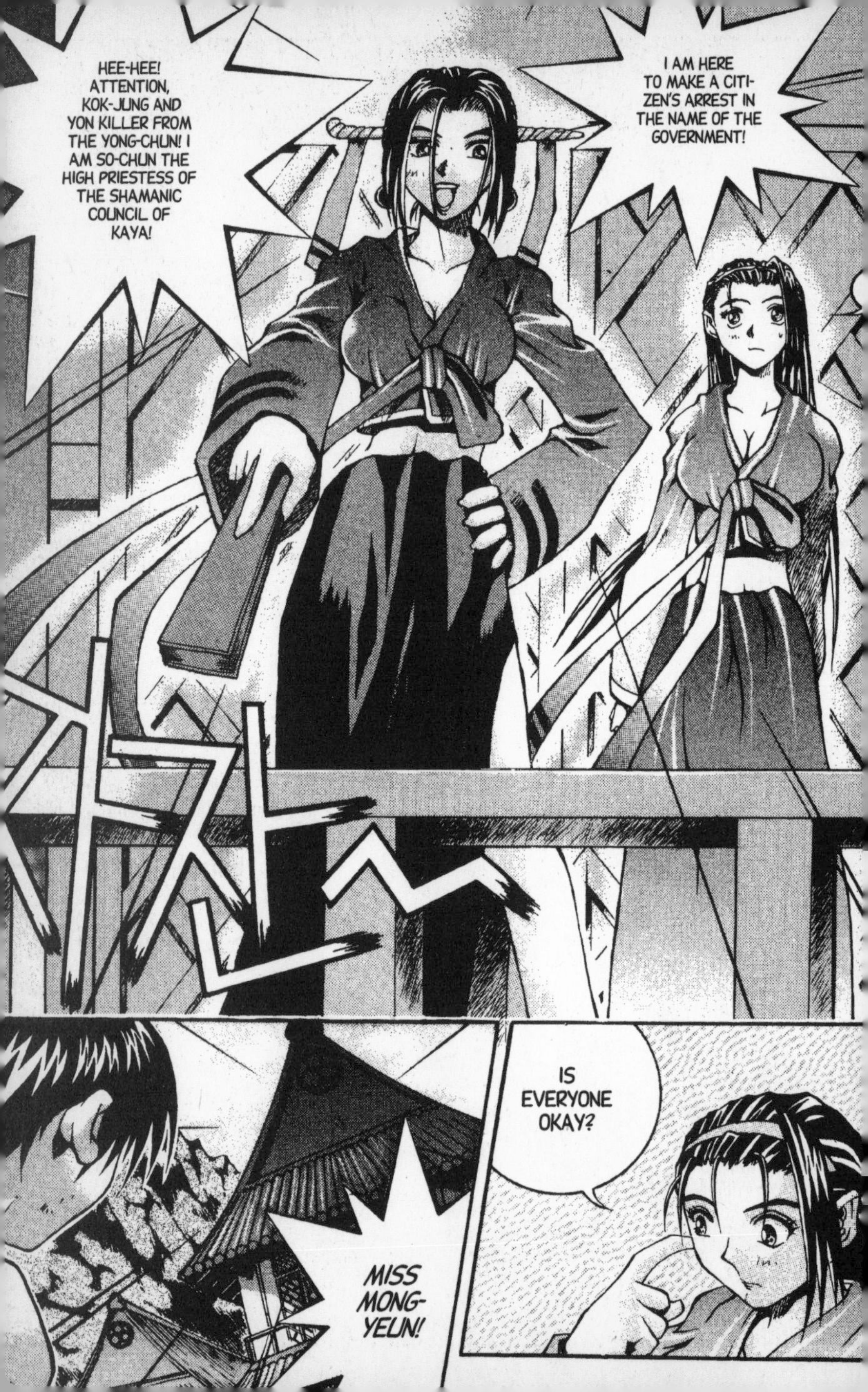
HEE-HEE! ATTENTION, KOK-JUNG AND YON KILLER FROM THE YONG-CHUN! I AM SO-CHUN THE HIGH PRIESTESS OF THE SHAMANIC COUNCIL OF KAYA!
I AM HERE TO MAKE A CITI-ZEN'S ARREST IN THE NAME OF THE GOVERNMENT!
MISS MONG-YEUN!
IS EVERYONE OKAY?

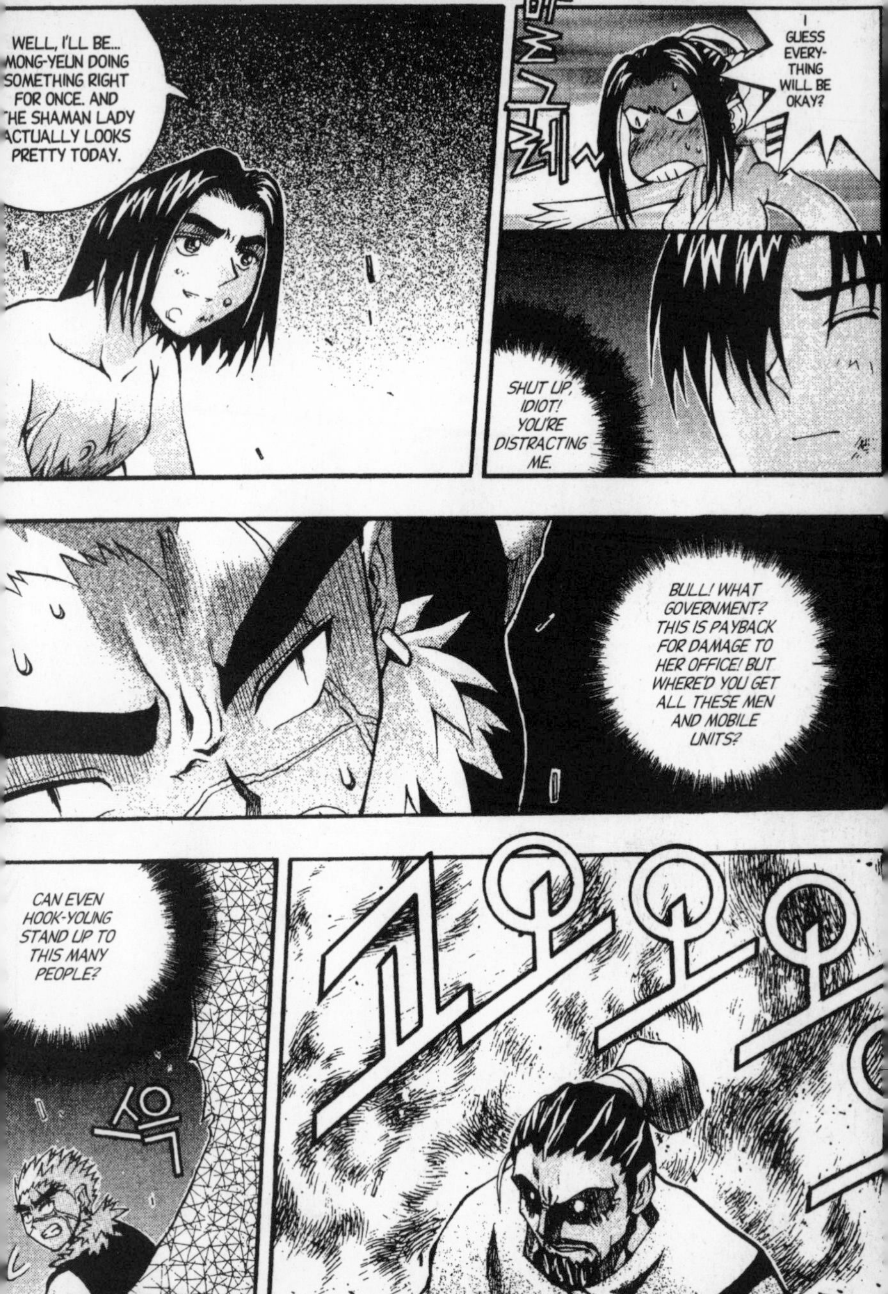
WELL, I'LL BE... MONG-YEUN DOING SOMETHING RIGHT FOR ONCE. AND THE SHAMAN LADY ACTUALLY LOOKS PRETTY TODAY.
I GUESS EVERYTHING WILL BE OKAY?
SHUT UP, IDIOT! YOU'RE DISTRACTING ME.
BULL! WHAT GOVERNMENT? THIS IS PAYBACK FOR DAMAGE TO HER OFFICE! BUT WHERE'D YOU GET ALL THESE MEN AND MOBILE UNITS?
CAN EVEN HOOK-YOUNG STAND UP TO THIS MANY PEOPLE?

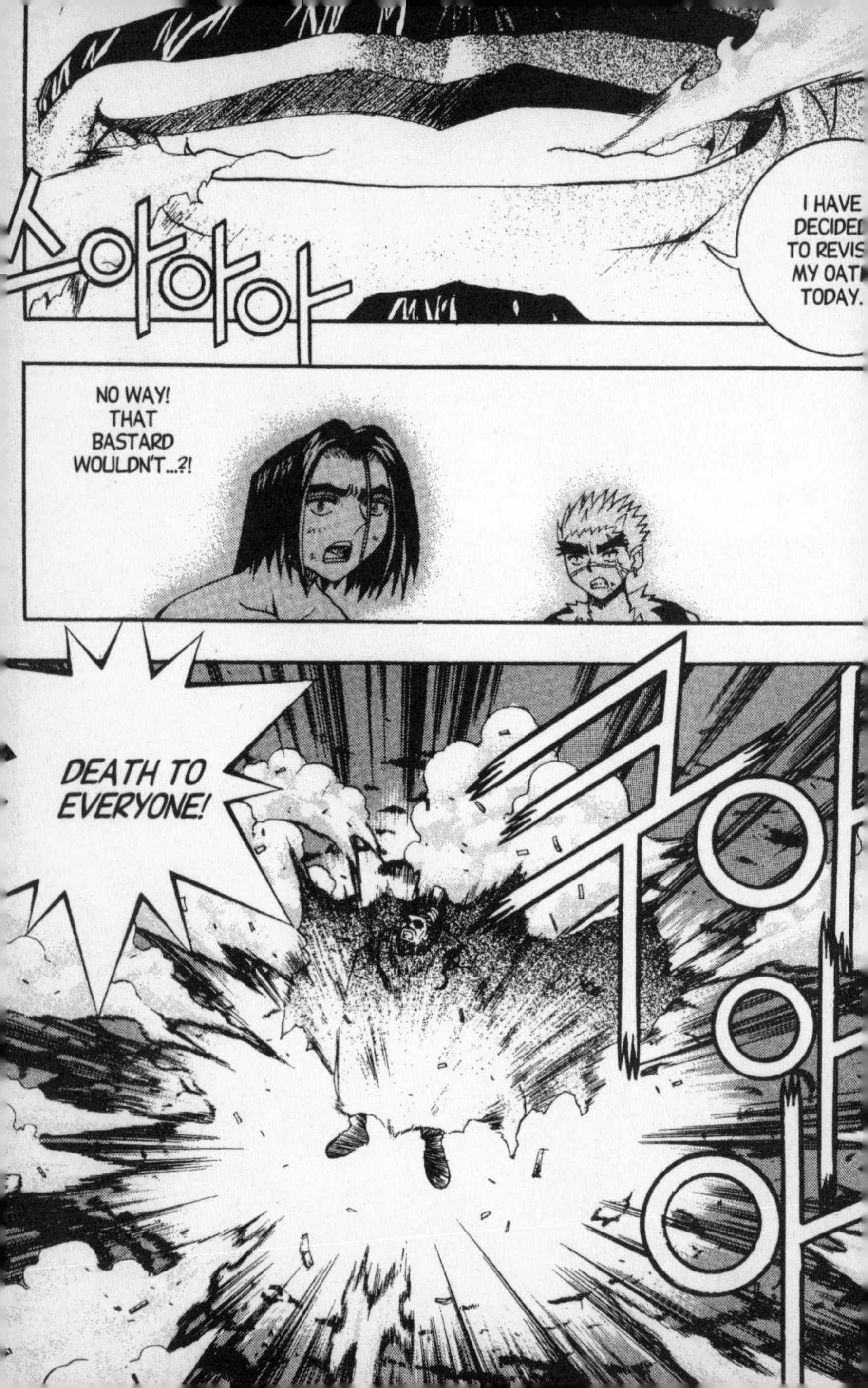

I HAVE DECIDED TO REVIS MY OAT TODAY.
NO WAY! THAT BASTARD WOULDN'T...?!
DEATH TO EVERYONE!

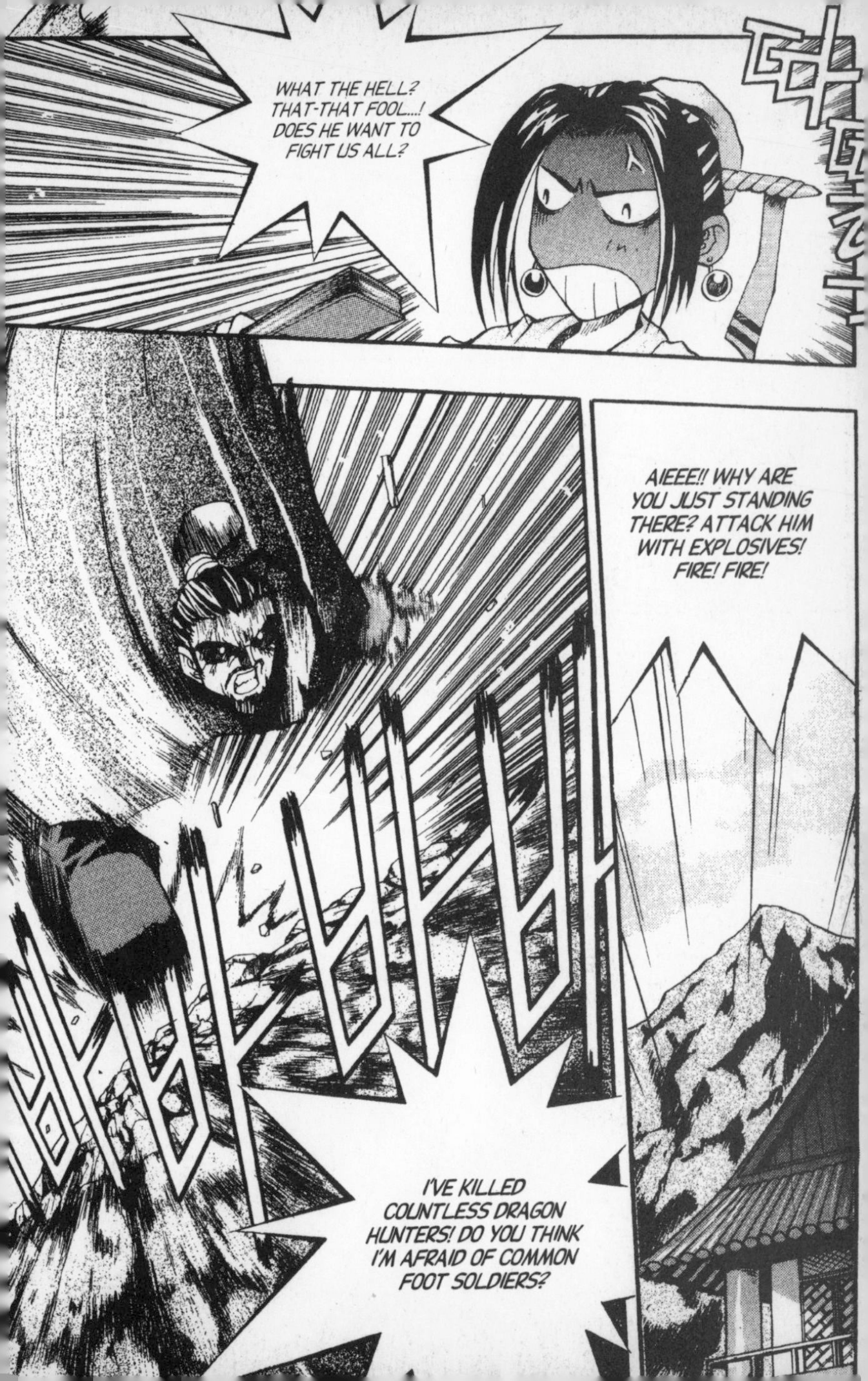
WHAT THE HELL? THAT-THAT FOOL...! DOES HE WANT TO FIGHT US ALL?
I'VE KILLED COUNTLESS DRAGON HUNTERS! DO YOU THINK I'M AFRAID OF COMMON FOOT SOLDIERS?
AIEEE!! WHY ARE YOU JUST STANDING THERE? ATTACK HIM WITH EXPLOSIVES! FIRE! FIRE!

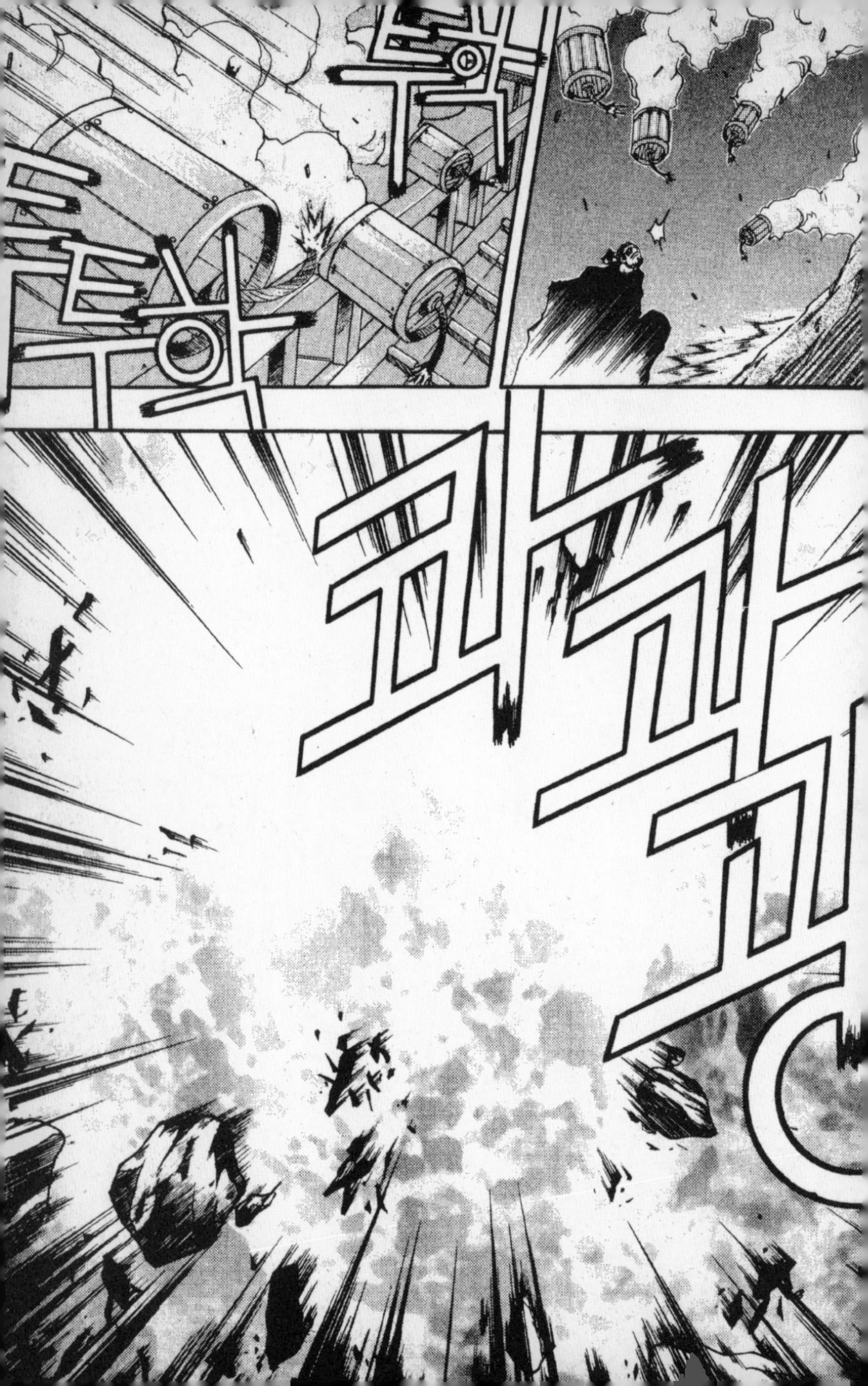
콰콰쾅

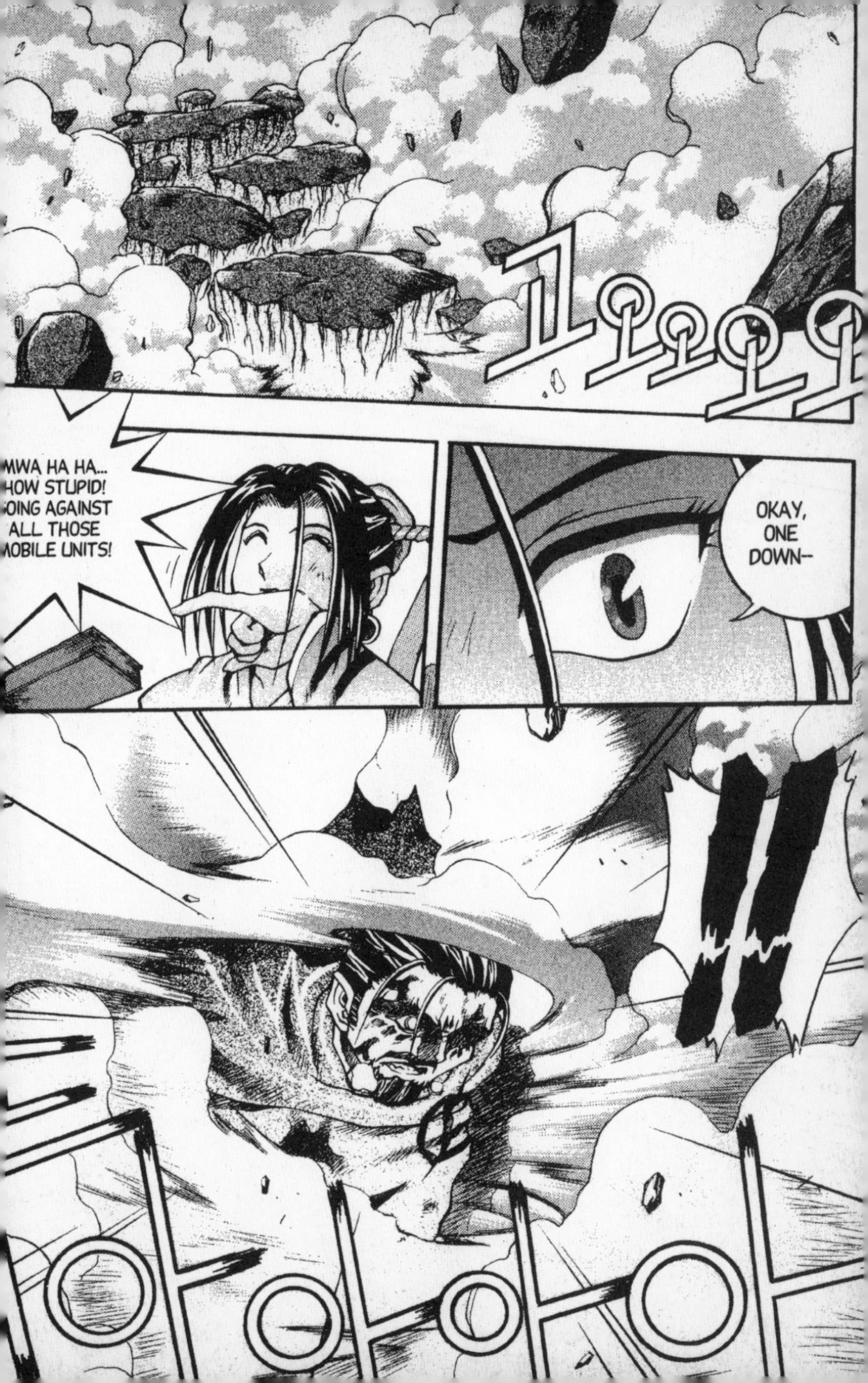
OKAY, ONE DOWN--
MWA HA HA... HOW STUPID! GOING AGAINST ALL THOSE MOBILE UNITS!

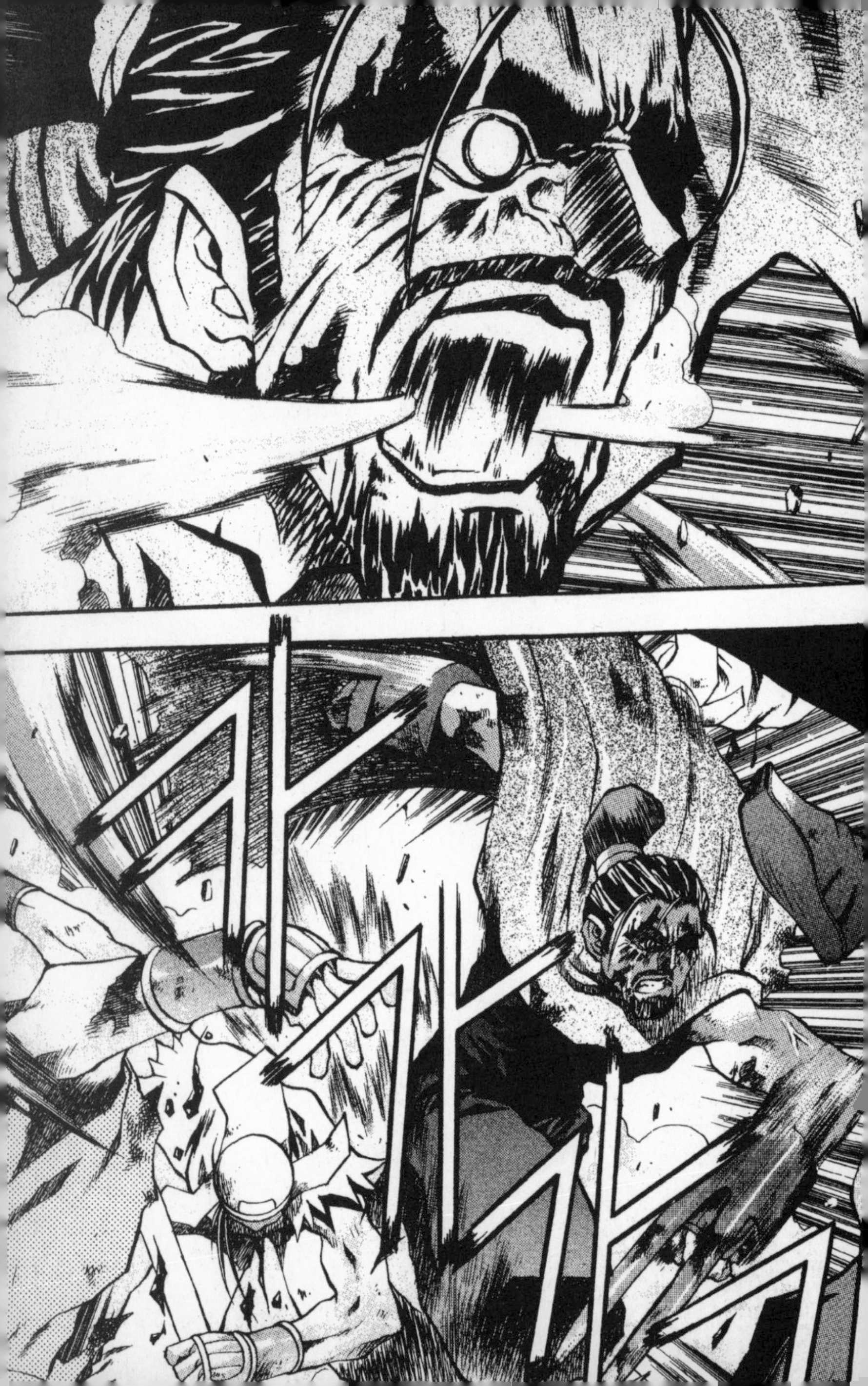

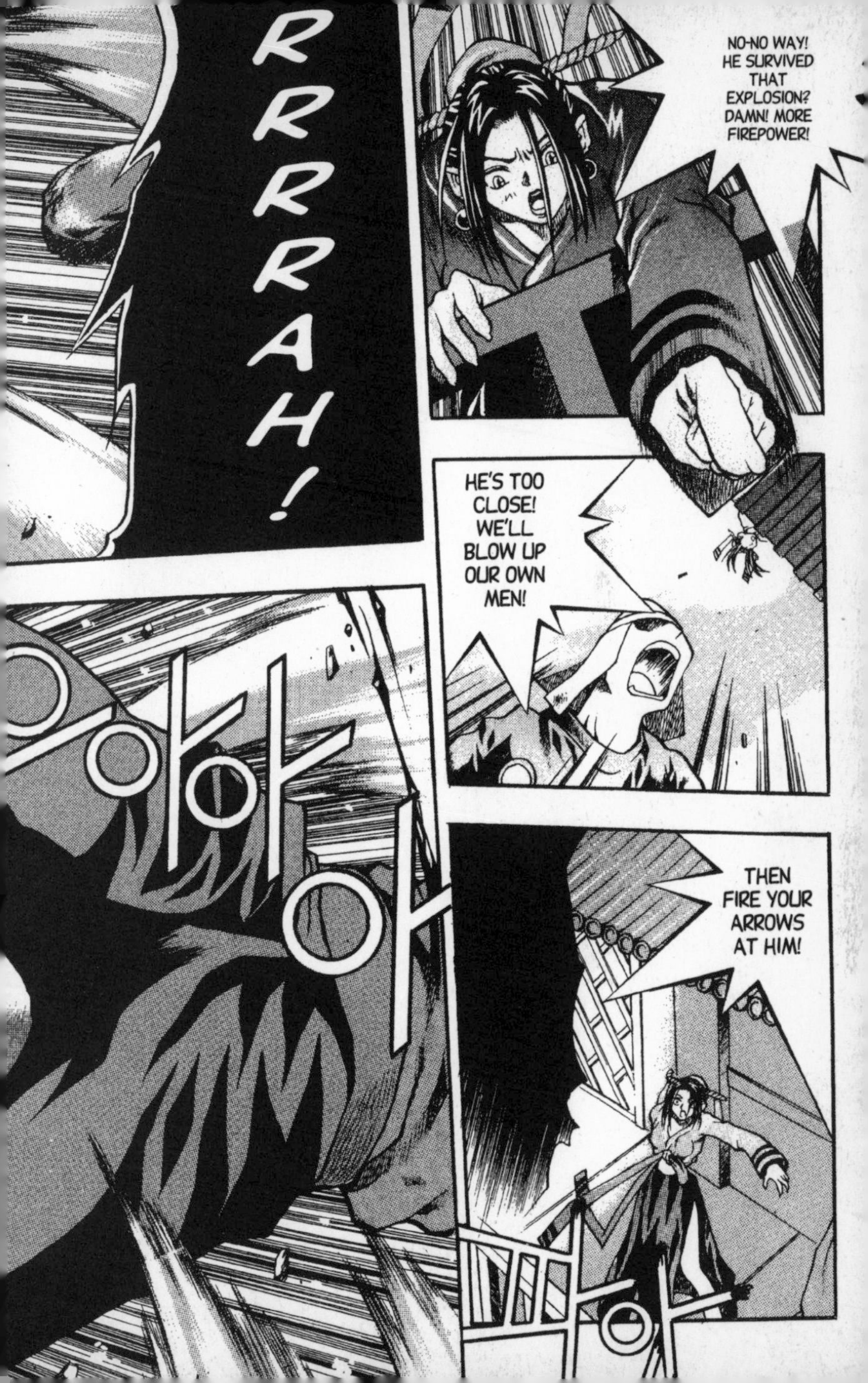
NO-NO WAY! HE SURVIVED THAT EXPLOSION? DAMN! MORE FIREPOWER!
RRRRAH!
HE'S TOO CLOSE! WE'LL BLOW UP OUR OWN MEN!
THEN FIRE YOUR ARROWS AT HIM!

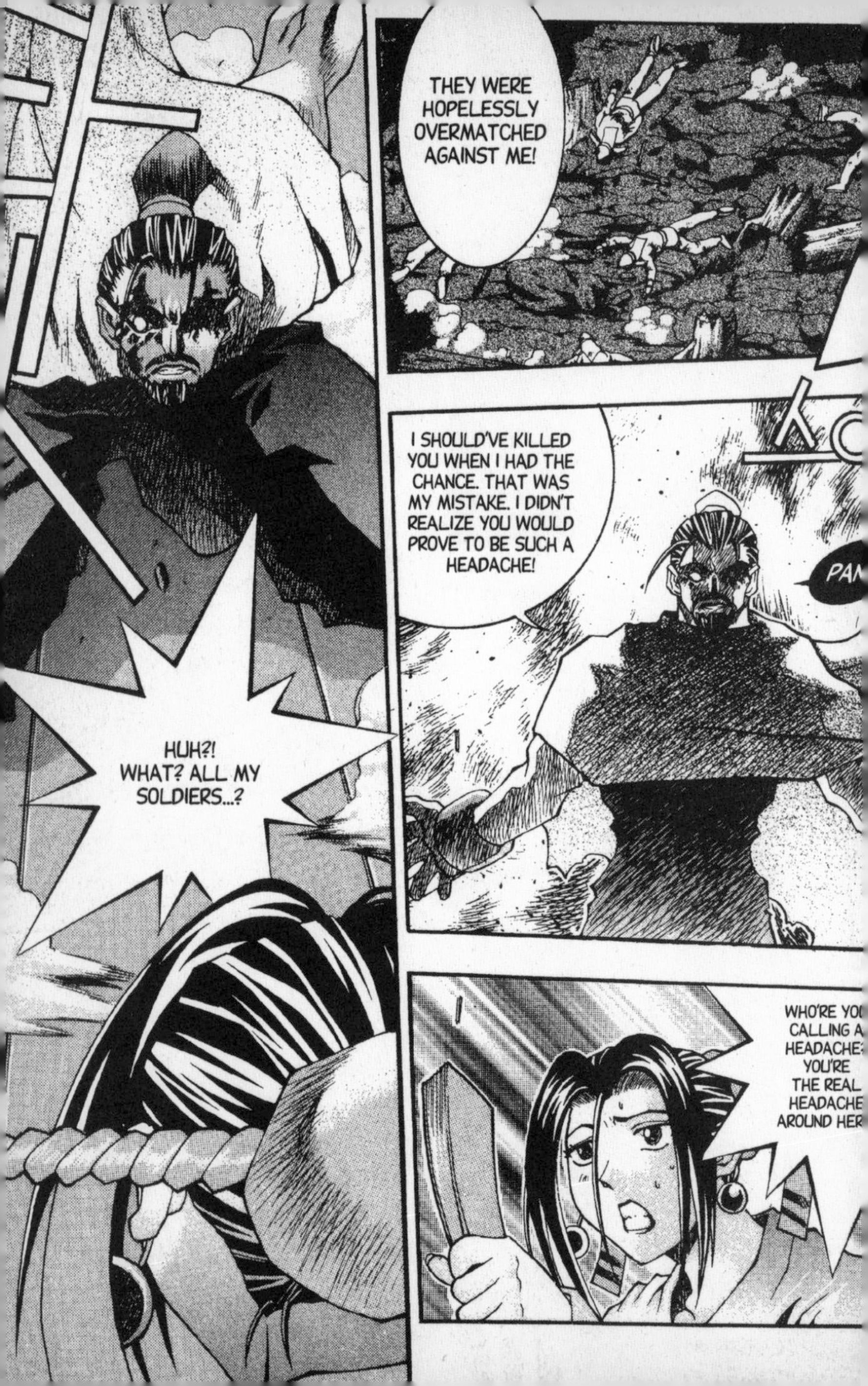
HUH?! WHAT? ALL MY SOLDIERS...?
THEY WERE HOPELESSLY OVERMATCHED AGAINST ME!
I SHOULD'VE KILLED YOU WHEN I HAD THE CHANCE. THAT WAS MY MISTAKE. I DIDN'T REALIZE YOU WOULD PROVE TO BE SUCH A HEADACHE!
WHO'RE YO CALLING A HEADACHE YOU'RE THE REAL HEADACHE AROUND HER

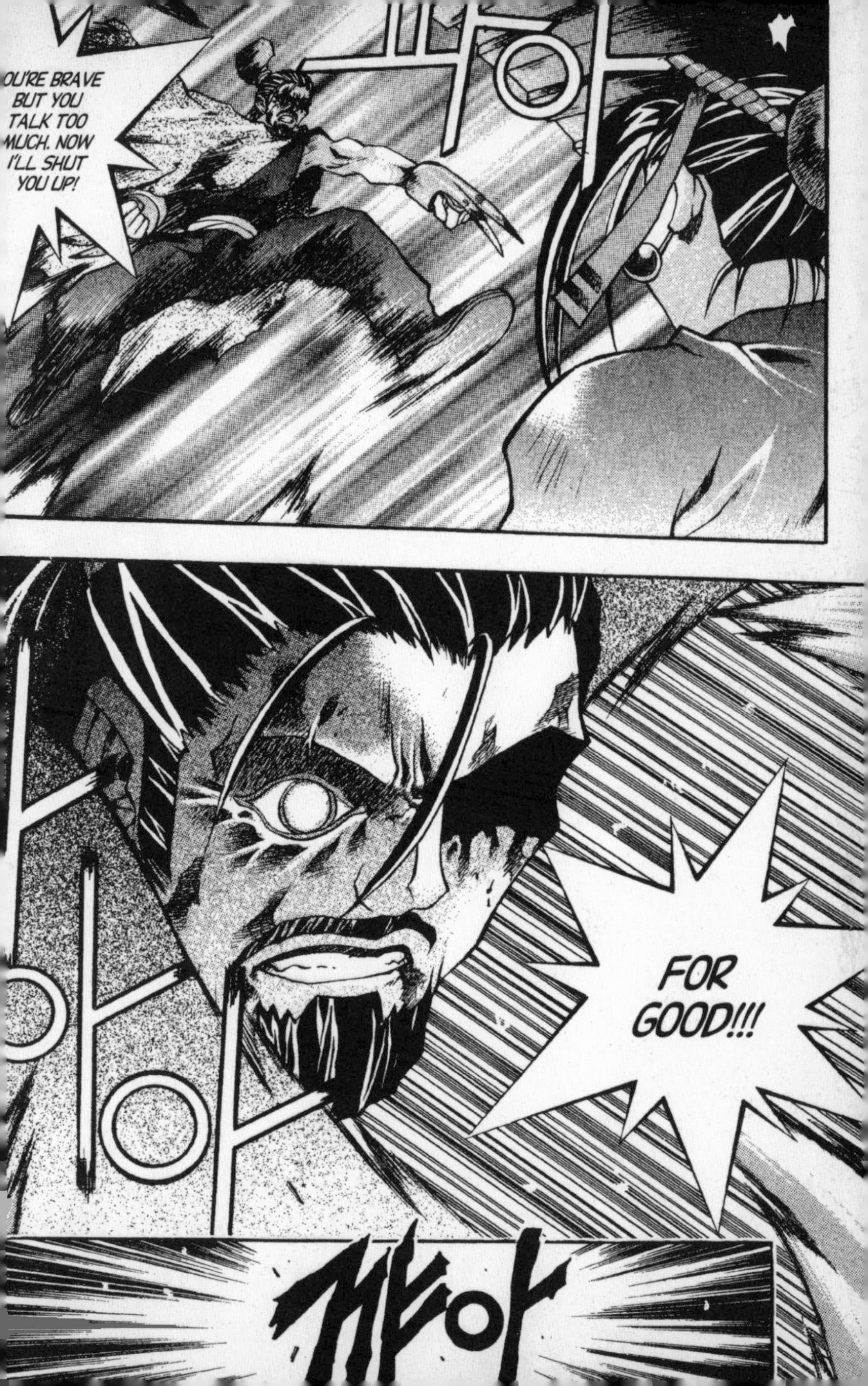
OU'RE BRAVE BUT YOU TALK TOO MUCH. NOW I'LL SHUT YOU UP!
FOR GOOD!!!

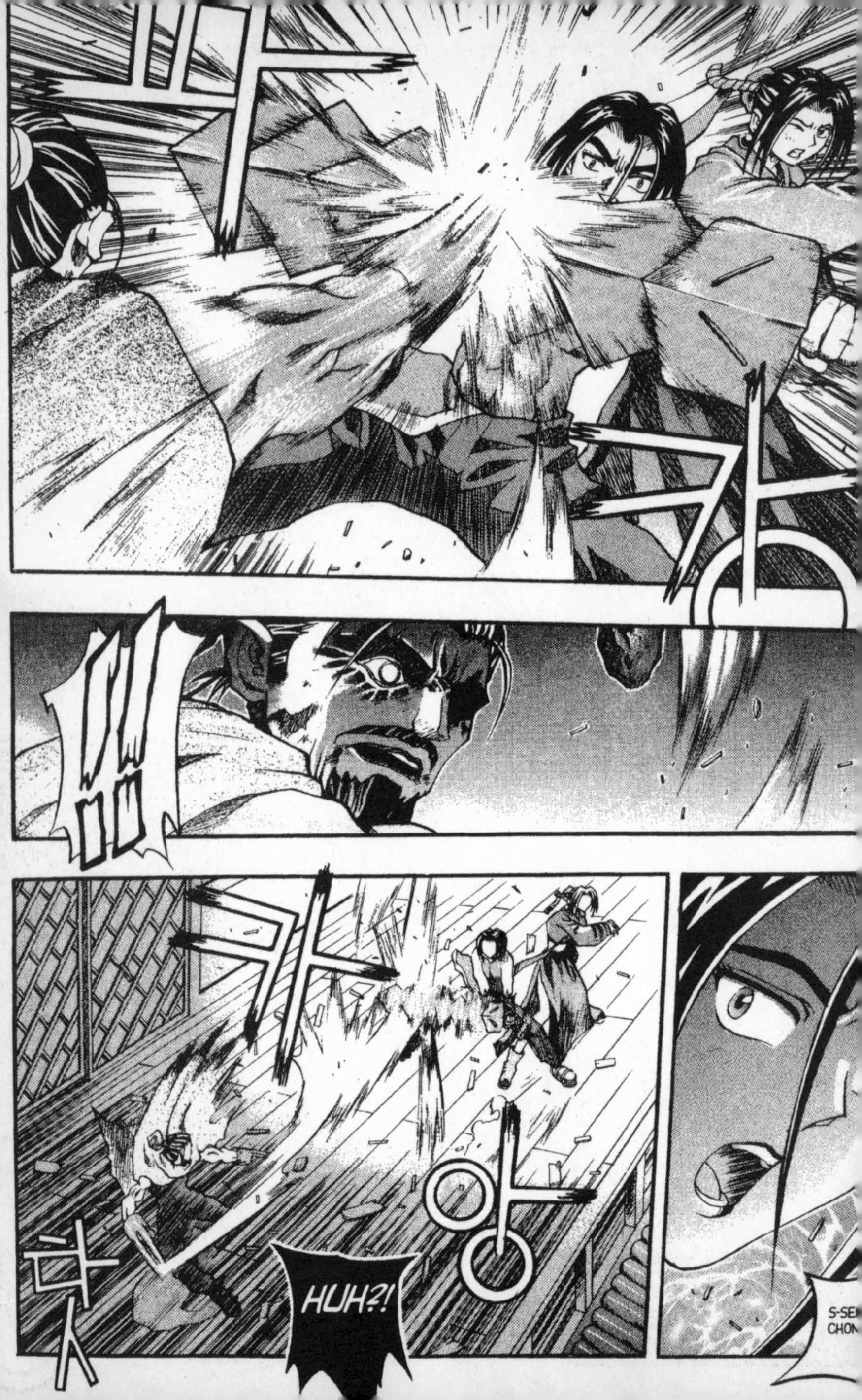
HUH?!
S-SE
CHON

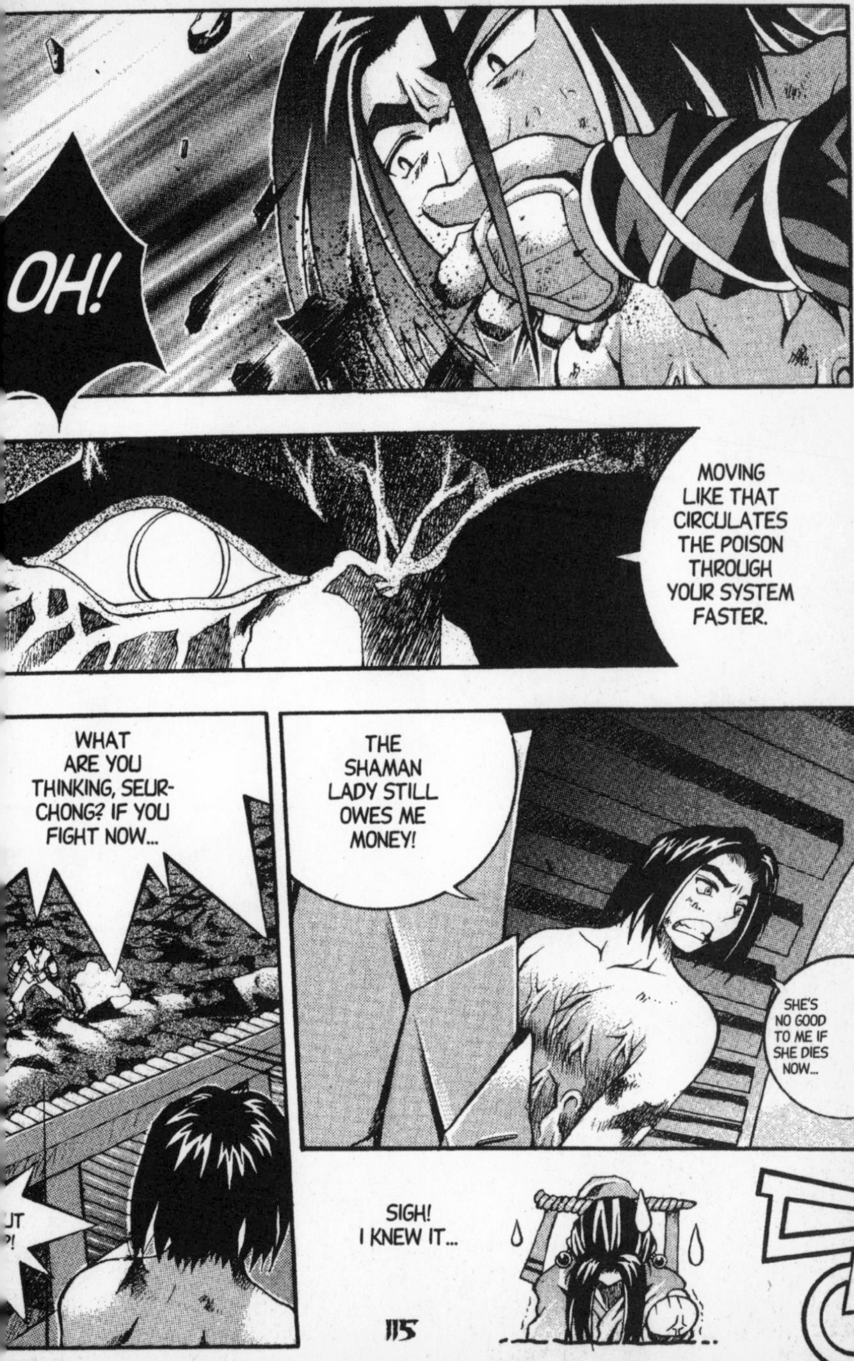
OH!
MOVING LIKE THAT CIRCULATES THE POISON THROUGH YOUR SYSTEM FASTER.
WHAT ARE YOU THINKING, SEUR-CHONG? IF YOU FIGHT NOW...
THE SHAMAN LADY STILL OWES ME MONEY!
SHE'S NO GOOD TO ME IF SHE DIES NOW...
SIGH! I KNEW IT...

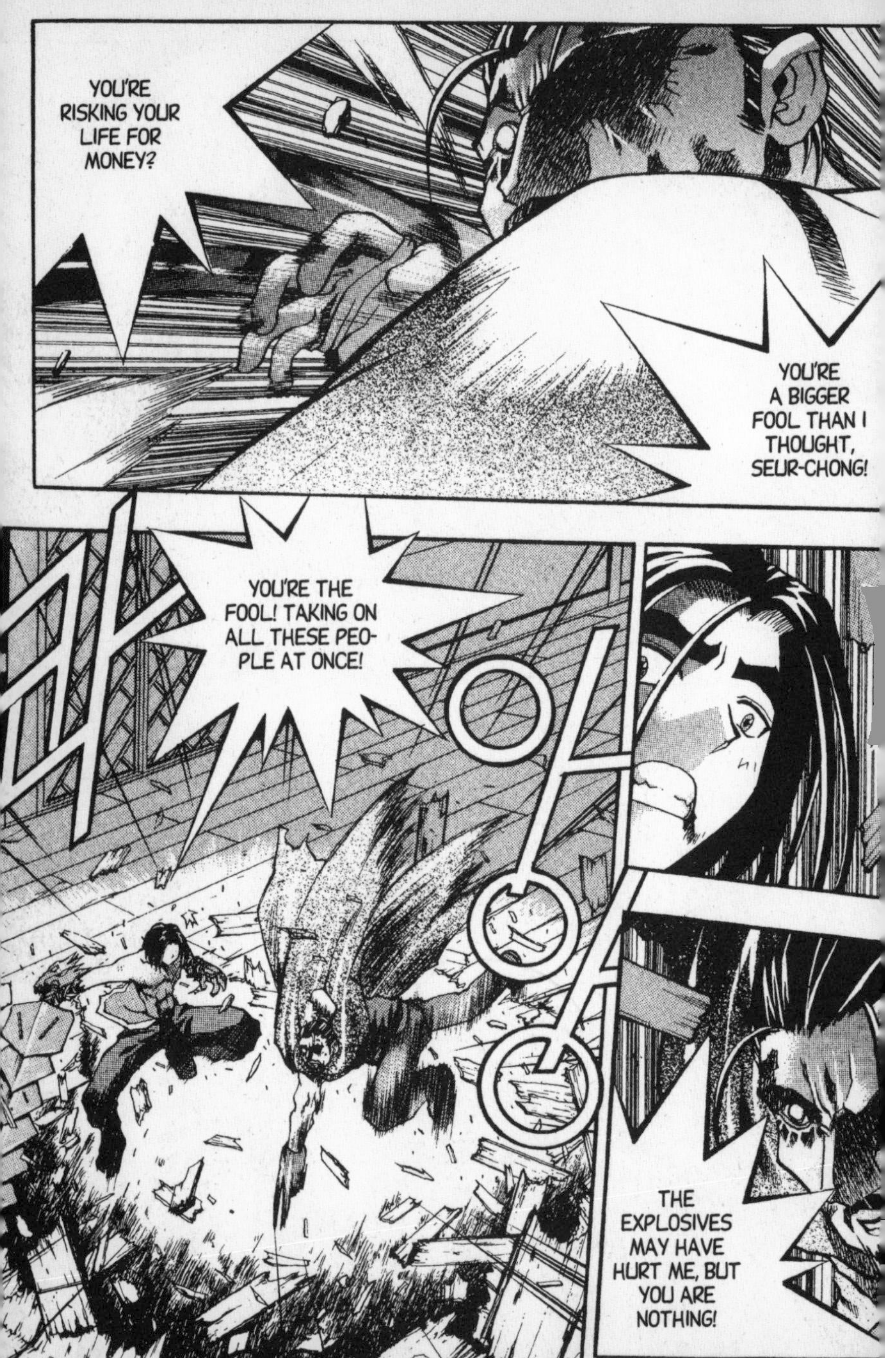
YOU'RE RISKING YOUR LIFE FOR MONEY?
YOU'RE A BIGGER FOOL THAN I THOUGHT, SEUR-CHONG!
YOU'RE THE FOOL! TAKING ON ALL THESE PEO-PLE AT ONCE!
THE EXPLOSIVES MAY HAVE HURT ME, BUT YOU ARE NOTHING!

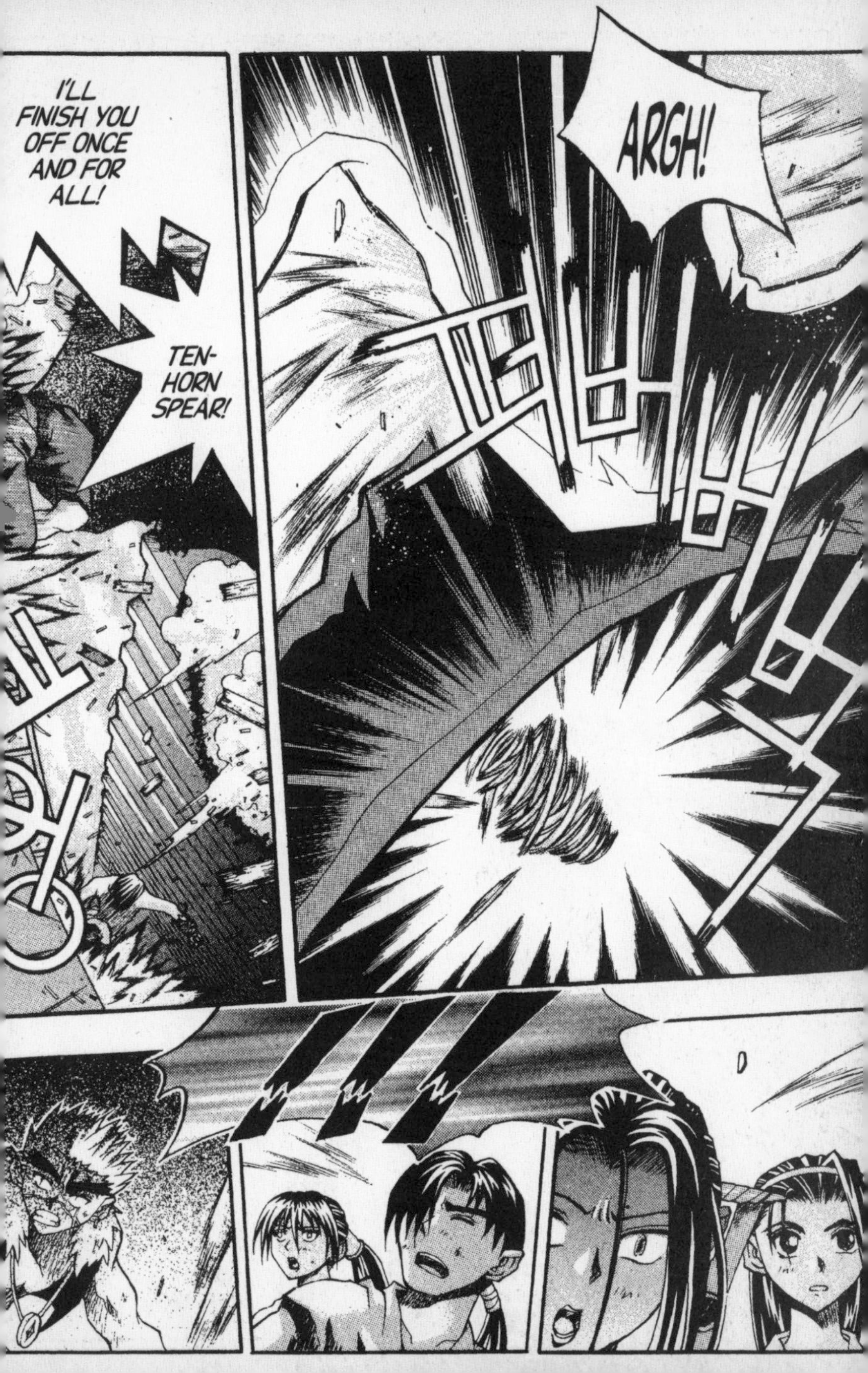
ARGH!
I'LL FINISH YOU OFF ONCE AND FOR ALL!
TEN-HORN SPEAR!

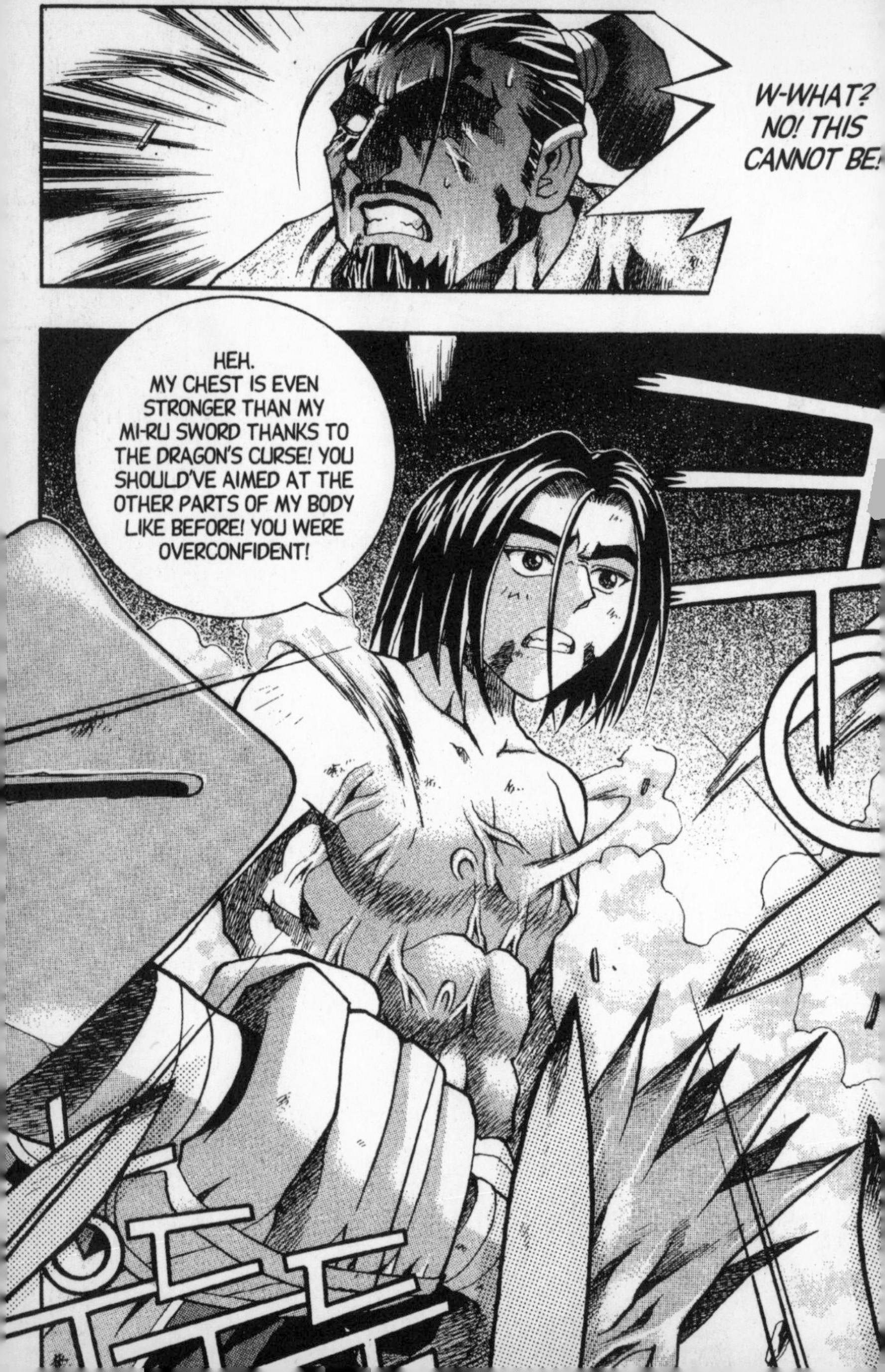
W-WHAT? NO! THIS CANNOT BE!
HEH. MY CHEST IS EVEN STRONGER THAN MY MI-RU SWORD THANKS TO THE DRAGON'S CURSE! YOU SHOULD'VE AIMED AT THE OTHER PARTS OF MY BODY LIKE BEFORE! YOU WERE OVERCONFIDENT!

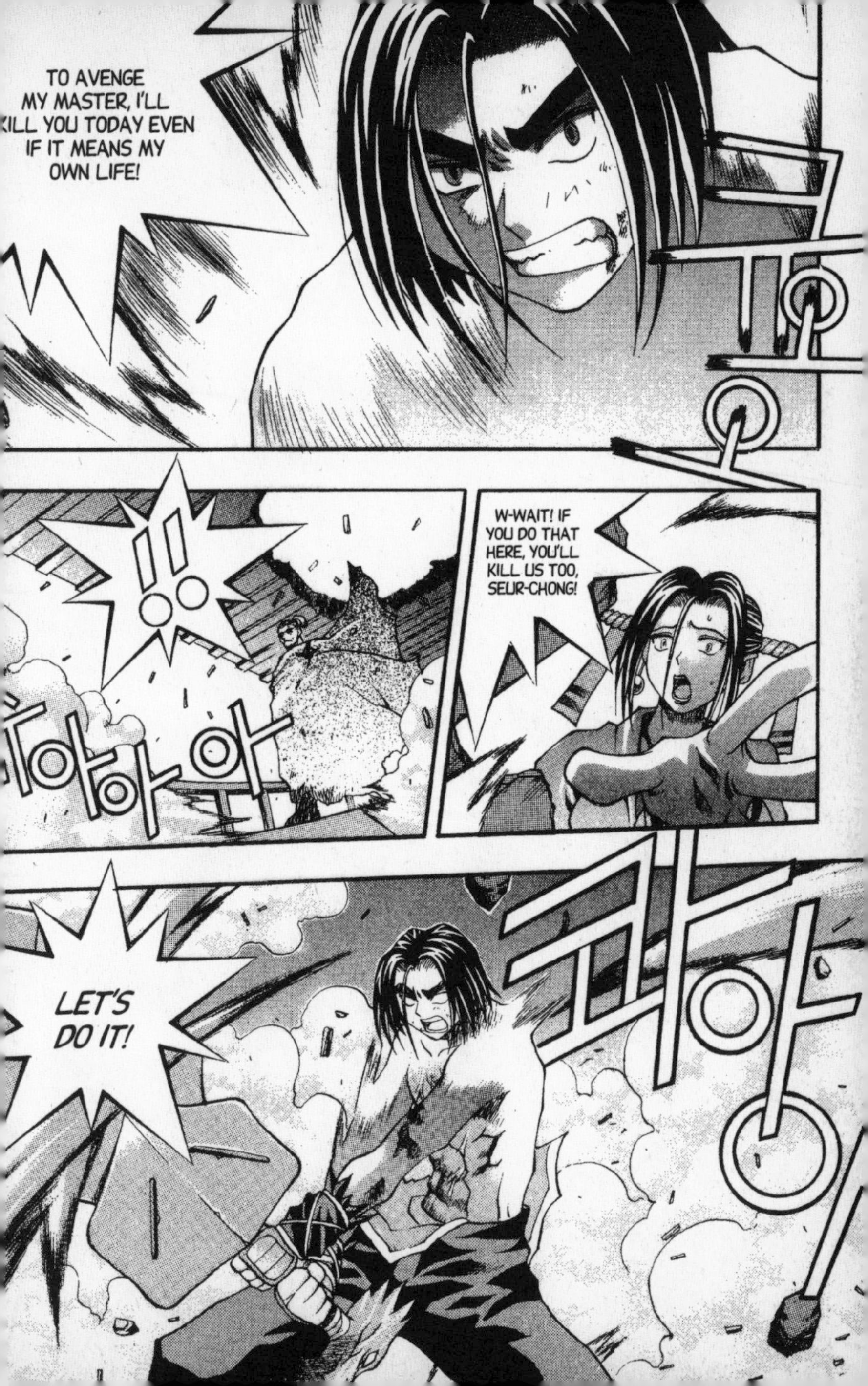
TO AVENGE MY MASTER, I'LL KILL YOU TODAY EVEN IF IT MEANS MY OWN LIFE!
!!
W-WAIT! IF YOU DO THAT HERE, YOU'LL KILL US TOO, SEUR-CHONG!
LET'S DO IT!

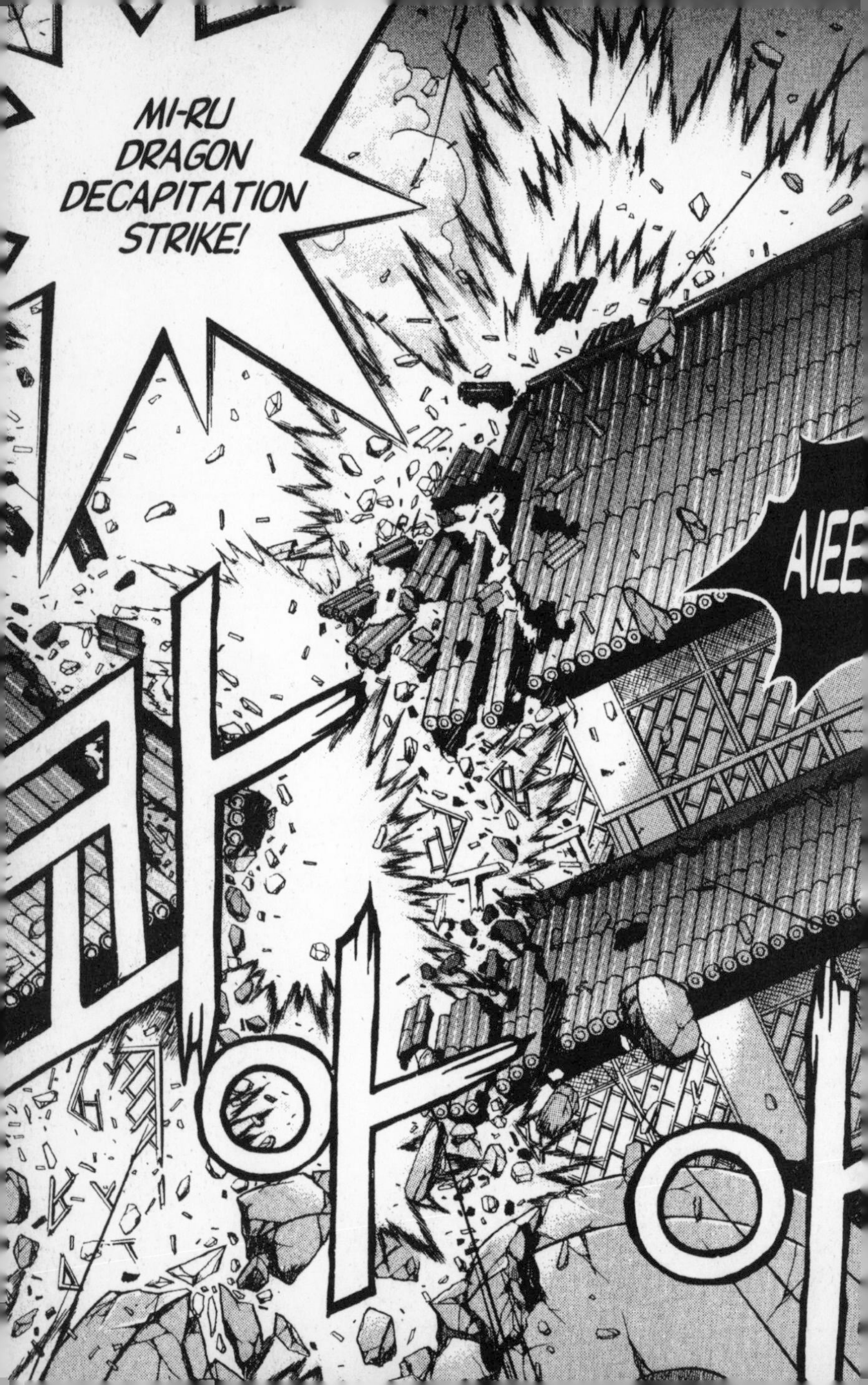
MI-RU DRAGON DECAPITATION STRIKE!
AIEE

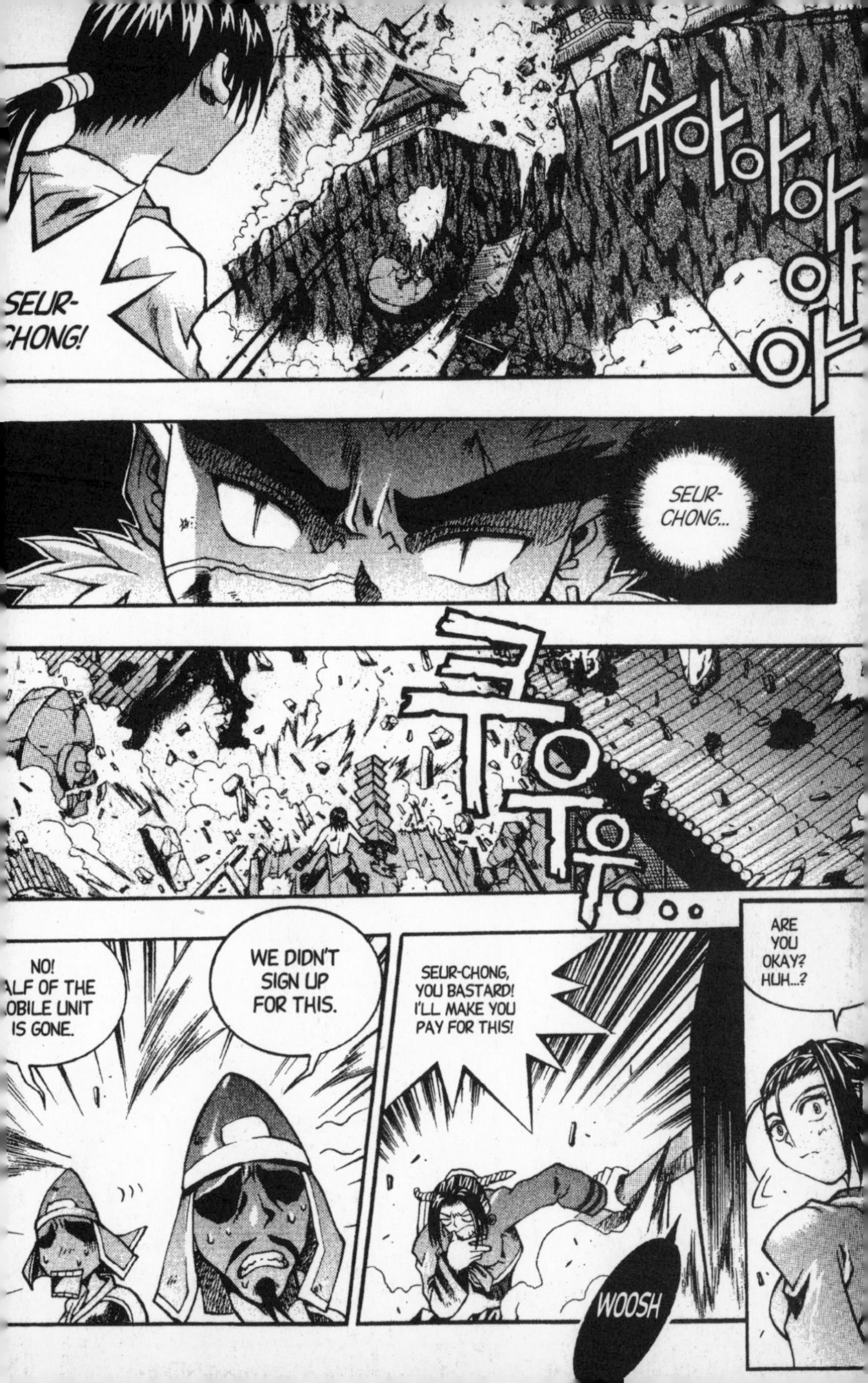

SEUR-
CHONG!
SEUR-CHONG...
NO! ALF OF THE OBILE UNIT IS GONE.
WE DIDN'T SIGN UP FOR THIS.
SEUR-CHONG, YOU BASTARD! I'LL MAKE YOU PAY FOR THIS!
ARE YOU OKAY? HUH...?
WOOSH

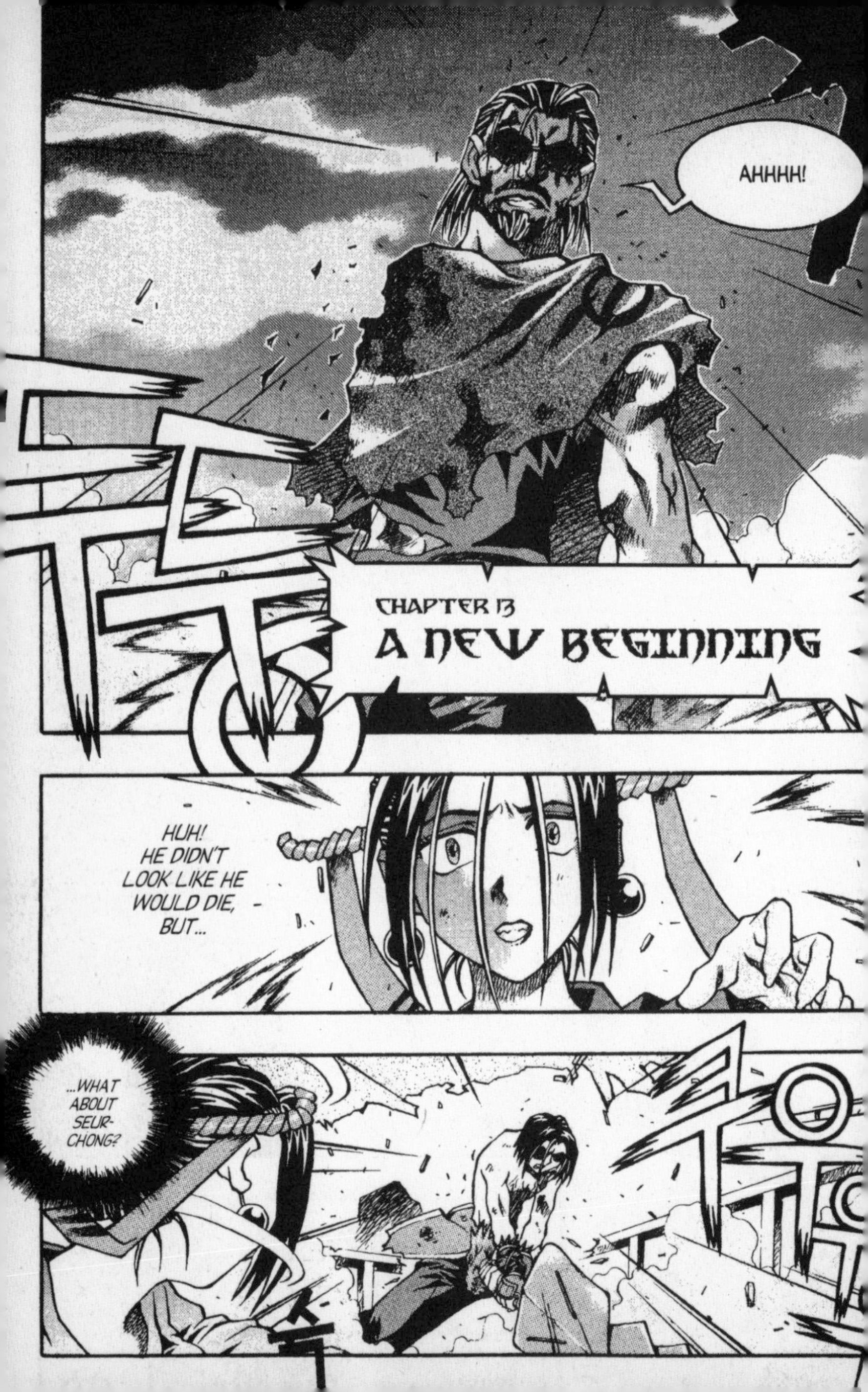
AHHHH!
CHAPTER 13
A NEW BEGINNING
HUH! HE DIDN'T LOOK LIKE HE WOULD DIE, BUT...
...WHAT ABOUT SEUR-CHONG?

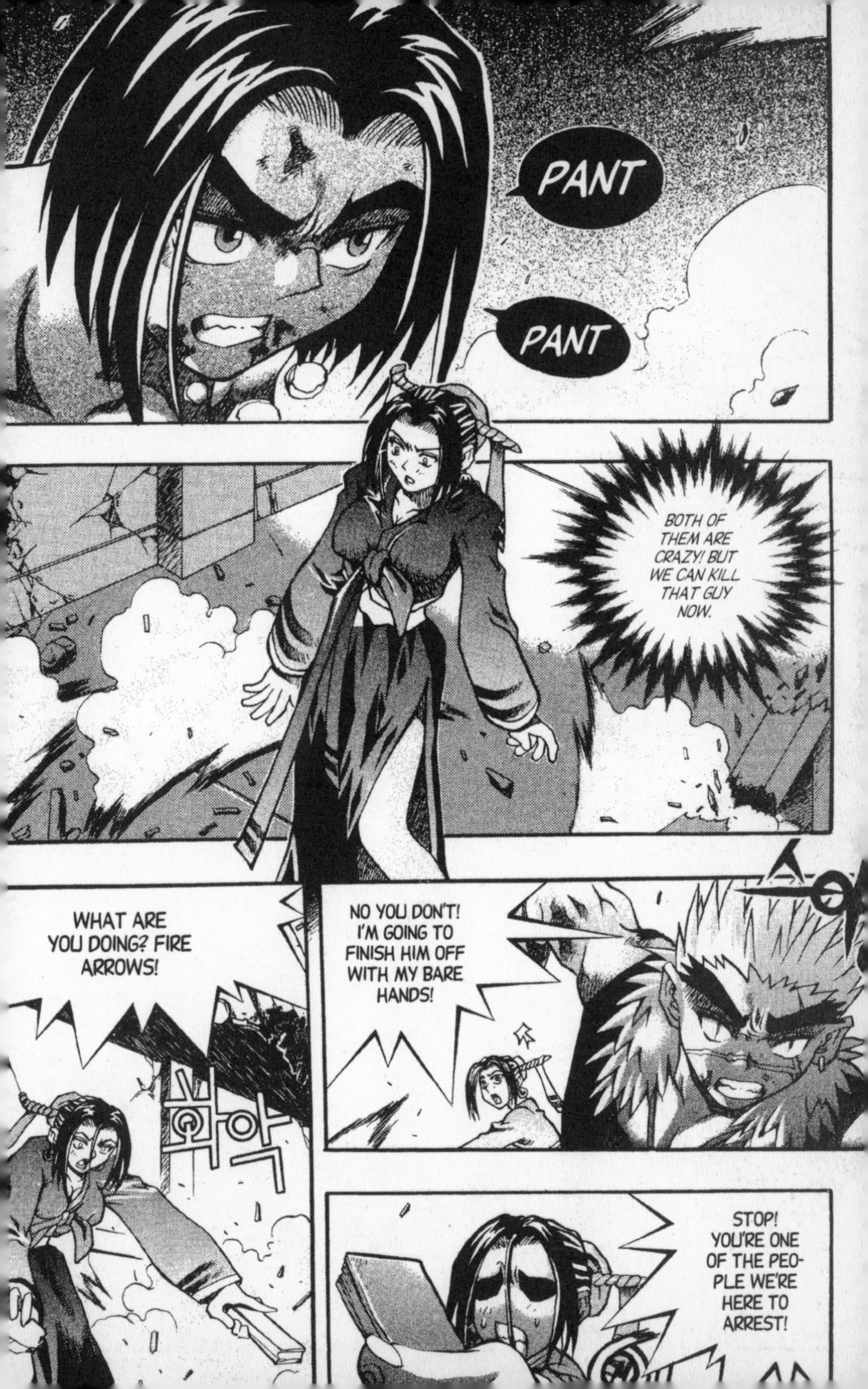
PANT
PANT
BOTH OF THEM ARE CRAZY! BUT WE CAN KILL THAT GUY NOW.
WHAT ARE YOU DOING? FIRE ARROWS!
NO YOU DON'T! I'M GOING TO FINISH HIM OFF WITH MY BARE HANDS!
STOP! YOU'RE ONE OF THE PEO- PLE WE'RE HERE TO ARREST!

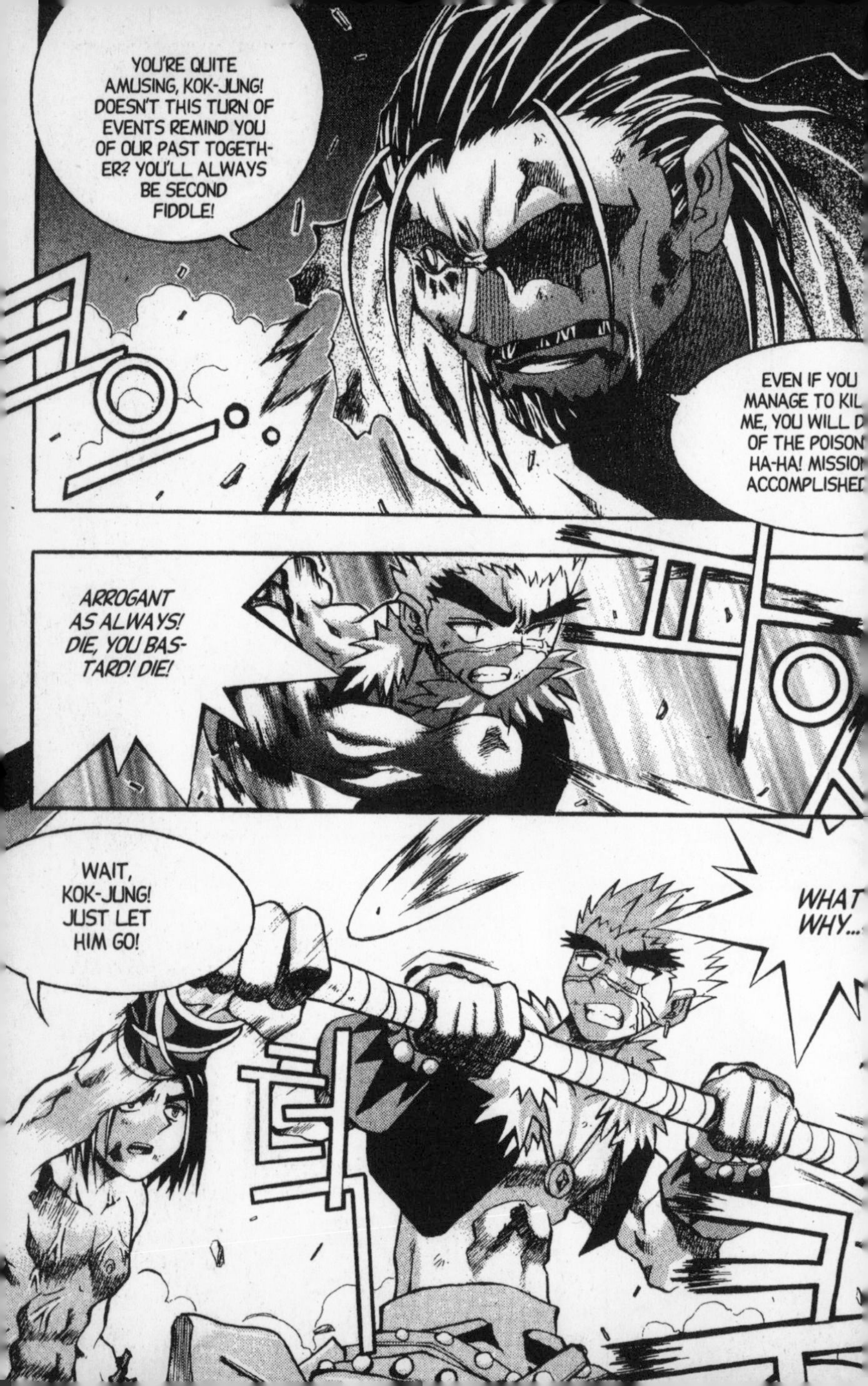
YOU'RE QUITE AMUSING, KOK-JUNG! DOESN'T THIS TURN OF EVENTS REMIND YOU OF OUR PAST TOGETH-ER? YOU'LL ALWAYS BE SECOND FIDDLE!
EVEN IF YOU MANAGE TO KIL ME, YOU WILL D OF THE POISON HA-HA! MISSION ACCOMPLISHED
ARROGANT AS ALWAYS! DIE, YOU BAS-TARD! DIE!
WAIT, KOK-JUNG! JUST LET HIM GO!
WHAT WHY...

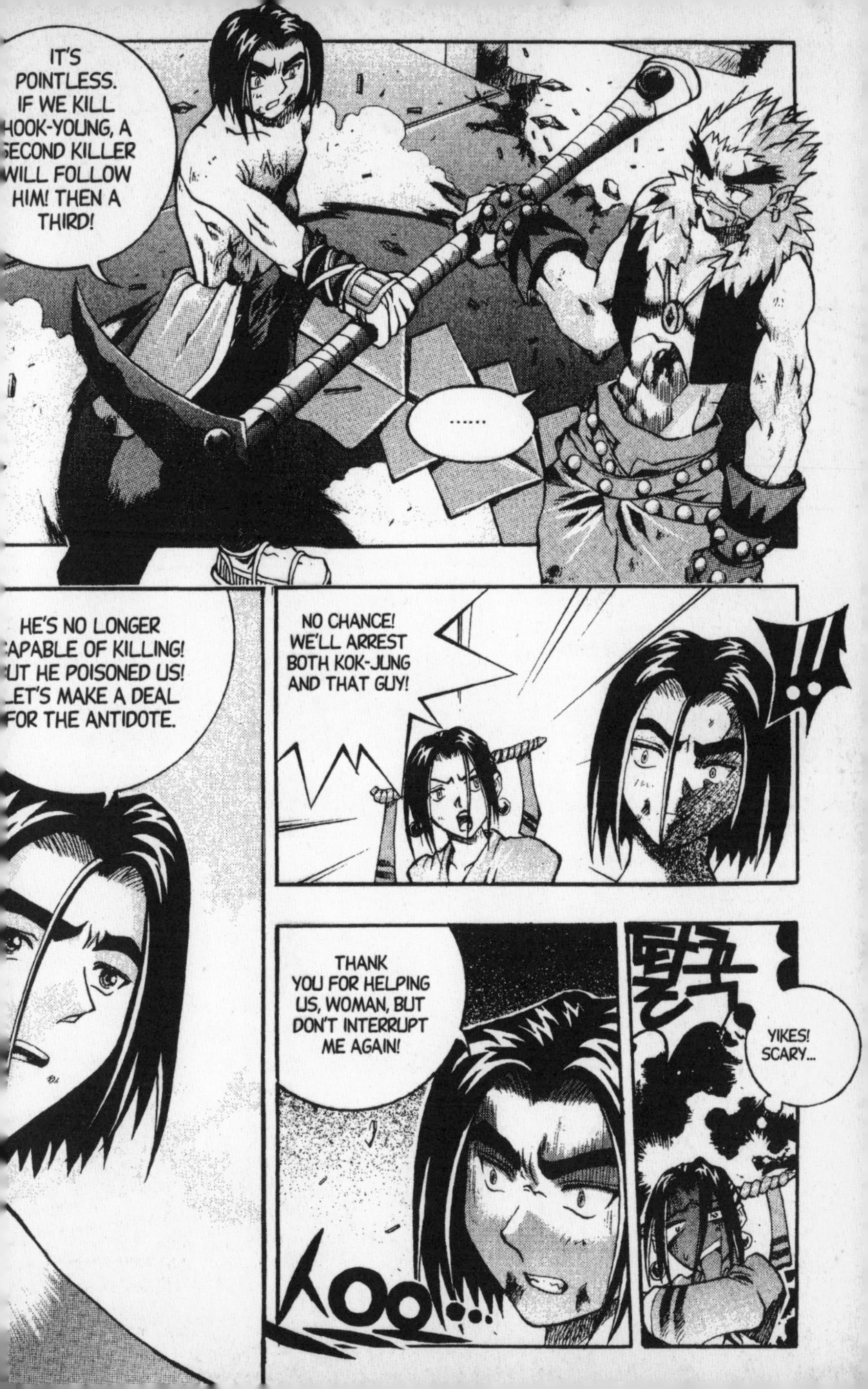

IT'S POINTLESS. IF WE KILL HOOK-YOUNG, A SECOND KILLER WILL FOLLOW HIM! THEN A THIRD!
......
HE'S NO LONGER CAPABLE OF KILLING! BUT HE POISONED US! LET'S MAKE A DEAL FOR THE ANTIDOTE.
NO CHANCE! WE'LL ARREST BOTH KOK-JUNG AND THAT GUY!
!!
THANK YOU FOR HELPING US, WOMAN, BUT DON'T INTERRUPT ME AGAIN!
KOO!!
YIKES! SCARY...

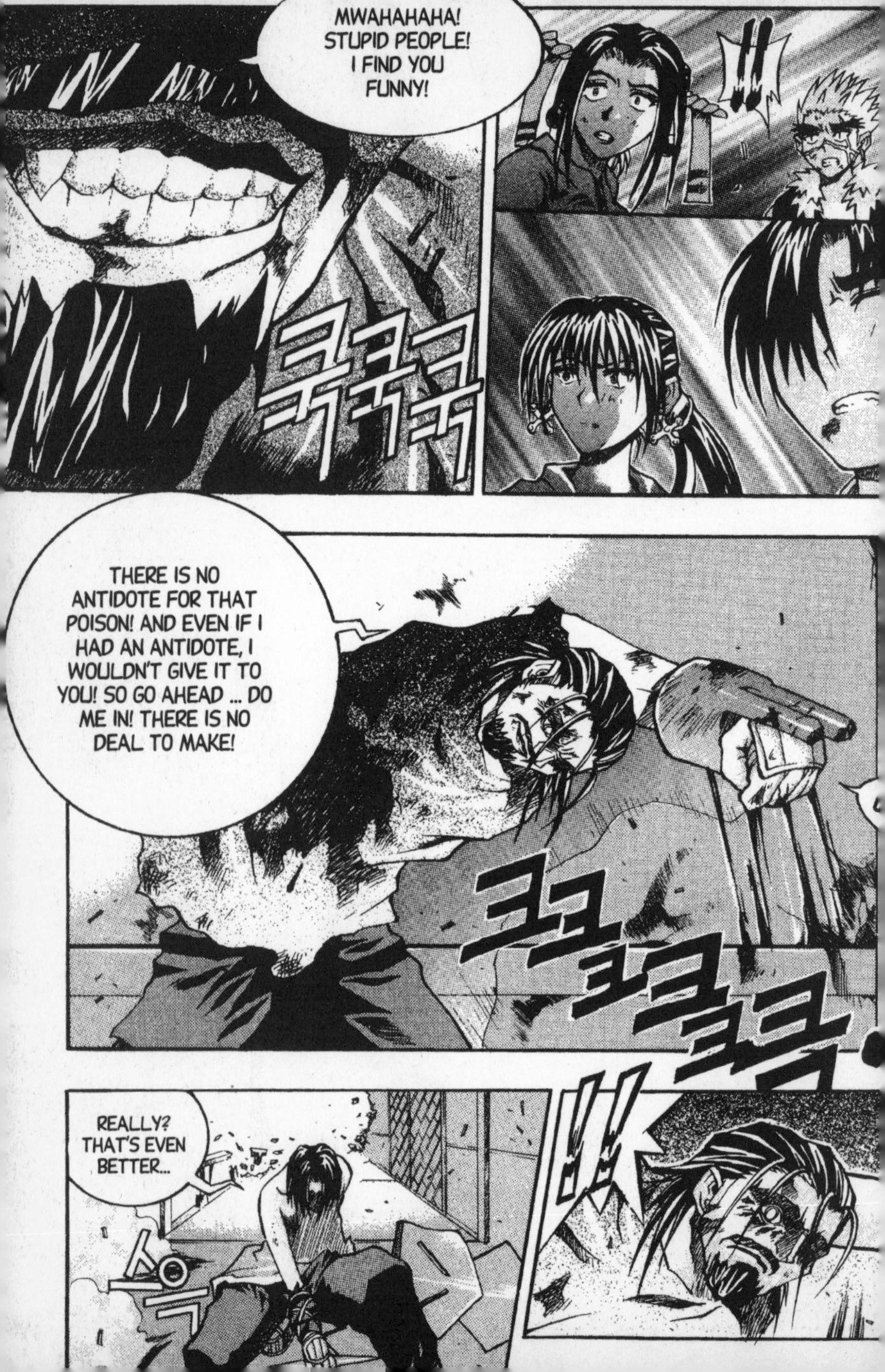
MWAHAHAHA! STUPID PEOPLE! I FIND YOU FUNNY!
THERE IS NO ANTIDOTE FOR THAT POISON! AND EVEN IF I HAD AN ANTIDOTE, I WOULDN'T GIVE IT TO YOU! SO GO AHEAD ... DO ME IN! THERE IS NO DEAL TO MAKE!
REALLY? THAT'S EVEN BETTER...

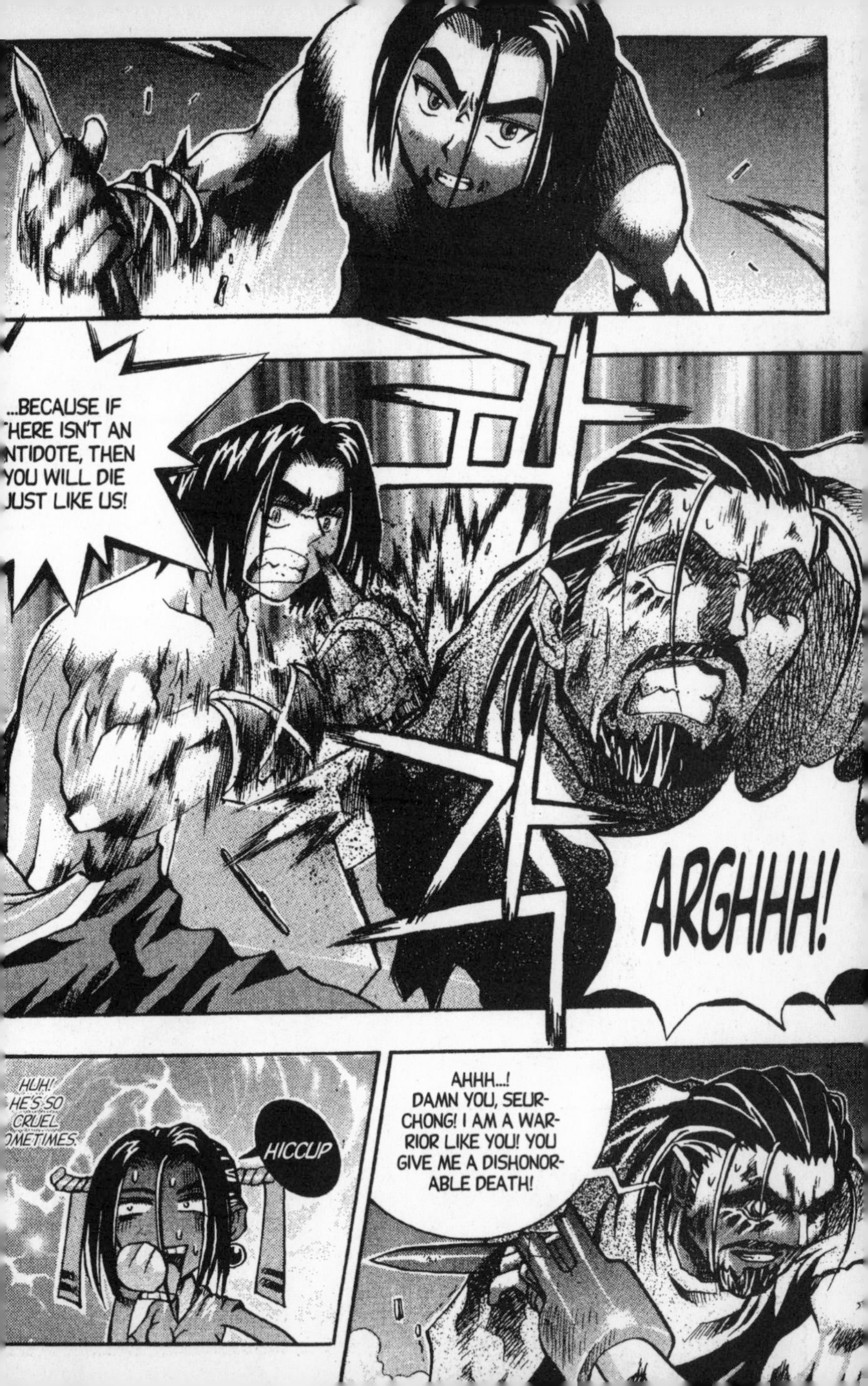
...BECAUSE IF
THERE ISN'T AN
ANTIDOTE, THEN
YOU WILL DIE
JUST LIKE US!
ARGHHH!
HUH!
HE'S SO
CRUEL
SOMETIMES.
HICCUP
AHHH...!
DAMN YOU, SEUR-
CHONG! I AM A WAR-
RIOR LIKE YOU! YOU
GIVE ME A DISHONOR-
ABLE DEATH!

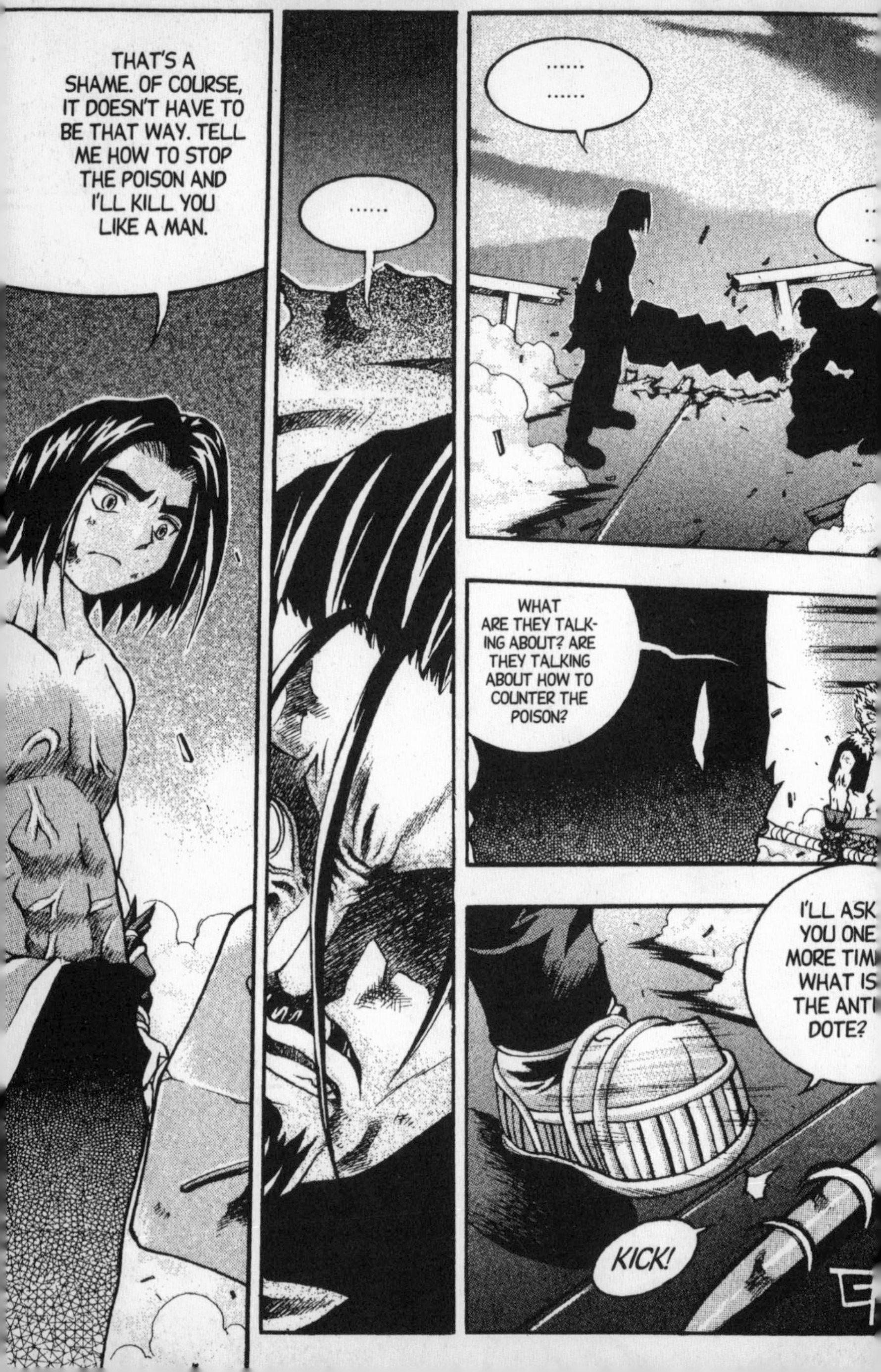
THAT'S A SHAME. OF COURSE, IT DOESN'T HAVE TO BE THAT WAY. TELL ME HOW TO STOP THE POISON AND I'LL KILL YOU LIKE A MAN.
......
......
......
WHAT ARE THEY TALKING ABOUT? ARE THEY TALKING ABOUT HOW TO COUNTER THE POISON?
I'LL ASK YOU ONE MORE TIM WHAT IS THE ANTI DOTE?
KICK!

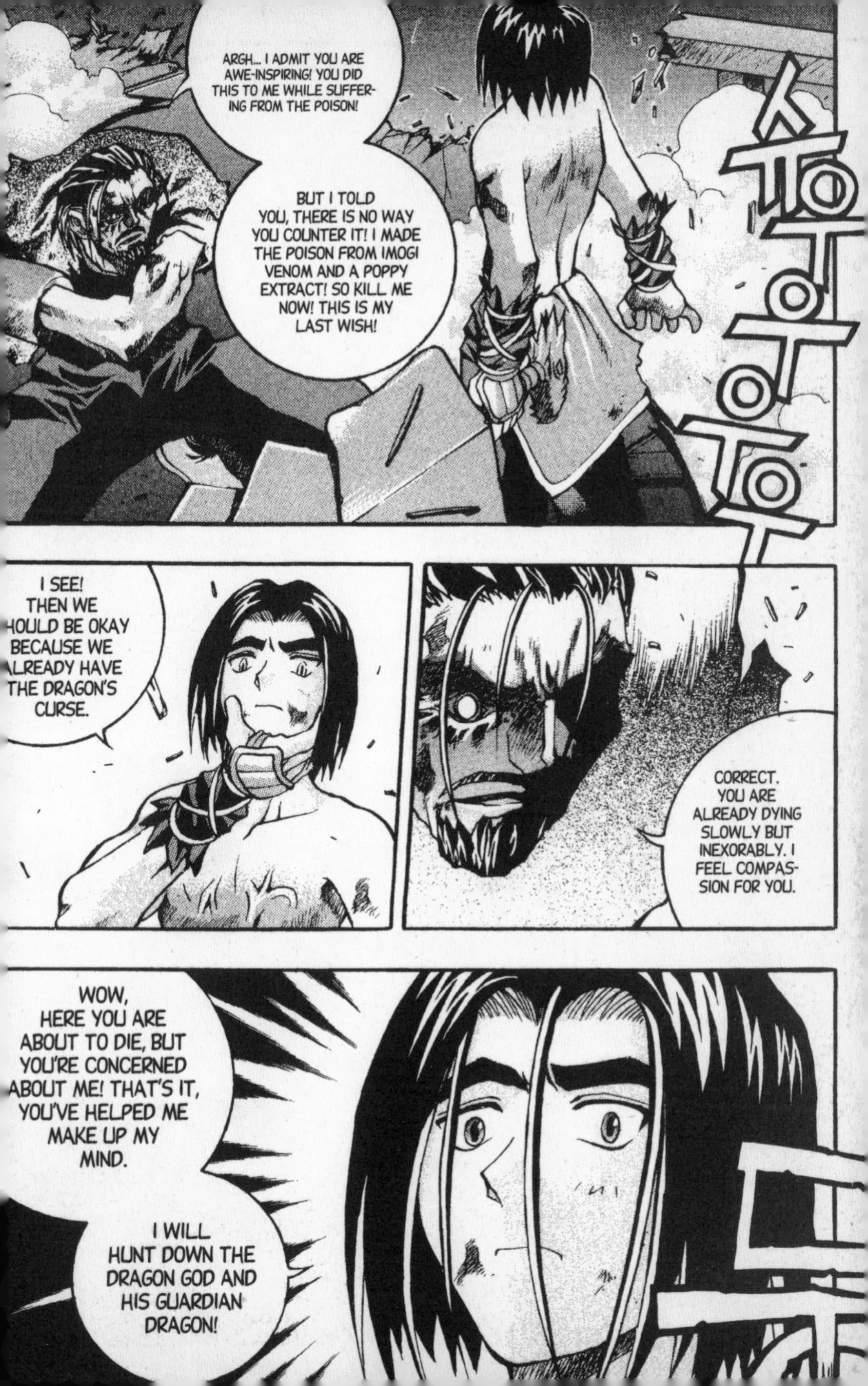
ARGH... I ADMIT YOU ARE AWE-INSPIRING! YOU DID THIS TO ME WHILE SUFFER-ING FROM THE POISON!
BUT I TOLD YOU, THERE IS NO WAY YOU COUNTER IT! I MADE THE POISON FROM IMOGI VENOM AND A POPPY EXTRACT! SO KILL ME NOW! THIS IS MY LAST WISH!
I SEE! THEN WE HOULD BE OKAY BECAUSE WE LREADY HAVE THE DRAGON'S CURSE.
CORRECT. YOU ARE ALREADY DYING SLOWLY BUT INEXORABLY. I FEEL COMPAS-SION FOR YOU.
WOW, HERE YOU ARE ABOUT TO DIE, BUT YOU'RE CONCERNED ABOUT ME! THAT'S IT, YOU'VE HELPED ME MAKE UP MY MIND.
I WILL HUNT DOWN THE DRAGON GOD AND HIS GUARDIAN DRAGON!

Dragon Hunter's Encyclopedia

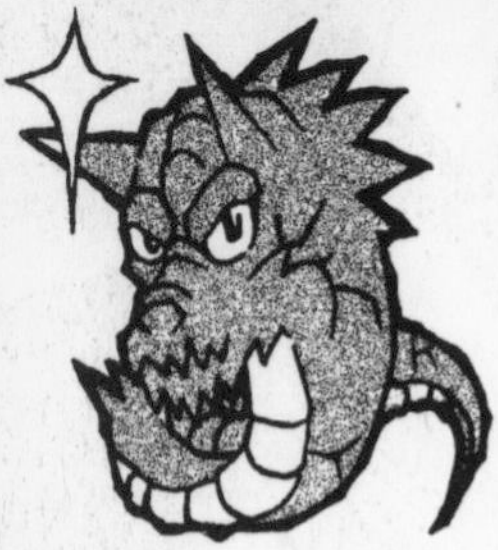

About Imogi, Part 2

Usually, Imogi do not have antlers but some who do--known as Chuk-Jok--can be found from time to time. According to myth, Imogi with antlers are male. Those with one antler are called "Gyu" and those with two antlers are called "Ghi." There are also Imogi called "Ban," which means "curled up on the ground." This name was used for one Imogi species, but I am guessing it was for lowly or less significant Imogi that couldn't fly since "Ban" is a name also used for earthworms and other underground insects. In Korean lore, there is also a son of the Dragon God in the west sea whose name was "Imock." The Chinese character for Imock is the same as Imogi. So, the Imogi is an animal with a duplicitous image. We will look at the different species of Imogi next time. For now, enjoy the rest of the book…

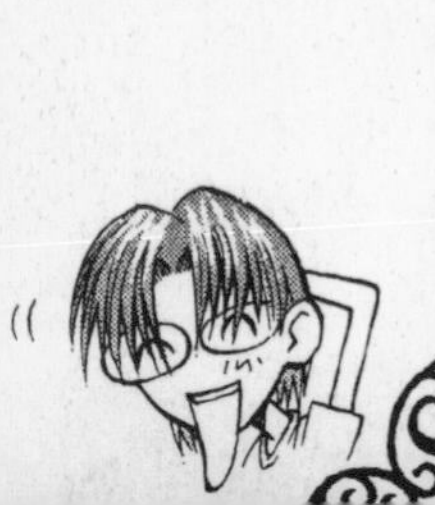

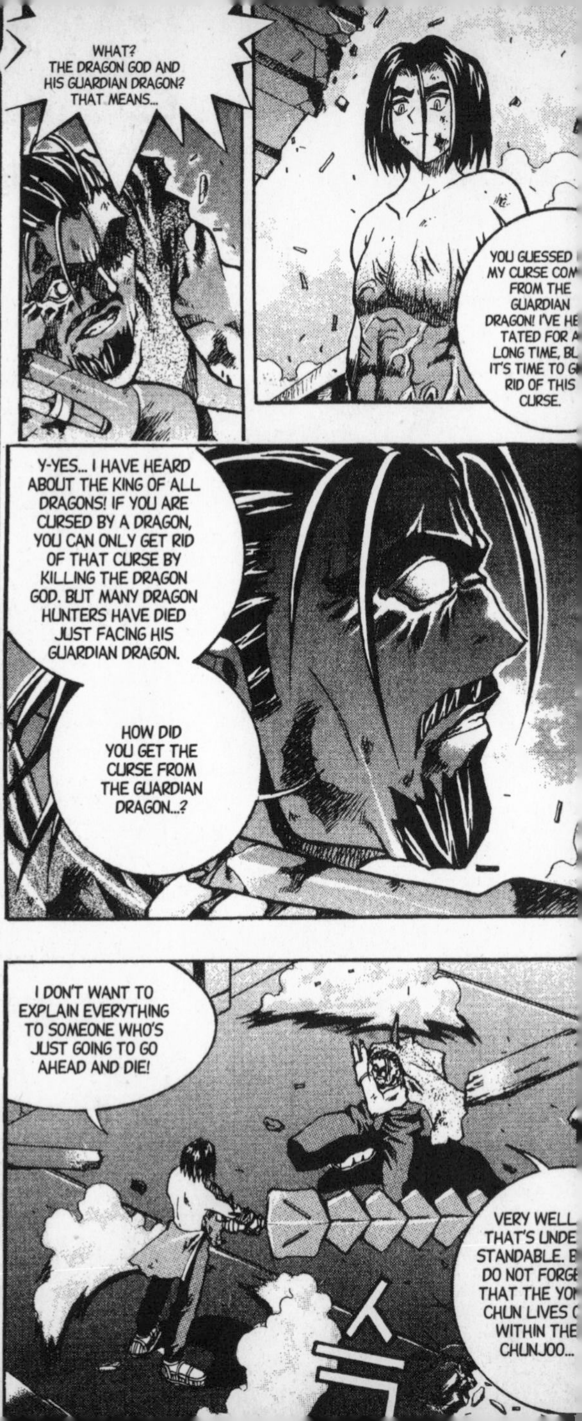
WHAT? THE DRAGON GOD AND HIS GUARDIAN DRAGON? THAT MEANS...
YOU GUESSED MY CURSE COM FROM THE GUARDIAN DRAGON! I'VE HE TATED FOR A LONG TIME, BL IT'S TIME TO G RID OF THIS CURSE.
Y-YES... I HAVE HEARD ABOUT THE KING OF ALL DRAGONS! IF YOU ARE CURSED BY A DRAGON, YOU CAN ONLY GET RID OF THAT CURSE BY KILLING THE DRAGON GOD. BUT MANY DRAGON HUNTERS HAVE DIED JUST FACING HIS GUARDIAN DRAGON.
HOW DID YOU GET THE CURSE FROM THE GUARDIAN DRAGON...?
I DON'T WANT TO EXPLAIN EVERYTHING TO SOMEONE WHO'S JUST GOING TO GO AHEAD AND DIE!
VERY WELL THAT'S UNDE STANDABLE. B DO NOT FORGE THAT THE YO CHUN LIVES WITHIN THE CHUNJOO...

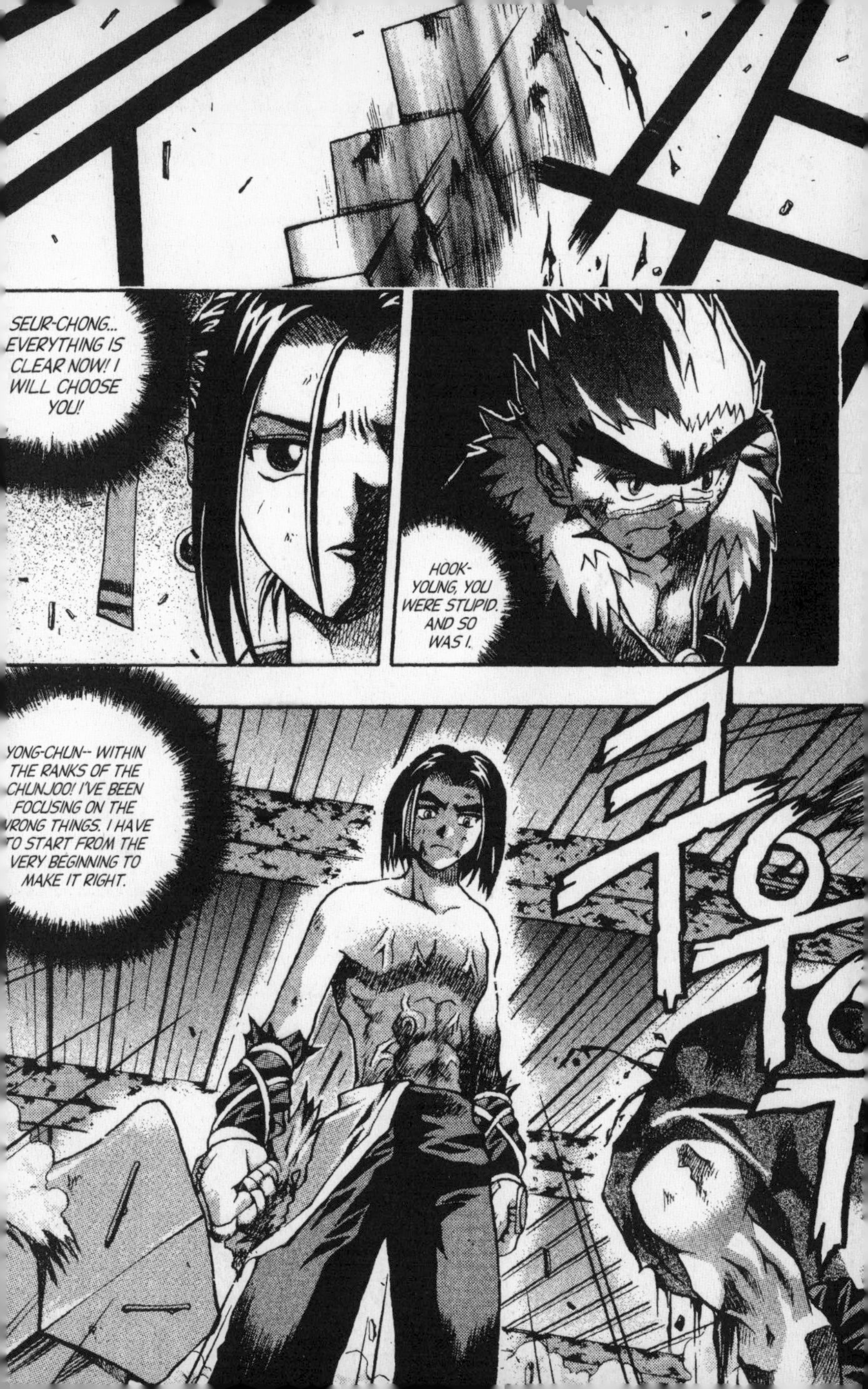
SEUR-CHONG... EVERYTHING IS CLEAR NOW! I WILL CHOOSE YOU!
HOOK-YOUNG, YOU WERE STUPID. AND SO WAS I.
YONG-CHUN-- WITHIN THE RANKS OF THE CHUNJOO! I'VE BEEN FOCUSING ON THE WRONG THINGS. I HAVE TO START FROM THE VERY BEGINNING TO MAKE IT RIGHT.

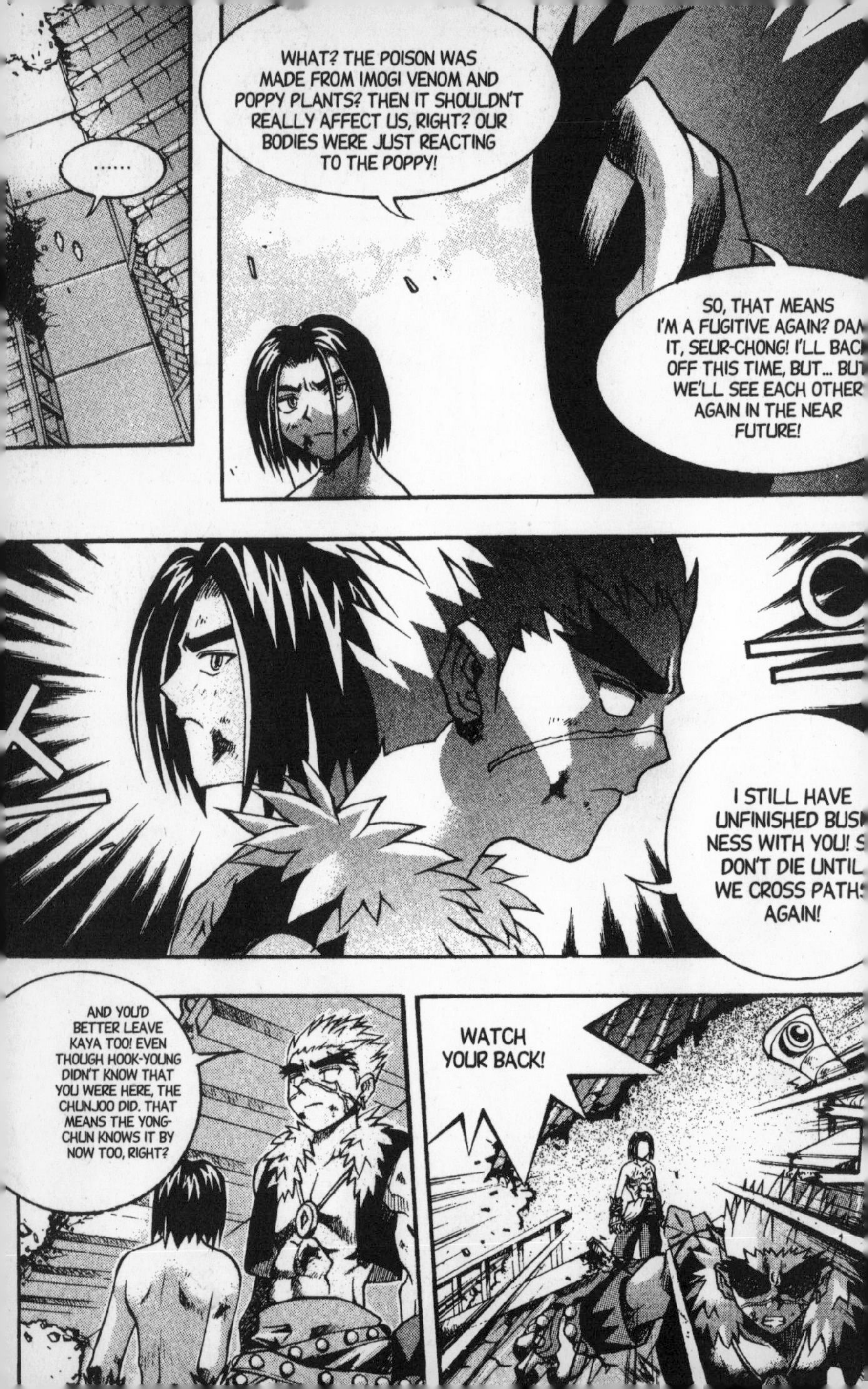
......
WHAT? THE POISON WAS MADE FROM IMOGI VENOM AND POPPY PLANTS? THEN IT SHOULDN'T REALLY AFFECT US, RIGHT? OUR BODIES WERE JUST REACTING TO THE POPPY!
SO, THAT MEANS I'M A FUGITIVE AGAIN? DAM IT, SEUR-CHONG! I'LL BAC OFF THIS TIME, BUT... BUT WE'LL SEE EACH OTHER AGAIN IN THE NEAR FUTURE!
I STILL HAVE UNFINISHED BUSI NESS WITH YOU! S DON'T DIE UNTIL WE CROSS PATH AGAIN!
AND YOU'D BETTER LEAVE KAYA TOO! EVEN THOUGH HOOK-YOUNG DIDN'T KNOW THAT YOU WERE HERE, THE CHUNJOO DID. THAT MEANS THE YONG-CHUN KNOWS IT BY NOW TOO, RIGHT?
WATCH YOUR BACK!

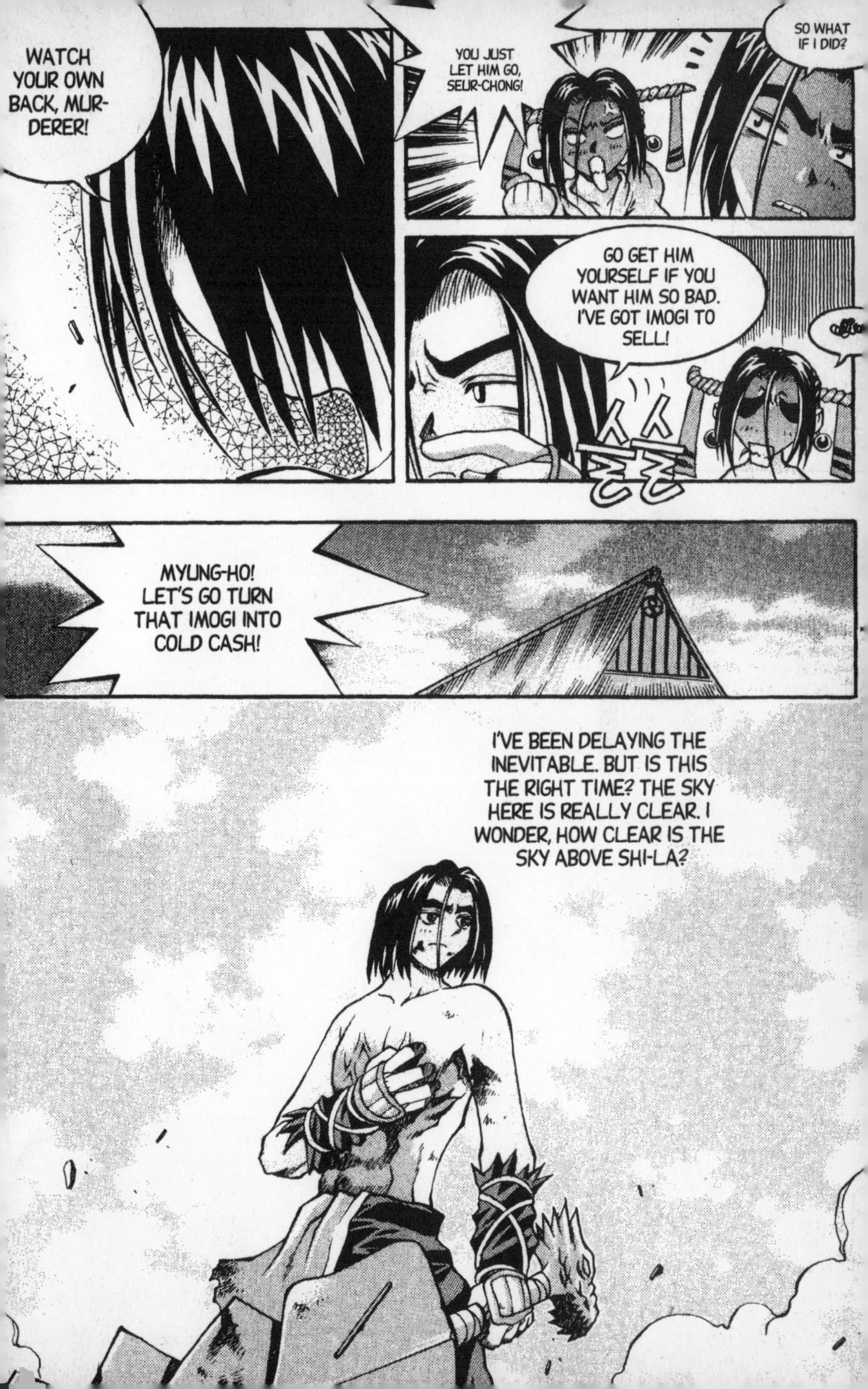
WATCH YOUR OWN BACK, MUR-DERER!
YOU JUST LET HIM GO, SEUR-CHONG!
SO WHAT IF I DID?
GO GET HIM YOURSELF IF YOU WANT HIM SO BAD. I'VE GOT IMOGI TO SELL!
MYUNG-HO! LET'S GO TURN THAT IMOGI INTO COLD CASH!
I'VE BEEN DELAYING THE INEVITABLE. BUT IS THIS THE RIGHT TIME? THE SKY HERE IS REALLY CLEAR. I WONDER, HOW CLEAR IS THE SKY ABOVE SHI-LA?

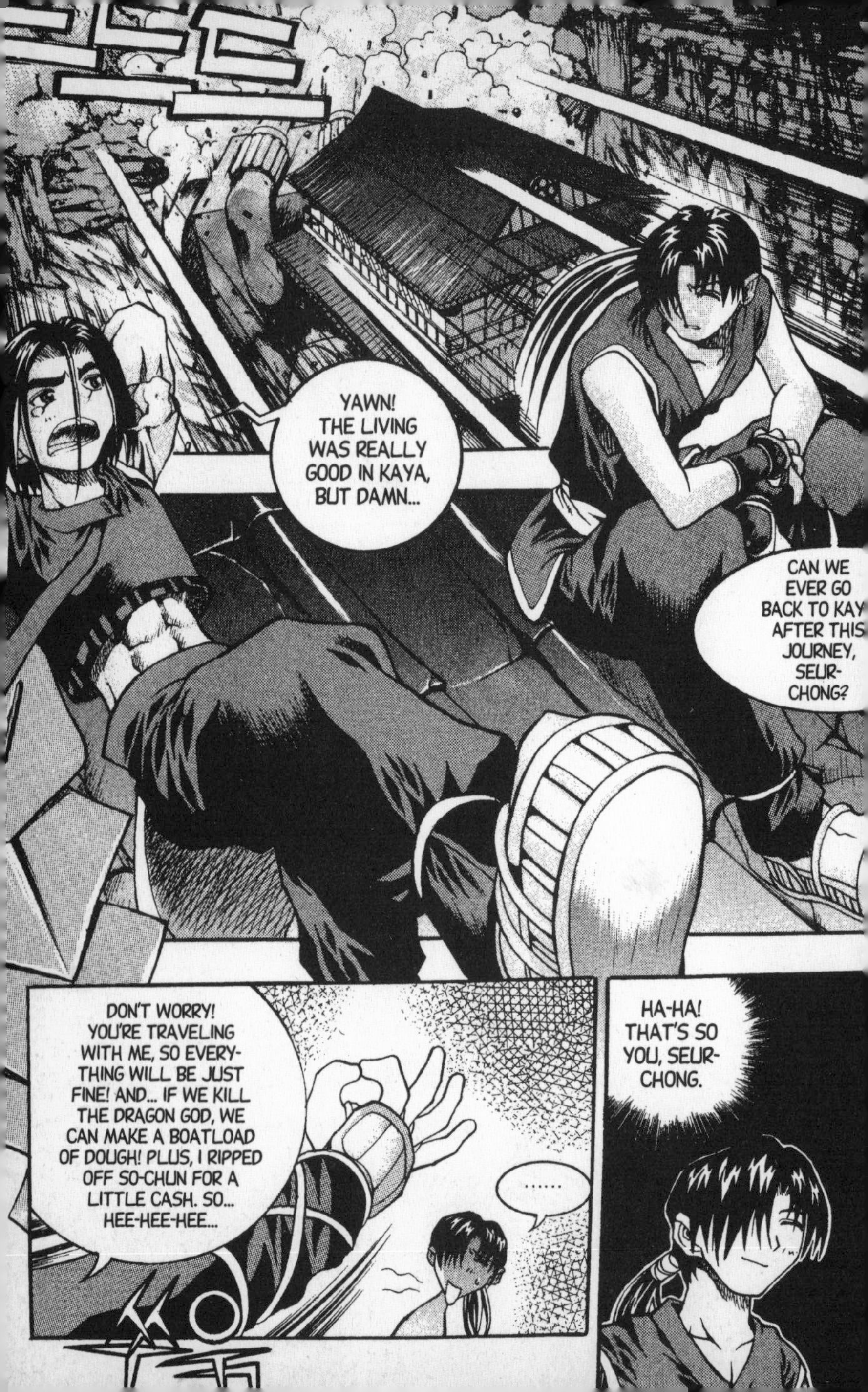
YAWN! THE LIVING WAS REALLY GOOD IN KAYA, BUT DAMN...
CAN WE EVER GO BACK TO KAY AFTER THIS JOURNEY, SEUR-CHONG?
DON'T WORRY! YOU'RE TRAVELING WITH ME, SO EVERY-THING WILL BE JUST FINE! AND... IF WE KILL THE DRAGON GOD, WE CAN MAKE A BOATLOAD OF DOUGH! PLUS, I RIPPED OFF SO-CHUN FOR A LITTLE CASH. SO... HEE-HEE-HEE...
......
HA-HA! THAT'S SO YOU, SEUR-CHONG.

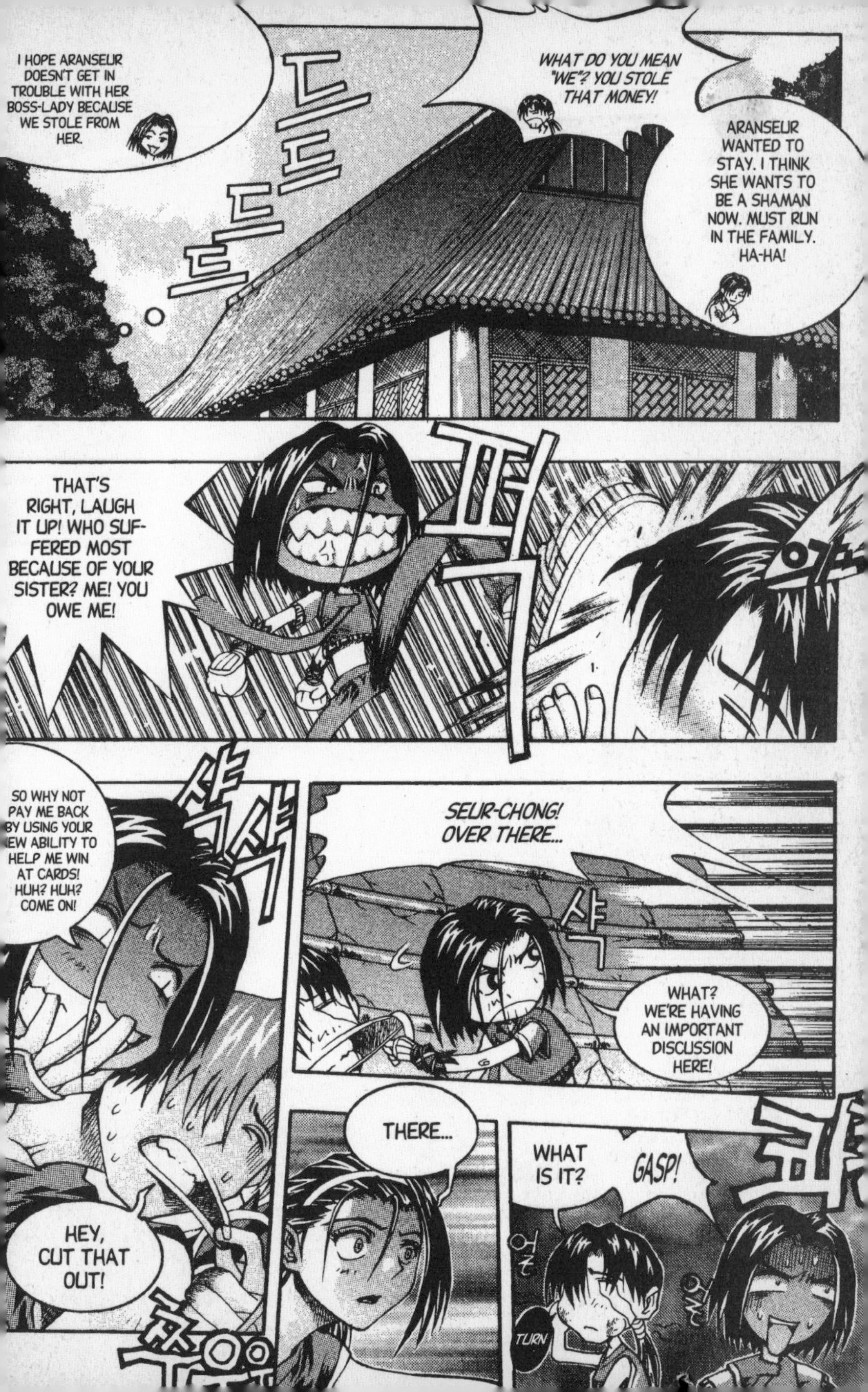
I HOPE ARANSEUR DOESN'T GET IN TROUBLE WITH HER BOSS-LADY BECAUSE WE STOLE FROM HER.
WHAT DO YOU MEAN "WE"? YOU STOLE THAT MONEY!
ARANSEUR WANTED TO STAY. I THINK SHE WANTS TO BE A SHAMAN NOW. MUST RUN IN THE FAMILY. HA-HA!
THAT'S RIGHT, LAUGH IT UP! WHO SUF-FERED MOST BECAUSE OF YOUR SISTER? ME! YOU OWE ME!
SO WHY NOT PAY ME BACK BY USING YOUR EW ABILITY TO HELP ME WIN AT CARDS! HUH? HUH? COME ON!
HEY, CUT THAT OUT!
SEUR-CHONG! OVER THERE...
WHAT? WE'RE HAVING AN IMPORTANT DISCUSSION HERE!
THERE...
WHAT IS IT?
GASP!
TURN

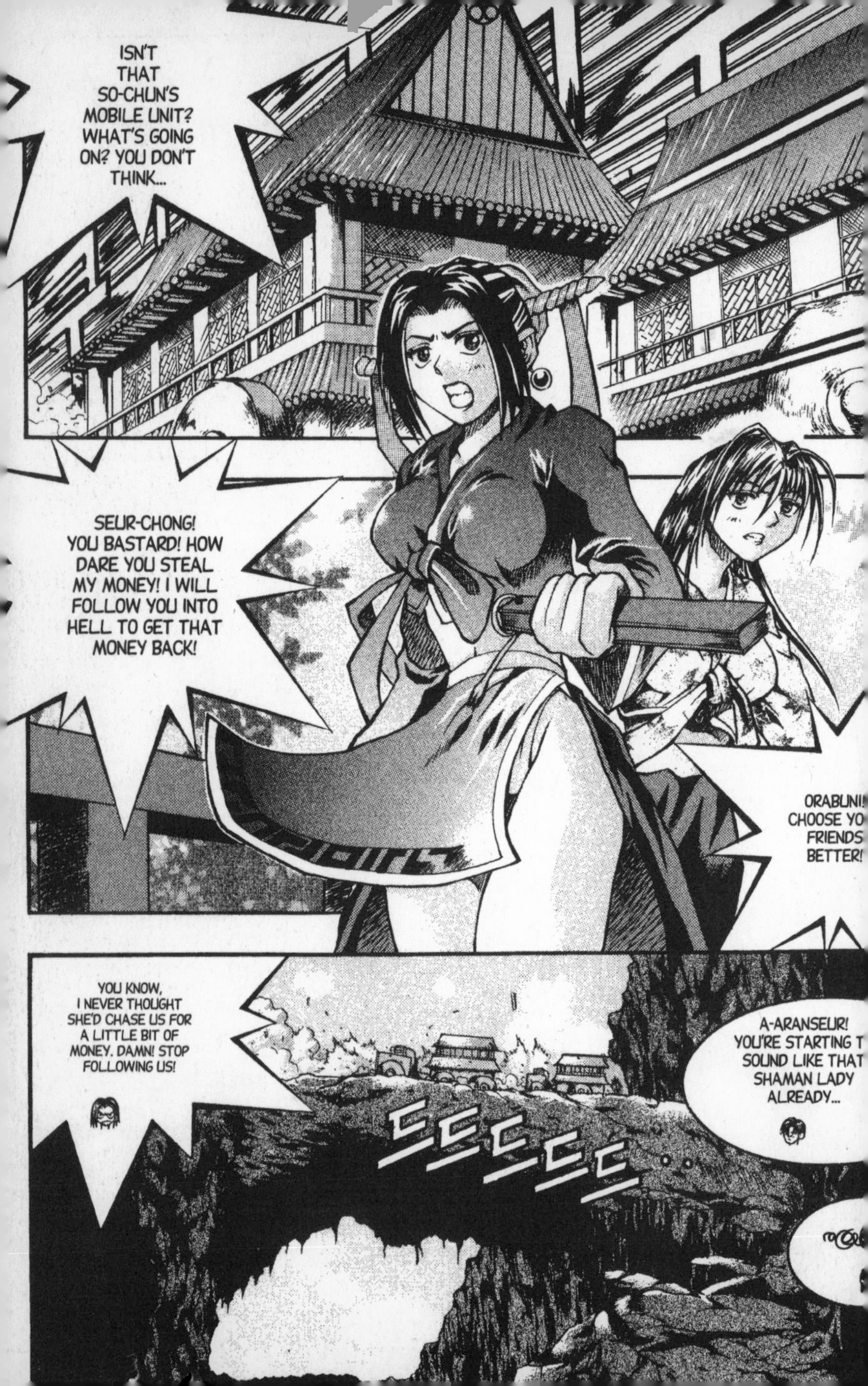
ISN'T THAT SO-CHUN'S MOBILE UNIT? WHAT'S GOING ON? YOU DON'T THINK...
SEUR-CHONG! YOU BASTARD! HOW DARE YOU STEAL MY MONEY! I WILL FOLLOW YOU INTO HELL TO GET THAT MONEY BACK!
ORABUNI! CHOOSE YO FRIENDS BETTER!
YOU KNOW, I NEVER THOUGHT SHE'D CHASE US FOR A LITTLE BIT OF MONEY. DAMN! STOP FOLLOWING US!
A-ARANSEUR! YOU'RE STARTING T SOUND LIKE THAT SHAMAN LADY ALREADY...

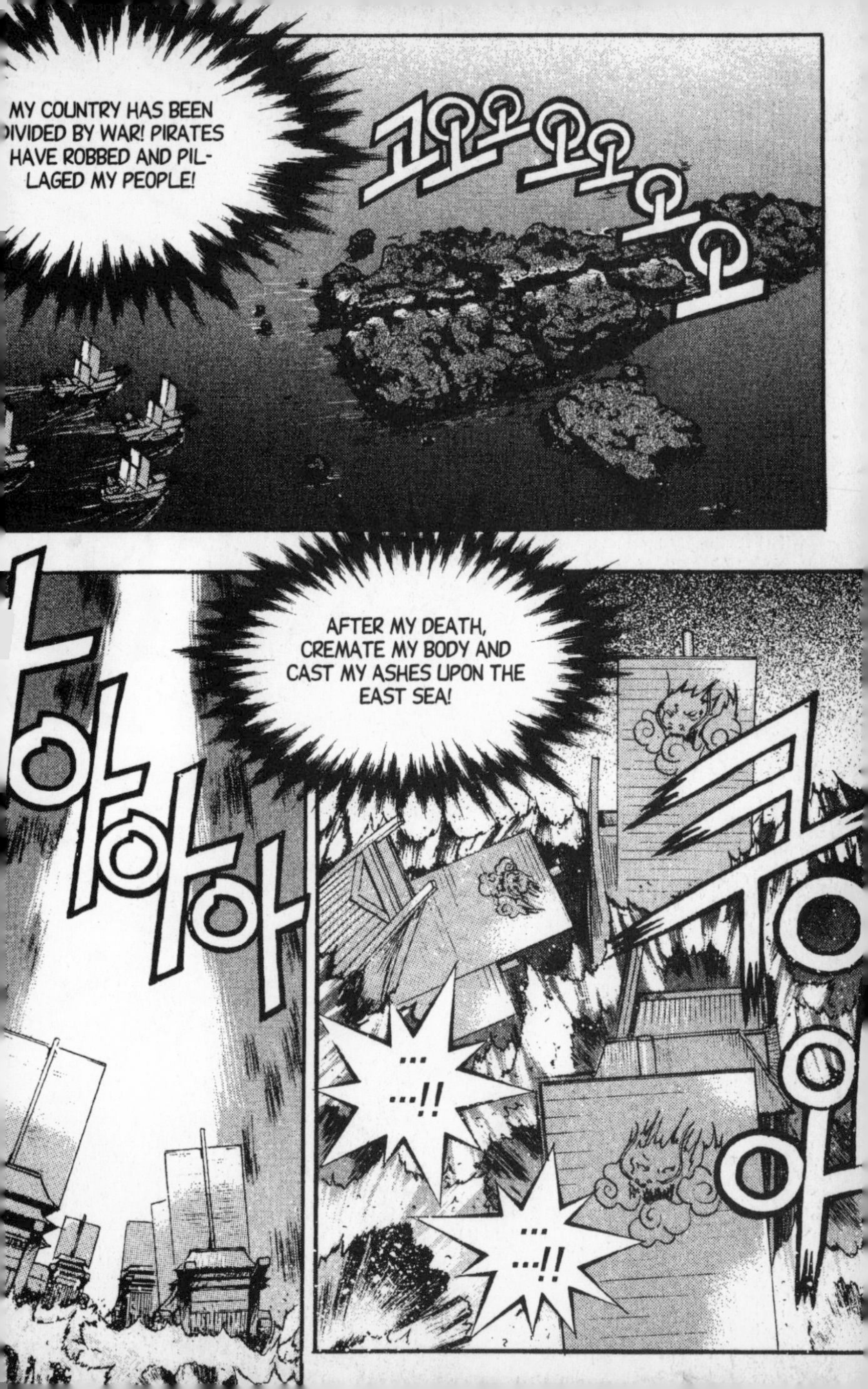
MY COUNTRY HAS BEEN DIVIDED BY WAR! PIRATES HAVE ROBBED AND PIL-LAGED MY PEOPLE!
AFTER MY DEATH, CREMATE MY BODY AND CAST MY ASHES UPON THE EAST SEA!
... ...!!
... ...!!

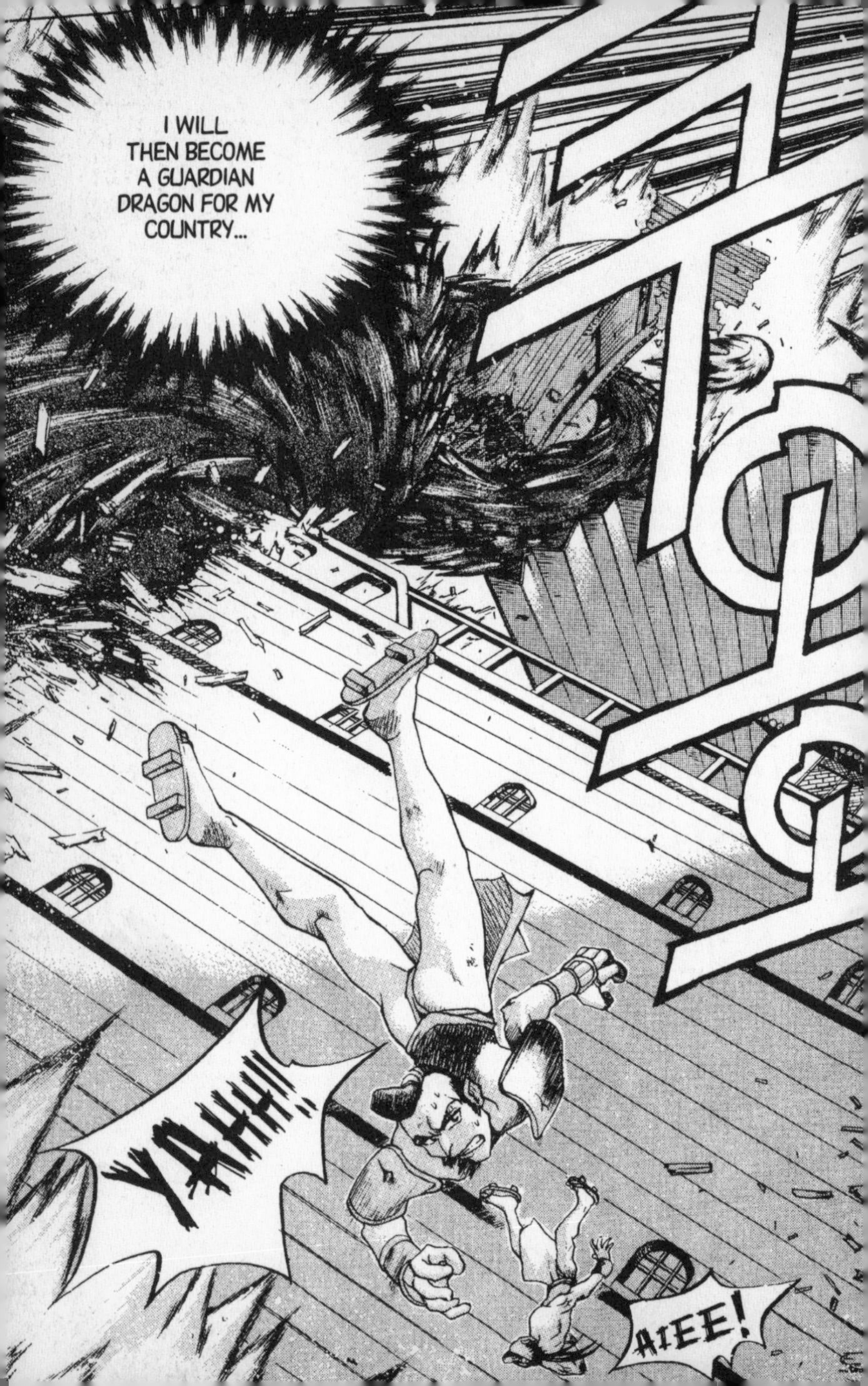
I WILL THEN BECOME A GUARDIAN DRAGON FOR MY COUNTRY...
YAHH!!
AIEE!

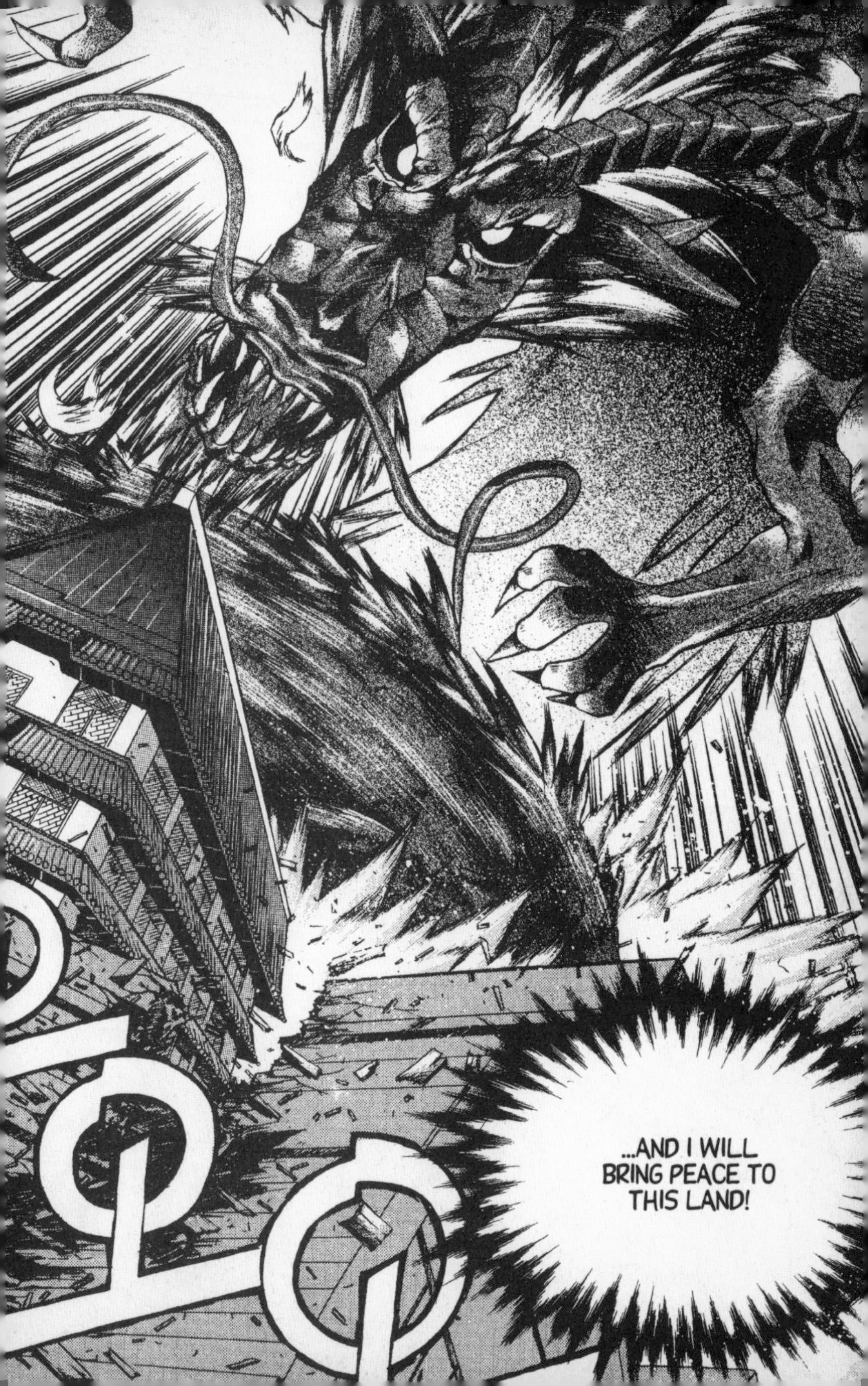
...AND I WILL BRING PEACE TO THIS LAND!

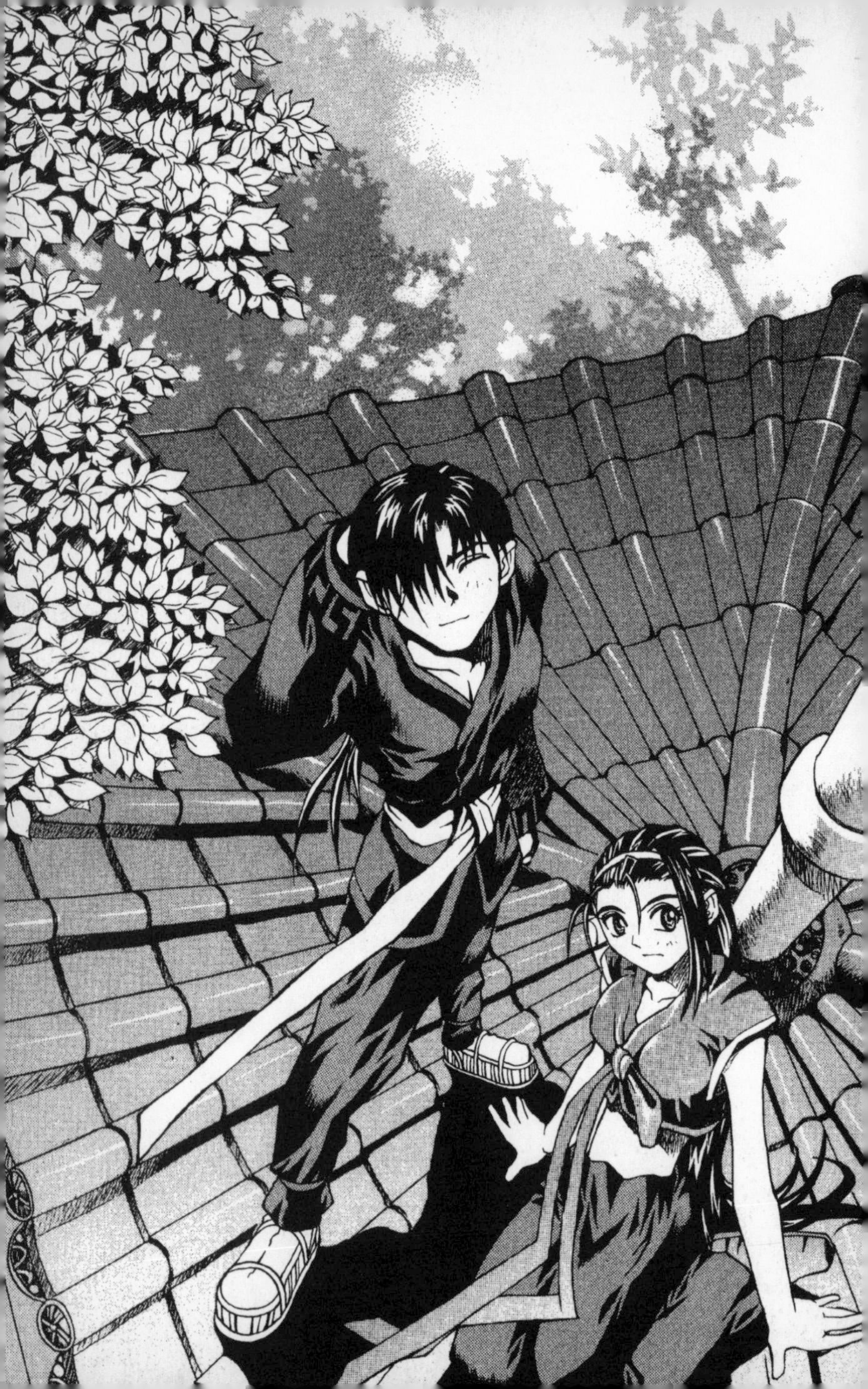

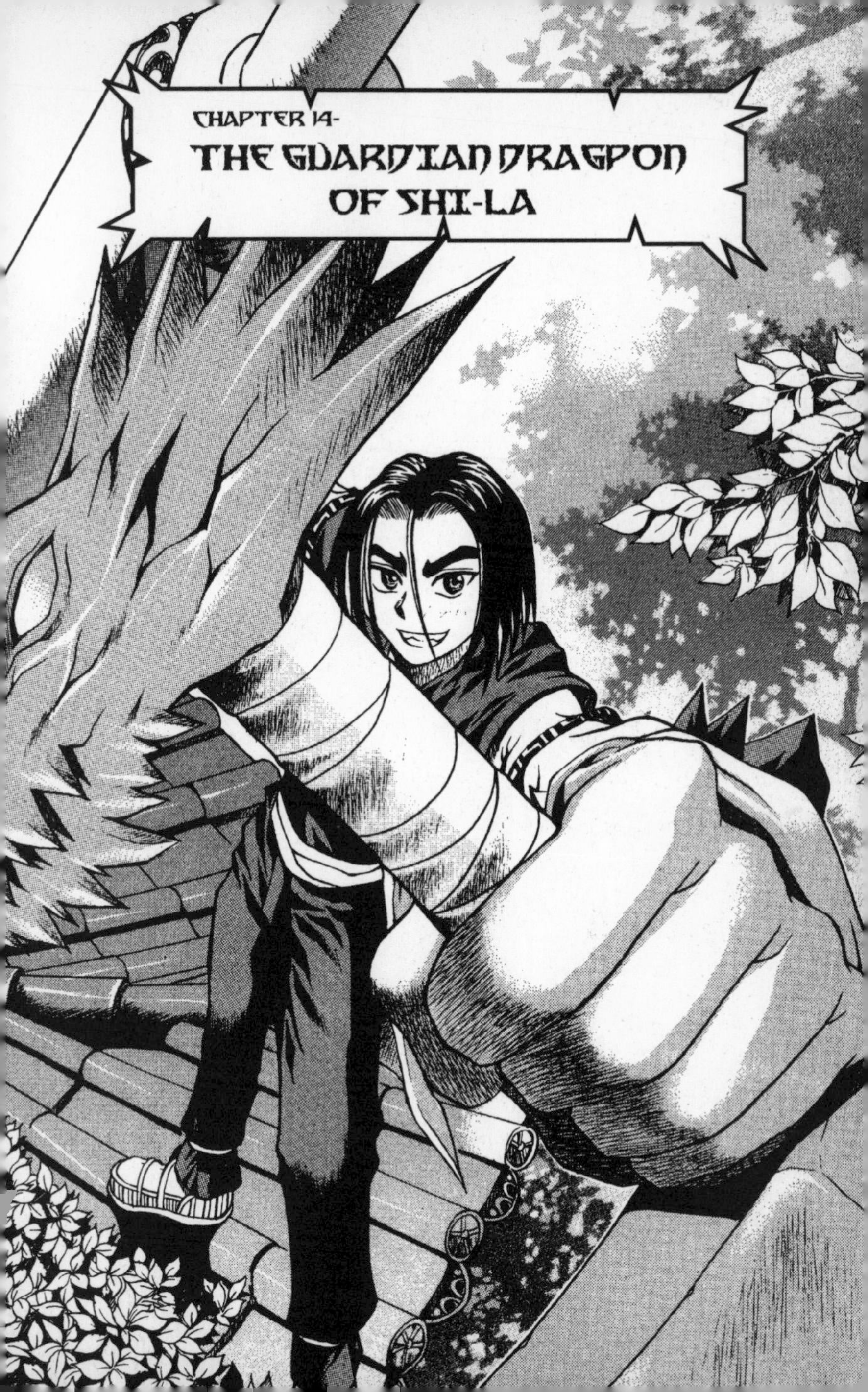
CHAPTER 14-
THE GUARDIAN DRAGPON
OF SHI-LA

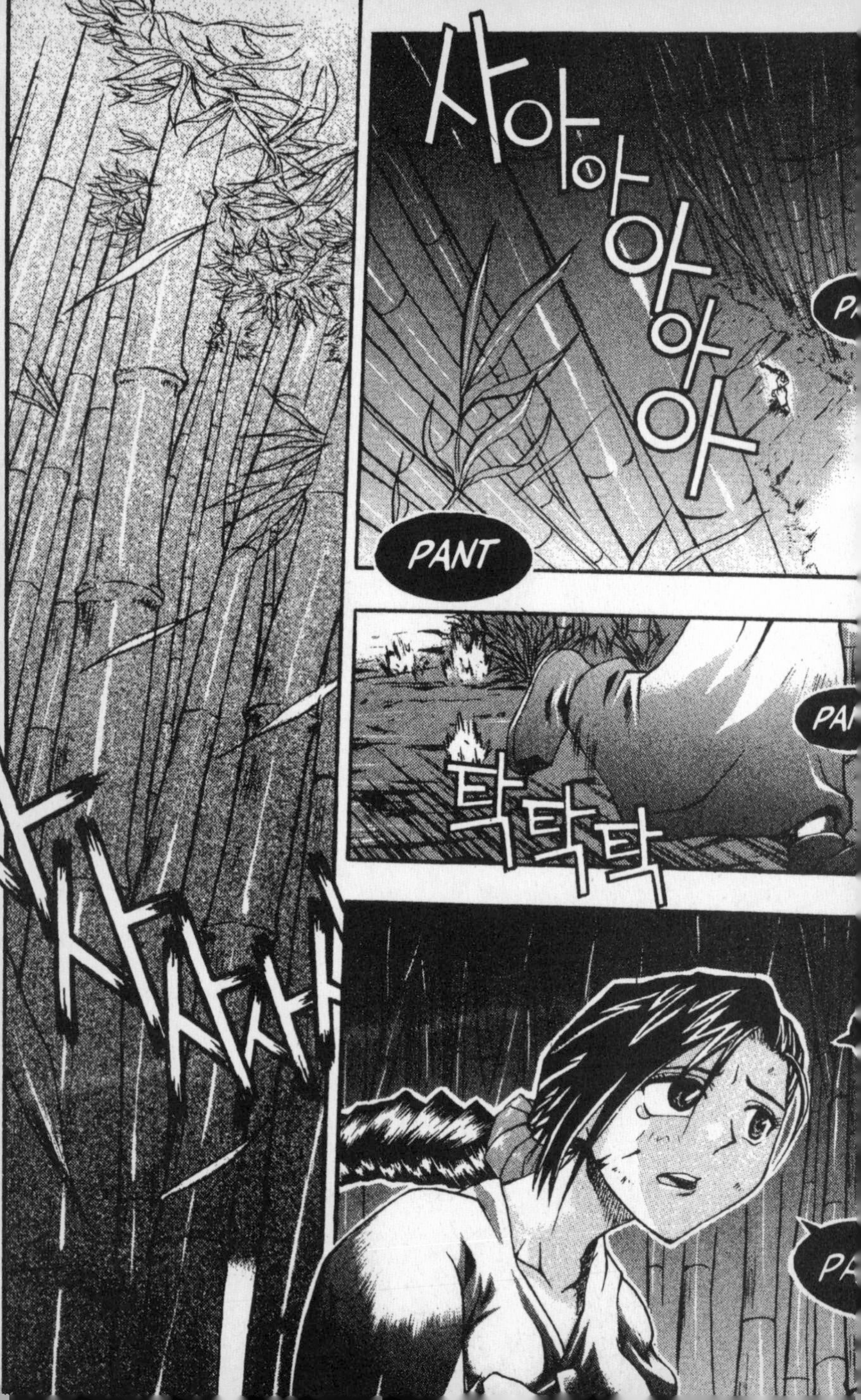
샤아아아아아
PANT
탁탁탁

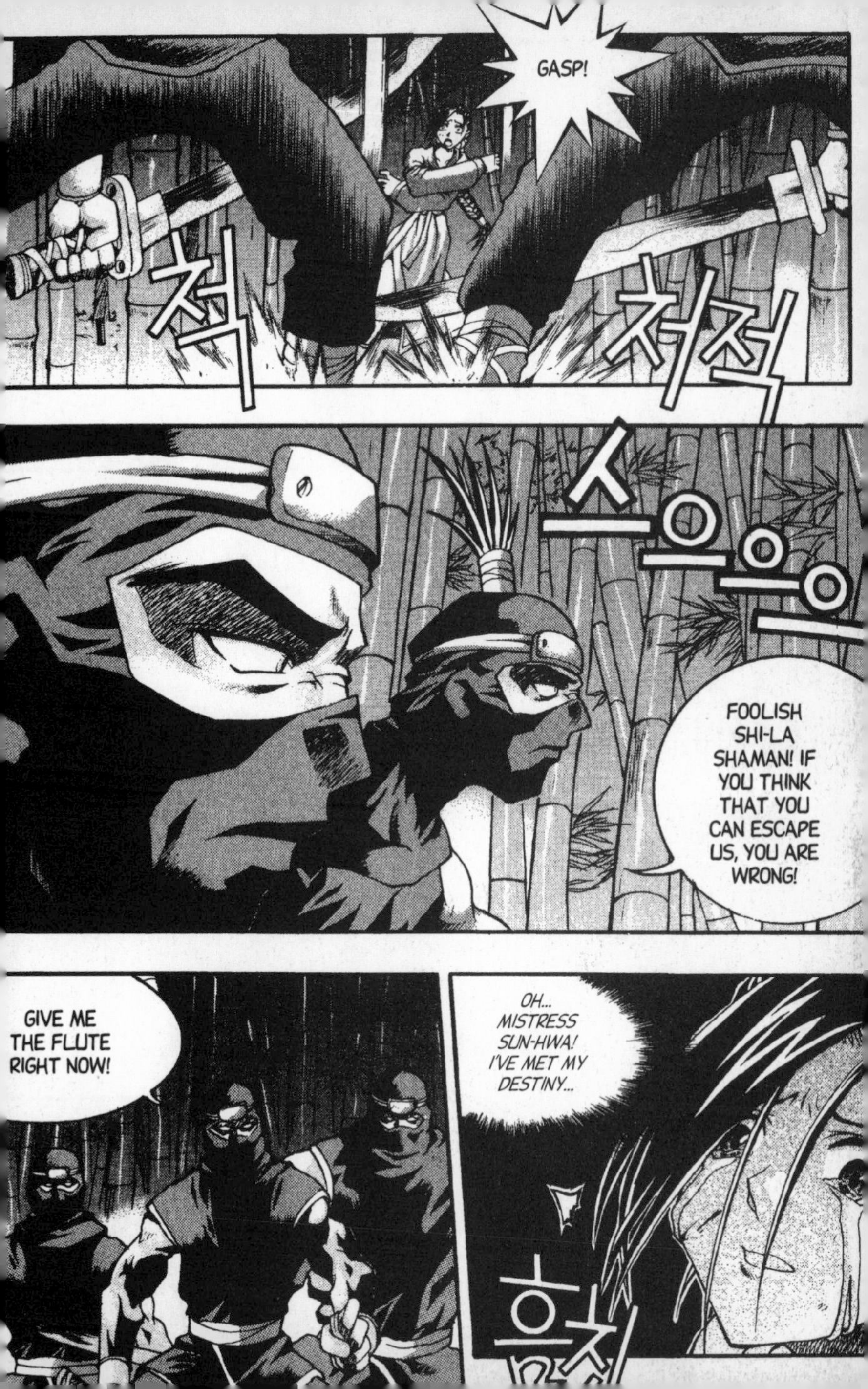
GASP!
척
처척
FOOLISH SHI-LA SHAMAN! IF YOU THINK THAT YOU CAN ESCAPE US, YOU ARE WRONG!
GIVE ME THE FLUTE RIGHT NOW!
OH... MISTRESS SUN-HWA! I'VE MET MY DESTINY...

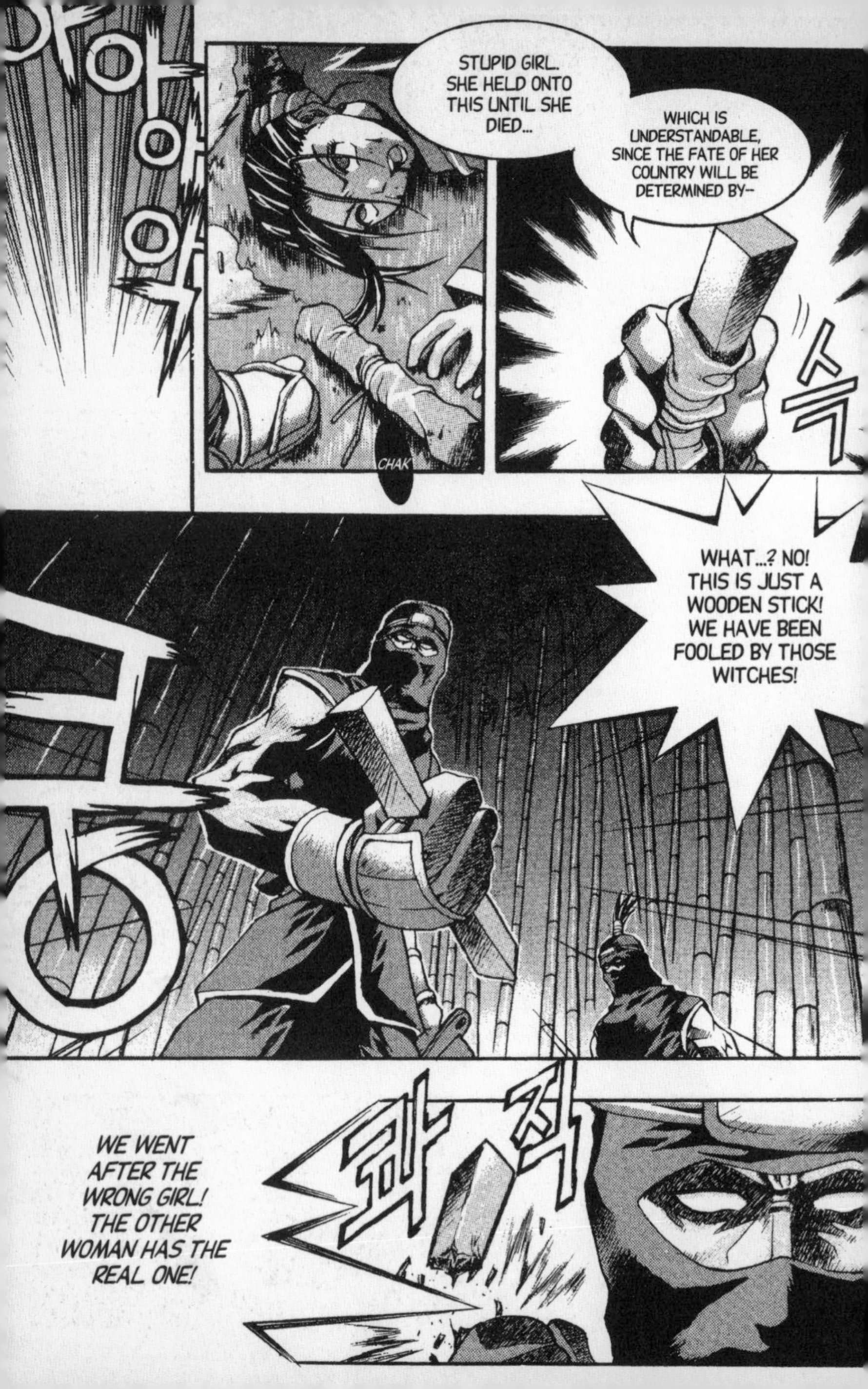

아아아아아악
STUPID GIRL. SHE HELD ONTO THIS UNTIL SHE DIED...
CHAK
WHICH IS UNDERSTANDABLE, SINCE THE FATE OF HER COUNTRY WILL BE DETERMINED BY--
스륵
WHAT...? NO! THIS IS JUST A WOODEN STICK! WE HAVE BEEN FOOLED BY THOSE WITCHES!
크으
WE WENT AFTER THE WRONG GIRL! THE OTHER WOMAN HAS THE REAL ONE!
파작

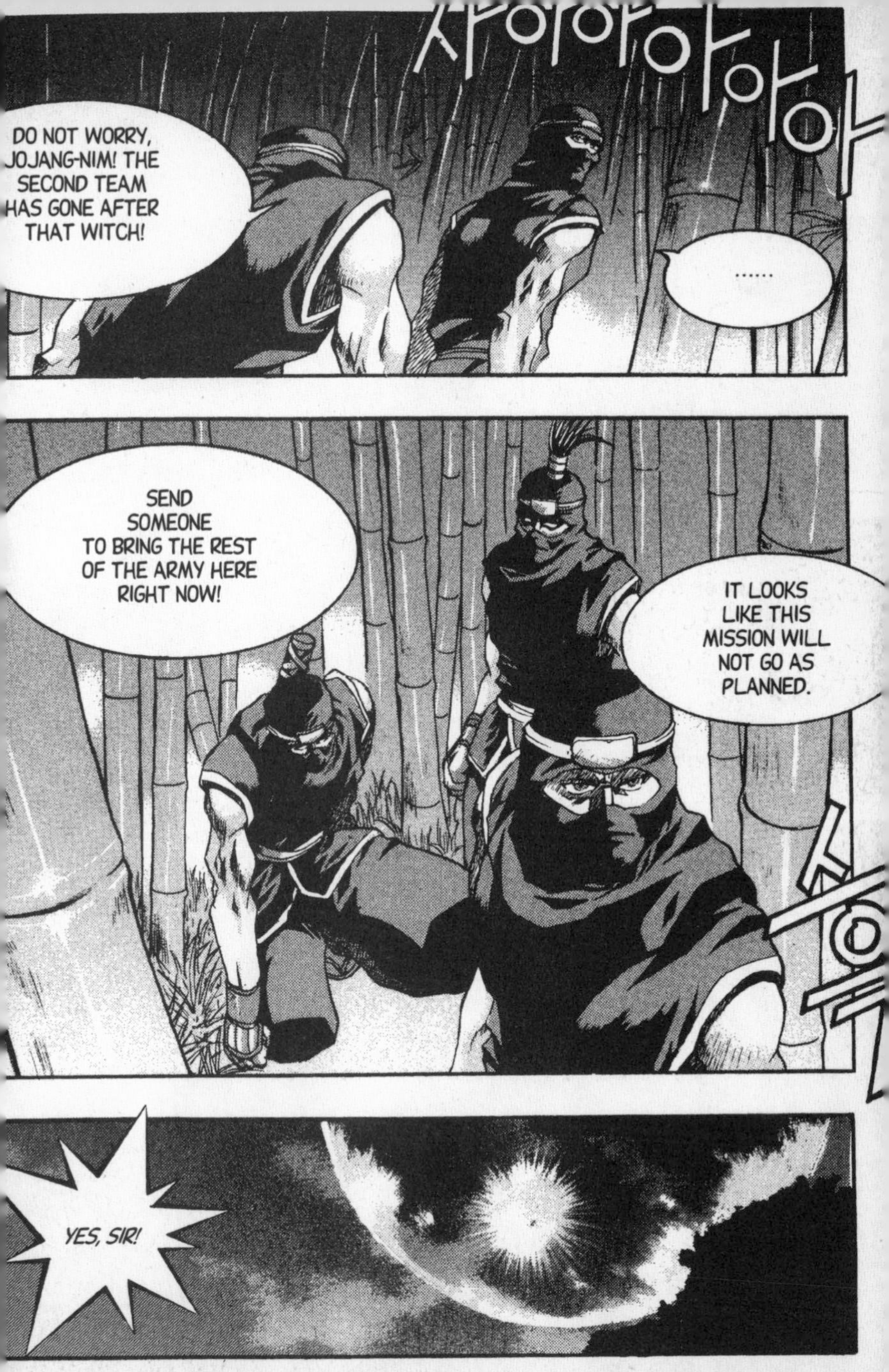
DO NOT WORRY, JOJANG-NIM! THE SECOND TEAM HAS GONE AFTER THAT WITCH!
......
SEND SOMEONE TO BRING THE REST OF THE ARMY HERE RIGHT NOW!
IT LOOKS LIKE THIS MISSION WILL NOT GO AS PLANNED.
YES, SIR!

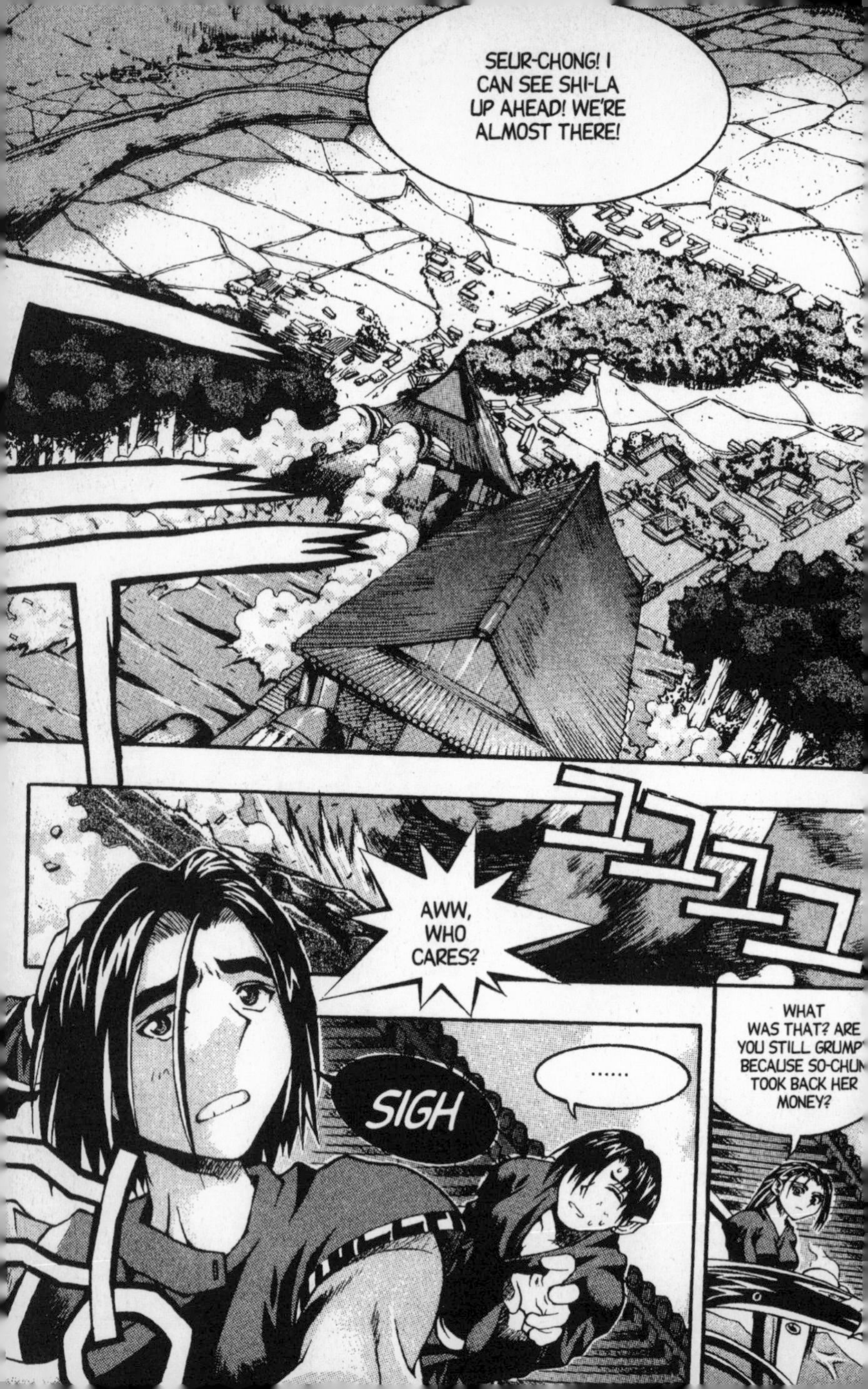
SEUR-CHONG! I CAN SEE SHI-LA UP AHEAD! WE'RE ALMOST THERE!
AWW, WHO CARES?
SIGH
......
WHAT WAS THAT? ARE YOU STILL GRUMP' BECAUSE SO-CHUN TOOK BACK HER MONEY?

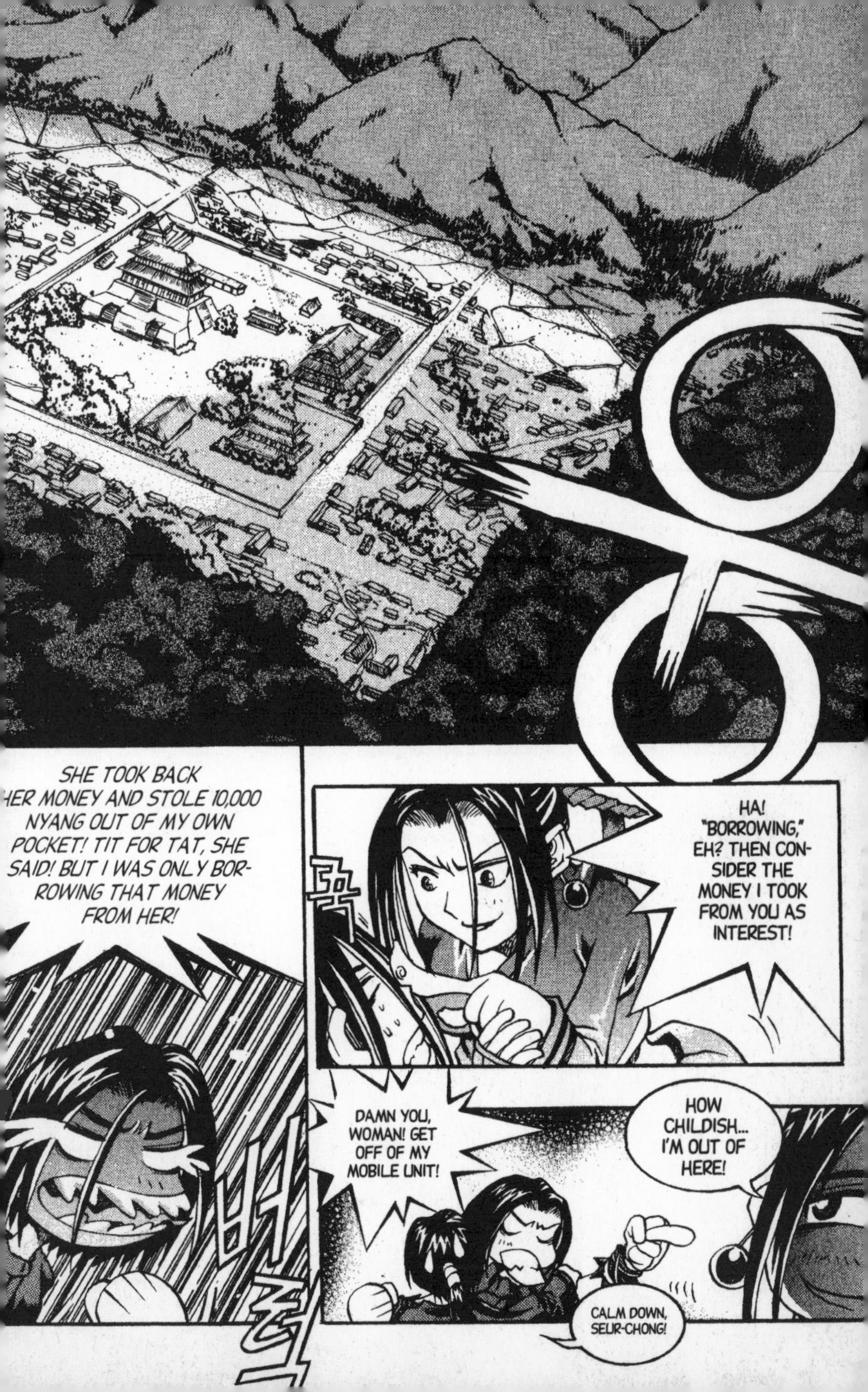
SHE TOOK BACK HER MONEY AND STOLE 10,000 NYANG OUT OF MY OWN POCKET! TIT FOR TAT, SHE SAID! BUT I WAS ONLY BORROWING THAT MONEY FROM HER!
HA! "BORROWING," EH? THEN CONSIDER THE MONEY I TOOK FROM YOU AS INTEREST!
DAMN YOU, WOMAN! GET OFF OF MY MOBILE UNIT!
HOW CHILDISH... I'M OUT OF HERE!
CALM DOWN, SEUR-CHONG!

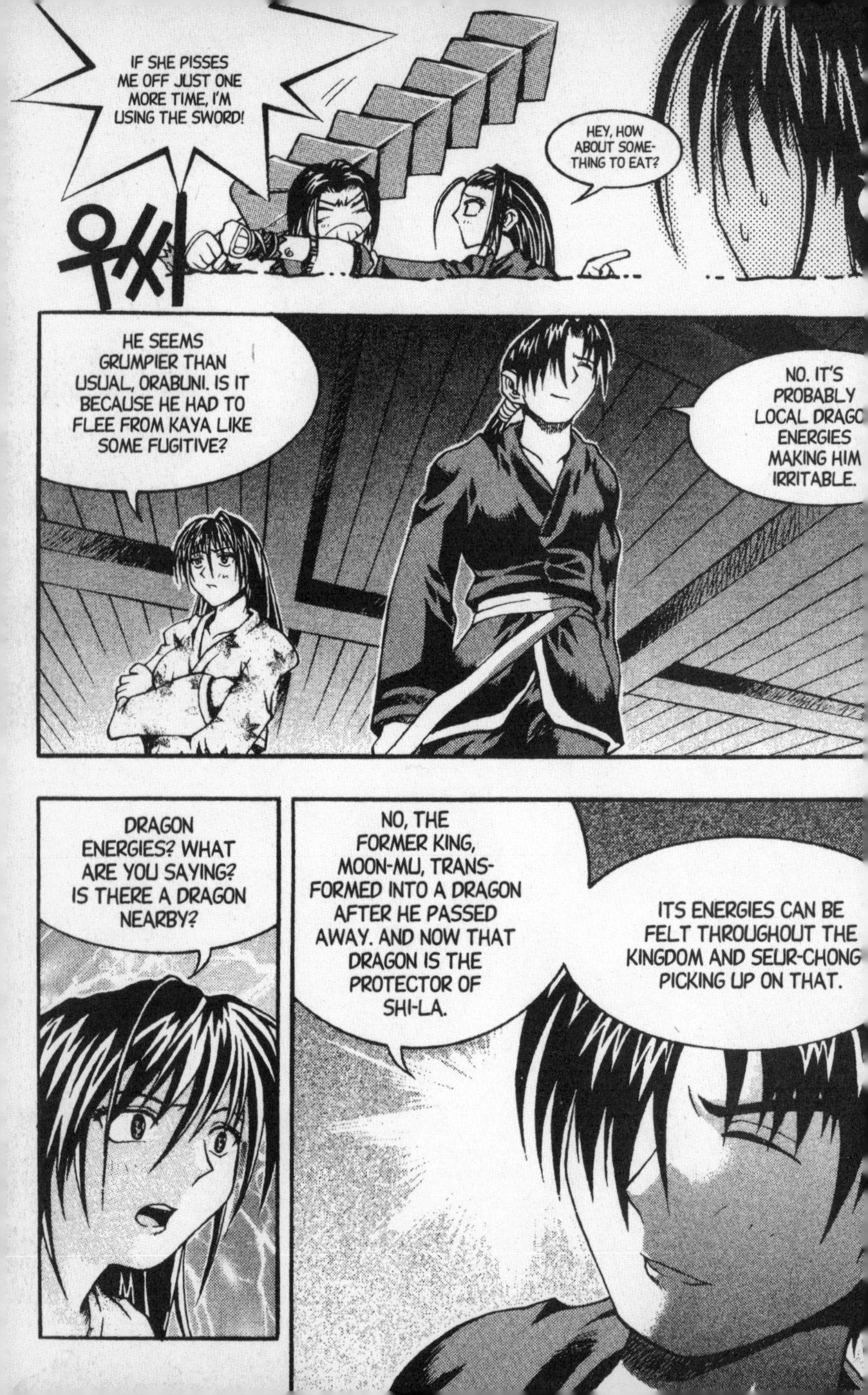
IF SHE PISSES ME OFF JUST ONE MORE TIME, I'M USING THE SWORD!
HEY, HOW ABOUT SOME-THING TO EAT?
HE SEEMS GRUMPIER THAN USUAL, ORABUNI. IS IT BECAUSE HE HAD TO FLEE FROM KAYA LIKE SOME FUGITIVE?
NO. IT'S PROBABLY LOCAL DRAGO ENERGIES MAKING HIM IRRITABLE.
DRAGON ENERGIES? WHAT ARE YOU SAYING? IS THERE A DRAGON NEARBY?
NO, THE FORMER KING, MOON-MU, TRANS-FORMED INTO A DRAGON AFTER HE PASSED AWAY. AND NOW THAT DRAGON IS THE PROTECTOR OF SHI-LA.
ITS ENERGIES CAN BE FELT THROUGHOUT THE KINGDOM AND SEUR-CHONG PICKING UP ON THAT.

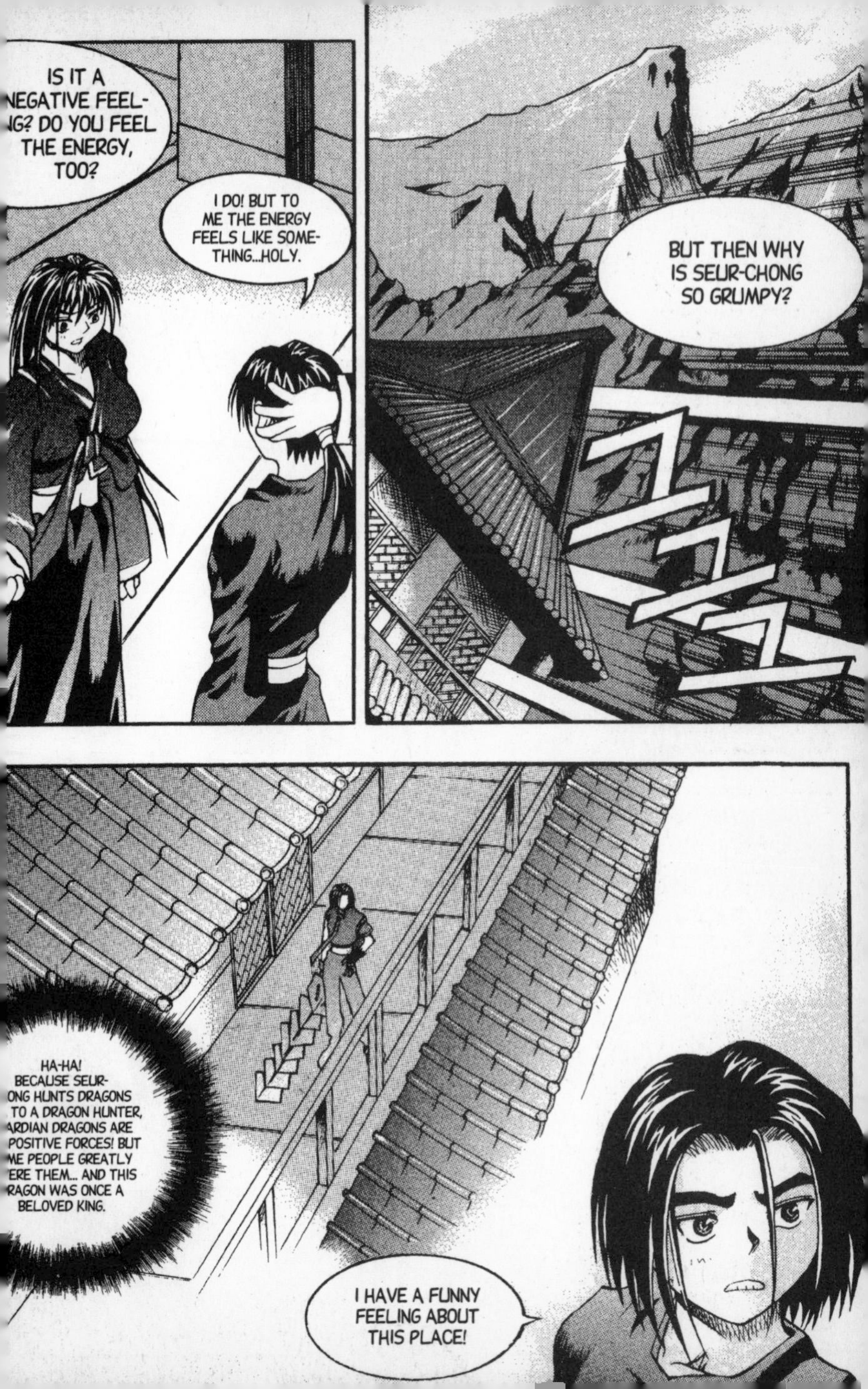
IS IT A NEGATIVE FEEL-ING? DO YOU FEEL THE ENERGY, TOO?
I DO! BUT TO ME THE ENERGY FEELS LIKE SOME-THING...HOLY.
BUT THEN WHY IS SEUR-CHONG SO GRUMPY?
HA-HA! BECAUSE SEUR-ONG HUNTS DRAGONS TO A DRAGON HUNTER, ARDIAN DRAGONS ARE POSITIVE FORCES! BUT ME PEOPLE GREATLY ERE THEM... AND THIS RAGON WAS ONCE A BELOVED KING.
I HAVE A FUNNY FEELING ABOUT THIS PLACE!

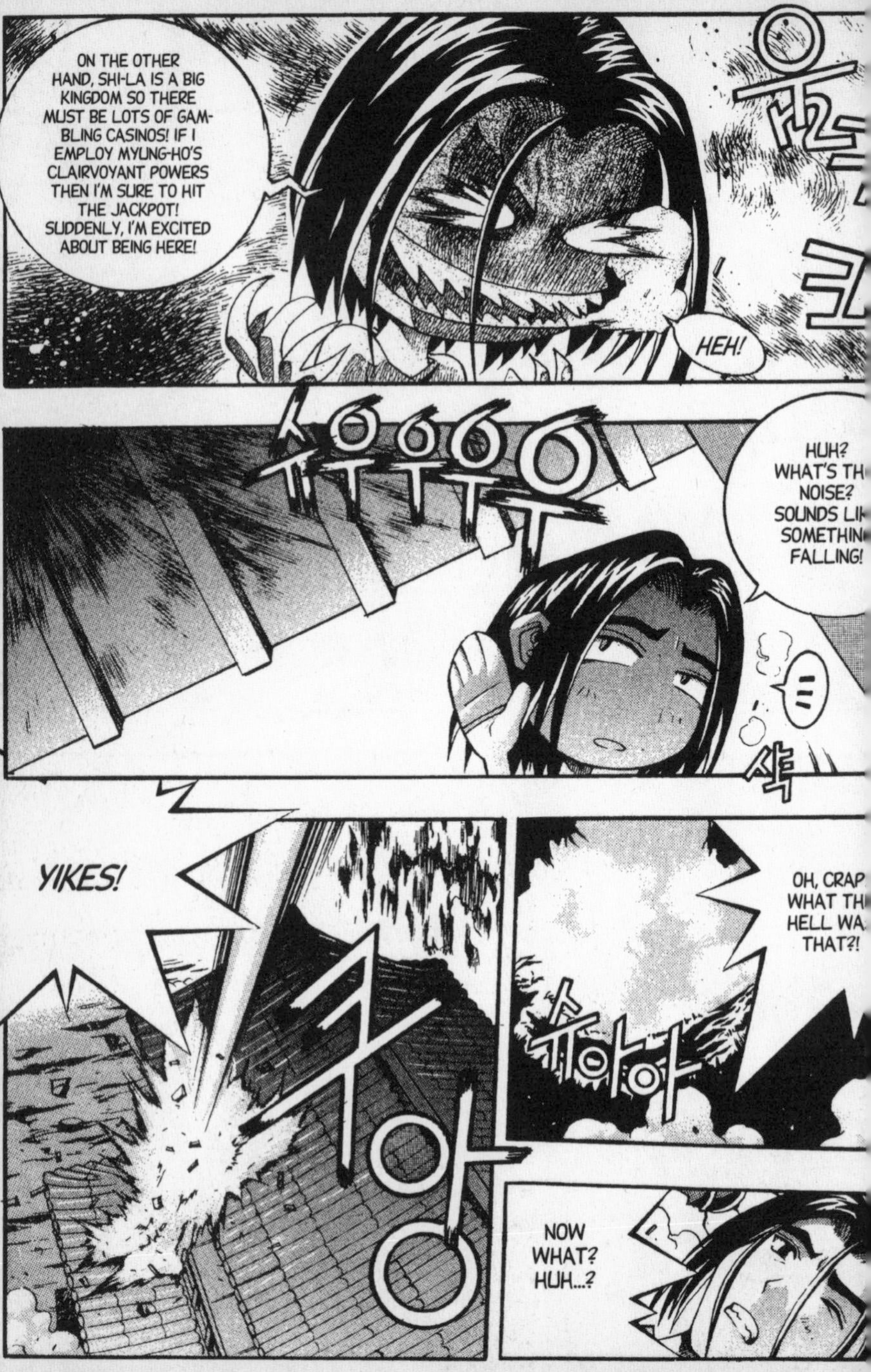
ON THE OTHER HAND, SHI-LA IS A BIG KINGDOM SO THERE MUST BE LOTS OF GAMBLING CASINOS! IF I EMPLOY MYUNG-HO'S CLAIRVOYANT POWERS THEN I'M SURE TO HIT THE JACKPOT! SUDDENLY, I'M EXCITED ABOUT BEING HERE!
HEH!
HUH? WHAT'S TH NOISE? SOUNDS LI SOMETHIN FALLING!
...
YIKES!
OH, CRAP WHAT TH HELL WA THAT?!
NOW WHAT? HUH...?

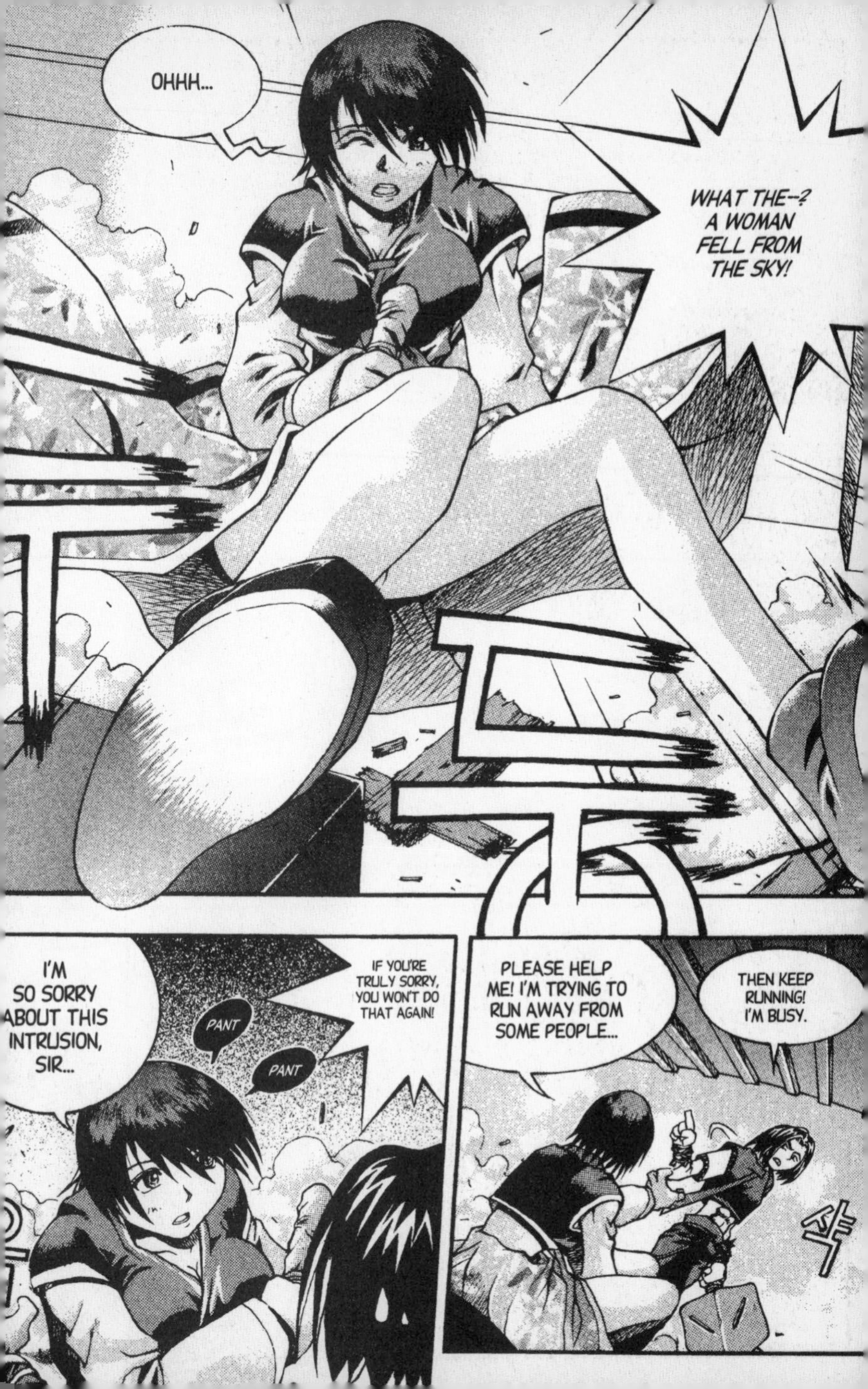
OHHH...
WHAT THE--? A WOMAN FELL FROM THE SKY!
I'M SO SORRY ABOUT THIS INTRUSION, SIR...
PANT
PANT
IF YOU'RE TRULY SORRY, YOU WON'T DO THAT AGAIN!
PLEASE HELP ME! I'M TRYING TO RUN AWAY FROM SOME PEOPLE...
THEN KEEP RUNNING! I'M BUSY.

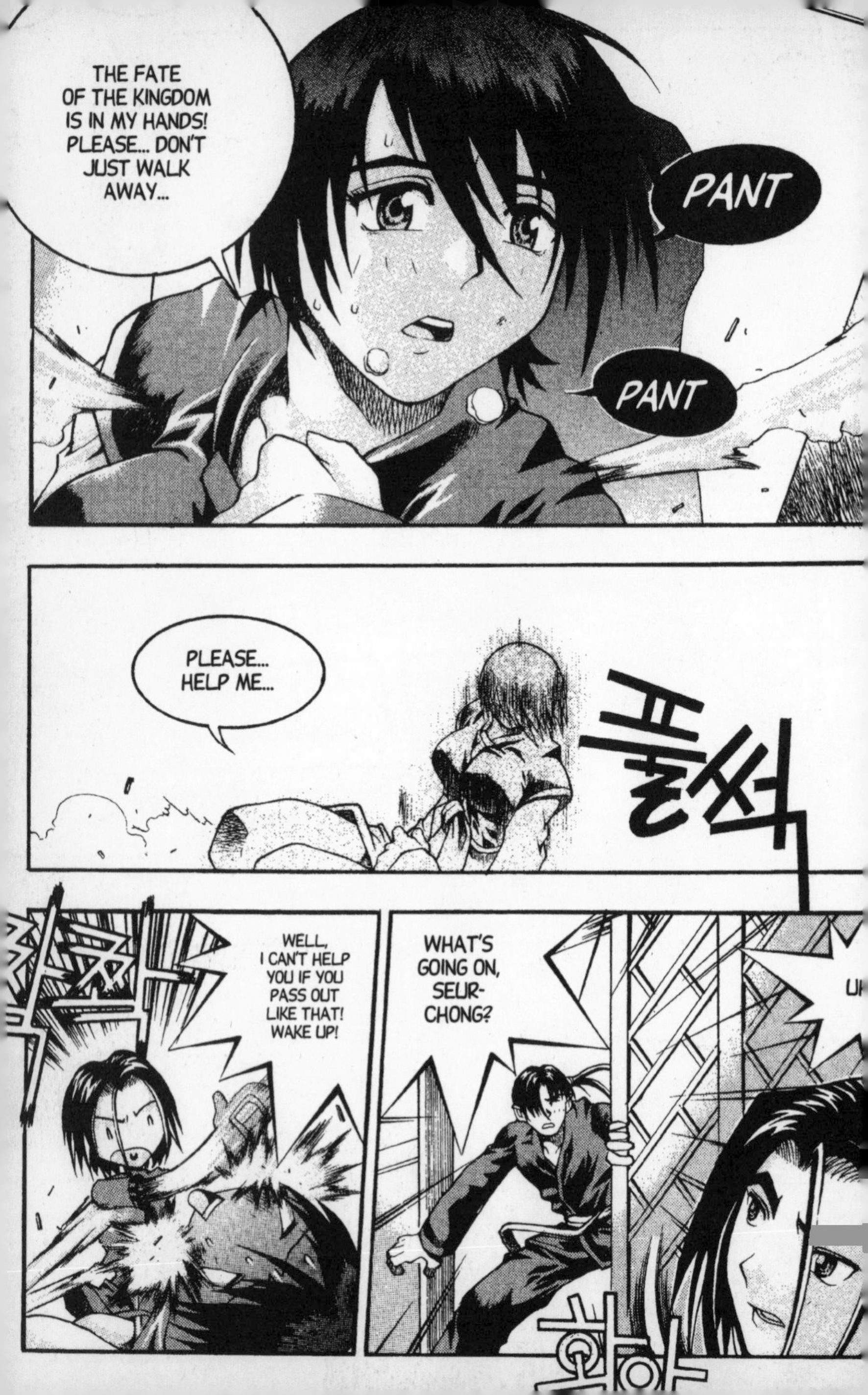
THE FATE OF THE KINGDOM IS IN MY HANDS! PLEASE... DON'T JUST WALK AWAY...
PANT
PANT
PLEASE... HELP ME...
풀썩
WELL, I CAN'T HELP YOU IF YOU PASS OUT LIKE THAT! WAKE UP!
WHAT'S GOING ON, SEUR-CHONG?

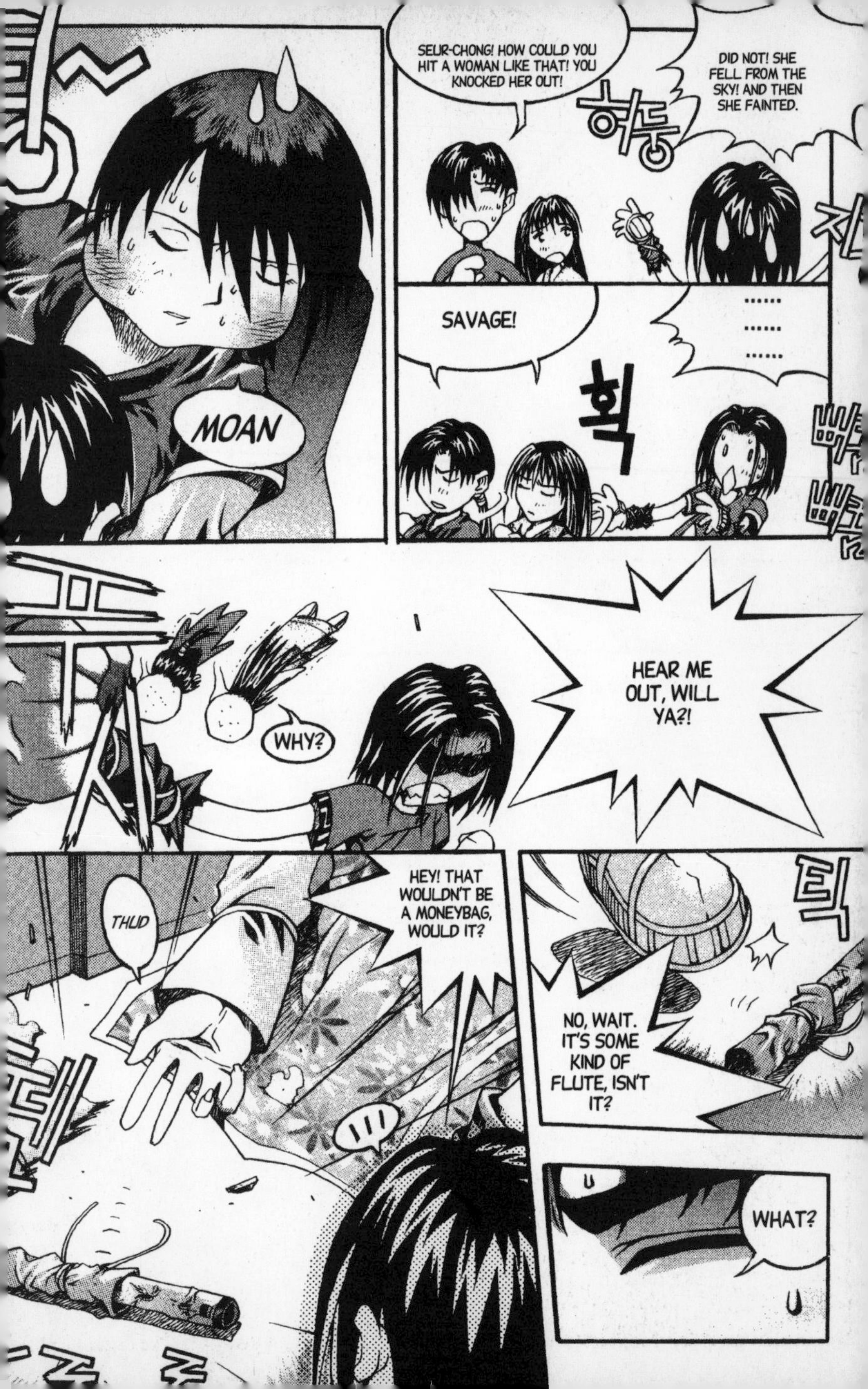
MOAN
SEUR-CHONG! HOW COULD YOU HIT A WOMAN LIKE THAT! YOU KNOCKED HER OUT!
DID NOT! SHE FELL FROM THE SKY! AND THEN SHE FAINTED.
SAVAGE!
......
......
......
WHY?
HEAR ME OUT, WILL YA?!
THUD
HEY! THAT WOULDN'T BE A MONEYBAG, WOULD IT?
NO, WAIT. IT'S SOME KIND OF FLUTE, ISN'T IT?
WHAT?

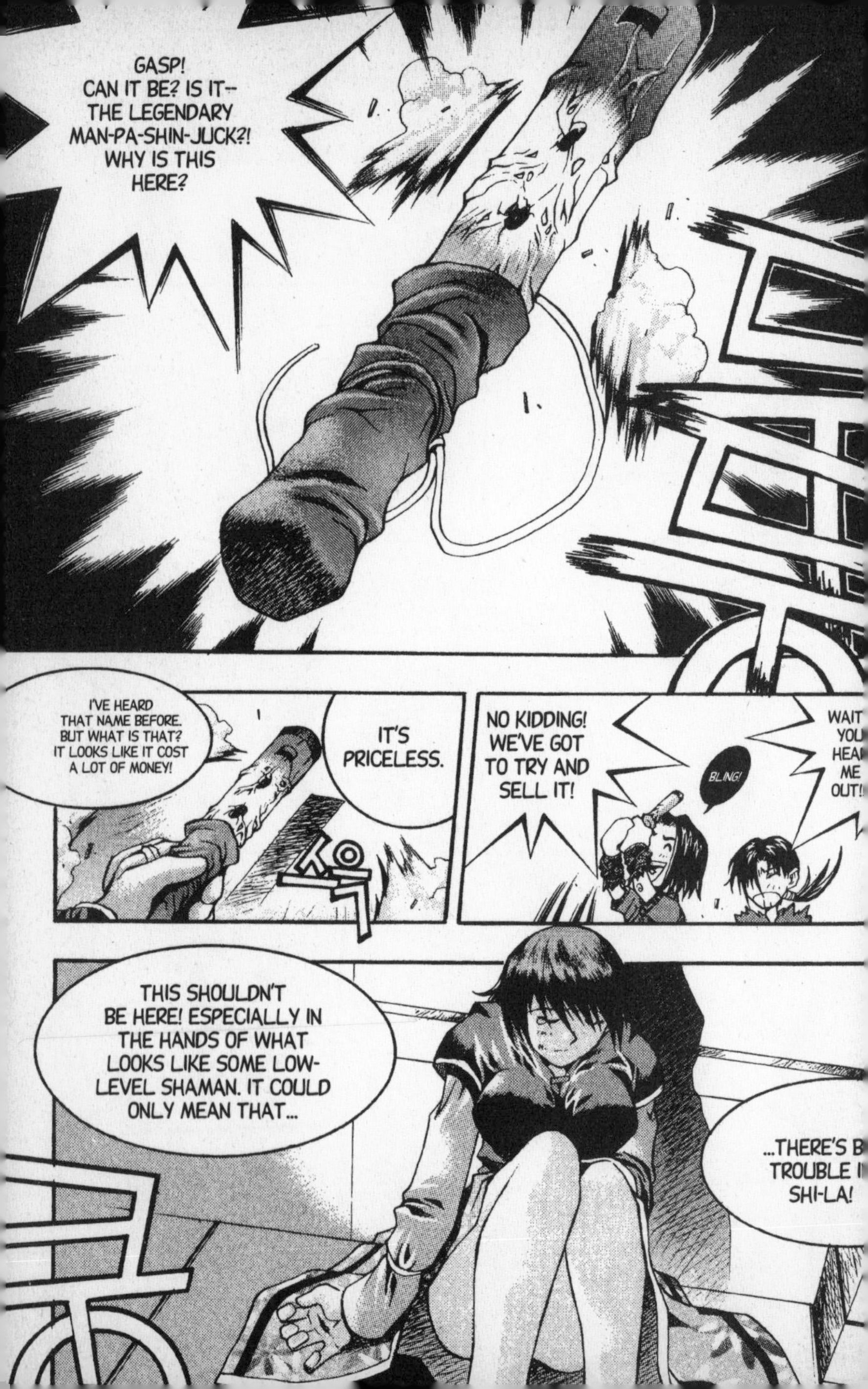
GASP! CAN IT BE? IS IT-- THE LEGENDARY MAN-PA-SHIN-JUCK?! WHY IS THIS HERE?
I'VE HEARD THAT NAME BEFORE. BUT WHAT IS THAT? IT LOOKS LIKE IT COST A LOT OF MONEY!
IT'S PRICELESS.
NO KIDDING! WE'VE GOT TO TRY AND SELL IT!
BLING!
WAIT YOU HEA ME OUT!
THIS SHOULDN'T BE HERE! ESPECIALLY IN THE HANDS OF WHAT LOOKS LIKE SOME LOW-LEVEL SHAMAN. IT COULD ONLY MEAN THAT...
...THERE'S B TROUBLE I SHI-LA!

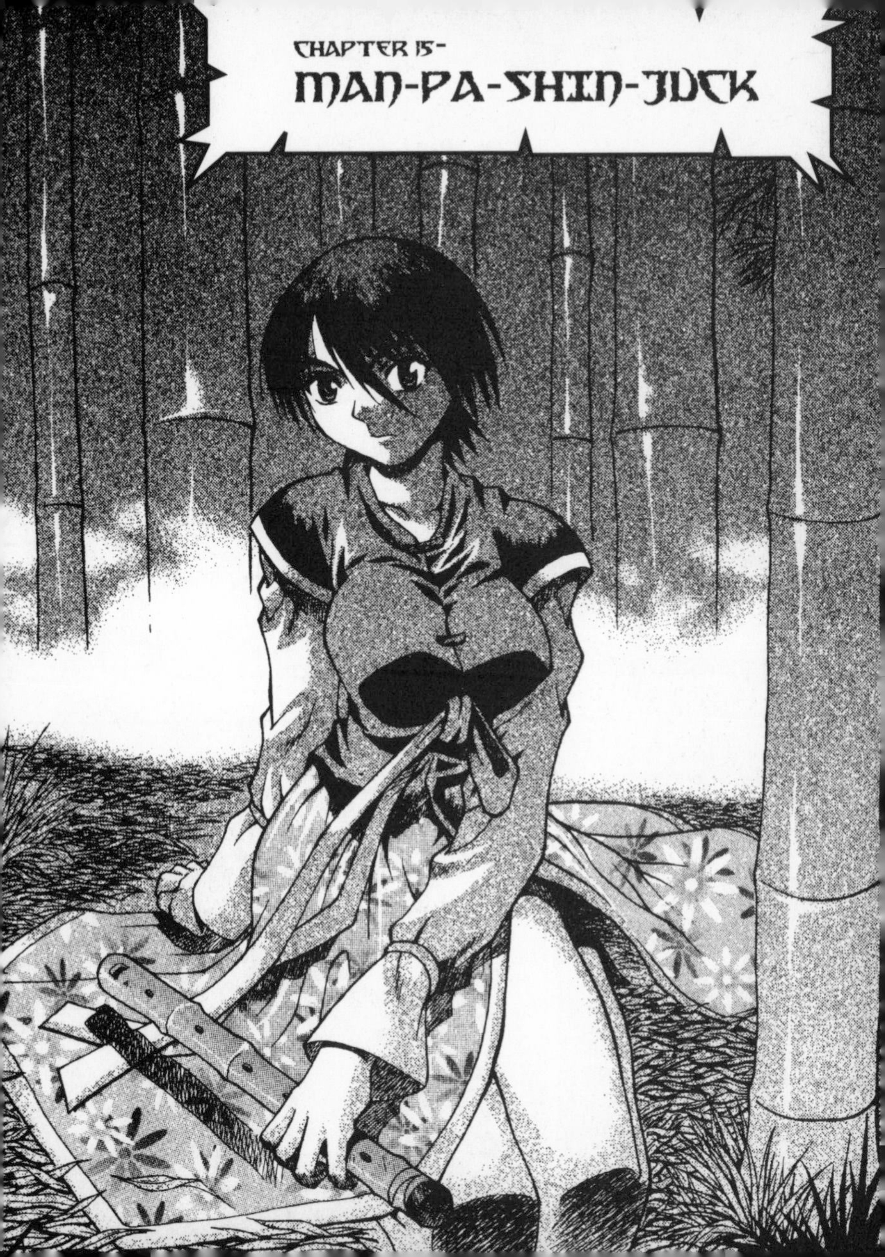
CHAPTER 15-
MAN-PA-SHIN-JUCK

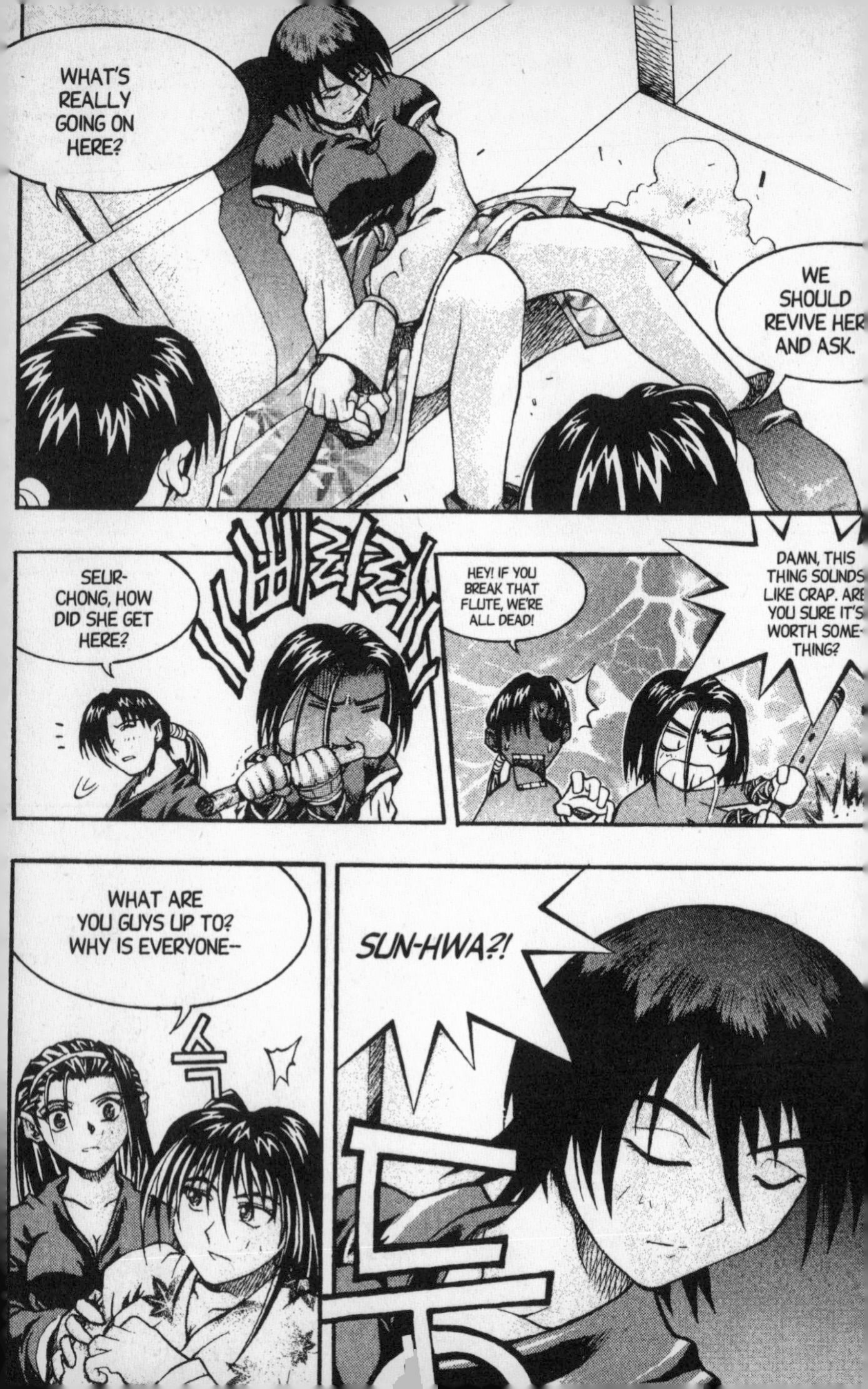
WHAT'S REALLY GOING ON HERE?
WE SHOULD REVIVE HER AND ASK.
SEUR-CHONG, HOW DID SHE GET HERE?
HEY! IF YOU BREAK THAT FLUTE, WE'RE ALL DEAD!
DAMN, THIS THING SOUNDS LIKE CRAP. ARE YOU SURE IT'S WORTH SOME-THING?
WHAT ARE YOU GUYS UP TO? WHY IS EVERYONE--
SUN-HWA?!

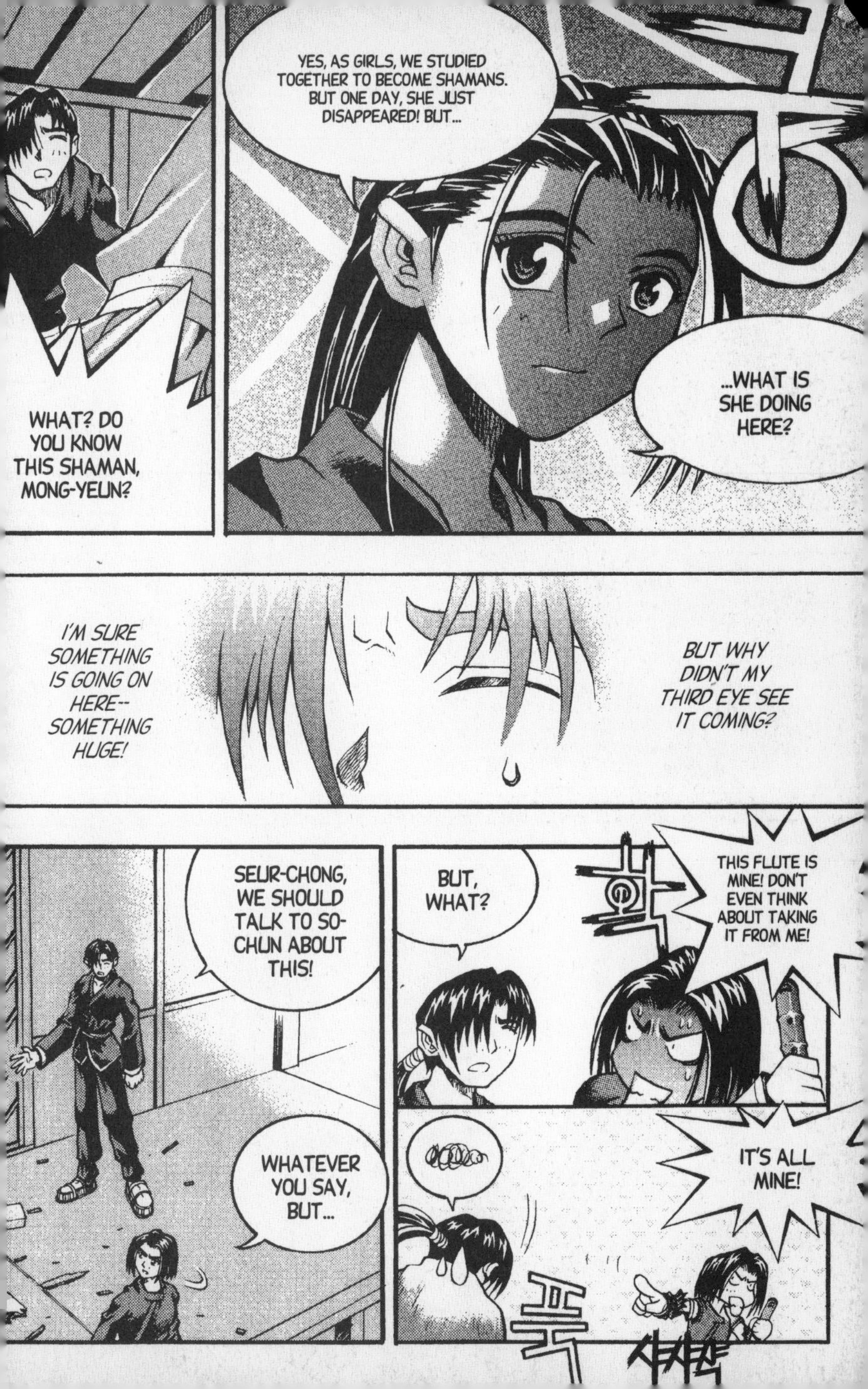
WHAT? DO YOU KNOW THIS SHAMAN, MONG-YEUN?
YES, AS GIRLS, WE STUDIED TOGETHER TO BECOME SHAMANS. BUT ONE DAY, SHE JUST DISAPPEARED! BUT...
...WHAT IS SHE DOING HERE?
I'M SURE SOMETHING IS GOING ON HERE-- SOMETHING HUGE!
BUT WHY DIDN'T MY THIRD EYE SEE IT COMING?
SEUR-CHONG, WE SHOULD TALK TO SO-CHUN ABOUT THIS!
WHATEVER YOU SAY, BUT...
BUT, WHAT?
THIS FLUTE IS MINE! DON'T EVEN THINK ABOUT TAKING IT FROM ME!
IT'S ALL MINE!

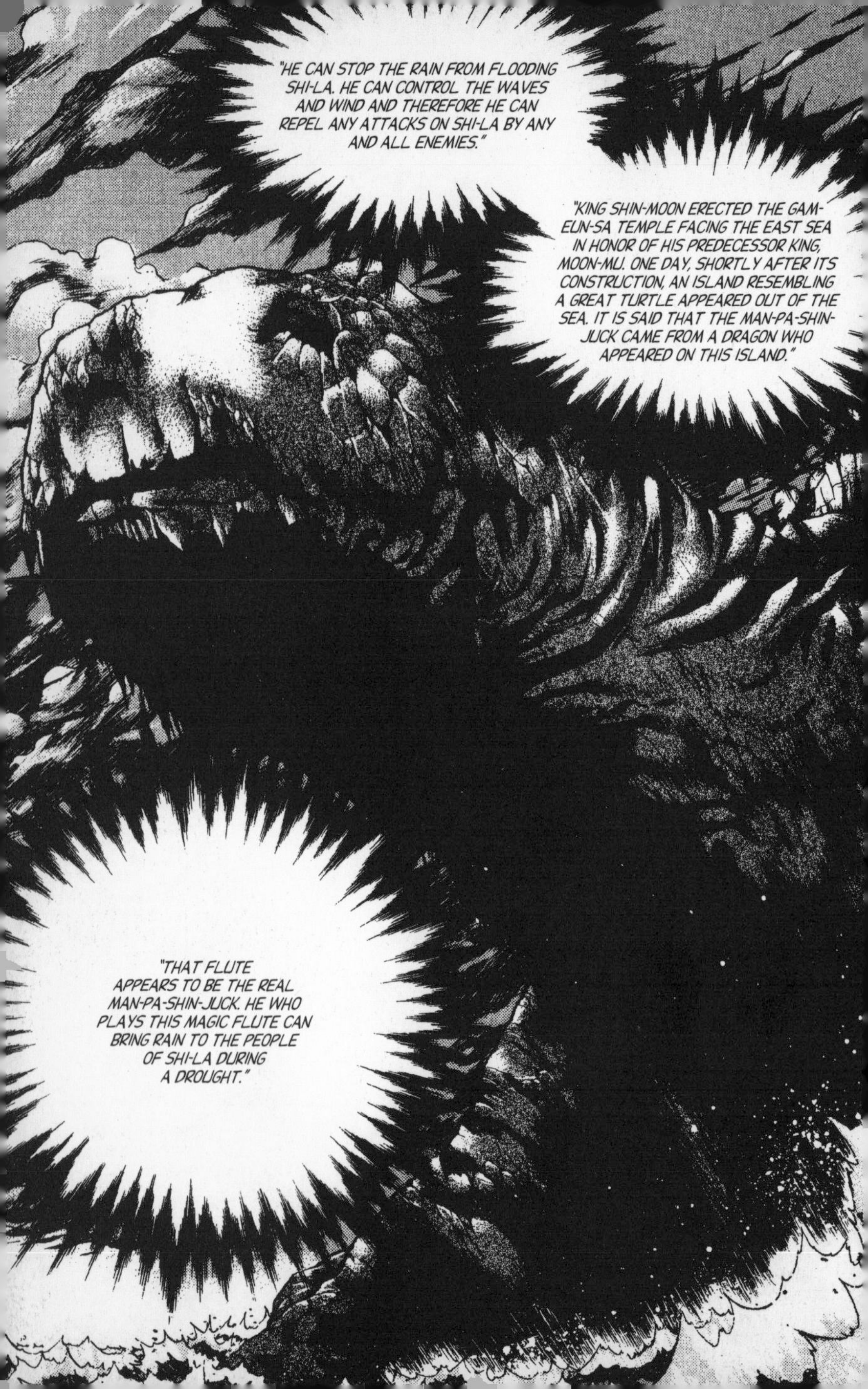
"HE CAN STOP THE RAIN FROM FLOODING SHI-LA. HE CAN CONTROL THE WAVES AND WIND AND THEREFORE HE CAN REPEL ANY ATTACKS ON SHI-LA BY ANY AND ALL ENEMIES."
"KING SHIN-MOON ERECTED THE GAM-EUN-SA TEMPLE FACING THE EAST SEA IN HONOR OF HIS PREDECESSOR KING, MOON-MU. ONE DAY, SHORTLY AFTER ITS CONSTRUCTION, AN ISLAND RESEMBLING A GREAT TURTLE APPEARED OUT OF THE SEA. IT IS SAID THAT THE MAN-PA-SHIN-JUCK CAME FROM A DRAGON WHO APPEARED ON THIS ISLAND."
"THAT FLUTE APPEARS TO BE THE REAL MAN-PA-SHIN-JUCK. HE WHO PLAYS THIS MAGIC FLUTE CAN BRING RAIN TO THE PEOPLE OF SHI-LA DURING A DROUGHT."

"I HEAR IT'S KEPT IN A SPECIAL VAULT CALLED THE CHUN-JON-GO IN THE CITY OF WAL-SUNG."
"THE NAME MAN-PA-SHIN-JUCK MEANS 'TAME THE WAVES AND BRING PEACE INTO THIS WORLD' AND THE FLUTE HAS BECOME A NATIONAL TREASURE."
"THE SHAMANS WHO TAKE CARE OF THE GUARDIAN DRAGON OF SHI-LA ALSO PROTECT THIS MAGIC FLUTE..."

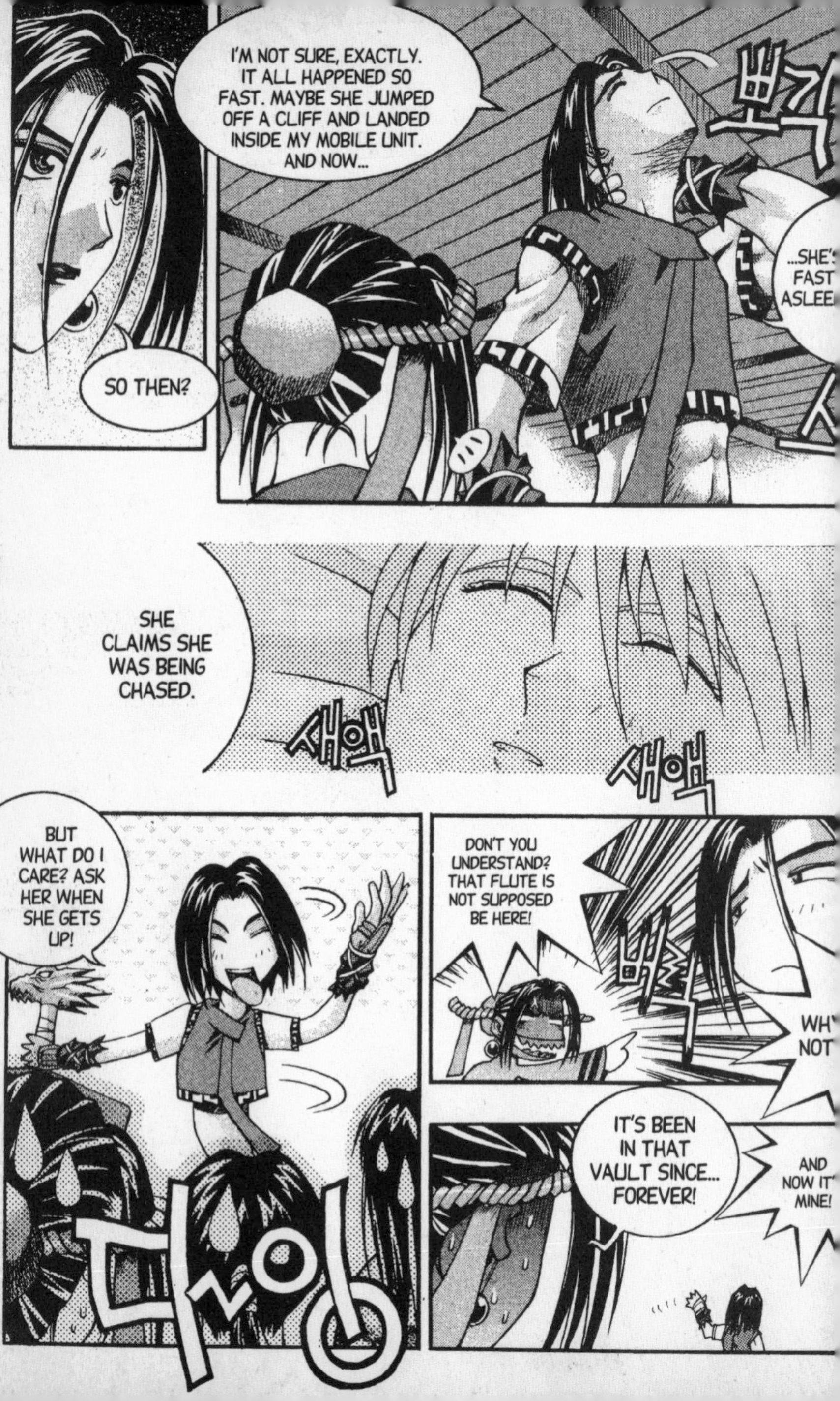
SO THEN?
I'M NOT SURE, EXACTLY. IT ALL HAPPENED SO FAST. MAYBE SHE JUMPED OFF A CLIFF AND LANDED INSIDE MY MOBILE UNIT. AND NOW...
...SHE'S FAST ASLEE
SHE CLAIMS SHE WAS BEING CHASED.
BUT WHAT DO I CARE? ASK HER WHEN SHE GETS UP!
DON'T YOU UNDERSTAND? THAT FLUTE IS NOT SUPPOSED BE HERE!
WH' NOT
IT'S BEEN IN THAT VAULT SINCE... FOREVER!
AND NOW IT' MINE!

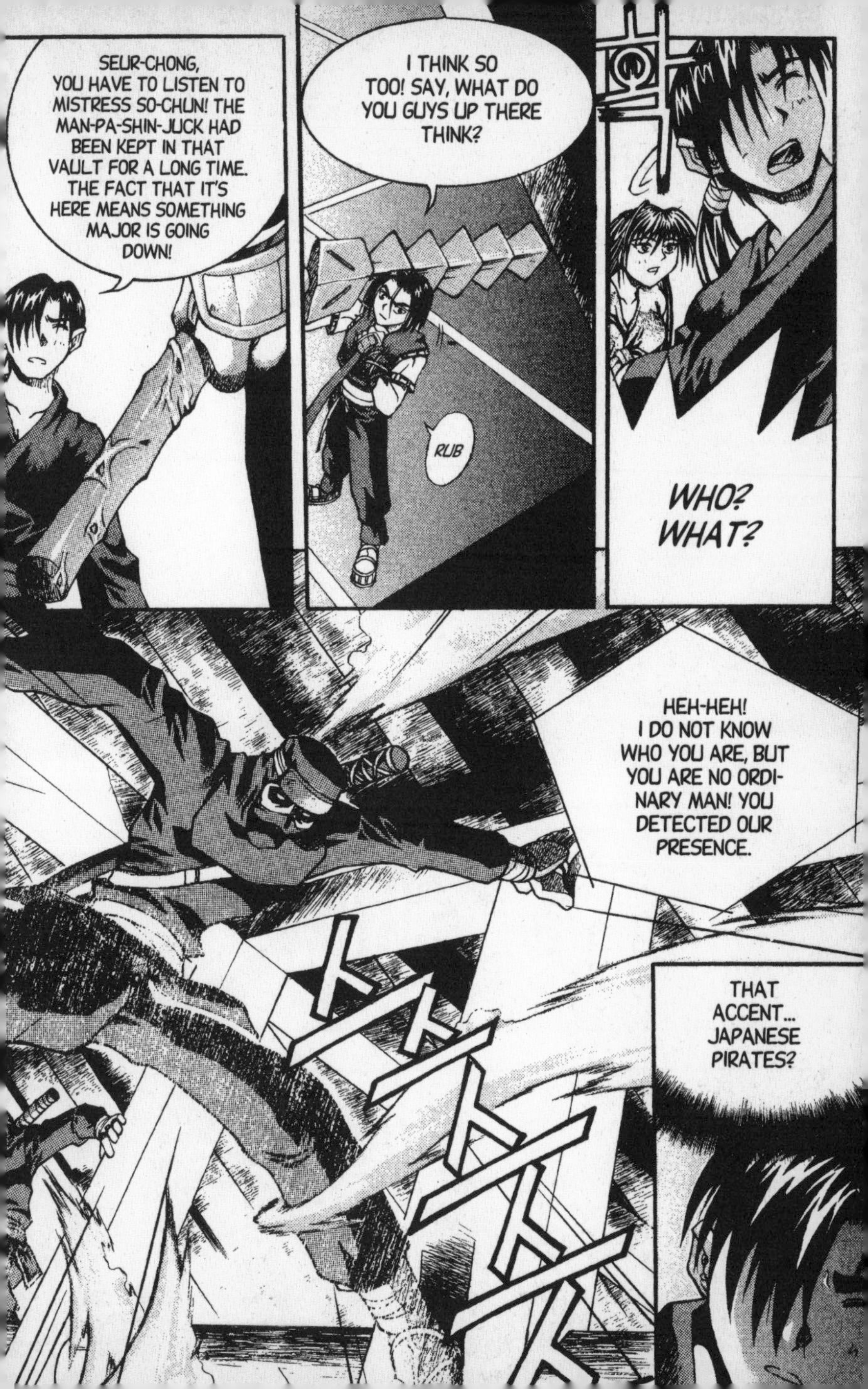
SEUR-CHONG, YOU HAVE TO LISTEN TO MISTRESS SO-CHUN! THE MAN-PA-SHIN-JUCK HAD BEEN KEPT IN THAT VAULT FOR A LONG TIME. THE FACT THAT IT'S HERE MEANS SOMETHING MAJOR IS GOING DOWN!
I THINK SO TOO! SAY, WHAT DO YOU GUYS UP THERE THINK?
RUB
WHO? WHAT?
HEH-HEH! I DO NOT KNOW WHO YOU ARE, BUT YOU ARE NO ORDI-NARY MAN! YOU DETECTED OUR PRESENCE.
THAT ACCENT... JAPANESE PIRATES?

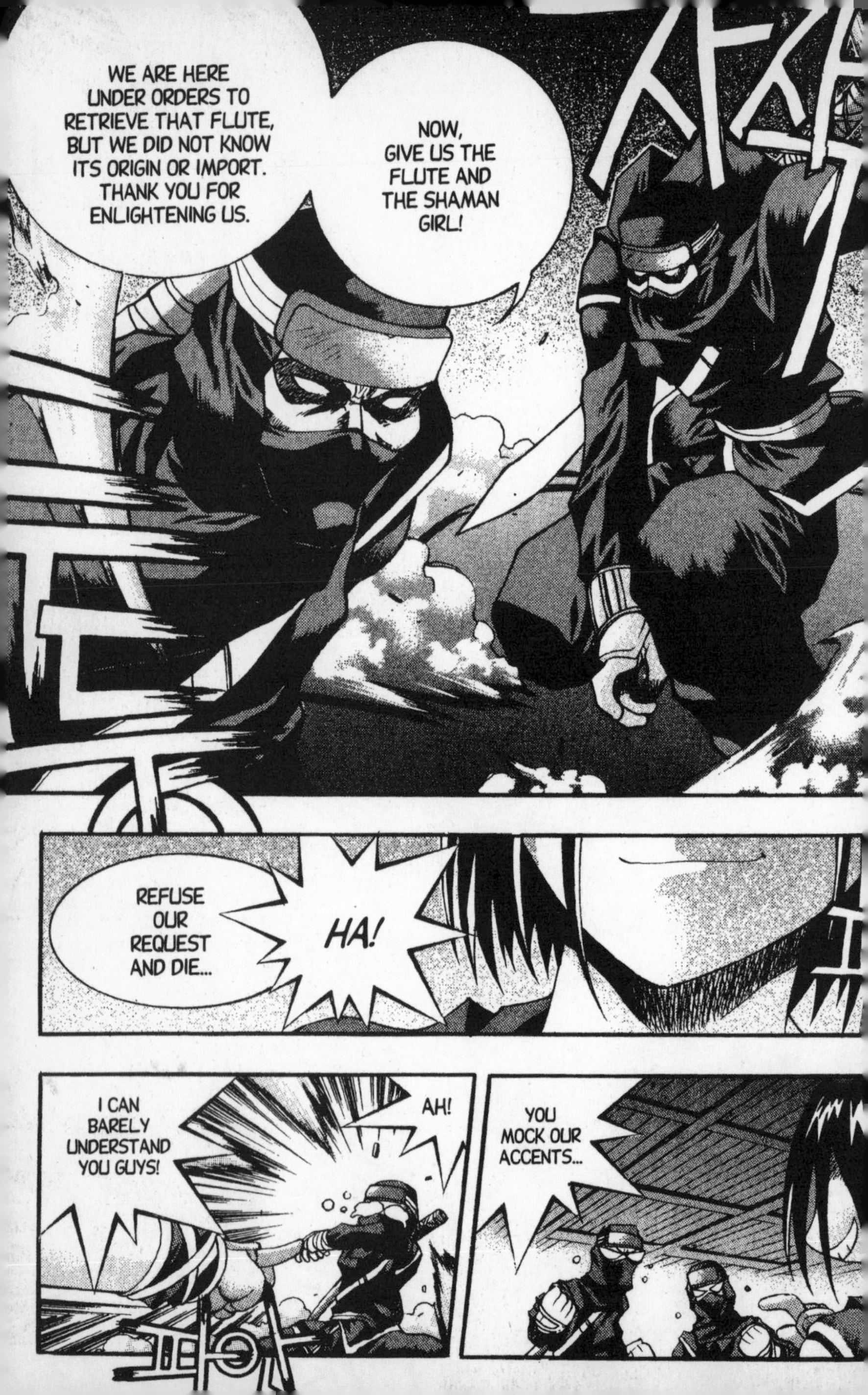
WE ARE HERE UNDER ORDERS TO RETRIEVE THAT FLUTE, BUT WE DID NOT KNOW ITS ORIGIN OR IMPORT. THANK YOU FOR ENLIGHTENING US.
NOW, GIVE US THE FLUTE AND THE SHAMAN GIRL!
REFUSE OUR REQUEST AND DIE...
HA!
I CAN BARELY UNDERSTAND YOU GUYS!
AH!
YOU MOCK OUR ACCENTS...

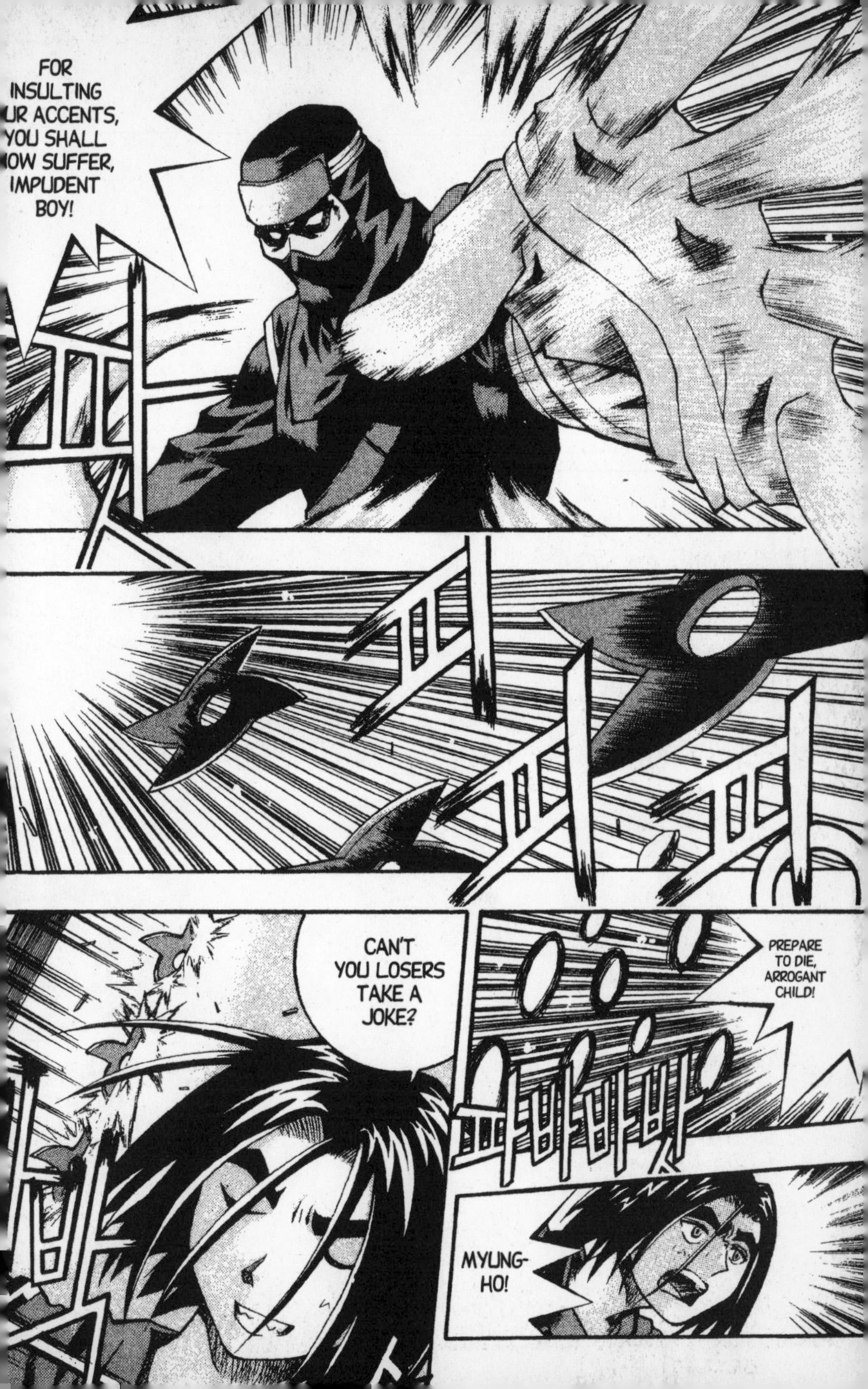
FOR INSULTING UR ACCENTS, YOU SHALL IOW SUFFER, IMPUDENT BOY!
CAN'T YOU LOSERS TAKE A JOKE?
PREPARE TO DIE, ARROGANT CHILD!
MYUNG-HO!

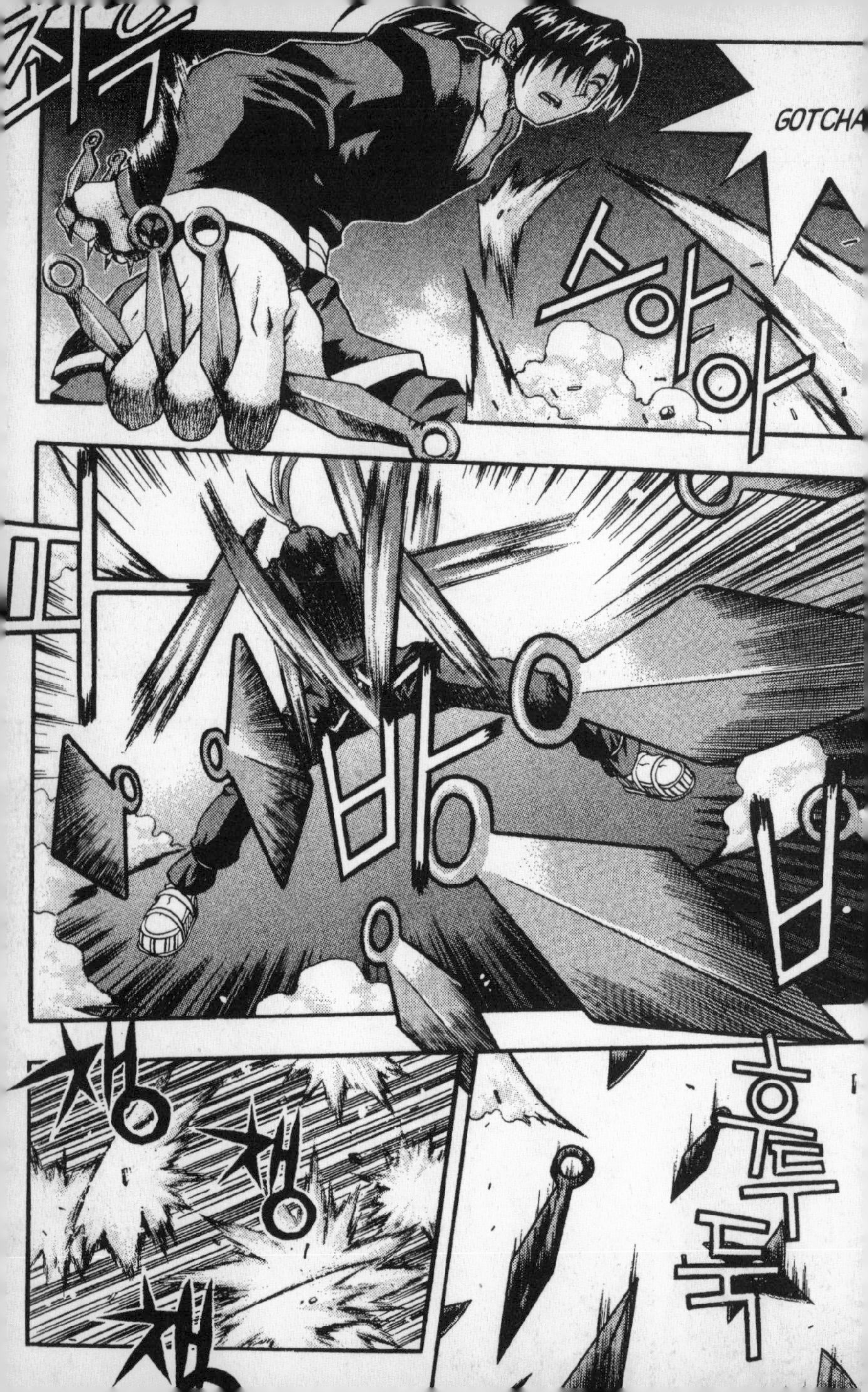
GOTCHA
챙
챙
챙

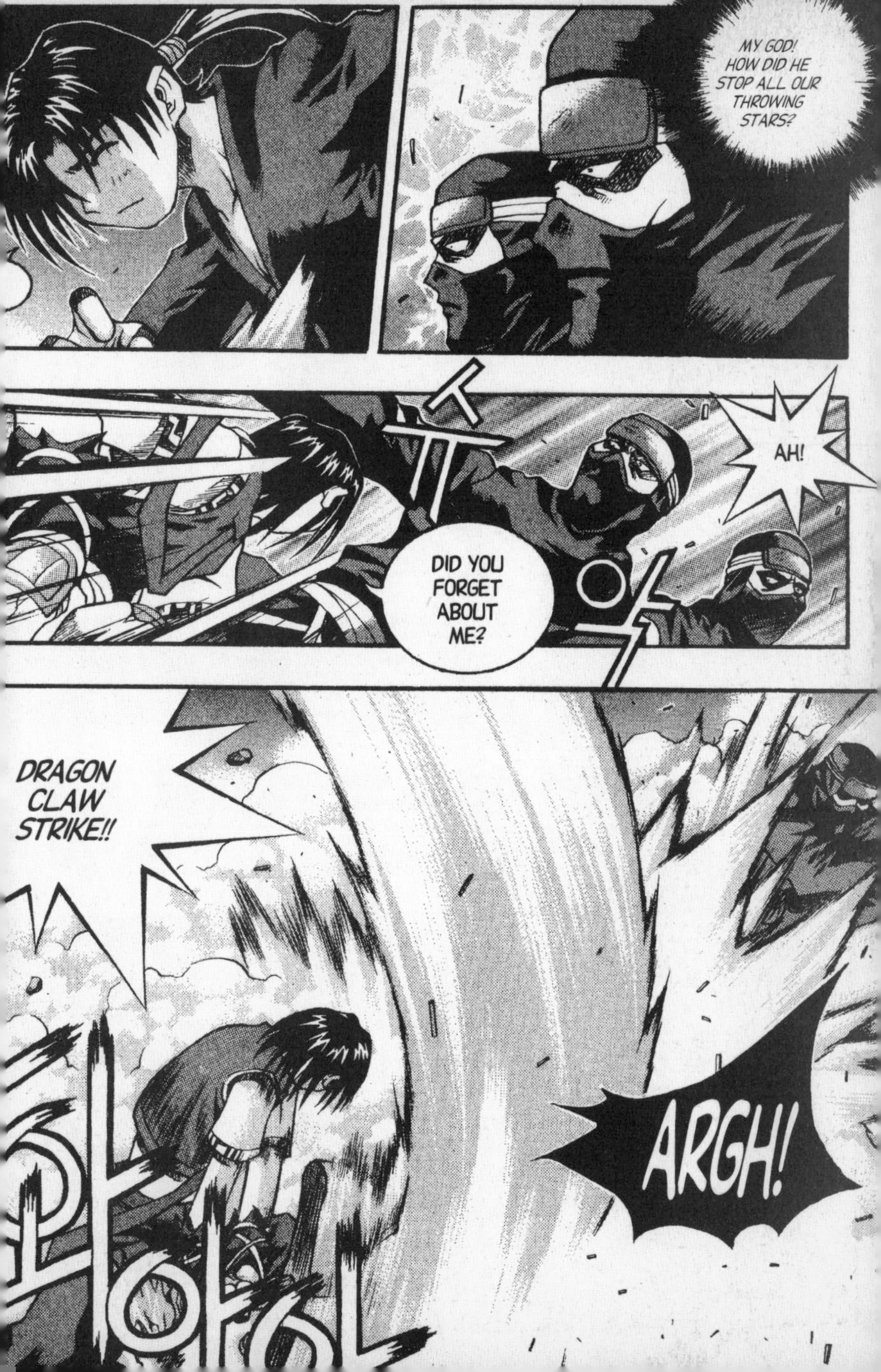
MY GOD! HOW DID HE STOP ALL OUR THROWING STARS?
AH!
DID YOU FORGET ABOUT ME?
DRAGON CLAW STRIKE!!
ARGH!

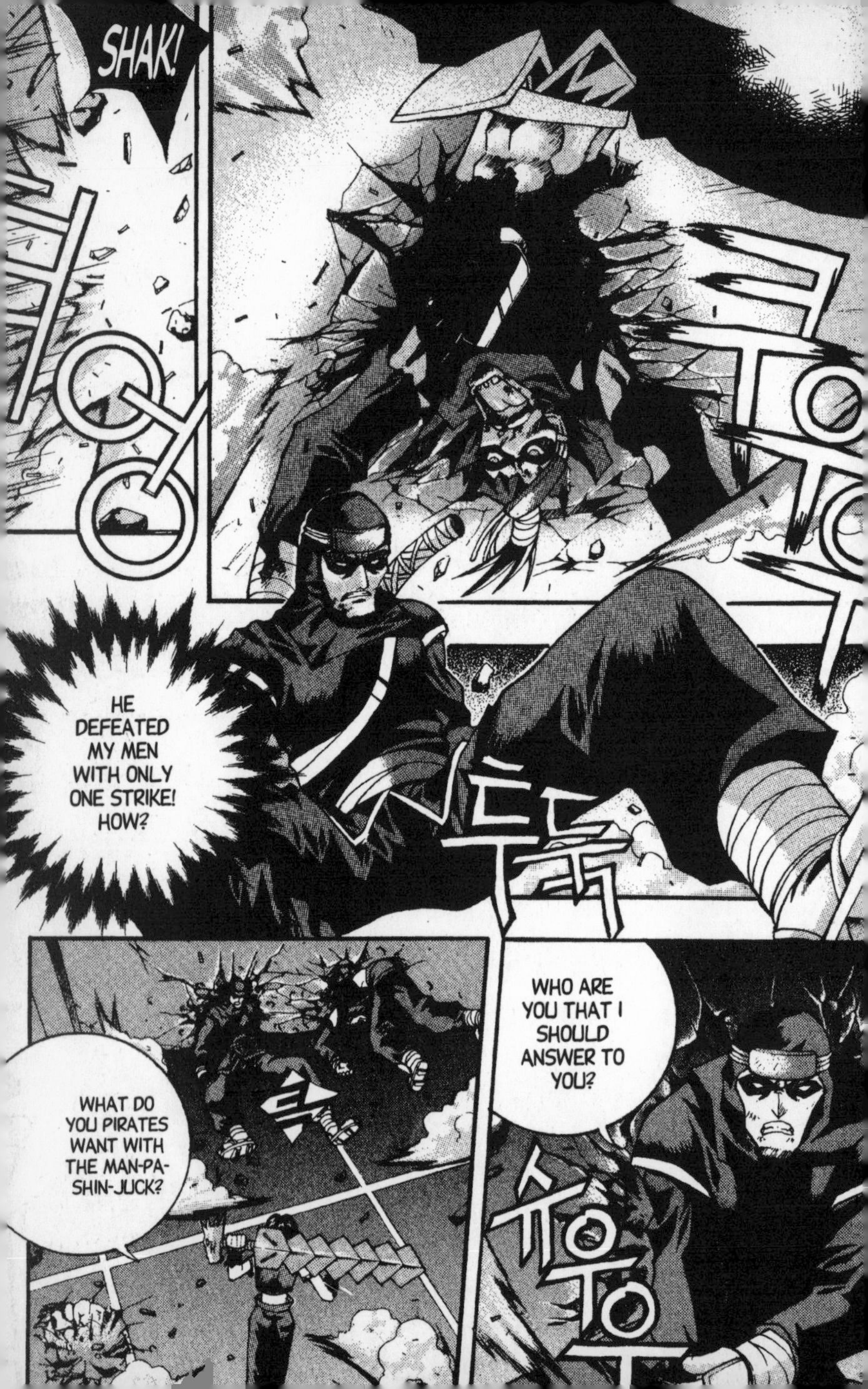
SHAK!
HE DEFEATED MY MEN WITH ONLY ONE STRIKE! HOW?
WHAT DO YOU PIRATES WANT WITH THE MAN-PA-SHIN-JUCK?
WHO ARE YOU THAT I SHOULD ANSWER TO YOU?

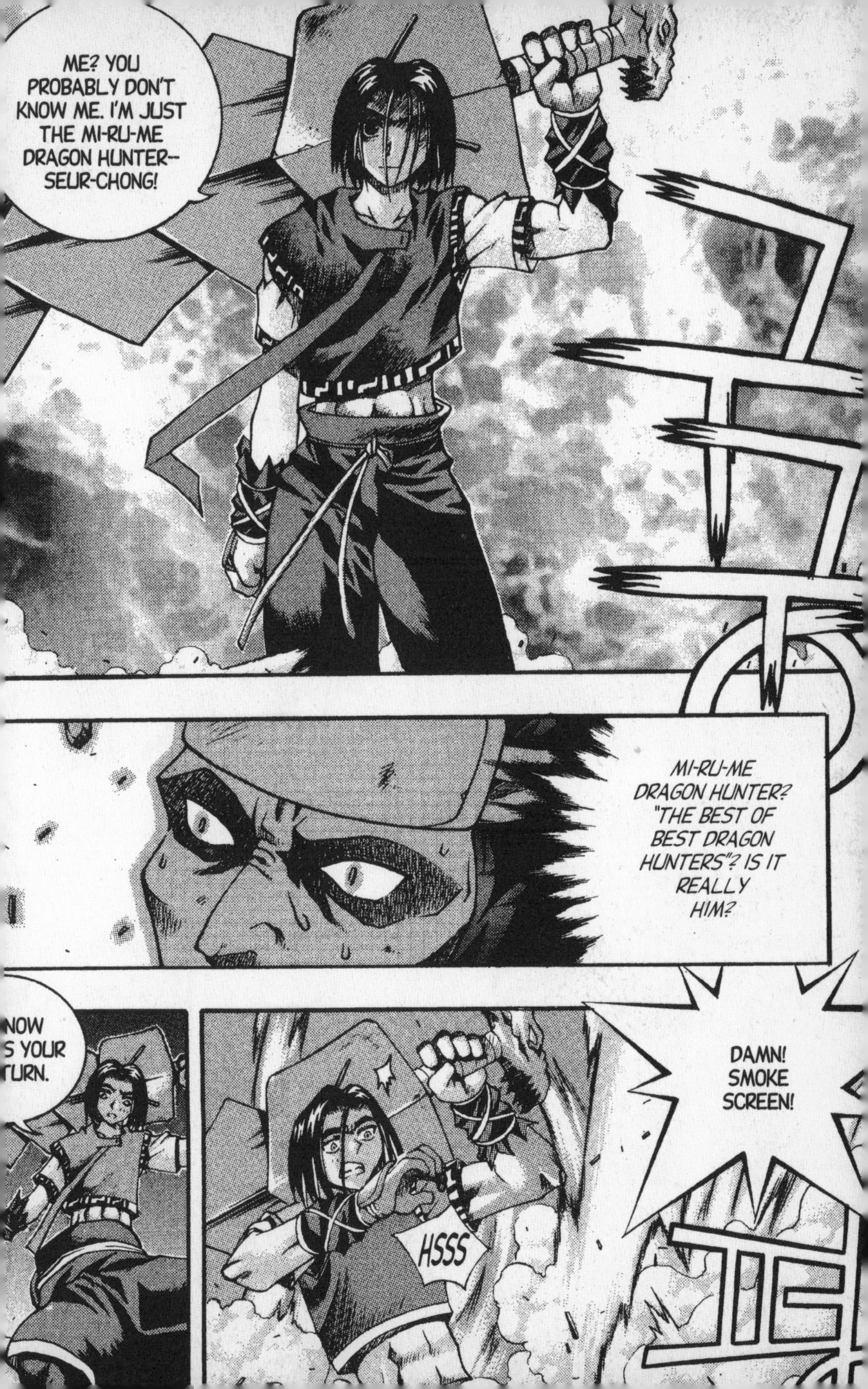

ME? YOU PROBABLY DON'T KNOW ME. I'M JUST THE MI-RU-ME DRAGON HUNTER--SEUR-CHONG!
MI-RU-ME DRAGON HUNTER? "THE BEST OF BEST DRAGON HUNTERS"? IS IT REALLY HIM?
NOW S YOUR TURN.
HSSS
DAMN! SMOKE SCREEN!

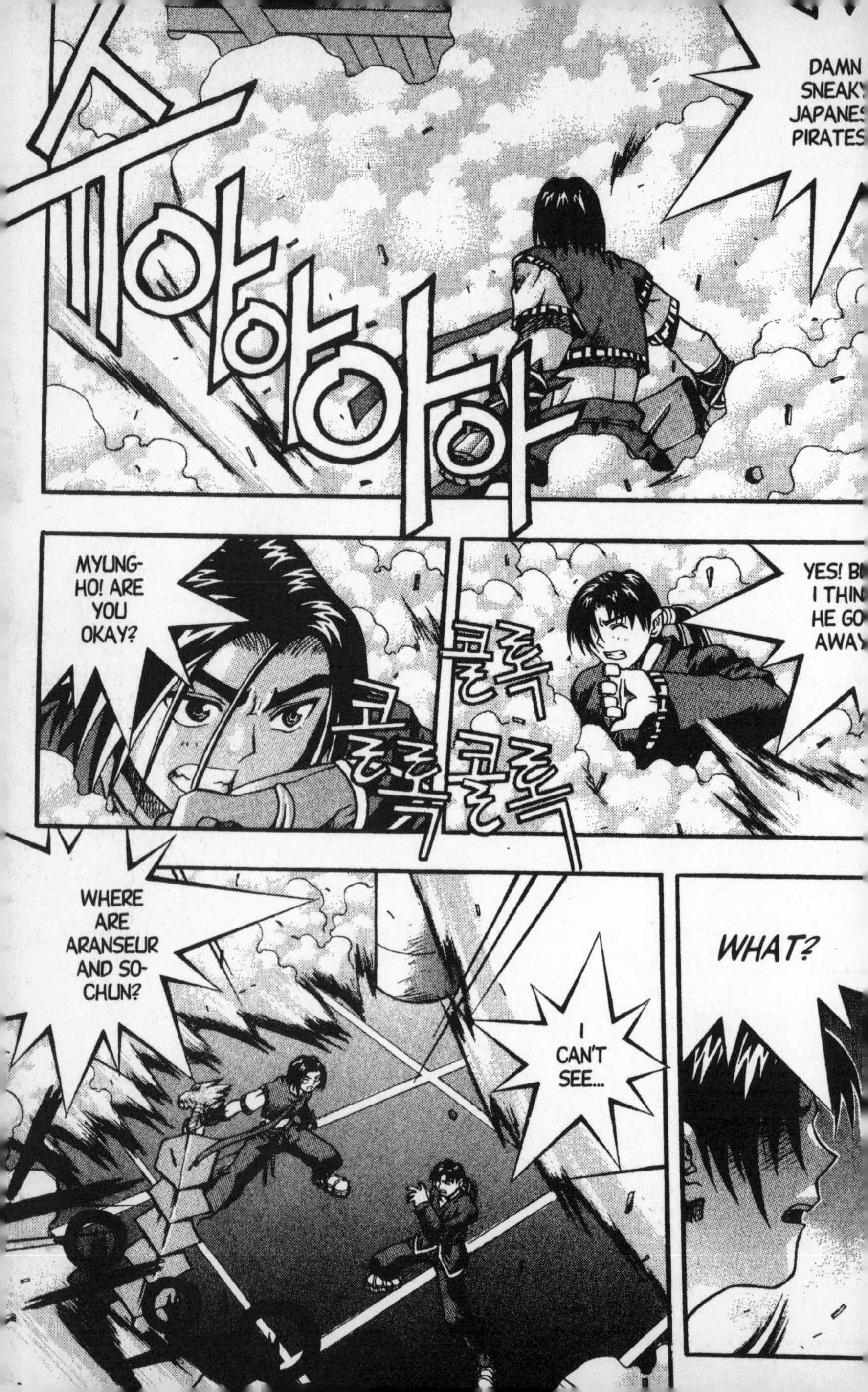
DAMN SNEAKY JAPANES PIRATES
끼야아아아
MYUNG-HO! ARE YOU OKAY?
콜록
콜록
콜록
YES! BU I THIN HE GO AWAY
WHERE ARE ARANSEUR AND SO-CHUN?
I CAN'T SEE...
WHAT?

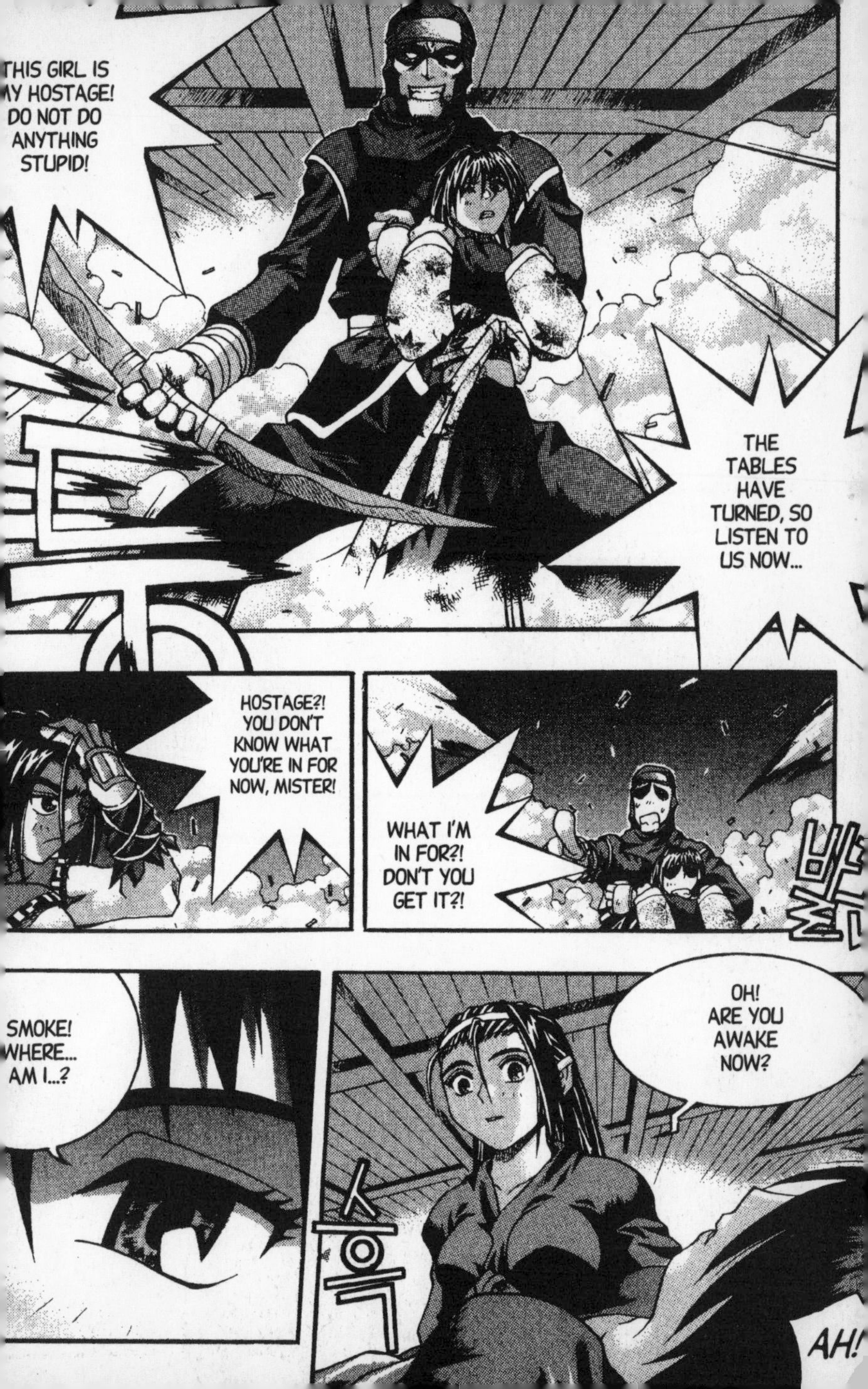
THIS GIRL IS MY HOSTAGE! DO NOT DO ANYTHING STUPID!
THE TABLES HAVE TURNED, SO LISTEN TO US NOW...
HOSTAGE?! YOU DON'T KNOW WHAT YOU'RE IN FOR NOW, MISTER!
WHAT I'M IN FOR?! DON'T YOU GET IT?!
SMOKE! WHERE... AM I...?
OH! ARE YOU AWAKE NOW?
AH!

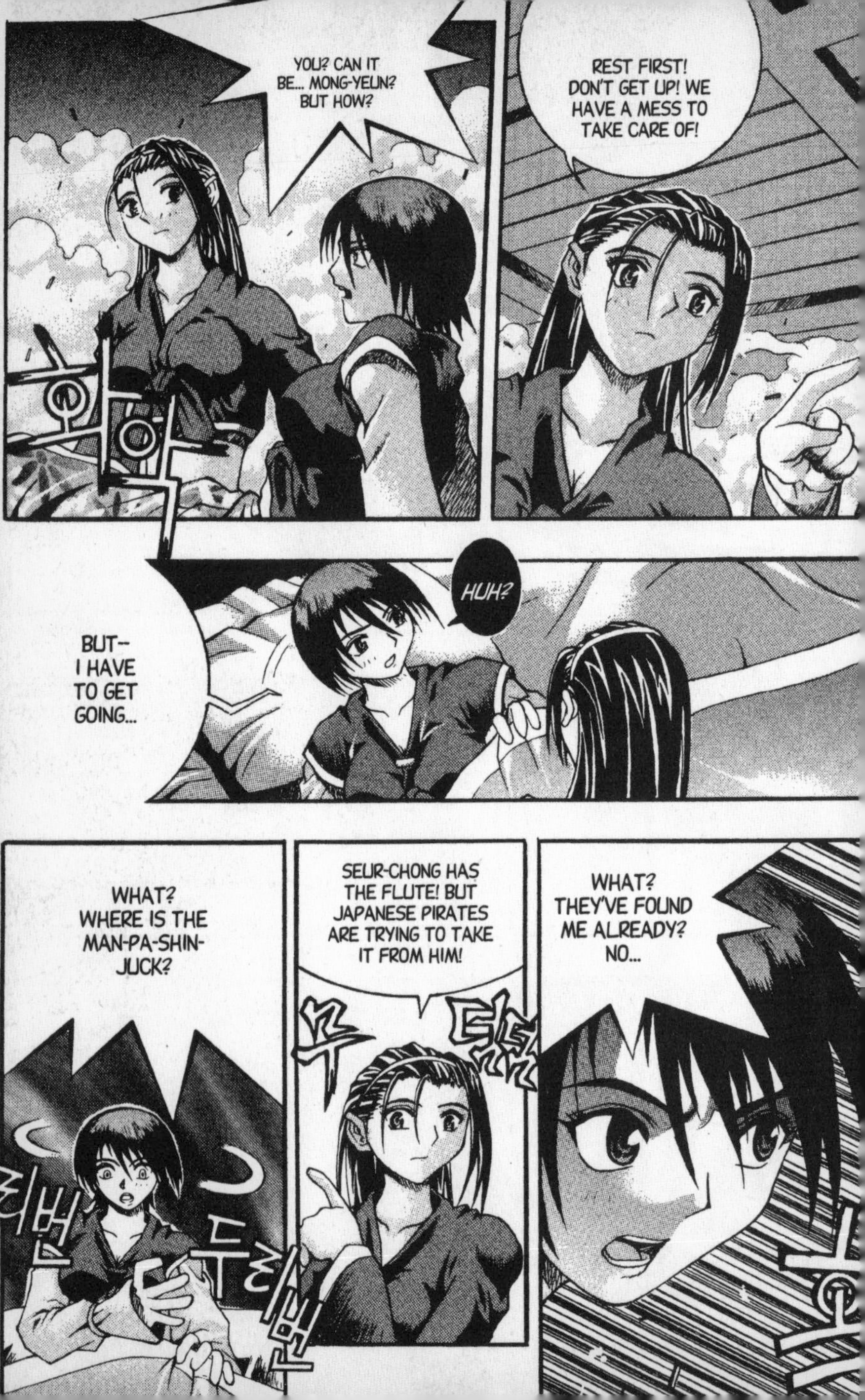
YOU? CAN IT BE... MONG-YEUN? BUT HOW?
REST FIRST! DON'T GET UP! WE HAVE A MESS TO TAKE CARE OF!
BUT-- I HAVE TO GET GOING...
HUH?
WHAT? WHERE IS THE MAN-PA-SHIN-JUCK?
SEUR-CHONG HAS THE FLUTE! BUT JAPANESE PIRATES ARE TRYING TO TAKE IT FROM HIM!
WHAT? THEY'VE FOUND ME ALREADY? NO...

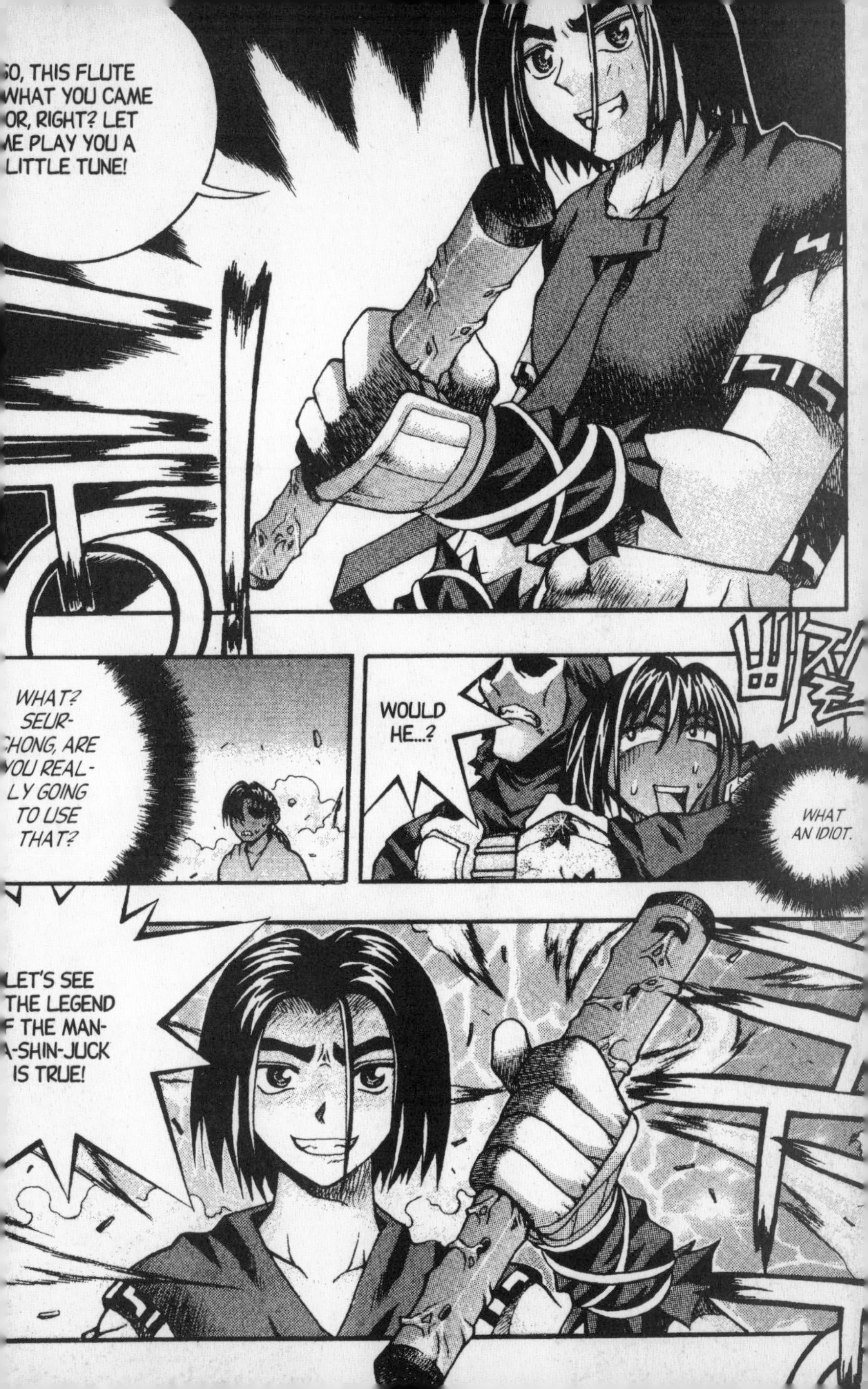
SO, THIS FLUTE WHAT YOU CAME OR, RIGHT? LET ME PLAY YOU A LITTLE TUNE!
WHAT? SEUR-CHONG, ARE YOU REAL-LY GOING TO USE THAT?
WOULD HE...?
WHAT AN IDIOT.
LET'S SEE THE LEGEND F THE MAN-A-SHIN-JUCK IS TRUE!

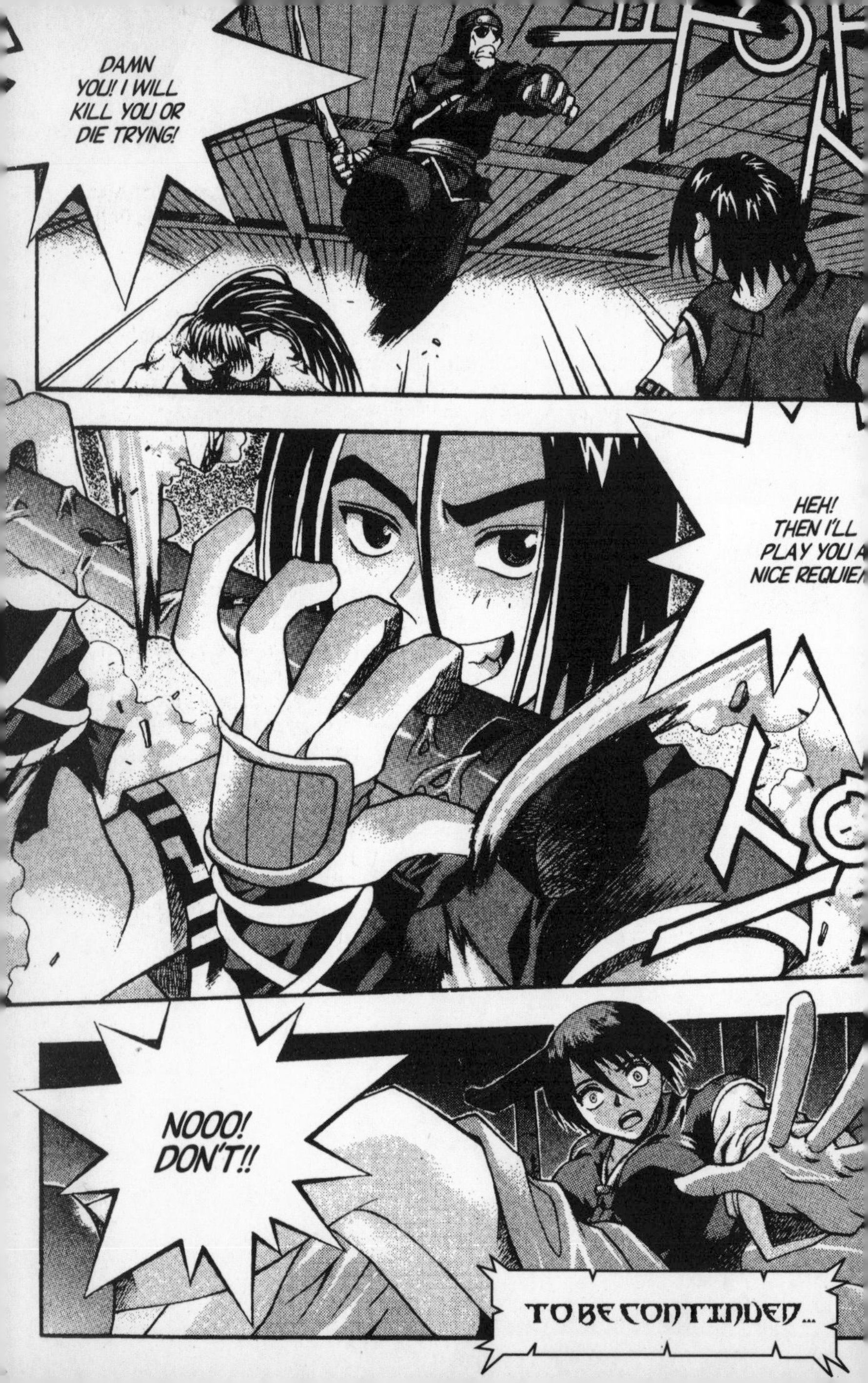
DAMN YOU! I WILL KILL YOU OR DIE TRYING!
HEH! THEN I'LL PLAY YOU A NICE REQUIE
NOOO! DON'T!!
TO BE CONTINUED...

The Studio Redstone Story (Chapter 3)

Ha-cha! We're only at our third issue and already I'm behind schedule. Not just because I'm lazy-- That's only part of it. Another reason is that I'm getting married in November (I may not be single by the time you read this volume). Due to wedding planning and preparation, I have been very busy and have fallen behind. I'm so sorry that production is behind schedule because of my personal life-- (deep bow)--I'll try to get back on track as soon as possible!

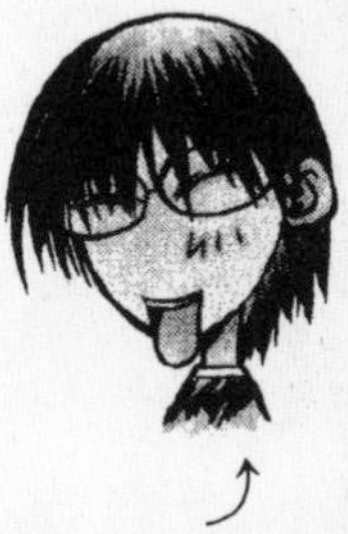

Hmm... I've become so obsessed with DVDs lately. Heh-heh. As I mentioned before, I have a PS2 but don't play it much. However, I started watching DVDs with my PS2 and have fallen in love with the system all over again. Sadly, DVDs are really expensive here and there is no DVD rental place in my area. The quality of the DVDs is really fantastic. I want to buy lots of DVDs but, alas, I don't have enough money. Sigh!

When I wrote to you in issue two, it was around early summer. As I write this, it is now late in the fall. I hope that my hands can draw faster than I write these things. Anyway, this married man will see you all in volume 4!

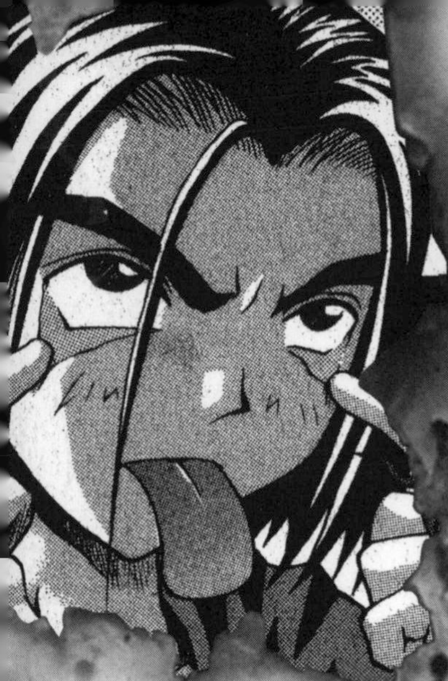

IN THE NEXT VOLUME OF DRAGON HUNTER

• • • • • •

Seur-Chong isn't known for his taste in tunes, but the sound of money pouring into his hands is always music to his ears. Even in the face of overwhelming odds, you can bet that Seur-Chong won't let go of the Man-Pa-Shin-Juck until somebody pays the piper--or, in other words, him!

Unfortunately for the young dragon hunter, the Japanese pirates aren't the only ones after him. When enemies both old and new join forces to beat the drums of war, will Seur-Chong be the one taking a pounding?

COWBOY BEBOP

shooting star

Story & Art by:
Cain Kuga

Original Concept by:
Hajime Yatate
©Sunrise

100% AUTHENTIC MANGA

TOKYOPOP®

NAMED TO THE N.Y. PUBLIC LIBRARY'S **Books** FOR THE *Teen Age* 2003 List

MORE SPIKE
MORE JET
MORE COWBOY BEBOP

Also Available:
Cowboy Bebop Volumes 1, 2, 3 & Boxed Set
Cowboy Bebop Anime Guides
Volumes 1-6 in stores now! Collect them all!!

T TEEN AGE 13+

www.TOKYOPOP.com

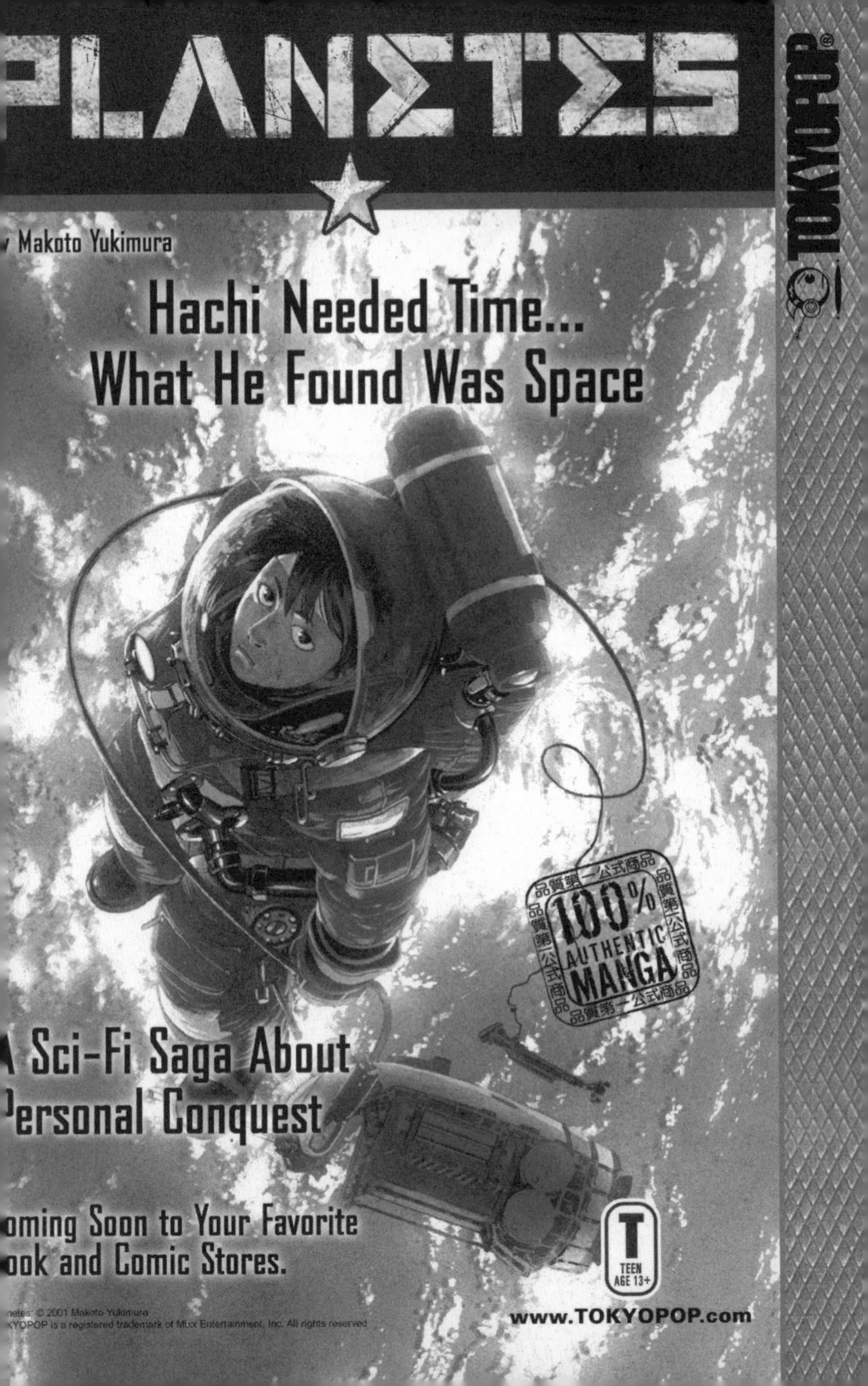
PLANETES
TOKYOPOP®
y Makoto Yukimura
Hachi Needed Time...
What He Found Was Space
100% AUTHENTIC MANGA
品質第一公式商品
A Sci-Fi Saga About
Personal Conquest
oming Soon to Your Favorite
ook and Comic Stores.
T TEEN AGE 13+
netes: © 2001 Makoto Yukimura
KYOPOP is a registered trademark of Mixx Entertainment, Inc. All rights reserved
www.TOKYOPOP.com

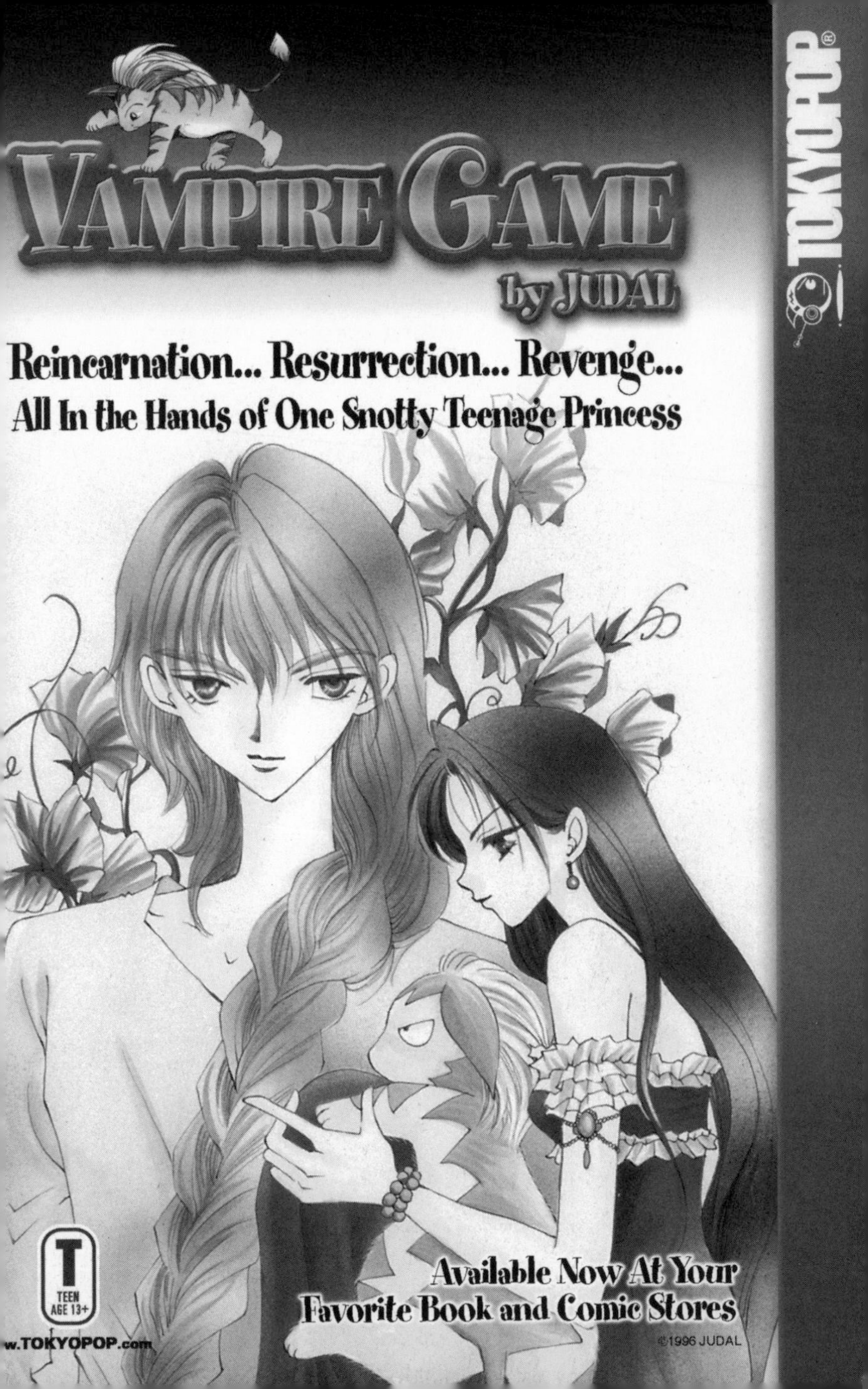
TOKYOPOP®
VAMPIRE GAME
by JUDAL
Reincarnation... Resurrection... Revenge...
All In the Hands of One Snotty Teenage Princess
T
TEEN
AGE 13+
Available Now At Your
Favorite Book and Comic Stores
w.TOKYOPOP.com
©1996 JUDAL

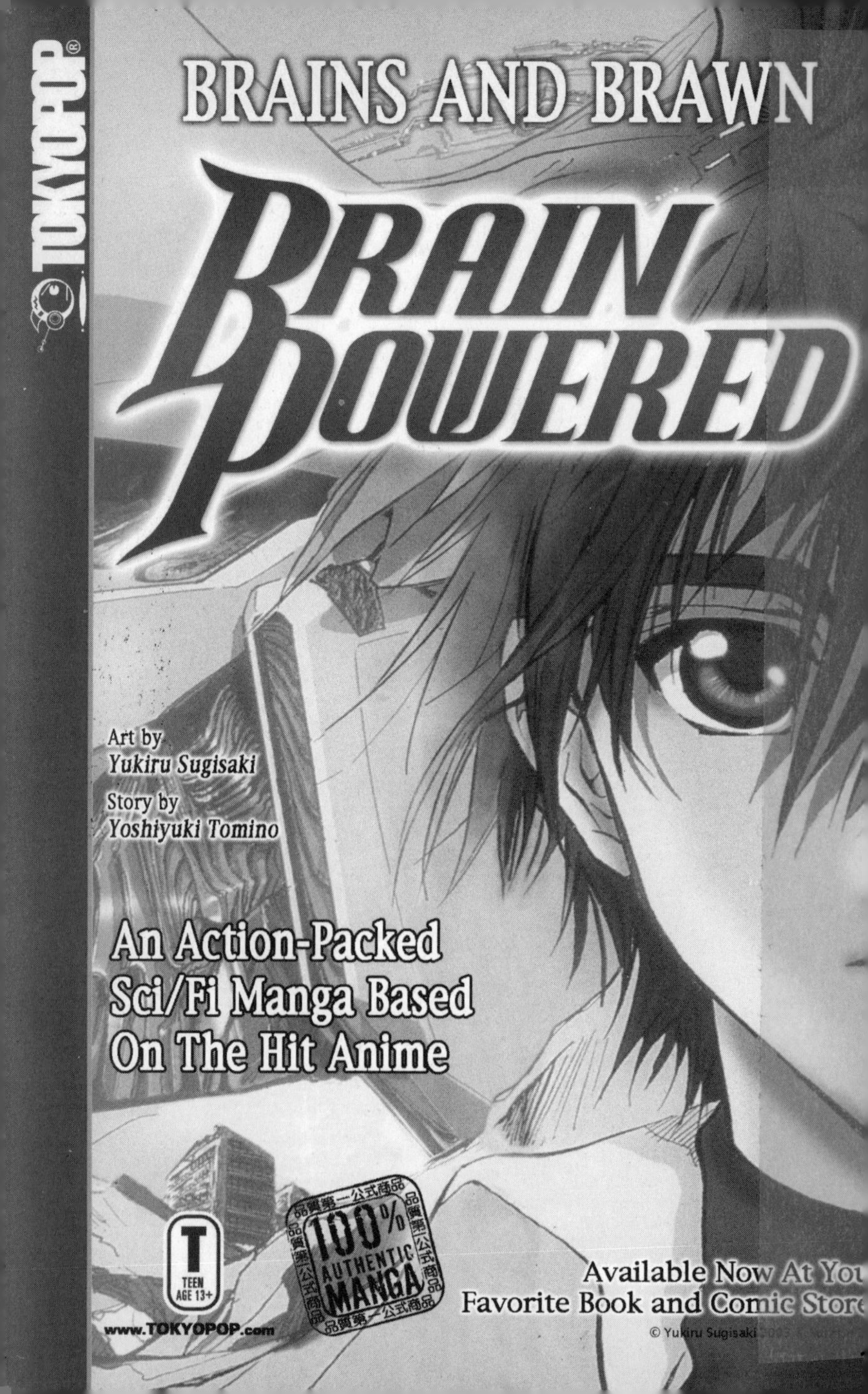
TOKYOPOP®
BRAINS AND BRAWN
BRAIN POWERED
Art by
Yukiru Sugisaki
Story by
Yoshiyuki Tomino
An Action-Packed
Sci/Fi Manga Based
On The Hit Anime
T
TEEN
AGE 13+
100% AUTHENTIC MANGA
品質第一公式商品
Available Now At You
Favorite Book and Comic Store
www.TOKYOPOP.com
© Yukiru Sugisaki